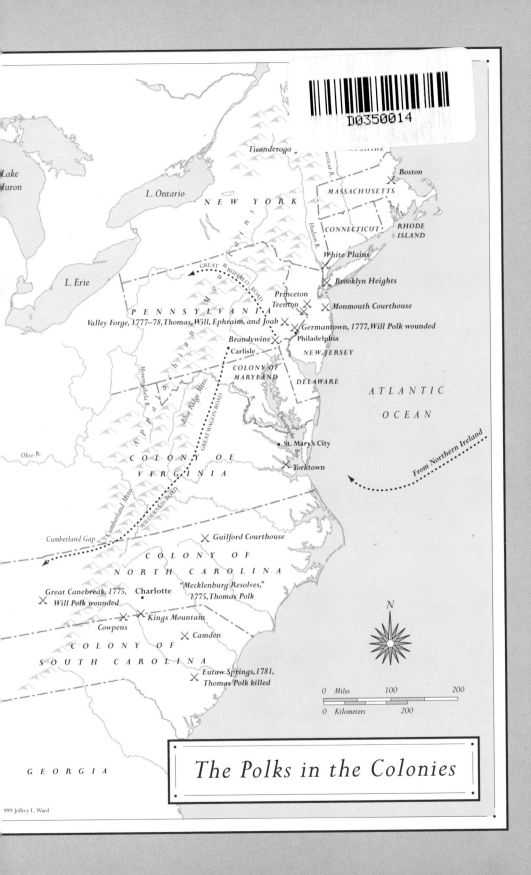

Lake Huron

L. Ontario

L. Erie

Ohio R.

Monongahela R.

Cumberland Mtns

Cumberland Gap

WILDERNESS ROAD

GREAT WAGON ROAD

Blue Ridge Mtns.

APPALACHIAN Mountains

GREAT BUFFALO ROAD

Ticonderoga

Boston

MASSACHUSETTS

NEW YORK

Hudson R.

Connecticut R.

CONNECTICUT

RHODE ISLAND

White Plains

Brooklyn Heights

Princeton
Trenton

Monmouth Courthouse

P E N N S Y L V A N I A

Valley Forge, 1777–78, Thomas, Will, Ephraim, and Joab

Germantown, 1777, Will Polk wounded

Brandywine

Philadelphia

NEW JERSEY

Carlisle

COLONY OF
MARYLAND

DELAWARE

Potomac R.

Chesapeake Bay

ATLANTIC

OCEAN

St. Mary's City

C O L O N Y   O F

V I R G I N I A

Yorktown

From Northern Ireland

Guilford Courthouse

C O L O N Y   O F

N O R T H   C A R O L I N A

Great Canebreak, 1775,
Will Polk wounded

Charlotte

"Mecklenburg Resolves,"
1775, Thomas Polk

Cowpens

Kings Mountain

Camden

C O L O N Y   O F

S O U T H   C A R O L I N A

Eutaw Springs, 1781,
Thomas Polk killed

N

| 0 | Miles | 100 | 200 |
| 0 | Kilometers | 200 | |

GEORGIA

The Polks in the Colonies

POLK'S FOLLY

POLK'S FOLLY

An American Family History

William R. Polk

DOUBLEDAY

New York   London   Toronto   Sydney   Auckland

PUBLISHED BY DOUBLEDAY
a division of Random House, Inc.
1540 Broadway, New York, New York 10036

DOUBLEDAY and the portrayal of an anchor with a dolphin
are trademarks of Doubleday, a division of
Random House, Inc.

BOOK DESIGN BY AMANDA DEWEY
ENDPAPER MAPS AND FAMILY TREE
DESIGNED BY JEFFREY L. WARD

Library of Congress Cataloging-in-Publication Data

Polk, William Roe, 1929–
Polk's folly: an American family history / William R. Polk.
—1st ed.
p.   cm.
Includes bibliographical references and index.
1. United States—History.   2. Polk family.   I. Title.
E179.P76   2000
973—dc21   99-24552
                                                        CIP

ISBN 0-385-49150-6
Copyright © 2000 by William R. Polk
All Rights Reserved
Printed in the United States of America
February 2000

First Edition
1   3   5   7   9   10   8   6   4   2

FOR MILBRY

Who made it possible

and then made it happen

❦

With love and admiration

ACKNOWLEDGMENTS

Above all others, I am indebted to my daughter Milbry Catherine Polk, who not only encouraged me to undertake this project but has been untiring and imaginative in the ideas, research and motivation required to complete it.

John Polk has read parts of the manuscript, tracked down documents and illustrations and offered the results of his own research in genealogy and ancillary fields. Ted Yeatman has been an able and persistent research assistant. Elsie Burch Donald also read the manuscript and offered valuable suggestions, particularly on the life and activities of her father, Lucius Burch. General R. R. Van Stockum provided information on the Andrew Jackson Polk branch of the family.

I am particularly indebted to Professor Wayne Cutler of the Polk Project at the University of Tennessee and the National Historical Publications and Records Commission of the National Endowment for the Humanities, who has done a masterful job of editing James K. Polk's correspondence.

Marylin Bell Hughes, archivist of the Tennessee State Library, Ted Teodoro of the Rare Books and Manuscripts division of The New York Public Library, Stephen E. Massengill of the North Carolina Department of Cultural Resources, Richard Richardson of the Maryland State Archives, William R. Massa, Jr., of the Yale University Library, Thomas Price of the James K. Polk Memorial Association, Joe Struble of George Eastman House, Ken Distler of the Ship and Aircraft Photo Collection of the U.S. Naval Institute at Annapolis, Ms. Candan Fuller of the Patton Museum of Cavalry & Armor and John E. White of the Academic Libraries of the University of North Carolina at Chapel Hill helped locate elusive documents and photographs.

Acknowledgment is here given to Manuscripts and Archives, Yale University Library, for permission to quote from the Frank Lyon Polk Papers.

Bill Thomas, Editor-in-Chief of Doubleday, has been a kind, sympathetic and thoughtful editor, and Sterling Lord, my agent, has been a constant source of encouragement and help throughout.

Many others have helped to track down illustrations, documents or sources. Included are James H. Polk III, Mrs. Jody Schwartz, John and Judy Clinton, Betty Lawson, William P. Polk, Michael Cody, Mary Tiegreen and Amon Carter Evans.

I have drawn heavily on the Library of Congress, the Yale University Library, the London Library, the University of North Carolina Library and the libraries and archives of the states of Maryland, North Carolina and Tennessee, all of whose staffs have been most courteous and helpful.

Finally, I appreciate the patience and warm support of my wife, Elisabeth, through what has been a long and consuming task.

—WILLIAM R. POLK

CONTENTS

Time is rapidly passing, the older members of the family are fast leaving us, and soon whatever might have been available in the past or at present or in the few years to come will have been lost forever. In fact, during the comparatively short time in which I have been engaged in collecting these records, I have felt and do feel now that, if they had not been preserved in this way, they would never have been available to any one. Important letters and books, especially family Bibles, have already been lost by fire or otherwise and soon it will not be possible to secure and preserve at any cost the records so essential for such a history as this.

—HERBERT BEMERTON BATTLE (ed.), *The Battle Book*

In this day of specialization, a social historian who undertakes to recount the life of people through three centuries and in three countries knowingly risks his scholarly head. Experts in Scottish, Irish, and American colonial history can only regard him as an unprofessional interloper, ignorant of the fine points within their special fields.

—JAMES G. LEYBURN, *The Scotch-Irish: A Social History*

We know only in the vaguest way who the hundreds of thousands of individuals who settled in British North America were, where precisely they came from, why they came, and how they lived out their lives.

—BERNARD BAILYN

. . . historical amnesia . . . has blotted out much of our past [leaving behind only a] white-oriented, hero-worshipping history.

—GARY B. NASH, *Red, White, and Black: The Peoples of Early America*

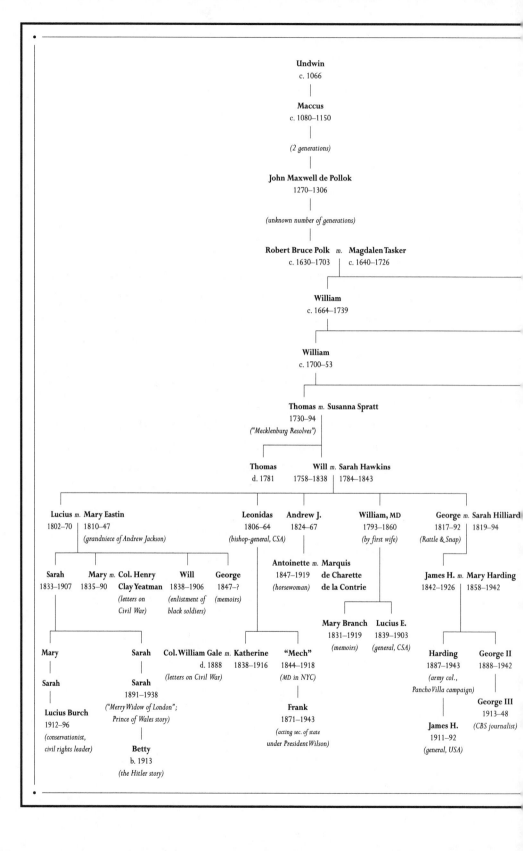

Undwin
c. 1066

Maccus
c. 1080–1150

(2 generations)

John Maxwell de Pollok
1270–1306

(unknown number of generations)

Robert Bruce Polk *m.* **Magdalen Tasker**
c. 1630–1703 | c. 1640–1726

William
c. 1664–1739

William
c. 1700–53

Thomas *m.* **Susanna Spratt**
1730–94
("Mecklenburg Resolves")

Thomas **Will** *m.* **Sarah Hawkins**
d. 1781 1758–1838 | 1784–1843

Lucius *m.* **Mary Eastin**   **Leonidas** **Andrew J.**   **William, MD**   **George** *m.* **Sarah Hilliard**
1802–70 1810–47   1806–64 1824–67   1793–1860   1817–92 1819–94
(grandniece of Andrew Jackson)   *(bishop-general, CSA)*   *(by first wife)*   *(Rattle & Snap)*

Antoinette *m.* **Marquis**
1847–1919 **de Charette**
(horsewoman) **de la Contrie**

Sarah **Mary** *m.* **Col. Henry** **Will** **George**
1833–1907 1835–90 **Clay Yeatman** 1838–1906 1847–?
(letters on *(enlistment of* *(memoirs)*
Civil War) *black soldiers)*

James H. *m.* **Mary Harding**
1842–1926 | 1858–1942

Mary Branch **Lucius E.**
1831–1919 1839–1903
(memoirs) *(general, CSA)*

Mary **Sarah** **Col. William Gale** *m.* **Katherine** **"Mech"**
| | d. 1888 1838–1916 1844–1918
Sarah **Sarah** *(letters on Civil War)* *(MD in NYC)*
| 1891–1938
Lucius Burch *("Merry Widow of London";* **Frank**
1912–96 *Prince of Wales story)* 1871–1943
(conservationist, | *(acting sec. of state*
civil rights leader) **Betty** *under President Wilson)*
b. 1913
(the Hitler story)

Harding **George II**
1887–1943 1888–1942
(army col., |
Pancho Villa campaign) **George III**
1913–48
James H. *(CBS journalist)*
1911–92
(general, USA)

Polk Family Members

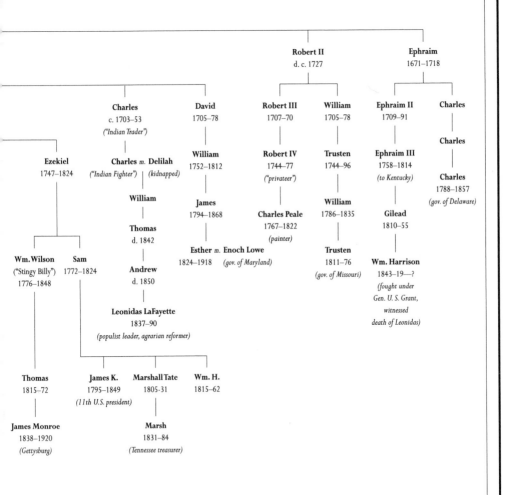

Robert II
d. c. 1727

Ephraim
1671–1718

Charles
c. 1703–53
("Indian Trader")

David
1705–78

Robert III
1707–70

William
1705–78

Ephraim II
1709–91

Charles

Ezekiel
1747–1824

Charles *m.* Delilah
("Indian Fighter")   (kidnapped)

William
1752–1812

Robert IV
1744–77
("privateer")

Trusten
1744–96

Ephraim III
1758–1814
(to Kentucky)

Charles

William

James
1794–1868

Charles Peale
1767–1822
(painter)

William
1786–1835

Gilead
1810–55

Charles
1788–1857
(gov. of Delaware)

Thomas
d. 1842

Esther *m.* Enoch Lowe
1824–1918   (gov. of Maryland)

Trusten
1811–76
(gov. of Missouri)

Wm. Harrison
1843–19—?
(fought under
Gen. U. S. Grant,
witnessed
death of Leonidas)

Wm. Wilson
("Stingy Billy")
1776–1848

Sam
1772–1824

Andrew
d. 1850

Leonidas LaFayette
1837–90
(populist leader, agrarian reformer)

Thomas
1815–72

James K.
1795–1849
(11th U.S. president)

Marshall Tate
1805-31

Wm. H.
1815–62

James Monroe
1838–1920
(Gettysburg)

Marsh
1831–84
(Tennessee treasurer)

INTRODUCTION

IN AN AGE OF INSTANT CELEBRITY AND USUALLY OF INSTANT Nirvana in which virtual reality often outshines reality and whose statesmen more frequently imitate movie stars than actors portray statesmen, *saga* is a literary relic harking back to an age when storytellers of great memory recounted the deeds and words of ancestors over generations.

Is the writing of saga today possible?

Saga is not only a relic but has always been rare. Consider a well-known classical example: within a century after the death of Caesar, none of the families that had been in the Senate during his time were still represented there. So to write Roman history through a family story is impossible.

But it is possible in the history of our young country. And it lends a continuity to our history that is otherwise unachievable.

By asking a reader to invest his time and effort in a book, particularly in such a long one as this, I believe an author assumes an obligation to explain why he wrote it, what it is about and why he thinks the reader might enjoy and profit from it. Here are my answers.

When I was a boy, growing up in Texas, my aged grandmother Mary Demoville "Molly" Harding Polk (then in her eighties) lived with my family. She was born on the eve of the Civil War, in which her husband, my grandfather James, had fought, and she spent *her* childhood in the company of an aged grandfather of hers who was born during the Revolutionary War. So, in just two memories, I had laid out for me tales of the entire history of the United States. Hers was, of course, a highly selective view, focused on the doings of relatives, but, being very personal, was particularly exciting to a small boy.

I also experienced a negative stimulus that was provocative. Part of my childhood was spent on a ranch west of Fort Worth in what had been, into the lifetime of my grandfather, Comanche country. Yet, except in the cowboy and Indian games I played with my schoolmates, the Comanche might just as well have been Martians.

In fact, we did not even know their name for themselves, *Nemene*. "Comanche," which we called them, was to them a foreign word, a borrowing from the Ute Indian language which came into English from the Spanish. In Ute, "comanche" means "enemy," and no people has ever called itself the Enemy. The Nemene were a proud and independent people who ranged over the Western plains before they were wiped out by the incoming Texas settlers and their diseases. In 1866, the Nemene were thought to number about 5,000, but twenty years later only 1,382 were left. They have now disappeared entirely from their old hunting grounds.

All over America, other Indian groups lived the experience of the Nemene. Each generation of Americans from about 1700 to about 1900 had its Indian war. Each ended in the misery of smallpox, starvation and broken spirit. Our stereotype of the Indian wars, Custer's "last stand," was only a moment of Indian glory in years of the cries of starving, diseased remnants of once proud, independent and colorful peoples who have given us much of our legendary past but whose far richer legacy we have largely forgotten.

Of all this, I knew nothing as a young boy. I was then governed in my attitudes toward the Indians by the message imparted by that great school of my generation, the movies. In childhood play, no boy wanted to be the Indian. The favored role was the cowboy or the cavalry trooper. He might die, always gloriously to be sure, as trumpets sounded the charge, but his side always won. As, of course, in reality it did. Our childish history was real history. But who the Nemene were, what they did, how they lived or thought, what they spoke, how they related to one another, these were not questions that even occurred to me.

Worse, I do not think they occurred to any adult I knew. For adult as for child, Indians were just anticowboys, bad guys, obstacles. I was later to find that my neighbors were not alone in this ignorance. When I began to read books on American history, I ran into what has been called the collective amnesia of historians. And it quickly became apparent that it was not only on Indians that large chunks of our past—and our society—were shrouded in shadow.

As a young boy, I spent a year in a primary school in a part of my city, Fort Worth, almost totally inhabited by Spanish Americans or Mexicans, yet I cannot remember ever having heard anyone speak Spanish there. In those years, Americans who were not white Anglo-Saxons did not advertise their ethnicity. Later I would find young Italian children in Boston ashamed because they did not consider themselves to be fully American. To them, Italian was the language spoken only by their embarrassing old grandmothers, not a language of culture and refinement. These feelings were echoed, I discovered, in group after ethnic group. And they were most marked in Texas in the 1930s in the black community. Yet, an American history without these peoples would surely be a poor, shallow, bowdlerized tale.

My studies of other peoples convinced me that such a version of history was not even believable. So, now armed with better intellectual tools and aided by the studies of many other scholars, I began to revisit the childhood stories that had originally so entranced me. Piece by piece, they fell into a pattern that has finally emerged as this book.

By personal preference and to give it coherence, I decided to treat it as saga—that is, to hang my tale of American history on a sort of "backbone" composed of my family. Doing so enabled me to make my story personal, in the way my aged grandmother had made it, and (as I hope the reader will find) both interesting and enlightening. From 1680, when the first Polk came to America, at least one person in each generation has played a significant, often a dramatic, occasionally an amusing and at least once a disreputable role in what the country was doing or experiencing.

In one respect, names, I warn the reader, the family is impoverished. Generation after generation is filled with individuals named James, William and George. It is a positive relief when an Ezekiel, Leonidas or Independence comes along. Where useful to avoid confusion, I adopt the device of attaching the middle initial to the name—so James K. refers to James Knox Polk, the president. But as the reader will find, this does not always suffice: my great-great-grandfather named one of his sons after his commander, George Washington, and after him was named his grandson, his nephew and his great-grandson, all of whom appear in my story.

THE FIRST POLK TO COME TO AMERICA WAS A SCOT BY THE name of Robert who had been an officer in Cromwell's army and who lived in county Donegal in what is now Northern Ireland. In the vicissitudes of the struggles between Parliament and the monarchy and between the established and the reforming sects of Christianity, he became a marked man. With his life in danger, he fled Ireland just as James II and Charles II took vengeance on many of Cromwell's officers and other

Republicans. His wife Magdalen's family's house, which is still standing, is one of the few that were not burned by the vengeful king. So I begin, not in America, where Robert got a land grant about 1680, but among those who would become the early Americans.

To become a colonist was no easy process. One first had to sail across the Atlantic. In the seventeenth century, that was at best a terrifying venture and was often fatal. Not only were ships small and unseaworthy, but navigation was rudimentary, without accurate maps or method to tell longitude. There was no means to forecast weather, on which sailing ships were wholly dependent; food could not be safely preserved; diseases could not be suppressed; and beyond all the other dangers loomed the risk of piracy. So, in Chapter 1, I give as clear an account as the record will support of Robert's and Magdalen's background in Scotland and Ireland, the forces that shaped their decision to come to America and the voyage that brought them here.

Robert could not have known—indeed, had he known, he might not have chanced the Atlantic—that in landing on the Chesapeake his troubles would just begin. Like a few thousand before him and many hundreds of thousands after him, he set out to create a new life for his family. What he encountered, how he struggled and the way in which he began to establish his family is, truly, the story of all Americans. Yet, I believe that tracking down exactly how, when and with whom this one man lived enables me to illuminate the whole.

Robert came to America in what I think of as the second wave of immigrants. Those who came half a century earlier had already displaced the resident Indians along a narrow band of Atlantic coast, laid claim to the better lands and stumbled upon a crop that had enriched them. Tobacco played a formative role in seventeenth-century America that is hard to exaggerate. But the lands Robert acquired were not suitable for tobacco—or indeed for much of anything else. So his sons padded out their meager incomes from farming by becoming artisans: one was a ship carpenter and another a blacksmith. Life was hard and diseases claimed the lives of many, perhaps most, of the immigrants as they adapted to the New World. The position of women was even harder than that of the men, but remarkably Magdalen lived into her eighties and was the real matriarch of the family. Theirs is the story I tell in Chapter 2.

Almost literally "over the next hill," in fact only about fifty miles north of the present city of Washington, was the end of white America about 1700. Beyond that frontier was Indian territory. Until relatively recently, no white American knew more about the native Americans than I knew as a boy in Texas, but tales were then on the lips of every traveler and trader. From the Indians came furs and skins, and to them were sent cloth, powder, shot and guns. And liquor. In the telling, stories about them must have grown as they always do about the unknown. Intrigued by what they heard and realizing that they had little opportunity where they were, two of Robert's grandsons, Charles and William, crossed into that wilderness about 1720 to try to make their fortunes.

In its own way, their venture was even more audacious than Robert's. Charles became well known as an Indian trader and was visited by George Washington—who actually *did* sleep at his house. What little can be reconstructed of his life enables me to tell about the Indians, the white traders and the process that moved the frontier westward. Charles's son, also named Charles, was known as "the Indian Fighter," and, perhaps fittingly, his wife, Delilah, and her son William were taken hostage by the Indians. Her story, told by her son in later life, is also the story of thousands of other white Americans. This is the essence of Chapter 3.

In Chapter 4, I describe the events and portray the people who made the American Revolution. To do this, I turn aside from the better-trod paths of American history, leaving Boston, New York and Philadelphia for the "backcountry" of North Carolina and putting aside the better-known leaders, Washington, Jefferson and Patrick Henry (who, incidentally, was also a cousin). I focus instead on two Polk family members, Thomas and his son William. Thomas, who is best known for having saved the Liberty Bell, fought General Cornwallis and proclaimed the so-called Mecklenburg Resolves. The British regarded those Re-

solves, which were proclaimed in May 1775, as the *first* American declaration of independence. They were, in fact, one of nearly a hundred
published during the year before *the* Declaration. Focusing on what led
Thomas to proclaim the Mecklenburg Resolves enables me to get at the
aspirations of the colonists and the underlying emotion of the buildup to
the Revolution.

The second man, Thomas's son Colonel William "Will", who was
my great-great-grandfather, enlisted in the Continental Line, as the main
Revolutionary army was known, at seventeen, fought for five and a half
years and took part in many of the major battles of the Revolution, including Germantown, and was one of the few who endured Valley
Forge. During the war, he formed a close friendship with Lafayette and a
number of the other volunteers from Europe. His story enables me to
give a rather different and more personal interpretation of the war than I
have read elsewhere.

As an officer in the Continental Line, Will was a staunch Federalist
and warm admirer of his commander, after whom he named one of his
sons, George Washington Polk. Will was one of the founders of the Society of the Cincinnati because, like many of the officers of the Continental Line, he feared that the forces of disunity, which had nearly
wrecked the Revolutionary army, might also wreck the new Republic.
He took his stand firmly on the side of Alexander Hamilton and against
Thomas Jefferson in the great question that would split the family and
the nation: was the United States singular, a union, or plural, a collection of sovereignties?

After the war, Will was appointed to high office by George Washington, became head of the first North Carolina state bank and played a
major role in the westward move into what became Tennessee. Alongside of his friend and occasional business partner Andrew Jackson, he acquired a vast amount of land and, in his later life, therefore, helped to
lay the foundations of what became the Old South. I use his story as a
key to open the young Republic.

Disagreeing politically with Andrew Jackson, Will remained a Federalist and thus opposed his first cousin, Jackson's protégé, James K. Polk, who during this period was a United States congressman and twice Speaker of the House of Representatives and then governor of Tennessee. The interaction of Will, Andrew Jackson and James K. enables me in Chapter 5 to discuss major American events ranging from the Indian Removal to the great crisis over the nature of the Union.

Chapter 6 focuses on the presidency of James K., in which the United States was nearly doubled in size. A firm advocate of Jeffersonian Democracy, he adamantly opposed the growth of the government role in private life, attempted to maintain what he thought of as the fundamental constitutional compromise between the states and the federal government and attempted to keep the issue of slavery separate from politics. Perhaps the hardest-working man who ever inhabited the White House, James K. dealt with issues ranging from a war with Mexico and incorporation of the whole western part of the United States to the creation of the magnificent Smithsonian museum and the U.S. Naval Academy at Annapolis. Somehow he also found the time and energy to write an extraordinary daily diary which gives a unique insight into the presidency.

Will's son George and his brothers built the group of plantations south of Nashville that more or less encapsulates the Old South. George's plantation, Rattle & Snap, is perhaps the most beautiful of the old southern houses. It was there that my grandfather James H. was born and grew to young manhood. His wife, Mary "Molly" Harding, grew up in another of the great plantations, Belle Meade. Although it did not last more than two generations, the Old South, along with the Wild West, is one of the two mythic periods in American history, and, needless to emphasize, it formed the core of the stories I heard from my aged grandmother. A portrait of the Old South forms Chapter 7.

Chapter 8 begins as events rushed toward the Civil War. James K.'s younger brother, William H., who grew from a wild young rake, involved in a disgraceful duel, to become a diplomat, army officer and lawyer, ran for governor of Tennessee on a pro-Union platform in 1860 and when war broke out became a federal official. James K.'s widow, Sarah, insisted on flying the American flag on her house in Nashville. No mistake about *their* Unionism. Meanwhile, George's brother Leonidas, after graduating from West Point and having resigned to become a cleric and, later, the Episcopal bishop of the Louisiana Territory, tried to stave off the war between the states, but, like everyone else in the Polk family, was swept into it. He and his branch of the family were leading Confederates. As a lieutenant general in the Confederate army, he fought in many of the battles on the western front. His correspondence (discussing prisoner exchange, care of the wounded and visits of wives and mothers) with General (later President) U. S. Grant strikes one of the few courtly notes in that horrible conflict. Leonidas was killed by the shell of a cannon fired, almost unbelievably, from within a few feet of a distant cousin who, having been trained by Grant, was fighting on the Union side. Around Leonidas, I discuss the major events of the Civil War, ending with the defeat of the Confederacy.

Quite a different war was the experience of Leonidas's nephew, my grandfather James H., who enlisted (as his grandfather Will had done in the Continental Line at the start of the Revolution) at seventeen. James H. is said to have been the youngest captain in the Confederate army, serving in General Nathan Bedford Forrest's famed 1st Tennessee Cavalry. He was captured during a raid behind Union lines and spent most of the rest of the war in three of the dreadful wartime prisons.

The aftermath of their war is the tale I recount in Chapter 9. Leonidas's brother Andrew Jackson Polk was a real-life Rhett Butler whose experience forms a leitmotif to the rest. A captain in the Confederate army, where he was badly wounded, he made a fortune during the war running cotton through the Union blockade to England, and then, at the end of the war, he escaped to Europe. In France, his daughter Antoinette, who had played a short but gallant role in the Civil War, married the Marquis Athanase de Charette de la Contrie.

In an amusing echo of that epoch, the black butler Pork at the fictional Tara in *Gone With the Wind* was played by Oscar Polk, whose ancestors may have played similar real-life roles at the Polk family plantations, Hamilton Place, Ashwood Hall or Rattle & Snap.

Less colorful than Andrew Jackson were two other Polks of the period of the Reconstruction. James H. and Leonidas's son William M. pose a dramatic contrast in their attempts to cope with the end of the Old South. More dead than alive, James H. was exchanged and walked back to Tennessee from prison camp to what can best be described as a shattered memory. The family plantations, all grouped around the family church at Columbia, were quite literally gone with the wind. Only the president's widow and her house in Nashville were left undisturbed. Everything else was burned or looted, and the economy, based as it was on slavery, was destroyed. Rattle & Snap was sold for taxes (and food) in 1867. Unable to do anything in Tennessee, James H. tried to re-create the old life by growing cotton in Mississippi but couldn't make a go of it and so, like many others, "went to Texas."

In Texas, he became a horse and cattle dealer, founding with his brother the Polk Brothers Stockyards. My favorite story of him is the family legend of his shooting the sheriff of the wild frontier town of Laredo. (All true Polks swear it was in self-defense!) The outlaws Jesse and Frank James were among his frequent visitors and purchasers of his horses. Meanwhile, his somewhat younger cousin, a second George Washington Polk, was helping to "sledgehammer" the railway west across the Great Plains, where he had to deal with such colorful (and dangerous) western characters as "Judge" Roy Bean, the "Law West of the Pecos." Thus, in their one lifetime, James and George participated in the two great myths of America, the Old South and the Wild West.

Meanwhile, William M., who had been a colonel of artillery in the Confederate army, went to New York, where he studied medicine, became a noted doctor and dean of the Cornell Medical School. On the side, he wrote a biography of his father the bishop/general. At this distance, he appears to have been perhaps the most "healthy" of the post–Civil War generation of Polks: while fascinated by the war, as his writing shows, he was not, as so many were, crippled by it.

For a while in the 1880s, it seemed that another Polk would go to the White House. After his bloody and miserable experience with the Civil War, Leonidas LaFayette Polk organized and led the mass movement of American farmers that developed into the Populist movement. A sudden death from cancer cut short, just at point of triumph, a career that might have changed American history.

The stories of Leonidas LaFayette, Andrew, James H., George W. and William M. form the core of Chapter 9, "Revolution and Diaspora."

William M.'s son, Frank, became a lawyer and was active in New York City politics. Then he was picked by Woodrow Wilson to be a one-man version of what today we call the operations center of government. As counselor and undersecretary of state, he handled every sort of issue that came before the government, from taxes on salt through discrimination against Asians to negotiations over trade embargoes. He was the man who handed the Zimmermann telegram to the president, the act that got America into the First World War. It was particularly ironic, or apposite, that the telegram in which the German foreign minister urged the president of Mexico to invade the United States went through Frank (whose cousin President James K. had fought a war with Mexico) to Wilson (through whose presidency hostilities with Mexico ran like a black thread). Frank was also a close confidant of Wilson's adviser, Colonel House and after being the acting secretary of state, led the American delegation in 1919 at the Paris Peace Conference. After the war, he founded one of the major Wall Street law firms with John Davis (who ran for president on the Democratic ticket in 1924) and took part in the establishment of the Council on Foreign Relations. Frank's story, in Chapter 10, enables me to discuss the First World War and the Paris Peace Conference.

The generation of my father, another George W., and his brother, Harding, both of whom fought in the First World War, was marked first by the heady days of the 1920s and then by the Great Depression of the 1930s, in which my father went bankrupt. In those days, bankruptcy was a shameful thing, and it evoked memories for him of the loss of the Old South. In two generations, his father's and his, struggles to bring the material life into accord with psychological expectations (or, put another way, to recapture the Old South) had ended in personal catastrophe.

Harding, who had attended West Point and was a career army officer, suffered in a different way. After a brilliant beginning as a dashing young cavalry officer, taking part among other things in the campaign against Pancho Villa, the last great campaign of the American horse cavalry, his career was stymied during the Depression years as the army was allowed almost to die, and came to a sad end just before the Second World War when his Virginia Military Institute (VMI) roommate and West Point classmate, George Patton, burst forth onto the world stage. Thus, both Harding and George, in their very different ways, show another face of the searing experience of the Depression, which has left so many traces on our lives.

Quite a different life was led by Sarah Polk from Nashville. She eventually married the man who became the equerry to King George VI, but along the way, there was a good deal of speculation that she might marry the Prince of Wales who became King Edward VIII. What a stunning change in the history of the British monarchy that would have caused. Her story casts quite an unusual light on the English royal family and London society. Sarah's daughter Betty grew up in the royal court and as a very young woman in 1929, was sent off to learn German in Munich. There she was taken to dinner one night with the rising young German radical politician Adolf Hitler. Hitler quizzed her most of the evening on life in Windsor Castle and Buckingham Palace, and at the end of the evening she said to the Englishwoman who had introduced them, Unity Mitford, that she had an eerie feeling that he had plans to attack England. Mitford's response was that this was nonsense; Hitler loved and admired England; and if such an unimaginable thing happened, she would shoot herself. She did.

Their experiences shape Chapter 10.

The Second World War and its aftermath lead me to the final episode, Chapter 11, with three great-grandsons of Colonel Will Polk: Harding's son, another James H.; George W.'s son, another George W., and Lucius Burch.

In the war, James led Patton's advance unit (the 3rd Mechanized Cavalry of the 3rd Army) across Europe. He was the first American officer into Germany and liberated one of the terrible concentration camps. He was later the commander of the Berlin Garrison (when President Kennedy made his famous *Ich bin ein Berliner* speech), and finally, wearing Patton's silver-plated (as required by army regulations) but solid-gold (as his snobbish taste required) stars, James was commander of all the U.S. forces in Europe. He was, incidentally, the last senior American general to have served in the horse cavalry and so took part in both the end of an epoch and the high point of the new, where he was regarded as the army's heir to Patton as a tank commander.

My brother, George, like most of the family, first attended military school, VMI, but then dropped out to work his way around the world. In the years just before the Second World War, he visited Alaska, Japan, China and the Philippines and became a journalist. He reported on the Japanese invasion of China for the *Shanghai Evening Post* and later watched the "phony war" in Europe while on the staff of the *Paris Herald Tribune*. At the time of Pearl Harbor, he enlisted in the navy and was the first pilot to land on Guadalcanal island, in the first American counterattack of the Second World War. There he established the airfield. Badly wounded in the grim and bloody fighting, in which half the men in his squadron were killed, he returned to journalism. Perhaps unique in his generation, he moved from a South Pacific foxhole to within a few feet of the Nazi hierarchy at the Nuremberg trials. Joining CBS, he became a member of the little team of outstanding reporters led by Edward R. Murrow and Howard K. Smith that set the ideal standard for later radio and television newscasting. It was as a member of that team that he was murdered in Greece in 1948. He has been described as the first casualty of the Cold War. Today, one of the major awards in journalism, the George Polk Award, is given in his name.

A recurring theme of the American experience is the struggle of the black community for civil rights. The record of the family goes full cycle from slave owning to participation in the civil rights movement. In this chapter, Chapter 11, I deal with the final phase of Martin Luther King's campaign when the lawyer who fought for his right to hold his march in Memphis was Lucius Burch.

Thus, my final chapter deals not only with the Second World War but also with the three great issues of postwar America: the Cold War defense against the Soviet Union, the attempt to establish a proper role for America in the war-shattered and underdeveloped world and the effort to bring into a just and respectable balance the quest for liberty, equality and the pursuit of happiness for all Americans.

Looking back, I find not only great diversity in the family's experience, and an almost unbelievable range of contacts with their contemporaries, but perhaps more significant a central theme: they moved, thought, acted restlessly. From Robert's journey from Scotland, frontiers always called them. In their ventures, they encapsulated the American experience—and dream. Robert started it all by coming to America, Charles took the family beyond the frontier into the wilderness, Thomas and Will helped to solidify the new nation and to move it to the Mississippi, James took it to the Pacific, Harding carried its writ into Mexico and separately he, Frank, James and my father and brother took it back into Europe to defend what America had come to mean. But beyond physical movement, there was a profound change in morals, politics and the physical aspects of American life which they also embodied. Robert could certainly not have conceived of the new American nation that Thomas and Will helped to call into being; nor could he have visualized the opulence of the Old South; nor could any of them have imagined the changes that were to be the thrust of the careers of Leonidas LaFayette, Lucius Burch or George. All grew with the country and helped to form it by their actions, their thoughts and their feet. Their history is the nation's history.

This, then, is the ''backbone'' of the book. Around my account of the major players, a great many other figures—wives, cousins, in-laws, friends and enemies and fellow participants—will necessarily come into play. My problem as the "teller," or chronicler—what in the Old Norse sagas would be called a *so gu-maðr*—has been to force myself (since we don't have those endless winter evenings around the fire) to leave out so much that I have found fascinating lest the book become unmanageably long. But I hope that enough remains to enrich, indeed perhaps occasionally contradict, what is now thought about our history.

WILLIAM R. POLK

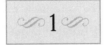

DEPARTURE

"All the Tryles, Hardships,
and Dangers of the Seas"

BROUGHT OVER FROM THE WILD SCOTTISH BORDERLANDS TO
fight in Ireland, Robert Bruce Pollok knew the exhausting and
bloody war of the guerrilla all too well. For him, combat became almost
a diversion; it was marching that wore men out. Across the mountains
and through the bogs that shredded seventeenth-century Ireland, trails
were just beaten furrows that stopped abruptly at the many streams and
gullies, forcing armies also to stop abruptly because bridges were then
more rare than roads. To carry the wounded even a few miles on bullock
carts was a wrenching experience which few survived. And to carry
food to the soldiers across the rugged land was a tedious and expensive
undertaking. As Robert had seen, the only way Cromwell could get food
to his troops was off of boats or barges. Indeed, Ireland's first line of defense was its very poverty: no army could live off the land for long, and

no army could feed itself at all if it moved far inland. But inland was where the Irish guerrillas were resisting English colonization; so inland the soldiers had to go.

Like most soldiers, Robert probably feared and distrusted the sea. True, he had sailed over from Scotland, but on a clear day Scotland was within eyesight of the northeastern Irish coast; so Robert had never been really out at sea. At least not in a sea like the one he would have heard about from sailors in the port of Derry or seen crashing remorselessly against the desolate cliffs of Dunluce Castle on Ireland's northern coast.

That coast he certainly knew firsthand in fights against the savage bands of robbers, pirates and even ordinary farmers who built bonfires to lure ships onto the rocks so they could prey on the stricken passengers. They were immortalized in the very names of their haunts— Tory ("outlaw") Sound, Bloody Foreland, Horn Head. No matter how strong the ship or how well armed the crew, once the sea and the shoals had done their work, no defense could be mounted against the raiders. Even the soldiers of the powerful Spanish Armada a century before had been stripped, robbed and often murdered; smaller merchant ships didn't have a chance. The fact that many of these robbers were fellow Scots gave Robert no comfort. He had often had to fight against Scots, and the pirates and outlaws on that coast were Highlanders who regarded Lowland Scots like Robert as virtual foreigners. No, there was no comfort in their national brotherhood.

More distant and more luridly painted in the wild tales of sailors were the Barbary pirates who pillaged and kidnapped up and down the Atlantic coast and around Ireland. Wild tales aside, no one could deny the infamous cutthroats who, despite brave talk from government after government, still kidnapped, sacked and burned whole villages. Even the lord deputy, as the English styled the viceroy of Ireland, had been captured by pirates less than fifty years before. Raiders often sailed right up the loughs to attack town walls, although a man who knew how to fight or who took shelter in a strong house could probably protect himself and his family. Ashore, Robert must have felt relatively confident.

He was a soldier. But encountering pirates at sea was quite a different matter. Indeed, an encounter with the sea itself was frightening enough.

Chilling tales of shipwreck, starvation and cannibalization were the staple conversation of sailors. Here in Londonderry, such tales were nearly all anyone talked about. Some claimed to have had personal experience. Maybe that was boasting, the way sailors and soldiers will when they measure themselves against one another. But to settle any doubts, a few of the stories had been printed by the famous Oxford geographer Richard Hakluyt.

Although Hakluyt's book *Divers Voyages Touching the Discoverie of America* had been published some years before, the dire portrait he painted of travel across the Atlantic would present the true dangers for at least a century to come.

Not that Hakluyt had intended to scare men like Robert away from voyages to America; far from it, he even wrote an enthusiastic treatise on agricultural possibilities in the New World. It was because he was engaged in promoting settlement there that he was taken under the patronage of Queen Elizabeth's powerful minister of strategic and intelligence affairs, Sir Francis Walsingham. England was already reaching toward empire, striving to catch up with Spain, and, surprisingly to our ears, was desperately worried about its ''surplus'' population. Its displaced peasants had begun to create an unruly, hungry and idle urban proletariat, as frightening to the ruling class as Rome's mobs had been to the caesars. Meanwhile, the younger sons of the aristocracy and the new commercial elite were greedy for the spoils of conquest and the riches of plantation; so, not surprisingly, government policy was to colonize the New World and Ireland.

And government policy was popular. Even more than whatever strategic and commercial aims the government espoused, people in the sixteenth and seventeenth centuries hungered for knowledge of the world beyond Europe. Some learned men, like John Locke (who was almost exactly Robert's age), avidly studied reports of the explorations. They thought they could find the basis of all human society, and perhaps its philosophical justification, in accounts of the newly discovered primitive nations like the Roanoke Island Indians who, Captain Philip Amadas thought, were living "after the maner* of the golden age." For Robert's contemporaries, the new discoveries were even more tantalizing than space exploration in our times. At the other end of their voyages were beings who, however exotic and bizarre their appearance and their actions, were human. How they got together to form communities or how they ruled themselves or were ruled by others was a sort of speculation more likely in the common rooms of Oxford or the drawing rooms of London, of course, than in rustic Ireland. There in Donegal, where Robert then lived, most people just loved a good tale of derring-do. And Hakluyt offered plenty of that. But a few, even in Donegal, thought they saw in the New World opportunity for riches and escape from the multiple tyrannies that afflicted their lives. Catering to each of these desires, and encouraged by government policy, Hakluyt and other paid publicists like the great poet John Donne had produced a stream of highly popular letters, pamphlets and books. Robert might not have read them, but he could not have avoided hearing their message; to him, that message was a mixture of hope and fear.

Whether or not hope was before him, fear was certainly behind him. For his service as an officer in Cromwell's forces, he had become a marked man when the monarchy was restored. With religion setting the parameters of politics, Robert found himself on the wrong side of the divide. The monarchy not only had defaulted on the salaries and compensations of Scots soldiers but now regarded them as enemies. As old scores were being called to account, Robert decided he must leave before disaster struck. Gamble he knew his venture to the New World would be, but in his position gamble was better than certainty.

In this state of mind, I imagine him sitting often on the walls of Londonderry looking down at the little bark moored in the calm, dark

---

* In quotations I will use the spelling and syntax of the originals without indicating (with "*sic*") misspellings or differences.

waters of the Foyle below, watching carpenters fitting new boards where storms had ripped them from the sides and deck. It would not have been a reassuring sight. And sitting there, he must often have mused over the tortuous path that had led him to this point of no return. It takes an act of imagination to follow him down that path, but from the effort, we can better understand both him and the America he and his family helped to build. So, let us begin where he did, in Scotland. Scotland was the anvil on which was hammered the cultural mold that shaped not only *his* life but also, in the more distant future, the lives of his descendants and many of the men and women who would form history in faraway America.

HISTORY HAD MADE THE SCOTS ONE OF THE MOST WARLIKE people of Europe. Calling them the Pictavi, the Romans fought them first in Gaul and then in the British Isles and finally drove them into the wilds of Scotland. To try to keep them at bay, the emperor Hadrian built his famous wall right across their land, but eventually the Romans gave up. In the long "dark ages" after the Romans left, the Pictavi were joined by other Celtic peoples, Britons from England, Scotti from Ireland and a smattering of Vikings from across the North Sea. For centuries, these people were distinct from one another, but from roughly a thousand years ago they were gradually bludgeoned together by that most persuasive tool, the sword.

Even the sword, however, could not produce unity. Domestic feuds and wars among the Scots were virtually constant. As a sixteenth-century Spanish ambassador commented, the Scots "spend all their time in wars, and when there is no war they fight one another." Fighting was the national pastime, but it reached a special intensity along the frontier with England. There, in Lowland Scotland, where Robert's family lived, society was comparable to the Sicilian. The separate clans living there were like so many mafias whose blood feuds with one another were unending. So strong were the imperatives of their hatreds that even in the

rare times when the English and Scots governments tried to control the
marches, their officials were afraid to execute outlaws for fear of revenge. In the savage warfare, a wild, bloody and desperate frontier life
was forged. Clan fought clan, sometimes to extermination and nearly always to impoverishment and abject misery.

A fourteenth-century observer described the clans collectively as
"a savage and untamed nation, rude and independent, given to rapine,"
and quoted with approval a much earlier writer who believed it common
for Scots fathers to give their baby sons their "first food on the point of a
sword so that they should desire to die not otherwise than under arms
. . . and be able to fight." He claimed that after every battle, the victors drank the blood of the slain and, as modern Scots deer slayers still
do with their prey, "besmear their faces with it."

Men believed that they had to fight to stay alive. They were probably right, since, if they fled the battlefield, it was not unknown for them
to be killed as cowards by their own wives: as Bishop Leslie wrote in
1578, "the women war wonte to slay thair men with thair awne handes
quhen frome the field they war cum hame ouircum be thair ennimies, as
to be ouircum war a takne of cowardnes . . ."

Nothing in the shared culture of the clans argued for peace or fellowship or mercy. No slight was allowed to go unpunished, and no overarching sense of law, or even of power, restrained them. Nor were they
softened by amenities of civilization. Food was primitive in the extreme:
oatmeal, eaten either as porridge or baked into little cakes known as *ban-
nocks,* was the staple. Cooking was over an open fire in metal pots, which
were also used for rendering suet from household animals into candles
and soap. Plates were made of wood or, as a sign of luxury, of pewter;
the principal eating utensils were fingers supplemented as necessary by a
dagger (which was used, more often, for other purposes). Dress was not
the colorful clan tweeds so fashionable now; they were not to be invented until centuries later. The kilt was unknown. Men and women
draped themselves in a length of coarse-woven cloth which was belted
by day to form a cloak and spread out at night to serve as a blanket. It

was either dyed gray or became so after long use. For fighting, men wore "jacks," quilted or leather coats on which plates of metal or bone were sewn to deflect or blunt the slash of a sword. There was no pretense of beauty.

Houses of the common people, resembling the tepees Robert's descendants would see in America, were slapped together from poles and sod and covered with thatch. Even among the gentry, "castles," despite the rather grand name, seldom had a floor area larger than a good-sized modern living room. On the ground level, behind a massive door, the owner stored his goods; up one flight, his servants cooked; on a third floor, he held court, and on the upper floor, he and his family slept. The only daylight came through narrow arrow or musket slits. Access to the upper floors was by a "turnpike," a word that gave almost exactly the opposite sense of the modern word: rather than a means of rapid travel, it was a narrow, screwlike staircase, just wide enough for a single person. It offered the last protection for the castle as the inhabitant could back up the stair as he slashed away at an intruder while his retainers or womenfolk poured boiling water or oil through the "murder hole." Visitors were not welcome.

Before the eighteenth century, in even the most elaborate of the castles, there was little or no decoration and only rudimentary furniture, usually restricted to wooden benches, tables and the occasional storage chest. Indeed, the chair was such a luxury that our word "chairman" comes from its high status. And some idea of how barren the buildings must have been is given by the fact that when an owner was forced to flee during a raid, he would often stuff his castle full of smoldering peat to keep the raiders from going inside. Even the castles of the great lords were well below what today would be considered the poverty line. It was this kind of hard and bare life that the Scots would take with them to the New World.

Constant warfare gave rise to the distinctive feature of Scottish life: clans. We would not be far wrong to define clans as protective associations, almost like modern street gangs, although the Scots thought of them, as the Gaelic word *clann* indicates, as kinsmen. Some members of clans were undoubtedly kinsmen, but many more were linked in the way indicated by the Gaelic term *gossipred,* which roughly translates as the American southern term "kissing cousins." Pushed together by neighborhood, a shared sense of hostility to the more distant and more alien and a recognition of their mutual dependence, Scots considered themselves members of a family whose patriarch was their chief. Tightly knit, intensely proud of their corporate identity and imbued with a sense of loyalty to kinsmen, they found in clans the most important identification in their lives. Indeed, not only peasants but "renegades, outlaws and 'broken men' " could, over time, merge into a clan, since every clan, being mobilized for feud and war, was willing to grant them membership. Thus, curiously, the clan system imposed a sort of democracy on Scotland and allowed even the poorest of men scope for personal pride. Later in America, as they went about subduing the forests and displacing the Indians, Scots frontiersmen would unconsciously re-create this heritage.

Imposed on top of a sense of nationhood and clanship was a third pattern of Scottish life, feudalism. It explains how Robert's ancestors entered Scotland centuries before, what happened to them in Scotland and why he and many others went to Ireland in the seventeenth century. To catch a ghostly glimpse of the first identifiable man among Robert's ancestors, we must turn back the pages about five hundred years.

IN ENGLISH HISTORY, THE BATTLE OF HASTINGS IN 1066 IS not only the most memorable date but also one that seems to provide a clean break, a sort of watershed: what went before was Anglo-Saxon England and what followed was Norman England. Against Duke William of Normandy, the Saxon knights and lords fought bravely but were utterly defeated and, in defeat, scattered across the known world. Some made their way even to distant Constantinople, where they enrolled in an elite corps in the Byzantine emperor's army, but most, including the

Saxon princess Margaret, who later married the Scottish king, fled to Scotland. Among them, perhaps in Margaret's party, was Robert's ancestor Undwin the Saxon.

As he imposed his rule on England, William realized that he must destroy the last hope of the Saxons; so shortly after the Battle of Hastings, he began a series of raids in which his knights turned much of northern England into a desolate no-man's-land. But the Saxon problem turned into the Scottish "problem" because Malcolm Canmore, king of Scotland (and the killer of Macbeth), welcomed Undwin and other Saxons, gave them lands and made them members of his court. Soon additional Saxons and even many Normans followed; profiting from their relative sophistication, the immigrants not only dominated the Scottish government but also introduced into Scotland the Norman military system of feudalism. In time, people who were originally Saxons or Normans became not only Scots but also clansmen and feudal lords. Their influence became so strong that the "Lowland" Scots put aside their Celtic or Gaelic tongue and customs to copy the new styles. We see this even in their names.

F OR CENTURIES, IN THE CELTIC TRADITION, THERE WERE NO family names. Some men were known by trade, as "Carpenter," "Baker," "Fuller"; others, whose fathers were prominent, were known by their first names, the father's name and the suffix "son." Thus, King Harold, who fought against William the Conqueror, was known as "Harold Godwineson," or Harold the son of Godwine. Sons of less well known fathers, particularly in Scotland, simply used the clan name; since they thought of themselves as descendants of the clan's founder, they called themselves "Mac" (Gaelic: "son of") so-and-so. Macdonald, for example, means simply "the son of Donald."

The European style, introduced by the Normans, derived names of noble families from locations; so the German *von,* the Italian *di* and the French *de* all mean "from." But the Scots did not slavishly adopt the European pattern; rather they joined it to clan names. Thus, among Robert's ancestors, the memory of the family's Saxon founder in Scotland, Maccus the son of Undwin, also became associated with a place. From the king of Scotland, Maccus had acquired a property on a tributary of the river Tweed by a well-known eddy (where, it is said, the fishing was particularly good). The Saxon word for eddy is *wele* or *well,* so the property became known as Maccus's *wele* or Maccuswell; a generation later, affecting the Norman style, Undwin's grandson called himself Herbert de Maccuswell. Eventually, Maccuswell was contracted to Maxwell.

Over time, the descendants of the founder became more and more separated from one another and acquired other kinship ties and interests. In the generation of Undwin's great-great-grandson, a Peter de Maxwell obtained a charter for a piece of land called Pollok, which in Gaelic meant a small lake or pond, just to the south of the modern city of Glasgow. So he became known as Sir John Maxwell de Pollok. The names of the Pollok *sept,* as the Scots call a branch of a clan, of the Maxwells appear in numerous documents over the following centuries.

A S THE MOST POWERFUL FAMILY ON THE SCOTTISH FRONTIER, the Maxwell clan encapsulates its history. Engaged in a bitter and centuries-long feud with the neighboring Johnston clan, the Maxwells were sporadically at war with the English forces across the frontier and were even more often engaged in cattle rustling. As in the much later wars on the range in the American West, rustling became a way of life. So furious with these "reivers," or outlaw-bandits, was King Henry VIII that he ordered his army to "Put all to fyre and swoorde . . . [to] remayne forever a perpetuel memory of the vengaunce of God." The soldiers were as good as Henry's word; they sacked and burned towns, hamlets and single houses, destroyed crops and drove away or slaughtered thousands of animals. This terrible onslaught, a veritable holocaust, lasted six years and has come down in Scottish folklore with the ironic name "the rough wooing." The "rough wooing" virtually destroyed the Maxwell clan; not until the American Civil War was the family again so close to extinction.

In the long years of penury and danger that were to follow, Robert Bruce Pollok was born, grew to manhood, became a soldier and found his way to Ireland. Like many of his family, he had by this time become a Protestant.

P OOR, PROUD AND BELLICOSE, THE SCOTS FOR CENTURIES HAD little interest in the religious conflicts that were later to shape their politics in the New World. Few were religiously inclined, but even had they been, the church they knew had offered little to attract them. There is a widely told anecdote of a visitor to one of the miserable little villages who, finding no chapel, asked if there were no Christians living there. "Na," came the inappropriate reply, "we's a' Elliots and Amstrangs."

While in many parts of Europe the medieval church was famously lax, in Scotland it made almost no pretense to spirituality. Prelates did their best to live well, and within the limits of the poor country, at least some notoriously succeeded. Without seeming to the medieval chronicler a shocking or unusual event, there is the account of one priest who was required to put up a bond to guarantee that he would not pawn or sell the silver, robes and books of his church or blatantly enjoy the services of "a continual concubine." Whether he lost his bond or not we do not know, but others certainly gave grounds to believe he may have. Many priests lived openly with their mistresses and children and treated the church's property as their own. That celibacy was not exactly a burning issue is shown by the allegation that nearly a third of all illegitimate Scottish children were the offspring of priests and/or nuns. So notorious was the conduct of the priests that in far-off Rome the pope punned that they were "Pilates rather than Prelates."

But even Scotland was not immune from the religious conflict that was wracking Europe. Cataclysmic change was presaged when in 1547

John Knox became the leader of the revolutionaries. Inspired by the better-known Martin Luther in Germany and John Calvin in Geneva, and particularly by his Scottish forerunner, George Wishart (who was burned for heresy in 1546), Knox proclaimed a new era: half a millennium of Catholicism was to be replaced by an austere form of what came to be called Protestantism. In 1561, he put before a convention of the nobility and lairds a program for reform: the "godly reformed Kirk," or national church of Scotland, was to be organized around congregations, each of which was to be governed by elders, or presbyters.

The governmental and church authorities recognized the revolution for what it was, and hounded Knox into exile, imprisonment and even slavery on galleys. But the Presbyterianism he proclaimed fit the Scottish national character, and they adopted it as their own. A true Scot, Knox was especially good at making enemies: Mary Queen of Scots borrowed French soldiers to try to suppress his movement, and Queen Elizabeth of England, however useful she found him in his attack on her enemy Mary, withdrew her protection when he published what must be one of the earliest attacks on the political role of women, *The First Blast of the Trumpet Against the Monstrous Regiment of Women.* But the new church emerged victorious, implemented a new "Scots" confession and abolished the Catholic authority. Thereafter, all Scots, willing or not, were under pressure to become members of the "godly reformed Kirk." After 1567, the saying of Mass anywhere in Scotland became a capital offense.

In keeping with the times, the message of Knox and his followers was stern and unforgiving: it held that we come into this world not innocent but ignorant and must be forced to conform to the will of God. Socially, it turned conservative after Knox witnessed the propensity to lawlessness of the poor. A statute of 1579, inspired by Knox, decreed that all "sturdy beggars"—the unemployed who were able-bodied and thought to be "fractious"—should be arrested and flogged. ". . . we are not patrons for stubborn and idle beggars who running from place to place make a craft of their begging . . . ," Knox had preached. His policy could not be fully implemented because there was neither enough land to support such people nor enough jails to house them; so, many were driven into crime or into military service abroad. This was a period in which many Scots went to fight as mercenaries in Germany, Holland and Ireland.

What the new kirk would not tolerate, above all, was the "backsliding" ways of the old: attendance at the Presbyterian church became mandatory; other faiths were not tolerated; paid spies were used to ensure that everyone participated and no one deviated; and the sexual laxness (both heterosexual and homosexual) associated with the past was savagely punished when discovered or suspected. Knox's followers would later enact many of his edicts into law in the new colonies.

In that age, religion was not just a matter of belief or social conduct but the hallmark of political loyalty, so religious difference ranked as subversion. In Robert's own family, this caused bitter conflicts because one branch remained Catholic while another became Presbyterian. And as families, ruling establishments and whole communities split over matters of faith, these conflicts became nationwide and spilled over into England, Ireland and the New World.

It was during these troubled middle years of the seventeenth century that Robert went to Ireland. This is a period for which few records in the outlying areas have survived, and little can be said with certainty about him. It appears that he was a second son, and so was unlikely to inherit even the meager remnants of the family property that had survived the terrible wars of the Scottish Lowlands; thus, a move to a more promising place would have been attractive. After what must have been a good deal of politicking among the clansmen, he was given a commission in a regiment that was being raised for service in Ireland and embarked to sail across the narrow Firth of Clyde from Glasgow, then across the sixty-five miles of the stormy Atlantic to Ballycastle.

By the time he arrived, more than fifty thousand Scots, including a number of his fellow clansmen, were already in Ireland. There Robert de Pollok must have felt right at home: not only was he among at least a few kinsmen, but Ireland, like Scotland, was a country of constant warfare. Unlike hostilities among the Scots, those in Ireland were defined by, sometimes caused by and always given a particular edge of savagery by religion. As a soldier employed by the English and as a Protestant fighting against the Catholics, he was buffeted by the changing tides of English and Irish politics, caught in dilemmas that he probably could not understand and hemmed in by forces over which he had no control. For years, he managed to survive, but particularly after his marriage to the daughter of a prominent member of what came to be known as the Protestant "Assendency," he realized that if he did not leave voluntarily, he might be sent away in chains. It was thus that he found himself on that hilltop, watching the repair of the little ship that was to take him to America and, he hoped, to safety. To understand the path he trod, let us briefly look at the forces that shaped his life and nearly caused his early death.

THE FIRST OF THESE FORCES WAS THE CONFLICT AMONG THE inhabitants of Ireland. Most were Gaelic-speaking Catholics whom their English overlords treated like the ancient Spartans treated the helots—as expendable labor and as permanent enemies. The Irish were not allowed even to enter cities except on certain appointed days; consequently, they had no political rights, since such rights as then existed in Ireland were derived from charters granted to cities. Kept from profitable trade, from most of the professions and from access to capital, most lived on the edge of starvation; they were described by a Spanish Armada captain as eating only once a day, and then just oatcakes washed down with *Bainne clabair,* or, as we call it, clabber. Only on feast days did they have meat, but whiskey, known in Celtic as *uisgebeatha,* had already become a national addiction. Probably, given their diet, their clothing and their houses, they needed its warmth.

Their main item of clothing, when they wore any (which to the amazement of the English they often did not), was a sort of drape of cloth, the *falaing,* which they also used at night as a blanket; their "wattle and daub'' huts contained no furniture, so they slept on rushes on the ground alongside their animals. Although the people were wretchedly poor and, like the Scots, were deeply divided—at times into as many as two hundred ''kingdoms''—they were led by their earls into unending hostilities against the English invaders. They had to fight to survive, but each battle brought terrible retribution. They gave and got no quarter.

Such contact as they had with foreigners, other than the English, was through the Franciscan order to Spain, upon which they were wont to depend for succor and, occasionally, for military support. This dependency increased in the half century before Robert arrived as England became more aggressive. The process fed upon itself: as the Irish felt more threatened, they drew closer to Spain, and as they did so, the English intervened more. But English policy was not consistent: as politics and religion in England itself swung violently in the seventeenth century, the rulers wavered in their attitudes toward Ireland, sometimes confiscating the earls' lands, imprisoning or exiling them, and sometimes encouraging them to enroll their peasants to fight for the monarchy; sometimes tolerating or even encouraging Catholicism and sometimes trying to destroy it. This was the vise in which Robert was caught.

But the Irish were not the only people in Ireland. Fighting was the specialty of another group, Highland Scots known in Ireland as galloglas (Gaelic: *galloghaigh),* mercenaries who resembled the *condottiere* of Italy. Despite generations or even centuries of residence, they betrayed their distant Viking ancestry in their choice of the battle-ax as their favored weapon. Employed by the earls, they were often Robert's antagonists in battle.

Ireland also housed two English communities. The ''Old English,'' like some of Robert's ancestors, were originally Anglo-Normans and lived apart from the natives in what came to be called the Irish Pale around Dublin. Sharing with the natives their Catholic religion, they thought of themselves as English. But being rich, they were often targets rather than allies of the usually impoverished and always avaricious English monarchy. Opposed to them were the so-called New English, who as fellow Protestants became the local agents of the home government. As events of the tumultuous seventeenth century unfolded, so powerful was the liability of religion and so attractive was the lure of wealth that the differences between the communities were submerged in blood. And what happened between them was not the worst.

By the time that Robert arrived in Northern Ireland, the great Irish clan of O'Neill had fought against the British for generations. The horror of that struggle can scarcely be imagined. Massacre followed massacre; prisoners not only were slaughtered but were often flayed alive; churches full of men, women and children were burned, and still the Irish fought on. Even in times of relative peace, no man dared to go out alone or unarmed. It was guerrilla war without end; so one of Henry VIII's advisers urged him "to exyle, banyshe, and expulsse therefro all the captaines, growen and dyscendeyd of the blode and lynage of Hugh Boy Onyll [the O'Neill leader] for ever."

While not remembered as a subtle man, Henry hit upon a more casuistic form of conquest than he was employing in Scotland. In a lull, after a particularly vicious bout of fighting in 1541, he laid a trap that was to set the shape of Ireland down to our own times: he offered the Gaelic lords what appeared to be only a face-saving deal. They were to surrender their lands to the Crown and then receive them back intact from the king. The deal is known in Irish history as Surrender and Regant. The Irish lords accepted it without realizing the catch. The catch was that the original title had been absolute, whereas the new title was conditioned by English feudal law. By feudal terms, the previously independent lords were to hold their titles only at the king's pleasure. His pleasure did not last long.

While the parallel is not exact, much the same process was used later in the New World to take lands from Indians, who similarly did not understand the "catch" in the treaties they negotiated with the incoming whites. In this, as in other ways, what was happening in Ireland and Scotland presaged events in far-off America and shaped the lives of Robert's descendants.

At first, what Henry had done did not seem to make any significant difference; life (and warfare) went on in the accustomed ways. But as Tudor England gained in power and influence, it became increasingly embroiled in Continental rivalries, particularly with France and Spain. And as Henry and subsequently his daughter, Queen Elizabeth, sought to secure the separation of England from the papacy, they stepped up their efforts to convert or suppress Ireland, both religiously and politically, to prevent it from being used by Catholic Europe against Protestant England. To the English, domination of Ireland was a defensive move and strategically vital; to the Irish, it was aggression not only against their homeland but also against their faith. And in the struggle, England seemed to have all the advantages. Among other things, it had created a military force armed with artillery, a weapon the Irish were almost completely lacking, and English armies, trained and blooded on the Scottish frontier, were better organized, more unified and better equipped. Yet, in Elizabeth's first attempts to project English power into Ireland, the failure was miserable. In despair, Elizabeth sought a truce, but Spain forced her hand.

As the first of three armadas (*the* armada as we know it) sailed in 1588 against England, the Irish "question" came to the fore. Several of the ships that were not sunk or turned back landed or were wrecked on the Irish coast, where they discharged about three thousand Spanish soldiers. For the English, this was a nightmare come true. In panic, the government ordered the English lord deputy of Ireland to immediately kill any Spaniards found by his troops and any Irishmen who succored them. But some escaped to form a sort of military assistance team.

By 1595, the Spaniards had taught some of the Irish earls to use firearms, the caliver (or harquebus) and musket, and to mobilize, for the first time, not only their free retainers but even the peasantry. And profiting from Spanish training and from their own bitter experience, they changed their tactics to guerrilla warfare. As Americans, French and Indians were to do years later in the French and Indian Wars in America, the Irish troops laid ambushes in forests, where they were safe from the

English cavalry, and fired from behind cover. With these tactics, they suddenly became a force to reckon with; in fact, they wiped out an invading Anglo-Scottish army. This stunning victory, much magnified in the telling, so elated the Spanish government that, despite its increasing poverty, it responded to Irish appeals by launching two new armadas to invade England and succor the Irish, but these, like the first, were mostly wrecked by storms with devastating losses for the Spaniards and fatal consequences for the Irish.

It was at this time that Elizabeth found her general. Lord Mountjoy decided to kill all the Irishmen of fighting age and starve their families: "We spare none of what quality or sex soever, and it hath bred much terror in the people . . ." A near contemporary, Fynes Moryson, in a book published in London in 1617, sought to catch the horror of the war-induced famine by describing a

> Spectacle of three Children (whereof the eldest was not above ten Years old,) all eating and gnawing with the Teeth the Entrails of their Mother, upon whose Flesh they had fed 20 Days past, and having eaten all from the Feet upwards to the bare Bones, roasting it continually by a slow Fire, were now come to the eating of her said Entrails in like sort roasted, yet not divided from the Body, being as yet raw.

In this warfare, the English were not moved by humane considerations, but they were learning that garrisoning the island was insupportably expensive. Queen Elizabeth, never a lavish spender, was particularly and vocally disturbed by the costs and was disheartened to discover that English troops could not be fed off the land; so she began to experiment with a very old form of imperialism, displacing the inhabitants and bringing new loyal settlers, soldiers who were also "good husband men, plow wryghtes, kart wryghtes and smythes . . . eyther to take habitation yf they be hable, or els to staye and serve there under sotche gentlemen as shall inhabyte there."

The first attempt failed in the face of bitter Irish resistance, so the English turned to treachery. As the epic of Catholic Ireland, *The Annals of the Four Masters,* recounts, the English invited the Irish leader to a banquet, and

> as they were agreeably drinking and making merry, Brian [O'Neill], his brother, and his wife, were seized upon by the Earl, and all his people put unsparing to the sword—men, women, youths, and maidens—in Brian's own presence. Brian was afterwards sent to Dublin together with his wife and brother, where they were cut in quarters. Such was the end of their feast.

Even such savage cunning did not stop the war, but the government was determined not to give up. It was after Elizabeth's death that her cousin, who became James I, found the formula. It was a combination of massive colonization and a brutal scorched-earth policy. Unwittingly, the earls played into the hands of the British by fleeing abroad. So the British took the position that the lands they had held at the king's pleasure had reverted to the Crown; the peasantry who actually lived on those lands were treated as mere squatters and were starved into "regroupment," and large numbers of Protestant English and Scots were imported into Ireland to establish "plantations" on the vacated lands.

DURING THESE CRUCIAL YEARS, KING JAMES I HAD A FIRM hand on the government in London. But his reign was the beginning of a period of great turmoil in English politics in which the monarchy and the Parliament were increasingly at odds. So complex are the events that historians today are themselves engaged in a virtual civil war in their attempts to analyze the period. But for our purposes, the complexity is precisely the point: the dramatic turns of fortune and shifting alliances of each of the several groups active in Ireland caused them to play varying roles in the collapse of the monarchy, in the creation of an English republic under Cromwell, in the restoration of the monarchy, in the reassertion of Catholic power and in the collapse of the monarchy of James II. It was this labyrinth through which Robert had to try to find his way and which ultimately made it impossible for him to stay in Ireland.

On the lips of contemporaries, the issue was religion, an increasingly Protestant Parliament and public with a probably Catholic royal family, but to both sides "religion" encompassed the nature of government, the right to levy taxes, the control of land and the distribution of wealth. James's son Charles I, who became king in 1625, lacked his father's political finesse and firmly believed in his divine right to rule; he did not, until much too late, comprehend the change of the political basis of the English monarchy, and he was encouraged in his pro-Catholic policies by events in Europe where the Counter Reformation and the Thirty Years War created a climate of bloody warfare, revolution and ever-shifting alliances.

This is the context in which contemporaries saw the flirtation of King Charles with the European Catholic powers, his personal preference for Roman Catholics or Arminian (near Catholic) Anglicans, his struggle against the militant followers of John Knox in Scotland and his opposition to the non-Anglican Protestants of England. Even the selection of a prayer book and even such symbolic actions as the choice between standing and kneeling in church services took on a political meaning that is virtually impossible for our age to comprehend.

Meanwhile, in England and Scotland, Charles was struggling to win a series of fights over the nature of government, the right to tax, the control of armies and the orientation of the church that we segregate but that in seventeenth-century Europe were encompassed in everyone's mind as religion. Thus, it was of the greatest importance what the king believed and what kind of religion he would espouse or tolerate and what he would suppress. In a series of complex moves, Charles tried but failed to work out accommodations with the Presbyterian followers of John Knox of Scotland; then, determining on war, he sought to raise money without Parliament's authority. Not only his struggle with Parliament, which was increasingly defined also in religious terms as the seat of the Puritans, but also the kinds of taxes, the incidence of fines, the threat that arbitrary confiscations posed to all forms of tenure and the ways these fell on selected groups, all combined to create a strong opposition to him in England and led Parliament to begin a process that would ultimately lead to civil war.

In Ireland, the Gaelic lords welcomed the Old English into their ranks to form the Confederate Catholics of Ireland and began to fight a very effective guerrilla war. This new group solicited papal and Spanish support. At least briefly, their alliance turned the tide of battle. So when General Robert Monro attacked the Irish in June 1646, he met with disaster. At the Battle of Benburb, about three thousand of his Scottish soldiers were killed. It was then, apparently, that with the Scottish troops that were raised to replace these losses Robert Pollok came to Ireland.

A FTER THE OVERTHROW OF THE MONARCHY, PARLIAMENT'S "man of the hour," Oliver Cromwell, determined to stop the Irish campaign before it completely bankrupted England. In 1649 (shortly after King Charles was executed), he led the New Model Army to Ireland to conduct a classical "counterinsurgency" campaign. His campaign was short and brutal. He not only massacred whole towns but deported thousands of Catholics to virtual slavery in the West Indies and outlawed Catholicism; all Ireland was treated as conquered territory, with the lands of all Catholics who could not prove their constant support for Parliament to be divided among Protestant "adventurers" (investors) and soldiers. This was the most violent swing of the political pendulum in favor of the Scots. It did not stay on their side long.

Shortly after Cromwell's death in 1658, one of his generals marched on London, dissolved Parliament and put the son of Charles I, Charles II, a covert Catholic, on the throne. That swung the political pendulum to the other extreme. The new "Cavalier" Parliament sought revenge against those who had fought for Cromwell, had taken part in the execution of Charles I or, more generally, were Protestants. Their policies came to fruition with a vengeance in the "bloody assizes" only after Robert had left Ireland, but the trend was clear years before as courts were manipulated, agents provocateurs were set loose and summary arrest, exile and execution became common.

Meanwhile, in Ireland, such civic order as had existed broke down as former soldiers and guerrillas, by then Protestant as well as Catholic, formed "tory" (or outlaw) gangs. Fresh English troops were sent over to hunt them down. How many were killed in combat is unknown, but hundreds were executed, 3,400 were packed off in exile to Europe and, adopting the harsh measures of the former Cromwell regime, about 12,000 were "sold" into quasi-slavery to the sugar plantations of the Caribbean. It was primarily the Protestants who had to pay for these counterguerrilla operations, so they watched their lands being confiscated, fines for real or trumped-up infractions levied and old obligations dishonored. These actions terrified the Protestants and culminated in near hysteria in 1678 when they believed that they were to be massacred. Everywhere Robert turned, he would have heard rumors of plots and counterplots.

It was during these events that Robert married Magdalen Tasker and further complicated his already exposed position. Magdalen's father, Roger, had also been a soldier and then held a small fief, about five hundred acres, in Ballindrait, south of Londonderry in county Donegal. Colonel Roger was at least as compromised as Captain Robert. Worse, Magdalen's first husband, John Porter, a colonel in Cromwell's army, had been Robert's commander. Robert was standing on the brink of catastrophe.

In fact, he got out just in time. A few years after he had left for America, an angry and vengeful James II, having just lost the throne of England, came to Ireland. There he got the Parliament to pass a bill of attainder condemning thousands of Protestants, and after he had failed in his attempt to force the main Protestant town, Londonderry, to surrender, he burned down the houses of most of the Scots and other prominent Protestants in county Donegal. Colonel Tasker's house was spared, legend has it, because at an earlier and happier time, he had given the king lunch under the giant sycamore in his garden. But had Robert been there, he might have been hanged from the same tree.

MORE WORRIED THAN EXPECTANT, ROBERT GAZED DOWN AT the boat in the bay. From his vantage point, the first thing that would have struck his eye was that the bark was not very large, only about thirty-five meters long. He would learn that sailors evaluated it at "fifty tons burthen" and that it was a former cargo carrier of a type called, by its Dutch makers, a *fluyt,* or, by the English, more alarmingly, a flyboat.

The best-remembered seventeenth-century ships were entirely different; they were grandiose floating castles built in the tradition of the Spanish galleons that had carried the wealth of the New World to the Old. Building each of these monsters not only was ruinously expensive but also required the chopping down of several thousand giant oak trees. Since England and Scotland were already largely deforested, the quest for new sources of timber was one of the spurs that caused the English government to encourage the plantation of settlers in the New World. Timber, in fact, was the first cash crop sent back from the new colonies at Jamestown and Plymouth.

The humble *fluyt* was as far removed from the great ships as a peddler's cart from the gaudy giant float of a parade. Built by merchants for merchants, the *fluyt* was strictly utilitarian. Ungainly-looking and drably constructed, it had a flat bottom so that it could sail into the mud-choked ports of the North Sea; instead of statuesque prows and high gilt sterns, its two ends were blunt—indeed, seemingly sawed off—so that lumber could be stacked inside, and being lightly and cheaply built, it lacked reinforcing planking and interior compartments. Unlike the clumsy and ill-rigged English and French ships of the period, which required large crews, the *fluyt* could be handled by only a dozen sailors. Consequently, it could do the job of a comparable English or French ship at about half the cost. While it would win no prizes for beauty and would seldom inspire artists, it was the workhorse of the seventeenth-century coastal trade.

Robert had probably made a good deal with the owners in procuring his boat, for in their recent wars with the Dutch, the English had captured more than twelve hundred, and when they were resold to English captains and adventurers (as venture capitalists were then known), they flooded the shipping market and brought down prices to the lowest ebb in the century.

From his military experience, Robert knew that armies travel on their stomachs. In Ireland, he had seen that even a disciplined and well-trained army could meet catastrophe as often in the failure to find food locally as in combat. And, of course, there was no "locally" at sea, and all the sailors' tales warned of voyages in which ships ran out of supplies, so that passengers and crew died or arrived as mere skeletons.

Loading food was too crucial a task to be entrusted to "victuallers." Anyway, they had a foul reputation for cheating on their contracts. From his old soldier companions, Robert had certainly heard about Cromwell's troopships, becalmed on their way to the West Indies in 1655, discovering that they did not have much of the food they thought they had and that even their biscuits were "most beastly rotten." A man of Robert's experience would have demanded to know every detail of supply.

Setting out across the Atlantic in a small boat is still, in our day, no casual venture, and in the seventeenth century it was far more daring: it was to be cast nearly blind and virtually defenseless into a void. What did this experience mean? How did Robert and the thousands who followed him to the New World feel about it? Why did some die while some survived? Answers to these questions shaped the growth of the American colonies. First, there was the ship itself.

Because they were so lightly built, *fluyts* were in need of constant repair. That fact together with the problem of accumulating stores and waiting out the changing weather in the North of Ireland probably meant that Robert's little boat spent months lying at anchor in the river Foyle just off Londonderry a few miles downriver from his wife's house in county Donegal. So he could often ride or take a barge down to watch the progress of the repairs and loading.

In planning on provisions, he would have had to consider how long the trip would take and how many mouths had to be fed.

The length of the trip was, of course, critical, but it was also unpredictable. When Robert sailed, very few ships had made the trip from Northern Ireland, so there was little experience to go by. And what little there was, was not reassuring.

These are some of the accounts he may have heard from sailors in Londonderry or Donegal. In 1669, on the first expedition to the Carolinas just fifteen years before he planned to sail, another, considerably larger *fluyt* sailed with two other ships to his destination, the bay named for the Chesapeake Indians. It took them nearly two months to reach Barbados, and once there, they were struck by a fearful gale that wrecked one of the three. Shortly thereafter, near the Bahamas, another ship was "cast away." The third reached Cape Fear but only after a month's sail. Watching the breakup of his little fleet, the captain was said to have gone mad and jumped overboard. And in 1670, another expedition, fitted out in part by the young philosopher John Locke, took some seven months, including stopovers for repairs, to reach the American coast.

Even today we do not know very much about the voyages of Robert's times, and he knew even less, but for many years after he had sailed, the ships about which we have some information were much like his. In the eighteenth century, when there was considerably more experience than in 1680, ships were reported to take from eight to ten weeks from the Irish ports to America. That was an average, however, and some took seventeen weeks or more. Others never made it. In that age of sail, the winds set the pace: strong westerly winds and calms could add weeks to the trip, bringing starvation to the passengers and crews. In 1729, some 175 passengers died on two vessels during their crossing, and in 1741, 6 of the passengers on the *Seaflower* were eaten by their starving shipmates. A writer in the June 7, 1729, *Dublin Weekly Journal* commented on "all the Tryles, Hardships, and Dangers of the Seas, by Storms, Shipwracks, Turks and Pyrates, to be starved, or cast away by the Villany of Ship Masters . . ." So grim were these voyages that, proportionally, about as many died as on the later slave ships.

While Robert (mercifully) could not have known of these floating disasters, there were many tales of woe he surely would have heard from the sailors. They must have pushed him to make every possible provision for the journey. And the journey itself was only the start: once they had survived the passage and landed, they would have to feed themselves until enough land could be cleared, planted and harvested to keep them alive. That would require at least a year. So to the question of how much food they should store, the answer must have been "as much as the ship can carry."

More urgent was the parallel question of how much water. How much they would need would in part depend on how long the trip would be. From Hakluyt's account and from sailors' stories, Robert would have learned that there was no certain answer, but he could estimate how much water each person would need in a day. He may have tried to figure out what he drank in a day and how much he used to keep reasonably clean, probably concluding that a gallon a day was about the minimum. But that answer was only a start toward what he needed to know. Indeed, as he puzzled over all the problems of the trip, each question seemed to lead to another. If each person needed at least a gallon of water a day, the total amount the ship should carry depended on how many people there would be.

A *fluyt* was generally manned by a crew of twelve, but that was for relatively short trips around the North Sea. So the captain would probably have put the figure considerably higher, perhaps another five or six, in case some fell overboard in a storm, got sick or broke arms or legs, or the little boat faced the unspoken dread of pirate attack.

Pirate attack! That would have raised to an old soldier an even more pressing question. Was the boat able to defend itself? Almost the first thing Robert would have noticed was that there were no cannons on board. The *fluyt* was, after all, just a coastal carrier, designed to transport lumber from one North Sea port to another at the lowest possible cost. Being so lightly (and cheaply) built, it would have been torn apart by the recoil of cannon. The builders and former owners had decided that the *fluyt* didn't need to be armed because pirates had ceased to be a major threat in the North Sea and because its planned cargo was not worth the attention of any who might slip past the English, Dutch and French navies. But all that was now changed. Out in the Atlantic, especially if the winds drove them down to the Canaries, and sailing as slowly as a *fluyt* did, pirates could be a real threat, even for such a modest little boat. Pirates would think that any ship heading across the Atlantic must have *something* on board worth taking. Being themselves often short of water and food, pirates would regard those basics as making any ship worth taking, and there was always the issue of kidnap for ransom. Even the governor designate of North Carolina had been captured by Barbary pirates on his way to America and was still in captivity when Robert sailed.

Not only out at sea but right in the Chesapeake Bay, there were frequent attacks by buccaneers. One could quibble over whether he started as a pirate or a semilegal privateer, but Richard Ingle had virtually conquered Maryland in 1644, captured the capital, St. Mary's, and taken the governor prisoner. Not only did he and his men pillage, burn, kidnap and kill, but they stimulated the Protestant Marylanders to do the same to their Catholic neighbors, so that what started as a raid turned into a vicious civil war. That war, in turn, converted the already strained relations with the neighboring colony of Virginia over ownership of Kent Island (adjacent to Annapolis) into an intercolonial war that sounded much like hostilities in Ireland. What the current status was, Robert probably did not know, but from his experience in Ireland, he would have ascribed to both sides an opportunistic approach to strangers who might have something worth taking.

Nothing in the intervening years argued to the contrary. The pirates were still there and would remain there long after Robert had sailed. Indeed, so bad was the situation that the government often appeared helpless. King Charles II in 1684 issued a high-sounding proclamation against piracy, which was so ineffective that it had to be renewed by King James II in 1687. James added the offer of a pardon for those pirates who turned themselves in. That didn't work either; so in the following year, he issued "A Proclamation for the more effectuall reducing and supressing of Pirats and Privateers in America" and sent out a seaborne search-and-destroy mission, promising its commander the profits from those ships he seized. The effect of this was to turn the king's force into a sort of pirate fleet itself, since the commander was apt to view any particularly attractive prize as a pirate.

Added to pirates, privateers and bounty hunters were England's enemies, the Spanish and the Dutch. England's wars with the Dutch, in which the English had carried off a large part of the Dutch merchant fleet including the *fluyt* on which Robert was to sail, had left the Dutch spoiling for revenge. Just about the time Robert proposed to sail, a Dutch man-of-war sailed boldly into the Chesapeake and destroyed a number of ships as the authorities, helplessly, watched from ashore.

While Robert probably had no opinion on how many sailors might be required, he must have thought that they should take aboard a half dozen stout men-at-arms. He would certainly have wished he still had some of the men of his old company, but after Cromwell died, the troops were impossible to hold together. (Later, of course, keeping them together was to risk arrest for conspiracy, and by then, in fact, no one wanted even to admit that he had served in the army or knew anything about handling arms for fear that he would be shipped off to slavery in the Caribbean.) By careful scouting and by word of mouth, however, Robert probably located half a dozen of his old men or their sons.

So he could count on a crew of at least twenty soldiers and sailors, in addition to his immediate family: himself, his wife, Magdalen, and their three boys. Such records as we have suggest that Magdalen insisted on taking along one or two Irish servant girls, a common practice among the émigrés, which we learn from the fact that various colonies passed laws in 1698, 1704 and 1715 against the importation of Irish servants. So "the family" made seven. And being a soldier, Robert probably figured that at least one of the men might smuggle aboard a wench. Women in those parts would do almost anything to get away from Donegal.

To cut costs, Robert and the shipowners would have cast about for others who would pay for their passage. It is likely that some of these people, like Robert, were former soldiers who had decided to leave for the New World on their own, and some of these would also have brought their families. We know that similar boats in the next century often carried a hundred or more passengers; this one, in the days before the massive migrations or the enforced exile of prisoners, would have probably taken fifty or so. How much water did that mean? A lot! Figuring on barrels of fifty or so gallons each, at least a hundred barrels would be needed.

But even that was not enough. There would be animals on board, and until they were slaughtered, they would need water too. Some, Robert hoped, would live to reach Lord Baltimore's Maryland plantation so the family could get established there.

But he probably cut down on barrels of water by replacing some of them with wine and beer. People in those days tried to avoid drinking water as much as possible because they feared it as a source of disease. He may not have known it, but the earlier Pilgrims landed at Plymouth Rock because they had run out of beer.

Most of the diet on the ship would be Scots' peasant food: oatcakes, porridge, some chicken every few days. To these Robert probably added stocks of cheese, onions, salted and dried fish and beef, marmalades, and large quantities of rusk, the ancestor of the southern "beaten biscuit." Not a very tasty menu, but the important thing was not to get things that would spoil in the salty wet hold, although at sea in the *fluyt,* that would have been just a pious hope. In case some of the food did rot, they would eat the animals. Chickens would have been the cheapest and easiest to handle, and they would also lay eggs. As they dwindled in number, though, Robert would have hoped that enough would survive that he could reestablish the flock in the New World. How many? The ideal would be the staggering and impossible number of about two hundred, but he would probably have compromised at about half that. We know they also took a few cows, because Robert's son John registered the earmark of a cow on September 8, 1680.

Magdalen and her mother meanwhile must have been hard at work assembling what they thought the family would need "over there."

They had little information on what they would find when they reached the New World. It might as well have been the moon they were heading for. There were no maps or drawings, and no one they knew, except for a few of the sailors, had ever been there and come back. They had to bring everything they would need to make cloth, cook, sew, make shoes. They were used to doing these things in Ireland, so they knew what they would need to turn raw materials into finished goods. But in Ireland, they had been able to get wool and flax and animal hides, and when they needed a new iron pan or kettle, as they did very rarely, they knew that an itinerant ironmonger was not far away. In the New World, however, metal was so rare that immigrants were advised to bring even hinges for their doors.

Magdalen and Robert may have seen the list of equipment and clothing provided to the would-be Maryland colonists in a more or less official pamphlet handed out by Lord Baltimore's brother-in-law in London in 1635. It specified everything from string (then called points) for mending clothing to aqua vitae to a "bandeleere and flaske."

Magdalen must have gathered an assortment of necessities as she saw them: yards of cloth, kettles, pots and lavers, a large pewter platter, a dozen or so pewter plates and bowls and a larger number of wooden plates. The centerpiece of any well-appointed Scots-Irish table was the saltfat, or saltcellar, that marked the boundary on the table between the "quality" and the "common," and Magdalen would certainly have carried hers. Had she not brought it, she would have been obligated, in the Scots tradition, to mark the social dividing line on the dining board with chalk. It was as well that no one then used earthenware or "china" plates or bowls or glassware, as they almost surely would have been broken on the trip. The men carried their knives with them at all times and used them to cut and spear the food at table. Forks were not yet in use, so everyone ate with the fingers, being careful for politeness' sake to use only the thumb and the first two fingers in taking food out of the common bowl lest he or she seemed greedy. But in keeping with the new fashion, Magdalen apparently (for they are later mentioned when they were settled) insisted on bringing a dozen silver spoons.

Magdalen apparently also insisted on taking her wooden bed with its feather mattress and the two *capamres,* or wooden chests, in which she had put her "hopes" since she was a young woman. These chests had followed her and her first husband and would, she must have said, go with her even if, God forbid, she had to marry a third time. Reluctantly, she put aside the *dressoir* that had ornamented the hall of her father's house and that he had given her at the time of her first marriage. Robert had argued that it was simply too massive to be carried on whatever primitive means of conveyance they would have in the New World; secretly, he probably thought it was too pretentious for the style of life they would have there. But she did bring the family clock, which for generations was to grace their house in Maryland.

In addition, there were probably many miscellaneous small items. These have disappeared over the generations and are not mentioned in wills, but the Polloks would have taken the things that they used to amuse themselves or to add comfort in the cold drafty houses. And certainly they would have packed a supply of the newly introduced tea leaves and coffee beans, brought into England in the 1660s by the East India Company, which everyone then regarded as medicine against "defluxion" (the discharge accompanying a cold). They had no carpets because carpets were only just coming into use in the North of Ireland, and it was common both in Ireland and in the New World to use only rushes on the floor.

Probably Robert would not have concerned himself so much with these "women's affairs," but he certainly would have given close attention to the weapons he and his associates would need when they arrived. People said the land was mostly empty but that the savages who lived in America were treacherous and vicious. The Indians were armed with bows and arrows, pointed with a shell or fish tooth, or with wooden, fire-hardened swords and war clubs with stag horns embedded in them. Not as effective as the steel sword Robert carried, but under the right conditions lethal enough. He and his men also wore breastplates of wood which would stop an arrow.

From his Irish experience, Robert would have assumed that some of the natives had acquired firearms from the Europeans against whom they fought and with whom they traded, just as the Irish had been provided with weapons by the Spaniards and the French. Indeed, unknown to Robert, the English themselves had supplied arms to the Indians so that they could bring the settlers fresh meat.

Already in 1618, an English governor of the Jamestown, Virginia, colony issued an edict prohibiting the teaching of Indians to use firearms on pain of death. But his edict apparently did little good, since a few years later another governor, this time in Plymouth Plantation to the north, lamented the widespread sale of muskets to the Indians: "O, the horribleness of this villainy!" The Indians were, he said, "ordinarily better fitted and furnished than the English themselves."

Robert was not sure exactly where he would land or whether, once he got there, he would have to move to another place. Whatever he heard about the Indians who would probably be his neighbors, others might be quite different and differently armed and organized. Battle experience in Ireland taught him it was wise to be as prepared as possible.

Robert's principal weapon had been the sword with a Dutch-forged blade, although he often carried a brace of pistols or a heavy carbine. Most of the soldiers he knew had been armed with the harquebus, which was a reasonably effective firearm, a little better than a crossbow, but very slow to load, dangerous to handle and fatally weakened by getting wet or having the powder blown out of the pan in a strong breeze. Moreover, the match, a coil of cord two or three yards long, had to be lit well in advance of firing. The musket, while firing a heavier slug and so useful against a man in armor, was so heavy and cumbersome with its four-foot-long barrel that it could be fired only with a supporting stake in the ground. The newer flint-firing mechanisms in the firelock, or *snaphanse,* were more reliable than the matchlocks, particularly in the rain, but, still, it took a long time to load them. And unless you were practically on top of your enemy, harquebuses and muskets produced more noise than harm. Because of his political past, Robert would have had to take whatever he could find on what amounted to the black market.

Robert also needed to plan for what tools he and his family would need to tame the land. These would have been simple but absolutely necessary: hoes, axes, saws, hammers, shovels, augurs, chisels, a pickax, a grindstone and a supply of nails. Most of these tools would look very different from their modern counterparts. The ax, for example, was as different from the ax we know as a musket is from a modern rifle: its head was a complex of metals of which only the cutting edge was hardened iron or steel, and the handle, unlike the Swedish or "American" ax, was just a straight pole. This would be important, although Robert would not have known it, because with such an inefficient tool, even spending nearly full-time and working hard, no one could clear more than about an acre of land a year—less in a lifetime than in most areas would support a family. Settlers had either to employ Indian techniques of land clearance or to acquire already cleared Indian land.

AFTER TOOLS, WEAPONS, CLOTHING AND FOOD SUPPLIES HAD been assembled, two questions remained unanswered: where exactly were they going and how would they find it?

Most ships bound for the New World took the southern route along the European coast, south past Madeira and the Canaries, almost to the Cape Verde Islands, west below the Tropic of Cancer to Dominica, then up to the west of Puerto Rico and east of the Bahamas to the Carolina coast. That route had been traditional since Columbus's time because the winds were usually favorable, provided the ships sailed well to the south of the Tropic of Cancer, but experienced sailors would have told Robert that they would do almost anything to avoid the violent and frequent storms encountered off Cape Hatteras, famous for demasting ships, starting timbers, carrying away longboats and caving in hulls.

On the northern route, the sea was usually rough, and when they hit, storms could last for days or even weeks. Then a ship would be out of control and might be blown onto uncharted reefs or sandbars. But, particularly from the North of Ireland, the distance was shorter and the risk of pirates was less.

There was no safe way. One chilling story in Hakluyt describes what it was like to be "cast away." When the survivors took to the longboat, their ordeal had just begun. As a survivor wrote,

Thus we continued the third and fourth day without any sustenance, save onely the weedes that swamme in the Sea, and salt water to drinke. The fifth day Hedly [the ship's master] dyed and another moreover: then wee desired all to die: for in all these five dayes and five nights we saw the Sunne but once and the Starre but one night, it was so foul weather.

Even if Robert's ship could avoid reefs and was lucky enough to miss the frequent storms, he must have been troubled by the many rumors and tales that warned of unknown or ununderstood natural, or supernatural, forces such as "the burnt line, whereby commonly both beverage and victuall are corrupted, and mens health very much impayred . . . [or] the frozen seas, which yeelde sundry extreme dangers." Knowing so little about the working of the physical world, Robert would have been disturbed to read in Hakluyt, by an unknown writer, that because passage of the sun over the Atlantic "doe qualifie and infeeble greatly the Sunnes reverberation . . . the Sunnes reflection is much cooled, and cannot be so forcible in the Newfound land, nor generally throughout America, as in Europe . . ."

A T LEAST AS LATE AS HALF A CENTURY BEFORE ROBERT SAILED, the area he hoped to reach, the Chesapeake, was thought to be an inland sea reaching ultimately to India or perhaps China. Of course, by the time Robert sailed, much more was known, and we would be mistaken to think of him or his fellow travelers as ignorant or stupid, but the boundaries of their knowledge were far more narrow than ours. There were no accurate maps, and for them "America" was a strip of land only a few miles deep along the Atlantic coast.

Even had they known more, they could not have better controlled where a ship went, since that was only partly a function of its rudder; more significant were the winds (which were unpredictable) and the tides (which were largely unknown). The *Endeavour* in 1747 off the Carolina coast lost her masts, rigging and longboat in "exceeding hard Gales of Wind" and wallowed in the Atlantic for six months before being carried by the Gulf Stream all the way to the Hebrides. It is truly remarkable that so many ships actually reached their destinations.

Navigational instruments had changed little since medieval times. To estimate latitude, astrolabes, both the simple and the "jackass" quadrants, and cross staffs were still common. But there was no means to ascertain longitude. Sailors relied mainly upon dead reckoning to try to fix the position of the boat. For this, they used two instruments, the compass and the combination of log lines and sandglasses. Every few hours, they noted an estimate of speed from feeding out a long rope fixed so that the end would remain more or less stationary in the water while they measured the time with a sandglass. This was extremely inaccurate, so they were usually miles away from where they thought they were. Since they had no accurate charts and the coasts and islands were unmarked and without any warning lights, they were in frequent danger of running aground on rocks or sandbars. To try to correct for this, they took samples of the bottom, when they could reach it, with a lead line, a sort of scoop attached to a rope, which they lowered off the side. By tradition and sometimes by markings on their "pilots," or sailing notes, they knew what kind of sand or rock they were likely to encounter in different areas of the sea. They also observed the flights of birds and the flotsam on the sea surface for signs of the proximity of land. But the danger remained clear and present that they would miscalculate and come unexpectedly, probably in a fog or moonless night, upon a reef, sandbar or shore. And with dreadful consequences. Thoughts along these lines made Robert check, as carefully as his landsman's experience would afford, the longboat stored above the main cabin.

THERE WERE PASSENGERS ON THE *FLUYT* FOR WHOM NO ONE could have planned: rats, vermin and various pathogens.

Virtually all small, wooden boats are infested with rats. We may be sure that Robert's was no exception, since it had been a cargo carrier during most of its career and had, like a later-day tramp steamer, gone from little port to port, loading and unloading cargo. That some species of rats carry typhus we now know, but in those days people did not. They did, however, find rats noxious and fought with them in their cramped quarters over food. In the account of a boat sailing about the same time as Robert's, however, we find that rats had their uses: driven

off its course by storm, the passengers of the *Virginia Merchant* were glad
to have them.

> Women and children made dismal cries and grievous com-
> plaints [in their hunger]. The infinite number of rats that all
> the voyage had been our plague, we now were glad to make
> our prey to feed on; and as they were insnared and taken, a
> well grown rat was sold for sixteen shillings as a market rate.
> Nay, before the voyage did end, a woman great with child of-
> fered twenty shillings for a rat, which the proprietor refusing,
> the woman died.

Rats may have had their uses, but lice did not. Unable to bathe
often and frequently confined in cramped and unventilated quarters during foul weather, almost all travelers were tormented by them. As one
French writer commented about his trip a few years later, "Each time
we left the tween-decks we found ourselves covered with vermin. I
found them even in my shoes." Unable to wash often or even to air out
bedding and clothes, the passengers picked away at one another's bodies,
but vermin were never defeated in crowded boats. They were a fact of
life.

A fact of death was mostly invisible. It was the billions of
pathogenes accompanying humans and animals across the Atlantic. This
was not so terrible a problem for Robert's group as it would become in
the next century when large groups of poor and undernourished people,
many of them prisoners, were jammed into small, poorly ventilated
boats. Then, "there is on board these ships," as a later German traveler,
wrote of his experience,

> terrible misery, stench, fumes, horror, vomiting, many kinds
> of sea-sickness, fever dysentery, headache, heat constipation,
> boils, scurvy, cancer, mouthrot, and the like, all of which

comes from old and sharply salted food and meat, also from very bad and foul water, so that many die miserably.

Children, he went on, rarely survived the voyage; on his trip, thirty-two died and were cast into the sea. Children not only were victims but became, unintentionally, the secret weapon of the whites against the Indians because they were carriers of the most lethal of the pathogens, smallpox. During the seventeenth century, virtually every person who reached maturity had been exposed to smallpox and so was immune, but children were often in process of being infected; so they were to prove the most deadly to the native Americans, none of whom had immunities to smallpox or other "childhood" diseases. No one then knew what caused smallpox, but malevolence or magic was often suspected. On one ship that sailed in the middle of the eighteenth century, the sailors thought it came about as a result of a macabre incident told by her grandmother to Molly Polk.

When they had been some days out at sea an old lady died. Her children of course were anxious to do the best for their mother and as there were no coffins to be had, they implied their household linens out of a chest, tied her in it and . . . At sunrise she was cast into the sea. Of course, it was very depressing, but later when everything had quieted down all the passengers were on deck for a sunbath. Some one spied a queer looking something that seemed to be following in the wake of the vessel. It proved to be the old lady. She was apparently sitting up in the box bowing to them for of course she went up and down with the waves. She was taken on board. This time sewed in a hemp sack and weighted down. This time she went over for good. Sailors are as a rule very superstitious especially in those days, and later on they attributed an outbreak of small pox on the vessel to the old lady's antics.

The terrible bane of all sea travelers then was scurvy. In Hakluyt's *Voyages* are descriptions of men whose legs were "swolne euery ioint withall With this disease, which . . . the Scuruie men doe call." Scurvy is exacerbated by eating precisely the sort of food sailing ships then carried, heavily salted meats. But there was then no other means of preserving meat than to salt it, and the cause of scurvy was not yet known in Europe, although the Chinese, Arabs and some American Indians had cures for it.

A T LAST THE REPAIRS AND THE LOADING OF THE LITTLE *fluyt* were complete. Robert must have been increasingly anxious in the final weeks as rumors of plots and counterplots, arrests and plans for rebellion and the possibilities of a French invasion of Ireland and even civil war in England had swirled around the streets of Londonderry.

In last-minute haste and in hushed and tearful good-byes to friends and relatives, the little band boarded the ship. It then was towed behind rowboats out into Lough Foyle and slowly floated down toward Inishowen Head.

The calm waters of the lough must have given a sense of security and delight to everyone on board. The sea breeze would have been fresh, salty and stimulating, and the adventure was still new and exciting. I imagine the children racing around the deck, exploring each nook and examining each new piece of equipment while the adults set about sorting their gear and examining the sleeping arrangements or just watching the scenery. All this peace and happiness was quickly to be shattered as they approached Inishowen and saw, for the first time, the waves of the North Atlantic. Within hours, their one wish would have been to stop the wretched boat from yawing and pitching or rolling from side to side.

The *fluyt* was simply not designed for the Atlantic. Long and narrow for its bulk, it was also flat-bottomed, so although it was ballasted with cobblestones, it rolled alarmingly even in slight swells, and in rough seas danced madly to the rhythm of the waves. The captain, of course, had expected this and so had ordered the carpenters to construct what resembled branding chutes on American ranches, to confine the cattle and keep them from being thrown against the sides and breaking their legs. For the people, however, no such protection was possible.

The hold of the *fluyt,* meant to carry bulk cargo and particularly long logs, was as little obstructed as possible by partitions. Only the braces for the masts and such beams as were required to support the sides were permanent. The hold was, in fact, just a single room—what the Dutch builders of the ship called the *koebrugdek*—only four or five feet high, between the upper deck and the floor covering the bilge. Some partitions had undoubtedly been cobbled together during the refitting, but most were probably canvas drapes. All the people and all the animals were literally cheek by jowl.

The hammock was not yet in common use on northern ships, and their fixed bunks caught each roll and pitch. People, equipment, furniture, stores and animals were hurled from side to side. Everything that was not fastened down skidded or flew from port to starboard and back every minute or so, and the bilge water, just below the deck on which people and animals were housed, boiled and sloshed in unceasing flow. At Inishowen, I am sure, everyone became violently seasick.

Rounding Inishowen Head, the captain would have tried to stand off as far to the north-northeast as he could to give wide berth to the rocks and shoals of the northern coast where professional pirates and casual brigands were known to lurk in wait for distressed ships. In the time of the Spanish Armada, men had perished in those cold and gloomy seas by the thousands. This course would have put the little ship athwart the worst of the winds and would have given the passengers a sobering baptism for the voyage ahead. In their minds, all thoughts of pirates and reefs were driven by the incessant pounding and rolling of wave and ship. For weeks to come, it would not stop.

In the hold, the animals could not be segregated from the passengers; so echoing the moaning and cracking of the timbers, their bellowing, squealing, clucking and whimpering must have produced a

discordant symphony, indeed, a ceaseless cacophony; the animals, perhaps even more than the adults or even the children, were terrified by
the new experience and gave vent to their terror with sound and scent.

In their distress, no one probably gave much thought to food for the
first few days, but gradually the demands of the body would have asserted themselves. For cooking, the crew had set up a "caboose." A recent innovation, the caboose was a small box or hut placed on the
quarterdeck to protect a barrel sawn in half and filled with sand, for a
fire over which a pot was suspended.

Fire was too dangerous to be made belowdecks, so there were no
lanterns. Such light as there was, was got from candles, which were extinguished in the almost constant rough weather. Since the hatch would
be battened down to prevent seawater from pouring in, the hold must
often have seemed to the miserable passengers, huddled in the pitch-
blackness and airless gloom, like a loose-fitting coffin.

The experience would have seemed worse for women. Coming
from a strict and private world, Magdalen, in that common bedroom,
probably seldom if ever felt that she could remove her clothing to wash.
Even when she wished to, fresh water would have been given out grudgingly for anything but drinking, and seawater would have left a crust that
would make clothes irritate the skin. For much of the trip, frequent rain
and fog would have made drying anything difficult or impossible, so all
clothes would have been mildewed. Worse, toilet facilities were merely
openings over the side which, as the ship rolled, must have terrified all
those who used them.

Little would these passengers have believed that, in comparison to
the misery suffered by the thousands who followed their path from Scotland, Ireland, England, Germany and other lands in the next century,
theirs was a pleasant cruise. But few who experienced it could ever contemplate going back.

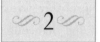

ARRIVAL

"Polk's Folly"

WHEN IN 1516 THOMAS MORE SET OUT THE DESCRIPTION of his ideal land, which he called Utopia, he wrote that it was an island bent in a five-hundred-mile crescent around an inland sea, "well secured from the wind [so that] the bay does not rage with great waves, but is quiet like a lake." He would have been astonished, had he been able to read the account written in 1584 by Captains Philip Amadas and Arthur Barlowe, of sailing into a real-life Utopia, the Chesapeake.

> . . . after we entred into the Haven, we saw before us an-
> other mighty long Sea: for there lyeth along the coast a tracte
> of Islands, two hundreth miles in length, adjoyning to the
> Ocean sea . . . most beautifull and pleasant to behold, re-
> plenished with Deere, Conies, Hares and divers beasts, and

about them the goodliest and best fish in the world, and in greatest abundance.

Indeed, Sir Thomas would hardly have believed a description of the Chesapeake: fed by nearly two hundred streams and rivers, of which many were large enough to accommodate boats the size of Robert's *fluyt,* the Chesapeake, like Utopia, formed a giant crescent, but New World nature was far grander than Old World art. The Chesapeake was comprised of nearly five thousand miles of shorelands, among which stretched a calm bay large enough, as one of the early English governors of Virginia boasted, to "harbour twenty Thousand Ships at once." Or as Father Andrew White wrote in 1634, England's "Thames is but a little finger to it."

Sir Thomas, of course, had been less interested in describing geography than people, since he was using his imaginary Utopians to comment on the manners and customs of Europeans. In Utopia, rulers were described as wise, stern and generous. Here again, nature appeared to follow art. To Captains Amadas and Barlowe, Wingandacoa, as the Indians called it, appeared an earthly paradise. Its rulers were depicted as virtual philosopher-kings, and "no people in the worlde cary more respect to their King, Nobilitie, and Governours, then these doe."

Beautiful people the early observers found them to be. The lovely consort of the crown prince was said to be adorned with "bracelets of pearles hanging down to her middle." Captain John Smith described one Indian he saw as "the goodliest man that ever we beheld." And a later observer, Robert Beverley, echoing these views, waxed lyrical when he described Indians who, he said, have the

cleanest and most exact Limbs in the World: They are so perfect in their outward frame, that I never heard of one single *Indian,* that was either dwarfish, crooked, bandy-legg'd, or otherwise misshapen . . . Their Women are generally Beautiful, possessing an uncommon delicacy of Shape and Features,

and wanting no Charm, but that of a fair Complexion . . .
[Women] are remarkable for having small round Breasts, and
so firm, that they are hardly ever observ'd to hang down, even
in old Women.

The incoming Europeans found the Indians not only beautiful but
friendly and welcoming. Amadas and Barlowe again:

when we came to the shore to him [the Indian leader] with our
weapons, hee neyer mooved from his place . . . nor never
mistrusted any harme to be offred from us, but sitting still he
beckoned us to come and sit by him, which we performed:
and being set hee made all signes of joy and welcome, striking
on his head and his breast and afterwardes on ours, to shewe
wee were all one, smiling and making shewe the beset he
could of all love, and familiaritie.

And, with the land itself being truly one of milk and honey, there was
much for the ruler to be generous with.

He sent us every day a brase or two of fat Bucks, Conies,
Hares, Fish the best of the world. He sent us diverse kindes of
fruites, Melons, Walnuts, Cucumbers, Gourdes, Peasse, and
divers rootes, and fruites very excellent good, and of their
Countrey corne, which is very white, faire and well tasted,
and groweth three times in five moneth [because] The soile is
the most plentifull, sweete, fruitfull and wholsome of all the
world . . .

As they composed their report, Amadas and Barlowe appear almost
to taste the fruits and vegetables. From what we know of the hardship of
travel on sailing ships, we are not surprised: getting off cramped, dirty
and meagerly supplied ships, hungry, tired and probably sick, they must

have been overwhelmed by the bounty of the New World. They were almost equally delighted by the natives. As they wrote,

> We found the people most gentle, loving, and faithfull, voide of all guile and treason, and such as live after the maner of the golden age . . . a more kinde and loving people there can not be found in the worlde . . .

How these words would be mocked by events of the next two centuries!

OF COURSE, THE CHESAPEAKE WAS NOT COMPLETELY AN earthly paradise. The aborigines had to cope with a nature that, while bountiful, was also capricious and sometimes pestilent, and with one another, who, while sometimes welcoming to outsiders, were often at ceremonial and occasionally at deadly war. What was this pre-invasion Eden truly like?

First of all, a price had to be paid for the hundreds of rivers and thousands of miles of coast: much of the land was swampy, and since the tidal action was insufficient to purge the bays and streams, much of the water was stagnant. These two features made for an almost perfect sanctuary for birds and fish but also for mosquitoes and a wide variety of pathogens. Before the arrival of the whites, the relatively few human inhabitants could avoid the marsh and set up their towns on high ground, but when the whites began to pour in, even the lands that the Indians had avoided were settled. There the colonists contracted a variety of "fevers," especially malaria, and "bloudie Flixe," or dysentery.

These diseases killed many whites, and the diseases that the whites unknowingly brought with them, against which the Indians had no immunities, caused an appalling mortality among them. Even a century before Robert sailed for America, the early visitor Ralph Lane described the lethal impact of contact with Europeans on the natives in Wingandacoa and Wingina. As he wrote,

within a few dayes after our departure from every such
Towne, the people began to die very fast, and many in short
space, in some Townes about twentie, in some fourtie, and in
one sixe score, which in trueth was very many in respect of
their numbers. This happened in no place that we could
learne, but where we had bin, where they used some practise
against us, & after such time. The disease also was so strange,
that they neither knewe what it was, nor how to cure it, the
like by report of the oldest men in the Countrey never happened before, time out of minde.

The lives of the Indians the whites first met have been obscured by
later experiences. One of the many misconceptions is that the Indians in
the Chesapeake were nomads; in fact, not only were they farmers, but
they lived "for the most part in Townes, like Countrey Villages in England." The houses, as Captain John Smith found on his travels, were so
commodious that the new arrivals often preferred them to the English
houses in which they had been born.

Moreover, the Indians were not "simple savages." Those who met
them found them to be politically sophisticated, with the individual
communities—what the whites thought of as "tribes"—linked into
confederations that often covered vast areas, and maintaining even more
extensive trade and diplomatic contacts with peoples distant from them
by days or even weeks of travel. True, their command of technology was
primitive vis-à-vis contemporary Europe, but it was in balance with resources and population pressures, and in some fields it was in advance of
Europe. In agriculture, corn (in the Algonquin language, *maize)* production had higher yields than almost any European crop, and the early colonists learned to cultivate it in the Indian manner. Even more was to be
learned by them in medicine, a field in which the early travelers and settlers regarded Indians as their teachers; particularly their beneficial use
of herbs astonished the arriving Europeans, whose own medical prac-

tices often rivaled diseases in their lethal effects. But since the Indians were almost totally devoid of metallurgy, it was mainly in warfare that their technology and practice shows to the greatest disadvantage.

"Violent theater" is how I have described an early stage of the warfare among tribal peoples in Africa and Asia, and the term is suggestive also of the customs of the American Indians before the spread of firearms. Battles were great ceremonial displays in which large formations of ornately costumed warriors performed an elaborate choreography in which relatively few were actually killed. Traditional Indian war was not about death: indeed, among such Indian nations as the Iroquois, to die on the field of battle was "a terrible prospect since the dead would not be accepted into the community of the afterworld but would have to wander alone seeking vengeance." Despite this danger, which of course always existed when arrows and spears were flying and warriors were packed together like European soldiers in formation, warfare was attractive, since only in it could warriors demonstrate the valor and skill that gave them status in their communities and assuage or work off sorrow and anguish for the deaths of loved ones.

"War" seldom destroyed property or harmed women and children; nor, generally, was it fought to acquire territory from the enemy. But as in all combat, defeat had its price: when prisoners were taken, they were sometimes adopted into a family of the victorious side, an act that the Algonquin and other Indians called "covering" or "raising up the dead," but at other times, to assuage the pain of loss, prisoners were viciously and painfully executed. Then their bodies might be eaten to imbibe their courage.

In this phase of violence, we see the world that the incoming Europeans found the most exotic. And the most barbaric. Indeed, whites referred to Indian warfare as proof that they were beyond redemption by civilization. But from our more dispassionate perspective and with a longer view of history, we can see that Indian warfare was not so outlandish as the incoming whites liked to believe. Cruelty has many faces, few of which had not been seen in sixteenth- and seventeenth-century Europe and especially in "that university of war" that Robert Pollok attended, Ireland.

B Y THE TIME ROBERT AND HIS FAMILY REACHED THE CHESA-peake, Virginia had been partially colonized by whites for nearly eighty years and Maryland for nearly fifty. During those years, the land had acquired a character, a society and an economy that made the entry of Robert and those who followed him very different from that of the "first wave" of immigrants.

The motivation behind the English government encouragement of colonization was as complex in the New World as in Ireland. Indeed, contemporaries drew no sharp distinction between them. Encouraged by Richard Hakluyt, the government adopted a religiously justified imperial policy that remained in place despite the turmoil in England. Whether the English kings were Protestant or Catholic, they were anxious to rid England of its "surplus" population. They were particularly keen to get rid of veterans who had returned from the wars in Europe likely to become indigent dependents or, worse, dangerous highwaymen. Hakluyt wrote to Sir Walter Raleigh,

> Seeing, therefore we are so farre from want of people, that retyring daily home out of the Lowe Countreys, they go idle up and downe in swarms for lack of honest intertainment, I see no fitter place to employ some part of the better sort of them trained up thus long [in military] service, then in the inward partes of the firme of Virginia against such stubborne Savages as shal refuse obedience to her Majestie.

What Hakluyt had hit upon was a policy of getting rich, getting rid of the poor and spreading the faith, surely as winning a combination as any policy planner ever put together.

Although Hakluyt was an unabashed proponent of imperialism, he spoke also for what we would call the enlightened "liberals" of his age. Even so benevolent a man as Thomas More, the friend of the great humanist Desiderius Erasmus, thought it was perfectly unexceptional that the people he invented and held up as exemplars to the Europeans, the people of Utopia, would conquer a more backward people, "a pack of ignorant savages," whom he named the Sansculottia, and enslave them to perform "rough and dirty work." The English were doing this in Ireland, so it was natural for them to try it also in the New World. Put the Indians in the place of the Gaelic Irish and the parallel comes into sharp focus. To some of the early settlers, indeed, the Indians even *looked* Irish, with their deerskin cloaks resembling Irish mantles.

But the way to empire in the New World would not be easy. In the first foray, in 1585, Sir Walter Raleigh's cousin Richard Grenville gave up before even planting any settlers. Then, when in his second attempt Grenville left a small group behind, they all died. The third venture, on Roanoke Island in 1587, left only a mystery: when a relief ship arrived the following year, all the would-be colonists had simply disappeared. The record was perfect: it was a catastrophe.

On the fourth attempt in 1606, a group of one hundred people set out for "Virginia," as the whole coast of North America was then known. After a voyage of six months, they landed on the James River. Most died, a fate that all would have probably met had it not been for the aid and comfort given by the Indians. Undeterred, the colonizing joint-stock company launched a vigorous propaganda campaign and enticed over six hundred men, women and children to follow them. It was the greatest venture so far, but it was a fiasco before it even reached North America. One ship sank in the mid-Atlantic and another foundered in the Bermudas. Those who arrived may have wished they had drowned too, for their ordeal, bad as it was, had only begun. In what has come to be known as the "starving time," many were forced to become cannibals "and rifled new made graves. One man murdered his wife and salted her body away like pork." The next ship to arrive, in May 1610,

discovered that only sixty of the five hundred or so people who had survived the crossing of the Atlantic were still alive.

The fact was quite simply that when the first settlers arrived in the
Chesapeake, they were few in number, ill supplied and ignorant of the
skills they required, whereas the Indians were relatively numerous,
skilled in agriculture and at home. This was not a time when Europeans
despised Indians. Indeed, not only were the incoming English grateful
for Indian help—although they usually attributed it not to Indian generosity but to divine intervention—they quickly learned to respect the
military prowess of the Indians. An early observer, George Percy, describes a scene in which the whites sought to impress the Indians with
their firepower but were themselves more impressed by the Indians.

> One of our Gentlemen having a Target [a shield] which hee
> trusted in, thinking it would beare out a slight shot, hee set it
> up against a tree, willing one of the Savages to shoot; who
> tooke from his backe an Arrow of an elle long [about 45
> inches], drew it strongly in his Bowe, shoots the Target a foote
> thorow, or better: which was strange, being that a Pistoll
> could not pierce it.

Yet, at least at first, it was not so much the military prowess of the
Indians as their openness and generosity that most impressed the newly
arriving Europeans. As one astonished Englishman remarked of the
neighboring Algonquin Indians, they showed themselves willing to share
their "Corne, weomen and Country." These happy days did not last
long. Relations soon began to deteriorate not only because the Indians
thought the whites were cheating them in trade or because the whites,
who were poor farmers, often stole Indian caches of food but also because the whites tried to force the Indians to convert to Christianity.

Conflict was inevitable. The first, fairly small-scale clash came just a
few years after the establishment of Jamestown in 1607, but this was a
local affair and was soon put aside. Over a broader area, relations re-

mained complex, with some Indians helping, trading with, even inter-
marrying with whites and forming alliances with whites against other
Indians. It was when the whites put all their energies into the production
of what they could not eat, tobacco, and needed the Indians to feed
them that problems multiplied. Individual ties with "our Indians" were
overridden by general fear and racial antipathy. As tensions increased,
they focused on the symbol and agent of white prowess, the gun. The Indians wanted guns and the whites were afraid to turn them over. In
1618, as we have noted, the governor of Virginia issued a proclamation
imposing the death penalty on any white who taught an Indian how to
use a firearm—and also on the Indian student. Having acquired new
"needs" for which the gun was the key, the Indians were desperate to
get them.

So in 1622 came the first of a series of white-Indian wars that
would rumble across the continent for more than two and a half centuries. Known among the whites, who, after all, were the ones who recorded the history, as the Powhatan Uprising, it came about, in the
words of the Powhatan chief, because he had concluded that the European colonists had arrived "not for trade, but to invade my people, and
possess my Country."

He was right. Once the colonists had landed at Jamestown, it was
inevitable that they would begin to take over Indian lands and that the Indians would resist. As whites became more numerous and the Indians
were decimated by the diseases brought by the whites, it was also inevitable that the Indians would be cowed, "removed," enslaved or exterminated. Colonial history illustrates in episode after episode the steps in
this process leading inexorably to the final drama at the end of the nineteenth century.

However, this was not at first so obvious. Despite European technology and superior armaments, the 1622 Powhatan Uprising was very
nearly successful. Ironically, it was their very success that caused the Indians' downfall. The terrified settlers concluded that the sinister and de-
vious Indians had no right to exist. No longer did they think of Indians as

"the people most gentle, loving, and faithfull, voide of all guile and treason . . ." From then onward, they saw Indians simply as dangerous
savages, lurking beyond the fringes of civilization, ready to rape, scalp
and kill the innocent whites. Their governor summed up the new mood.
". . . our first worke is expulsion of the Savages to gaine the free
range of the countrey," he proclaimed, "for it is infinitely better to have
no heathen among us, who at best were but thornes in our sides, [than]
to be at peace and league with them."

In 1626, what amounted to apartheid was instituted as colonists
were ordered not to admit Indians to their houses or to "converse, play,
or even trade with the savages unless he had procured a special license to
do so." Taking the cue, the whites embarked upon what would become
a pattern of search-and-destroy operations (then called marches) in
which the Indian men were to be massacred and the women and children
sold into slavery "to defray the expenses of the campaign." Whatever
rapport that might have been created between white "civilization" and
Indian "savagery" was ended, and whatever respect whites may have felt
either for individual Indians or for Indian culture in general was wiped
out.

But pragmatic considerations at first modified this attitude in practice. The new settlers on the Chesapeake and elsewhere needed the
nearer Indians to block incursions from the still-wilder Indians in the interior. Moreover, the whites fell out with one another, and in the first
intercolonial war Virginia and Maryland both engaged Indian allies.
These coalitions did not last long; when Virginia resolved its dispute
with Maryland, shortly before Robert Pollok arrived, it turned on its
Susquehannock Indian allies and destroyed them.

Nor was the Chesapeake unique. Virtually the same pattern of
events—cordial relations, coalition of whites and Indians against other
Indians and then destruction of the Indians—was played out in what is
now Connecticut in what became known as Pequot's War. There, in the
1620s, the whites and Indians had got along without excessive violence
and with mutually beneficial commerce; gradually, as in Virginia, how-

ever, the Indians came to realize the danger to their way of life posed by the whites. The flash point was reached in 1636 when a white militia expedition, aided by Mohegan and Narraganset Indian allies, stormed the main Pequot town at what is today Mystic and either burned alive or massacred the inhabitants. The white militia then hunted down and either killed or sold as slaves to sugar planters in the West Indies all the remaining Pequot.

The process was taken to its logical and bloody conclusion in what the white historians have called King Philip's War. "King Philip," the Indian chief Metacomet of the Wampanoag people, had put together a coalition of northeastern Indian tribes to resist further white encroachment. In 1675, just about five years before Robert and his family landed in the Chesapeake, a full-scale war broke out in Connecticut and Massachusetts. When it was over, some six hundred colonists had been killed, but the Indian tribes were destroyed or driven out of their ancestral lands. They were soon followed by the Seneca and the Iroquois, so that by the time Robert arrived, Indians were rarely seen anywhere along the coast.

No one thought this any more unusual or reprehensible in the New World than in Ireland. If anyone doubted, John Locke provided a rationale in "An Essay Concerning the True Original, Extent, and End of Civil Government." Published in 1690, the essay argues that it was labor that "gave a right of property." While Locke does not explicitly say so, the inference is that those who do not use or inefficiently use land have little or no right over it. Colonists did not need Locke to tell them that it was nearly a crime to "waste" land, and, as farmers, they considered the Indian hunting lands wasted. By the middle of the seventeenth century, those who had seen Indian production of corn—"a graine of marvellous great increase: of a thousand, fifteene hundred, and some two thousand folde"—were long dead.

And Indian lands were not just *land;* they were *cleared* land. That was crucial, since the whites did not have the manpower or the technology to clear land rapidly, and except for lands already taken over from

the Indians, almost no open fields existed. At first, this was relatively un-
important, but in 1612 John Rolfe created a revolution in white-Indian
relations when he brought in the first commercial export crop of tobacco.

When introduced into Europe, tobacco had a mixed reception. Officially, it was discouraged. In a statement that sounds strikingly like that
of modern campaigners against smoking, King James I of England commented that tobacco is "loathsome to the eye, hateful to the nose,
harmful to the brain [and] dangerous to the lungs"; yet, like cocaine in
our times, tobacco set off a virtual revolution among consumers. Within
a few years, smoking was the rage in London, with tobacco selling for its
weight in silver. And in the Chesapeake, the colonists saw tobacco as the
means to purchase all the weapons, tools and luxuries for which they
yearned. Indeed, within a year or two, colonists so desperately sought
space to grow it that they even planted the lanes between the houses in
Jamestown.

And the Chesapeake proved to be the ideal place to produce it.
Since tobacco was damaged if moved long distances over the bumpy,
rutted trails that were typical in the seventeenth century, water transport turned out to be the solution waiting for that problem: the Chesapeake offered hundreds of inlets and easy landings within reach of
virtually every agricultural area. The colonists did not enter the market;
they stampeded. So their exports to England shot up from 1622, when
sixty thousand pounds were delivered, to over 20 million pounds by
1700. The Chesapeake became, in Arthur Middleton's phrase, the Tobacco Coast. Tobacco rescued a faltering Virginia and turned it into the
most valuable of England's overseas possessions.

To grow it, the colonists needed good, already cleared land, and
usually that meant Indian land. Indians often surprised the whites by appearing willing to give away or sell (for tokens of little value) their lands.
This exchange rested on a fundamental difference in concepts of landownership. Indians did not think of land as subject to absolute ownership
but as coming under what might be called priority of right of use. A

hungry man, for example, had the right to kill an animal on someone else's land (unlike the European idea that "poaching" was theft and so often punishable by death), but he did not have the right to keep the fur of the animal, which was a trade item and which was not therefore justified by the need to prevent starvation. Thus, when whites "bought" land, the Indians thought they were giving only the right to what is known in European law as usufruct—that is, use for a special purpose—and that the property remained as much theirs as it had always been.

Neither did the Indian peoples consider land as "private" or individual property; for them, it was the common property of the people or nation.

The white misunderstanding of Indian property came into focus on the individual who appeared most likely to be able to exercise control, the "chief." The colonists thought of chiefs, known first to them from the Powhatan Indians as *werowances,* as the equivalent of European kings; consequently, they believed, or chose to believe, that the chief not only commanded his people but personally owned (and so could alienate) the lands occupied by his people. To the Indians, this was an alien idea. For them, the chief was a "first among equals," usually a respected elder, sometimes a war leader, but in no sense did he own or could he alienate tribal lands.

WITH TOBACCO VIRGINIA WAS PROVING A SUCCESS, AND THE English Crown decided to extend colonization to the other side of the Chesapeake. So it was that in 1632, George Calvert, Lord Baltimore, a favorite of King Charles, was granted the right to win for himself a "plantation" in the New World. The site was an obvious choice on strategic grounds: by granting him the area just north of Virginia, the Crown aimed to block the Dutch from extending their domain south from New Amsterdam.

Maryland was an aberration among the colonies. First of all, it was granted to a practicing Catholic. That was surprising enough, but even more surprising was that Lord Baltimore hoped to turn it into a haven for the by-then-persecuted English Catholics. Few were attracted. From the beginning, more Protestants than Catholics engaged to go there. Recognizing the inevitable, Baltimore decided that "Mary Land" should be one of the few places in the intolerant seventeenth century where religious diversity might actually be allowed. He was determined that the colonists live under "a Lawe by which all of all sorts who professed Christianity in Generall might be at Liberty to Worshipp God in such Manner as was most agreeable with their respective Judgmts and Consciences without being subject to any penaltyes whatsoever for their soe doeing . . ." His was a wholly unrealistic hope for the times. Relations steadily soured until in 1655 Maryland replayed a version of the English Civil War with Puritans seizing Catholic property, hanging some professing Catholic laymen and driving out their priests.

Perhaps Lord Baltimore had read *Utopia,* because he also hoped to turn Maryland into an idealized kingdom. This appeared not so wild a dream, since the Crown had given him the rights of a "dependent king" over Maryland's 12 million acres. Since the land was empty of Europeans when he began, he was almost as free to invent his kingdom as Thomas More had been to invent Utopia. His only subordination to the English king was in a symbolic rent specified as "the yearly payment of two Indian arrows at the castle of Windsor . . ." He, in turn, could rent, give away or sell the land as he wished and to whom he wished. In effect, Baltimore had, uniquely, the mandate to create a nation-state.

The first Lord Baltimore died before he could initiate the project, but his son sent off the first group of colonists in 1633. They sailed on two ships, of which one, the *Dove,* was about the size of the one on which Robert and his family were later to sail. The trip, from Cowes along the southern route to the Canaries to Barbados and north along the Virginia coast, took three months, during which time the *Dove* disappeared and was feared lost. But, reunited, the two ships sailed into the river known to the Indians as Attawomech.

From the day they landed, the colonists made serious efforts to cultivate good relations with the Indians. They did not have to work very hard at it, since the five thousand or so Indians living in what became Maryland were remarkably friendly and supportive. The incoming three hundred settlers took up residence, under a sort of invitation, in the Indian town of Yoacomaco. This town and the surrounding areas they "purchased," as they understood the transaction, and renamed it St. Mary's. Both because the surrounding land was already cleared and under cultivation by the Indians and because the Indians supplied them with food, the first Marylanders avoided the terrible "starving time" of the earlier Virginia colonists.

At first, they lived in the Yoacomaco Indians' houses *(wigwang* in Algonquin). Gradually, the colonists began to build crude and uncomfortable houses with sod which, in rainstorms, must indeed have become sodden. Since their houses had only bare-earth floors, they covered the earth with rushes and leaves. A generation would pass before much improvement would be attempted. Then the settlers tried to build houses along the lines of what they remembered from England. Lacking a number of materials, including paint and plaster, they often had to mock the Tudor style: where the English plastered between beams, for example, they used a sort of whitewash to look like plaster. For years, houses had no windows; then, when the builders began to cut openings in the walls, the windows were covered with oiled paper. When they began to acquire glass, it came in small pieces, and the distinctive style of multiple "lights" arose.

Not surprisingly, since the Chesapeake was colder than England, they emphasized the chimney. But having no brick, they built chimneys out of logs, which they daubed with mud to keep them from catching fire. Such records as exist indicate that they could hardly have done worse. The chimneys had no flues, and fireplaces were said to have consumed as much as twenty cords, or roughly 2,500 cubic feet, of wood a year. Even with roaring log fires, water would freeze just a few feet away from the fireplace, so families huddled virtually inside them. As Jaspar Dankers and Peter Sluyter wrote in 1680, "if you are not so close to the fire as almost to burn yourself, you cannot keep warm, for the wind blows through [the walls] everywhere.''

It would be nearly a half century before even the best of the colonists' dwellings were more than "mean," as a contemporary observer described them in 1678. To make that observation concrete, one seventeenth-century "gentleman's house" was described as fifteen feet square, but both floored and "lofted" with planks. Such a house in 1680 was valued at about eight hundred pounds of tobacco, or roughly £4.

Furnishings matched the architecture. Since few people owned beds, they slept on bedrolls or wrapped themselves in blankets. Such light as they had came either from the fire or from burning pine knots. Candles were a luxury, as both suet and cord were expensive. When a family splurged on candles, they were made by itinerant craftsmen from bear grease or deer suet. Very few enjoyed the luxury of a chamber pot. Benches were the common seating, since they were relatively easy to make: often they were just a split log held up by four pegs. A chair was a prized rarity.

The colonists ate off a board set on a sort of trestle, and food was often poured directly onto the board. If the family had tableware, it was probably mainly wooden "trenchers," blocks of partly hollowed wood in which stews were ladled to be shared and eaten by several people. If they were better off, they might have earthenware or pewter.

The fork came into general use only at the end of the seventeenth century and was not common even well into the eighteenth. For stews, porridge or the "samp" that took the place of the Scots oatmeal as the most common dish, the spoon, sometimes just an oyster shell, was the favored implement. (It is probable that the way Americans use the fork, as distinct from Europeans, arises from the way one has to use a spoon.) Other household tools were adapted from whatever was handy: gourds were used as dippers, and clamshells helped to skim milk.

Yet, for all the primitive style of living, Lord Baltimore had grand pretensions. To our ears, they sound rather like playacting. He wanted to reconstruct a medieval barony which he saw as divided into manors, each of which was to be held by a lord who, in turn, ruled over holders of fiefs in the feudal fashion. Land was not to be held by private owner-ship (as in contemporary Virginia) or in common (as among the Indians) but by "patent" or what was known in medieval law as socage, in which the tenant acquired limited rights in return for services or payment of rent.

The nature of the right to land and the even more sensitive issue of religion were nearly to wreck the colony in its first half century. The settlers, of whom a majority were Protestant, did not want the land they cultivated to "belong" to a distant and unseen feudal lord. Particularly not to a Catholic. Baldly put, they didn't want to pay rent for what they regarded as the fruit of their labor. So in the 1650s, the new colony was wracked by what amounted to a civil war. They lost because the home government supported Lord Baltimore, but they continued to struggle.

By this time, Maryland was a one-crop economy, wholly dependent upon tobacco prices in England and even more upon access to the Euro-pean market, neither of which it could influence, much less control. For a while, no one cared because under the Protectorate the price was high and production was sufficient only for the English market. Tobacco pro-duction soared so that supply far outstripped English demand, but when Charles II banned trade between the colonies and foreign countries, the price of tobacco began to collapse. The price fell from the heady early days of its entry into the English market when it was worth its weight in silver to a penny a pound.

Meanwhile, people flooded into Maryland. Population increased from about 4,900 in 1634 to about 19,000 or 20,000 in 1680. Since many died of disease, more than 25,000 Europeans had immigrated to the colony by the time the Polks arrived. Almost half of the immigrants were indentured white servants, virtual slaves for a given term of years, who could be bought and sold at the whim of the master. When the Polks arrived, there were some Indian slaves but virtually no black slaves.

As they set about organizing their colonies, the lords proprietor naturally copied the British system. They established familiar offices, such as the sheriff, land registrar and judge, and enforced the system of criminal justice then in force in England. Because it was thought that jailing a person was too heavy a burden on the community, which then had both to feed and to guard him, jails were not introduced into Maryland until about 1650. Punishments were savage. About three hundred crimes in Maryland carried the death penalty; lesser punishments had evolved little from medieval times and they were, in truth, garish, painful and grisly. Convicted political offenders who were not lucky enough to go directly to the block were usually disemboweled while still alive. Then they were quartered. Women who murdered their husbands were often burned at the stake. Accused but not-yet-tried prisoners who refused to plead were often slowly pressed to death under heavy weights.

Execution was seen not just as revenge against the offender for his already committed act but as *prospective* punishment of all those citizens who were likely to commit acts in the future. Consequently, the act of execution had to be not only terrifying but conspicuous. Killing served only a limited purpose if no one knew of it. Terrible pain had no benefit if it merely grieved the dying. So to fulfill its role as a deterrent, execution was turned into a public spectacle.

The colonials had less capacity to put on spectacles than contemporary Londoners, but they probably had as much taste for them. Perhaps even more than in England, the crowds were fascinated with sexual crimes and made punishment a titillating public event. Many of the offenders were women who were considered guilty of fornication if their babies were born prematurely or they were not married; they were stripped to the waist and whipped on their bare backs as crowds ogled.

With gossip a favorite means of entertainment and heterosexual intercourse suppressed as much as possible, homosexual activity was probably fairly common and when detected was savagely punished. Sodomy was regarded with particular horror. Perhaps the most bizarre case recorded was of a young boy convicted of sodomy and buggery with a cow, two goats, five sheep and a turkey. We are not told how witnesses were brought forward for this astonishing collection of acts. But the boy was duly tried and found guilty. Then, after being forced to watch the animals being executed (since they were regarded as defiled), he was hanged. "A very sade spectakle it was," the governor remarked.

ORE IMPORTANT THAN LEGAL FORMS IN SHAPING THEIR SOCI-ety, Marylanders inadvertently imported a collection of diseases, pests and weeds that until the seventeenth century had been unknown in the Chesapeake. The catalog would horrify any modern customs inspector. It includes the black fly, the cockroach, the gray rat, various weeds, typhoid, dysentery, malaria, smallpox, influenza, measles, bubonic plague and other diseases common in Europe.

High mortality rates produced a curious mixing of generations and relatives. Marriages did not usually last more than a decade before either the husband or the wife died. As the records of one community show, "nearly a third lost one parent by the age of nine, another quarter lost both by the age of thirteen, and fewer than a third had both alive at the age of eighteen." It has been estimated that 70 percent of immigrant men died before they were fifty, and women lived even shorter lives. The survivor usually immediately remarried and often to a parent with several children. This might happen several times in the life of a person, so that households were often filled with full, half and actually unrelated siblings. Orphans were counted in the thousands.

As dreadful as diseases were among the Europeans, they struck with terrible intensity those without acquired immunities to them, the Indians. It has been estimated that some Indian tribes lost half or more of their population by the middle of the seventeenth century to epidemics of bubonic plague, influenza, smallpox, measles and other European ailments. Whites, unintentionally, were engaged in what amounted to biological warfare. Their very infirmities constituted "a deadly, invisible ally of the English . . ."

And the Indians assisted, as they would continue to do for the next two centuries, in their own destruction. Their warfare with one another ceased to be what I have called violent theater, in which the principal objective was the demonstration of valor, and after the introduction of firearms, turned to conquest and extermination. The introduction of firearms set off an arms race, forcing Indians to do whatever was necessary to acquire arms to defend themselves against their Indian enemies and the white invaders. Whatever was necessary came to mean both raiding white settlements to seize arms and hunting, on a hitherto unknown scale, animals for whose fur the whites would pay. In area after area, animals were hunted virtually to extinction. And as their own hunting grounds became depleted, tribes began to raid the territories of their neighbors in the desperate search for the wherewithal to buy arms. Thus, tribes that had only rarely fought one another became engaged in increasingly frequent and deadly combat in which the losers were usually driven from their traditional hunting grounds.

Meanwhile, as the Indian threat receded, control over the settlers by the home government also weakened. During the English Civil War, and in the confused period of the Restoration, the colonies schooled themselves in self-government. In Maryland, the legislature was constantly at daggers drawn with the proprietor. The colonists usually lost or compromised, but a few years after Robert had arrived, with him taking part in the action, they declared themselves virtually a separate republic under the distant monarchy.

THIS, THEN, IS THE NEW WORLD INTO WHICH ROBERT POLlok brought his family to become Americans.

How marvelous it must have seemed to those who stood on the deck of the little boat to finally sight land; then to enter the Chesapeake, skirting what we now call Fishermans Island to turn north. Somewhere past Cape Charles the by-now-bedraggled *fluyt* was joined by a pilot. That pilots skilled in the bay were already available to incoming boats was, in itself, a sign of the changes that had taken place over the preceding century. This pilot, according to a family tradition, which was written down a century and a half later, was able to guide the *fluyt* right up to the very piece of land on which Robert and his family would settle.

How wobbly must have been their land legs. How worried their faces as they searched the trees and bushes for the expected wild savages. And how confused they would have been about knowing what to do upon leaving the little world of the boat. But the crew, less baffled and more sure of their return, began carrying kegs, barrels, boxes and trunks onto the shore, leading the animals down an improvised gangplank and letting them graze among the nearby trees. As the children ran along the shore, the worried parents must have hovered close to the boat and yelled to the children not to stray. For the first few days, they probably sheltered aboard the *fluyt* while the captain was searching for cargo—tobacco, beaver pelts and deerskins—for the return trip.

Then Robert and the other men had to arrange temporary housing. At earlier times, the new arrivals might have built an Indian-style wigwam by leaning poles together, tying them at the top and covering them with canvas or skins or even moved in with an Indian family. But by this time, Indians were not to be seen, so they probably arranged to stay with the nearest already established English or Scots neighbor.

Then, if they did not already have some piece of land assigned to them, Robert would have had to go across the Chesapeake to St. Mary's City and negotiate for one. It was at this point that he got caught in a process that would be of profound importance to the growth and character of America: he found that the best land was already taken and that what was left was marginal or worse. Like scores of thousands of later arrivals, he faced a painful choice: he had either to move to the frontier, which was difficult and might have been impossible, or to make do with the dregs of "paradise." Robert made do.

Almost the first thing anyone did was to register the cattle brought from Ireland, because cattle were then regarded as being far more valuable than land. John, the son of Robert and Magdalen, is recorded as having done this on September 8, 1680. In this, apparently one of his first acts, Robert followed the local custom in which fathers would register a separate livestock mark for each child.

Maryland's lords proprietor had stopped giving out automatic grants of land to all immigrants just at the time the family arrived, so there is no record of the Polloks or, as they now began to style themselves, Polks or Polkes having received title to lands until four years later. However Robert acquired it, he established his family in what was then known as Damned Quarter (later bowdlerized to Dames Quarter) in what became Somerset County, Maryland.

Records mentioning previous grants may be missing, but the first grant of 125 acres in Locust Hammock, dated June 1, 1685, was to Robert's son John. According to the records, Robert acquired two tracts of land, Polk's Folly and Polk's Lott, two years later, on March 7, 1687. It is probable that Robert actually took possession of these (and perhaps other) pieces of land months or perhaps years before the title was actually "patented."

Polk's Folly and another piece of land called Forlorn Hope were aptly named. The Indians had been too wise to live on or near them because the land was too swampy to farm. Indeed, as the early settlers soon found, they could not even bury the dead underground in that area because the caskets would literally be swimming (and a number are recorded as having floated out to sea in the occasional floods). The whole area was also a perfect breeding ground for mosquitoes, and as malaria increased in the second half of the seventeenth century, the death toll of "fevers" rose apace. Fittingly, the area has now become the State of Maryland Deal Island Wild Bird Refuge.

R OBERT COULD HARDLY HAVE PICKED A WORSE TIME TO LAND in Maryland. Not only had the best land long since been taken, but a long and deepening depression was well under way in the tobacco market. It was so bad a year after he had arrived that a "stint," or total ban, on tobacco production was declared. The next year was even worse. Those with reserves fared better, but Robert had no reserves.

And in what was nearly a final blow, the years of deforestation and exhaustion of the land by growing tobacco produced a terrible flood in 1683. The surging waters drowned or swept away much of the little he had been able to make of the marginal lands he had acquired.

Yet, like his new neighbors, Robert struggled on, clinging to the Forlorn Hope because it was the only hope he had. But he must have taken perverse amusement from the name Polk's Folly—as his whole venture to the New World began to seem a folly indeed. By then, we must assume, land had come to seem to him of transcendental value: behind in Ireland, there was no hope at all. Such news as he received from Magdalen's father would have confirmed that he had got out just in time and that under no circumstance could he go back.

Closer to home in Maryland, Robert and his neighbors rankled over the issue of land. No matter how poor it was, they had put themselves into it, and it was all they had, folly though it might be; yet the land was still not completely theirs. Feeling deprived, Maryland Protestants formed a sort of political party determined to better their condition vis-à-vis the proprietor. Much of the action was played out in the nearest equivalent Maryland had to the House of Parliament. Here the colonists made speeches that were consciously patterned on those that had been heard before the English Revolution in London. And the reaction of the proprietor, Lord Baltimore, resembled that of Charles I: in 1684, he vetoed all of the laws that had been passed by the Maryland Assembly.

Finally, there was a widely believed rumor that the Catholics were conspiring with the Indians to attack the Protestant settlers. The rumor was probably insubstantial, but those who had lived through the turmoil of seventeenth-century Ireland were inclined to believe it. On military men, particularly those like Robert who had come out of the turmoil of Ireland, it was not lost that Lord Baltimore's regime supplied arms and ammunition to the Catholic subjects while denying them to Protestants.

It was at this point that the Civil War in England was ended by the flight of James II and the crowning of William and Mary. No one knew exactly what that would mean to Lord Baltimore; in any event he was in London, out of touch with his resident officials. Into this void Robert and his neighbors stepped in the spring of 1689 to form an "Association in arms for the defence of the Protestant religion and for asserting the right of King William and Queen Mary to the province of Maryland." In July of 1689, the "associators" made a coup d'état and called for a freshly elected assembly. Seconding this, an "Address of the Inhabitants of the County of Somersett Nov^{er} th 28th 1689" was signed by a large number of people including Robert and his son William, both now styled "Polk" rather than "Pollok." They requested that Maryland cease to be a proprietorship of Lord Baltimore and become a royal colony. The new monarchs were pleased to agree, and so it became in June 1692.

For Robert, Maryland was the last stage in a hard life. It had not been so hard for him as it was for the early colonists in the "first wave" and certainly was not so hard as it was for the many Scots prisoners of war who began to arrive, branded to prevent their return to Scotland, after the defeat of the Earl of Argyll's rebellion in 1685 or for the thousands of Indians who died of disease or wounds, but still it was a life that can be characterized as hardscrabble, in which he struggled to make a place for himself and his family, and when his end came in 1703, his estate was valued at just twelve hundred pounds of tobacco, or £50. Included in it were a feather bed, a small chest, five books, various pots and pans, thirty-eight pounds of bacon, twenty-eight hogs, thirteen cattle, some cloth and leather, and one (probably indentured Irish) servant girl valued at £6. Not much, but he had succeeded in planting his family in the New World.

WESTWARD FROM MARYLAND

"The Young Chief of the Long Knife"

THE CHESAPEAKE HAS BEEN APTLY CALLED THE TOBACCO Coast because events there cannot be fully understood apart from the influence of tobacco. In the early years of the century, tobacco saved the faltering economy of Virginia; then, by creating an economic boom, it lured thousands of immigrants to Virginia and Maryland, setting the pattern of their settlement and enriching many of them. But by the last part of the seventeenth century, the costs of growing it were becoming apparent. Tobacco proved to be a voracious plant, depleting the land and causing erosion while draining the energies of the farmers and putting them under the control of economic forces beyond their ken. And by creating a desperate hunger for land, it helped to destroy the nearby Indian societies and set in motion forces that would sweep across the continent like a prairie fire. Thus, tobacco is a key to much of the history of early America.

With the technology of the seventeenth century, the only way to keep tobacco land in production was to let it lie fallow every few years. Obviously, this was difficult or impossible for small farmers. Having enough land to be able to diversify crops or temporarily abandon a piece of land was one of several advantages that accrued to those who had arrived early. A second advantage was that the early arrivals got the best land. As judged by tobacco growers, the better lands were not just well drained and with good-quality soil; they were also adjacent to the water, since transport costs were thereby reduced. Small farmers, who by definition were usually the late arrivals, had to make do with plots that had few or none of these advantages.

To work the land, a farmer had either to throw himself and his whole family—with children above the age of three then considered to be potential workers—into the task, which was the way the small leaseholders were forced to operate, or to acquire the labor of others. In seventeenth-century society, that meant ''renting'' indentured servants for a period of years or buying slaves.

An indentured laborer was acquired from a jobber or wholesaler at a Chesapeake landing or was engaged through English agencies whose ''crimps'' often worked like naval press gangs, ''shanghaiing'' vulnerable people. In either case, the indentured person's way across the Atlantic had to be paid, his upkeep had to be provided and, usually, some sort of ''severance'' pay had to be given to him when he completed his term. Early in the century, many Englishmen, some Irishmen and a few Scots were willing to rent themselves out in return for their passage and what they thought would be a new opportunity for a better life. By the time Robert and his family arrived in the Chesapeake, however, the ''push'' of unemployment in England had diminished, so that fewer free people were willing to undergo indenture. And as rumor circulated that the boom days of opportunity had passed, this source of labor virtually dried up. A relatively small number of convicted felons and prisoners of war continued to come, but, obviously, they were less eagerly sought by the Chesapeake farmers. Even including them, the supply of workers declined, and as it did, their cost went up. On average, this amounted to at least twice as much as the indentured servant could produce in a year.

Slaves were another alternative. While not very much is known about them, many were Indians. In the Carolinas at the beginning of the eighteenth century, they made up about 15 percent of the population. Like African slave traders, planters encouraged friendly societies to raid their neighbors and to exchange their captives for arms, tools, cloth and liquor. In each of the many conflicts, whites also seized Indians, often killing the grown men and nearly always enslaving the women and children. But Indians were not considered reliable (they could run away) or a good investment (they had few immunities to white-borne diseases and died quickly).

More attractive to tobacco farmers were black slaves, of whom the first were brought to the Chesapeake in 1619 on a Dutch ship. Ten were reported in Jamestown in 1625. More arrived periodically, but until the very end of the seventeenth century, black slaves were relatively rare. Many of those who were imported came not directly from Africa but from the older, mainly sugar plantations of the Caribbean, where they had been "seasoned." New Negroes, as they were called, were more highly regarded than the "outlandish" Africans, since they had learned rudimentary English and had been "broken" to bondage. Because they were very productive, there was a significant shift in the 1680s and 1690s to employment of black slaves.

Slaves played a significant part in the growing division of rich and poor immigrants. Since they were between twice and three times as expensive as indentured servants, they were beyond the means of farmers with small amounts of land or marginal land, like Robert. For those who had good land, however, slaves were the key to wealth. They enabled the earlier settlers to form a plantation establishment. Thus, the coming of slavery altered not only the economy but also the mores and outlook of the white community. As they explained this change to themselves, the settlers thought that it made them more "English" and less colonial.

Slaveholders, then as later, put a kindly mask on the grim face of slavery. In his *History and Present State of Virginia,* Robert Beverley protested against the notion that the colonials were backward or primitive by saying that "generally their Slaves are not worked near so hard, nor so many Hours in a Day, as the Husbandmen, and Day-Labourers in *England.*" In early colonial times, slaves were usually treated about the same as indentured laborers and often shared their living quarters and meals. Many, we now know, cohabited and produced children, and of these not a few had black fathers and white mothers. The conditions of both servants and slaves, by modern standards, were wretched, but the blacks do not seem, at least in the early years, to have been treated notably worse than the whites. Except, of course, for the ultimate misery of slavery—that it was permanent—whereas the indentured servant knew that there would be an eventual end to his servitude.

A grandson of Robert Bruce Polk is the first member of the family who is recorded as having owned slaves. When this William died in 1739, his will mentions four slaves whom he divided among his children.

Holders of large blocks of land had another option for the acquisition of labor: they could let out some of their lands to sharecroppers. Many did, but as the frontier in Pennsylvania, Delaware and lands beyond the mountains began to open, fewer landless people were willing to stay on the terms the owners offered. Since their migration contributed to the rising cost of labor, some of the larger owners tried to block westward movement. They did this both by periodically banning settlement beyond certain barriers and by encouraging the still-free Indian communities to hunt them down.

Keeping their labor force in place, however, was not the larger planters' only motivation: they also wanted the more distant Indians to keep on supplying them with valuable furs and skins on which they earned a considerable part of their fortunes. But these restraints on movement were never effective for very long. The lure of the richer, deeper soils across the mountains was simply too strong. Attempts at restraint did, however, set the tone of the earliest conflict within the white community and created the conditions in which each wave of new arrivals had to "leapfrog" the already settled areas to colonize beyond the fugacious frontier.

As labor costs rose, markets for tobacco and sugar matured. Stagnation was bad, but worse were the results of European wars, particularly those between England and Holland, which virtually ruined the export trade. Many small farmers were forced into bankruptcy while the wealthy used their advantage to solidify their political and administrative powers. In the 1680s and 1690s, between 75 and 85 percent of the delegates to the Maryland Assemblies owned more than one thousand acres and almost none owned less than five hundred acres. What amounted to a resident oligarchy had come into existence, and as opportunity came, as it did in the 1689 "revolution" against Lord Baltimore, the oligarchy solidified its power.

Despite these major and long-term changes, a casual visitor to Maryland would probably have noticed little difference in the way people lived from half a century earlier. As late as the third decade of the eighteenth century, almost all houses were still furnished drably and sparsely and only a few houses were painted. But after the first quarter of the eighteenth century, the houses of the rich began to take on a patina of elegance. Brick came into more general use, and attention began to be paid to design. Furniture and decorations, often imported from England, became more usual and more opulent; such hitherto rare items as clocks, like the one Magdalen brought over from Ireland, and even books, like the five Robert owned at his death, began to appear in wills.

Society also began to change. By roughly the end of the seventeenth century, people born in Maryland became more numerous than immigrants. Also significant was a change in social mobility. Whereas in the early days of Maryland and Virginia, indentured servants could hope that when their periods of service ended they could acquire land, servants and slaves, such opportunities virtually ceased by the 1680s.

Families remained weak because so many people lived outside of them. Over a quarter of the men who died in southern Maryland around the turn of the century were unmarried, while many of those who were married had been married several times, with confusing and often conflicting patterns of kinship (or lack of it). With families temporary and divided, often unhappily, young people escaped as quickly as they could. In Somerset County, where Robert and his family were established, the *average* age of marriage of girls was sixteen—many were recorded at fourteen—and more than a third of the brides were already pregnant.

How did Robert and his family fit into this "typical" Maryland society?

Judging by the assessed value of his estate, about £50, Robert fell in the middle or lower-middle social category. "Class" is still too formal a word for seventeenth- and early-eighteenth-century Maryland, and with his Scots pride, Robert certainly considered himself an aristocrat. In any event, the value of his holdings must be viewed as only approximate, since appraisers of probated estates assessed only what the more evident goods would bring in a forced sale. But judging by the same criteria, Gloria Main found that two-thirds of the estates inventoried in Maryland before 1720 were worth less than £66.

We get a more concrete and surer estimate by the acreage Robert possessed at the time of his death. His plots of land (Polk's Folly and Polk's Lott) are recorded at just 150 acres. In the only indication of how he used his land, a petition to the court on March 10, 1697, he mentions that he had cleared a cornfield, from which we can infer that the land was not up to growing tobacco. Perhaps this does not give us a full picture, however, since his sons, perhaps with his help, were beginning around the time of his death to acquire their own holdings. Robert "Poalk," Jr.—in the early documents the name was variously spelled

Polk, Polke, Poke, Poalk, even Pulke, as well as the older forms of Pollok and Pollock—got title to 200 acres of marshland in 1700; Ephraim
Poalk got 374 acres (known as Long Delay and Clonmell) between 1700
and 1705, and James acquired 200 acres (known as James' Meadow) in
1705. I have mentioned the names of these plots because they, perhaps
more than the sizes indicated, show that the lands were not prized acqui-
sitions.

It is not clear how Robert or his sons made a living on such small
and marginal lands; Robert must have used whatever savings he had
brought from Ireland, together perhaps with remittances, like later
émigrés, and worked in some nonagricultural trade or profession. His
military background would not have helped him much, but, one way or
another, he did manage to acquire a house, known as White Hall (which
was still standing in the late nineteenth century), and got his sons
started. But the meagerness of his life can be graphically inferred by the
inventory of his possessions at the time of his death. Those things worth
recording are listed as,

  1 feather bed and covering [for] a small chest
  1 yard and half of serge and handmill
  5 books and 17 pounds of Pewter and 1 iron pot
  1 frying pan and 3 iron wedges
  1 grubing hoe and 1 small gun
  2 tin pans and 1 pot hanger
  4 reaphooks and a parcel of linnen yarn
  38 pounds of bacon and a grin[d] stone
  1 servant girl and 1 old bed tick
  28 head of hogs and 1 mans[?]
  13 head of cattle
  1 hide of tanned leather and 1 iron pot
  a parcel of old lumber
  Total value: £50-15-8.

Robert's fourth son, James, worked as a ship carpenter. Perhaps that gave him just the additional income he needed because he moved out of the swamp on which his father had started, and acquired about five hundred acres of slightly better tracts—although their names still ring alarm bells: in addition to James' Meadow, he acquired White Oak Swamp and Green Pasture. All are located in Damned Quarter. A later owner, Colonel William T. G. Polk, described the area as "a low, flat strip of land but little above tide water . . ." Marginal land at best.

James and his mother, Magdalen, both died in 1727. James was then about fifty-one or fifty-two, but he had already had eleven children, and a twelfth was born after his death. He divided his lands among his sons and gave each of his seven daughters £10; in addition, he set aside "unto the Child my wife is now with ten pounds if please God it lives." So he must have done well as a carpenter or in some other, unrecorded way. (The family Bible, dated 1669 and brought over from county Donegal, which might have given clues on his life, was destroyed, along with many other family papers, by a fire in 1847.) Finally, James arranged that his wife "have full Privilege of my dwelling plantation and Marshes during the time of her widowhood." Thus, even leaving aside the value of his lands, house and movable property, James left an estate that was considerably larger than his father had left a quarter of a century earlier.

All in all, by 1742 Robert's heirs had some form of title to 4,150 acres, but much of it, like James' Swamp, was useful only for pasturing animals. The results of the Polks' first half century in America were meager when compared to the plantations and fortunes acquired by many of the "first wave" settlers.

So far in my narrative, I have focused on Robert and his sons, but in many ways the most extraordinary person in the family was the matriarch, Magdalen. In almost every respect, she was outstanding for her time. It is ironic that we must reconstruct her long, fecund and eventful life from her will, but it is from tombstones and wills that much of our information on colonial America derives.

The very fact that Magdalen wrote a will was unusual; in the seventeenth and early eighteenth centuries, only about one person in three wrote one, and almost none of those was a woman. In hers, Magdalen gives us more personal information than her husband and son did in theirs. The first remarkable feature is her age. At a time when most men died in their forties and women considerably earlier, she lived to a truly astonishing great age. From her marriages, first to Colonel John Porter and then to Captain Robert Bruce Pollok, we can infer that she must have been born about 1640. Her will is dated 1726; so she lived nearly three times as long as the average for women in Maryland.

One of the major causes of early death among Maryland women was pregnancy. Not only was the act of giving birth a significant killer, but even unexceptional pregnancy lowered resistance, so that many normally healthy women succumbed to such common sicknesses as "fevers" and "bloudie Flixe." As a consequence, marriages seldom lasted more than a decade, and women usually had fewer than three children before they died. To the contrary in both ways, Magdalen was married to Robert for about forty years and had by him nine children.

In the contrasting fate of her children, we see how surprising her life had been. Her oldest son, John, who had been born in county Donegal before the trip across the Atlantic, was married twice, with each marriage lasting less than a decade. The first wife died on October 28, 1700, a week after giving birth to her third child, a son, who died a day later. John then remarried, this time to the sister of his brother's wife, Joanna Knox. John himself died within seven years. His widow, like practically all colonial widows, speedily remarried and had other children by her second husband. Whether her new husband had children by a previous marriage is not recorded, but colonial "families" were commonly composed of "his," "hers" and "neither's" as one or even both of the spouses inherited stepchildren. The position of the unrelated children, to judge by court cases, was unfortunate. Commonly, they were "put out" as indentured servants by the now-otherwise-engaged foster parents.

John's children were in an exposed position as "neither's" in the household of Joanna Knox and her new husband: as children of John's first wife, they were stepchildren of Joanna and were legally unrelated to her husband. Perhaps foreseeing the danger, John's brother William applied to the Somerset court in 1708 to be appointed their guardian:

To the Worshipfull ye Justices of Somerset County now in Court sitting Wm. Polk humbly sheweth That whereas your petitioners Brother Jno. Polke late of this County, Dec'd left two children behind him towit Wm. & Anne Polke wch upon his death bed he requested of your petitioner & wife to take care of them to see them educated and brought up Christian life & alsoe to bring up ye boy to learn a trade wch your petitioner humbly craves yt we may have ye two children ordered unto him pr your worships and he shall be willing to doe by them as his Brother John Polke requested & what your Worships shall in your Prudence & discretion think fitt to be done (Reasonably) for ye Orphans and your petitioner as in duty bound shall ever pray. William Polke

The court found the petition convincing and ordered that the two minors and such movable property as their father had left be delivered to William with the admonition that he teach the boy a trade along with reading and writing. In this decision, as in nearly all cases involving orphans or distressed people, the courts' primary concern was not so much to protect the welfare of the children as to ensure that the public not be burdened by orphans. To this end, William and his brother James were required to put up "ye sum of tenn pounds sterling to be levied on their goods and chattles Lands & Tennements for ye use of ye Orphans Wm. & Anne Polk."

Ultimately, upon their reaching maturity, "Wm. & Anne" received a piece of land known as Locust Hammock, which John had conveyed in trust. John had done what he could, but he could not protect his children from the real bane of Chesapeake life, the many virulent kinds of fevers and diseases. Thus, William of "Wm. & Anne," like well over half the inhabitants, died while still a young man; what happened to Anne after her marriage is unknown. It is likely that she also died quite young and probably without children.

This pattern of early death was repeated by Robert's and Magdalen's second, third, and sixth sons, who all died before they were forty-five. The oldest daughter, who was married twice, died in her early twenties, and her younger sister lived only until she was about thirty-one. Women had a harder time than men, but life was usually short for everyone. In her great age, Magdalen was a rare exception.

Despite the fact that under contemporary Maryland law, "a woman could not legally own property or make any contracts while married," Magdalen retained, independent of her husband, "a tract of land called Moneen" in Ireland, which she had inherited from her father and which she bequeathed to her youngest son, Joseph.

One of the reasons that we do not know more about Magdalen was that she was not involved in litigation. That, too, was unusual, since early colonists were exceptionally litigious. From the lack of court records, we can infer that she and her husband must have been at least reasonably happily married.

I imagine that Magdalen must have been proud to watch her numerous children and, in due course, grandchildren grow up; merely to do so made Magdalen remarkable—the records suggest even the word "unique"—since, in southern Maryland, "between 1658 and 1705, 67 percent of married or widowed male decedents left all minor children, while only 6 percent left all adult children." Avoiding the pitfalls of colonial society and law as they had survived the dangers of Ireland and the Atlantic, Robert and Magdalen had well and truly launched their family in the New World.

Just as Robert had struck out into the unknown New World, gambling his life and the lives of his family to escape the dangers and confinements of Ireland, so two of his grandsons would launch themselves beyond the already settled fringe of the Atlantic coast to carve out new opportunities on the frontier. It is sobering to reflect that in the early part of the eighteenth century, the frontier was located on the north bend of the Potomac, about fifty miles north of the present site of Washington, D.C. Politicians today should perhaps take note of this new definition of "outside the beltway." But in those days, to venture even that short distance required a major, even a reckless, throw of life's dice.

These two young brothers were sons of Robert's son William, the man who had intervened with the court to protect his niece and nephew. In the meantime, William himself had moved from the original lands to a more prosperous area to practice the then prized and rare trade of blacksmith. From his strong arm, he became relatively wealthy, for in 1723 he conveyed some five hundred acres of land to his son, also called William, and when his first wife, Nancy Knox, died, he remarried. Perhaps their father's remarriage caused a rift in the family—we know only that he left them nothing in his will—but in any event, it was at this time that William Jr. and Charles decided to leave home and move across the frontier.

In southern Maryland during their childhood, they probably heard tales from Accoomac or Occohannock Indians working as seasonal laborers or slaves about the wonders of the hinterland. They even probably learned some Algonquin, since Charles was later said to have spoken "the Indian tongue well."

Besides a few words of some Indian language, they could have had little preparation, since no white person then knew even as much about the hinterland as their grandfather had known about the New World. They did not know even the rudiments of nearby geography. Possibly they meant to stay within Maryland, but they walked right out of Maryland and penetrated two or three days farther into Pennsylvania to establish themselves near the modern city of Carlisle.

Except for whatever tales they may have heard from the Indians, the boys would not have known much about the severe conflicts between whites and Indians that were to shape their lives, but they would certainly have learned of the vicious search-and-destroy missions of such colonial leaders as Virginia's Colonel Nathaniel Bacon and the more recent and equally vicious wars by Indian proxies, armed and incited by the governors of New York, Pennsylvania and Connecticut against one another's citizens. Charles and William were jumping into a den of lions.

Adding to the complexity and danger were the larger hostilities of Great Britain and France. Vying for control over the Ohio and Mississippi Rivers and over Canada, they, too, subsidized, encouraged and occasionally fought alongside their Indian allies. Circulating among them were settlers intent on carving out farms, traders swapping cloth, guns and liquor for pelts and Jesuit missionaries intent on spreading their faith. Over several generations, this confusing and conflicting congeries was further enriched by half-breeds who were outside all the major groups. All this produced constant anarchy and frequent war.

Because they ranged most widely and most freely over the vast area centered on the Ohio River, the traders were most in contact with the Indians and were most distrusted by the governments. The French government often treated the men they called *coureurs du bois* ("woodland wanderers") as outlaws, in part, no doubt, because many were Huguenots. They were the precursors of the trappers and "mountain men" of the American West and were the most successful and most knowledgeable of all those who moved among the Indians. Much of their knowledge and some of their success resulted from the fact that they lived in the Indian style, among Indians, and employed "sleeping dictionaries." The Jesuits were horrified by their sexual relationship with the Indians and lobbied to get their government to ban it, as Louisiana did in the 1730s, but it remained common throughout the eighteenth century.

Sexual relations with Indians were more common among the French—one French nobleman boasted of having sired over sixty *métis*—than among the coastal English. Virginia had outlawed intermarriage in 1691, but it remained common among Englishmen, even senior officers, beyond the frontier. Among white traders, as the missionary David McClure commented, it was accepted practice: "the greater part of the Indian traders," he said, "keep a squaw." Provided some deference to Indian customs was maintained, Indians were said not to have opposed whites cohabiting with unattached Indian women, but traders rarely paid even limited deference: they often got the Indians drunk and raped their wives. To this, not surprisingly, the Indians reacted violently.

Violence was produced not only by sexual relations but also by the introduction of new items of trade, particularly guns and liquor, by the spread of imported diseases and by the frequent seizure of Indian hunting grounds. In all these ways, traders provoked bloody conflicts not only between Indians and whites but among the Indians. In the process, Indian societies were militarily crushed and culturally debased. An Indian envoy to the Mohawk in 1756 explained his ineptness in diplomacy by saying, "the Rum we get from the English hath drowned the Memory of all antient Customs & the Method of treating on public affairs."

"Rum-debauched, Trader-corrupted" was Benjamin Franklin's description of Indians he observed. Reflecting on what had been "normal" in the earlier contacts in his part of the frontier, the Scots traveler and trader James Adair wrote,

> Before the Indians were corrupted by mercenary empirics, their good sense led them to esteem the Traders among them as their second Sun, warming their backs with British fleeces, and keeping in their candle of life, both by plentiful support and continual protection and safety, from the arms and ammunition which they annually brought them. While the Indians were simple in manners and uncorrupt in morals, the [white]

traders . . . were kindly treated and watchfully guarded by a society of friendly and sagacious people . . .

As societies broke down and as whites selectively armed or withheld arms from different groups, Indians turned on one another in their scramble for living and hunting grounds. To win access to the arms and tools they needed to survive, many were willing to give up their religion and culture under the prodding of missionaries and the demands of government. But such moves rarely saved them. Bewildered and frightened, they concluded, in the words of a chief of the Lenni-Lenape (whom we call the Delawares), that they were fighting for survival, since "We have great reason to believe you intend to drive us away and settle the country."

So the interior of North America became a sort of no-man's-land in which only the desperate, the brave or the young and the foolhardy among the whites sought their fortune. As their chronicler Charles A. Hanna wrote, they were "a few score of brave but inglorious men, known as the Indian Traders, the most of whom have passed into deep and, to judge their lives by modern standards of conduct, well-merited oblivion." Among them shortly would be Charles Polk.

CHARLES LEFT NO RECORD OF HIS LIFE, BUT WE CAN BE SURE it was grim and dangerous. He lived, metaphorically, on the edge of the tomahawk. His Indian hosts tolerated him, for he performed a service for them, but this service involved bringing, storing and trading goods that the Indians coveted, which created a tense and hostile relationship. To survive, Charles would have had to fit himself into the society in which he traded. We do not know exactly how he did it, but we know that most traders took Indian wives and begot half-breed children; in this way, they acquired "ascriptive" relatives who, in times of danger, could protect them. Charles probably dressed like an Indian, ate Indian food, learned to speak the local dialect and took part in the sports and contests the Indians enjoyed. But, finally, we are left not with a portrait of him but little more than a blur. This, I suspect, is not only because such men as Charles would rarely have written about their lives but also because they protected themselves: camouflage became their way of life.

Not all, however. A few traders did talk or write about their lives. Some were brutally critical. James Adair, who spent nearly forty years as a trader himself, describes one group as "generally the dregs and offscourings of our colonies . . . crowds of disorderly people infest the Indian countries, corrupt the morals, and put their civilization out of the power of common means." Most were dangerous men, outcasts from their own societies, semisavages. But even those who had started out on more constructive and law-abiding paths found it difficult or impossible to maintain a sense of civilization when operating beyond their own society and its laws. Their lives were balanced on the sharp edge of two hostile civilizations: outside the law of both the white and the Indian societies, they often obeyed neither. Moreover, they were aided and abetted, indeed cynically manipulated, by those who profited from their activities; thus, they often pioneered invasion trails through Indian territory to facilitate what were, even by the lax colonial standards, illegal land seizures. In the world in which they lived and operated, it was the lowest common denominator that usually set the tone. That denominator was liquor.

Despite occasional and usually halfhearted attempts by various colonial, British and French authorities to respond to the scores of recorded Indian requests that they ban the flow of liquor, whites flooded the Indian communities with it. The reason was simple: as the German traveler John Lederer wrote in 1670, "Sometimes you may, with brandy or strong liquor, dispose them to an humor of giving ten times the value of your commodity . . ." Liquor proved as effective a weapon as disease and more effective than the musket. Finally, at least some Indians realized this and took steps to stem the flow: in 1738, the Shawnees smashed the kegs of rum that traders had brought into their villages and warned the traders that they would continue to do so. But for reasons that are still debated, Indians took to liquor like addicts to heroin, and, at times, they became so drunk as to be defenseless. In 1704, the chief of the town of Conestoga wrote to William Penn that his people "are ruined by it, having nothing left, but have laid out all, even their clothes, for rum, and may now, when threatened by war, be surprised by their enemies when besides themselves with drink, and so utterly destroyed." Years later, in 1744, Governor George Thomas addressed the Pennsylvania Assembly, saying,

> Our Traders, in defiance of the law, carry spiritous liquors amongst them, and take advantage of their inordinate appetite for it to cheat them of their skins and their wampum, which is their money, and often to debauch their wives into the bargain. Is it to be wondered at then, if, when they recover from the drunken fit, they should take severe revenge? . . . If I am rightly informed the like abuses of the Traders in New England were the principal causes of the Indian Wars there . . .

One Indian put the liquor-induced cheating even more graphically: at a congress in Mobile in the winter of 1771, a Chocktaw complained that traders provided them with loincloths so skimpy that they "dont cover our secret parts, and we are in danger of being deprived of our manhood by every hungry dog that approaches."

Liquor was not, of course, the only trade item, although, at times, it appeared to the Indians that it was. The most popular "normal" trade good was cloth, particularly a coarse woolen material called stroud. A length of stroud made a "matchcoat" (Powhatan: *matshcore* = garment), which traded for a buckskin. In time, a "buck" became a unit of trading measure, so we read one of the Indian traders writing to his partner that he had "sold eight bucks worth of goods." Hence the slang word for a dollar. In addition to material, which was the most popular trade item, the Indians wanted guns, powder and shot, none of which they could manufacture and all of which they needed both to protect themselves from their enemies (red and white) and to hunt.

THE ACTUAL FUNCTIONING OF THE TRADE IS DIFFICULT TO reconstruct from the scattered and meager records. A man desiring to trade with the Indians was legally required to get a license from his colonial government if he was English or from the authorities in Canada or Louisiana if he was French. At least some did not go through this procedure but simply set off on their own. Most of these men have left no record, but the licensed traders (and their "servants") usually set up trading posts adjacent to an Indian village. One such location was the Indian village of Conestoga in what became Pennsylvania.

To get goods to the store and to bring out furs, which were the most desirable products the Indians had, and particularly to procure salt from often distant "licks," travel was essential for both Indians and whites, so the "wilderness" was interlaced trails. They have left us a remarkable heritage, as Paul A. W. Wallace has written:

> . . . it was the Indians who deserve first praise for the highway system in which we today take so much satisfaction . . . the Indians had laced our hills and valleys with a complex system of paths which not only drew local communities together but spread out into a vast continental network that linked the Atlantic seaboard with the prairies and the Gulf of Mexico with the Great Lakes and Hudson's Bay . . . Its forests were not lonely and trackless, but penetrated by well-trodden paths . . .

The need for a virtually indestructible and commodious wagon was what gave birth to the ancestor of the prairie schooner, originally called a Conestoga wagon. To give it passage, Indian trails, worn by moccasined feet and suitable only for a single person, were soon enlarged.

At Conestoga, the leading traders were the Quakers John and his brother Edmund Cartlidge (or Cartledge), who became the father-in-law of Charles Polk. Like Charles, the Cartlidges were second- or third-generation descendants of Scots who had migrated from Northern Ireland. In fact, so many of the traders were "Scotch-Irish" that one trading post was named Donegal; traders like Charles, who appears in that area about 1724, were often called Donegal traders. Some, like Charles, had been born in America, while others were new arrivals who had been driven from Ireland by renewed attacks on religious dissent in 1719. The newcomers brought with them an attitude toward "natives" that easily translated Irish to Indian. It was a violent, lawless society in which whatever morality that had been associated with religion was lost. The two Cartlidge brothers, Quakers that they were, were briefly jailed for having murdered an Indian in a dispute over the swap of rum for furs.

How the traders lived usually gets a simple answer: like the Indians. But that is not quite true; their living conditions were often worse. Indeed, in Pennsylvania, the colonial officials ordered that caves inhabited by some of the traders be filled in. Most lodged in "half-faced" lean-tos. When they built their own cabins, they used the available local material, logs, notched to hold together, since, as late as the middle of the eighteenth century, they had no nails. Chimneys, when built at all, were just as the first settlers had built them a century before, logs daubed with mud or clay. Floors were bare earth.

Families who lived in such primitive houses were not necessarily poor. While the Indian trade was certainly risky—not only for life and limb but also because the market for furs swung wildly—it could be quite profitable. Moreover, since it was almost entirely based on credit, one could become a trader with very little capital. So it was that when Charles's father-in-law, Edmund Cartlidge, died in 1740, he left an estate valued at more than twice what Robert Bruce Polk had accumulated roughly forty years before, some £107.

By the nature of the trade, houses tended to be widely separated from one another. A Moravian missionary who stopped at Charles Polk's house, which at that time was located near the modern town of Hancock, Maryland, on the northernmost bend of the Potomac River, about seventy miles northwest of Washington, D.C., said that beyond Charles's there was no house for forty miles. The missionary continued, "I arose early, being very glad and thankful to the Lord for having delivered me from this house."

It is one of the jokes of American history that if George Washington had actually slept in all the places he is alleged to have visited, America would still be an English colony. Certainly, Charles's cabin would not have figured high on the list of suitable accommodations, but in the journal he kept on his surveying mission, the young George Washington wrote in March 1747,

Sonday 20th finding y. River not much abated we in y. Evening Swam our horses over and carried them to Charles Polks in Maryland for Pasturage till y. next Morning . . . *Monday* 21st We went over in a Canoe and travell'd up Maryland side all y. Day in a Continued Rain to [the house of Colonel] Collo Cresaps right against y. Mouth of y. South Branch about 40 miles from Polks. I believe y. worst Road that was ever trod by Man or Beast.

Charles ate what the Indians ate. Hominy (Algonquin: *uskatahomen)*, ground corn, was their staple. When pigs were available, bacon and various kinds of "drippings" slightly livened the mush, and before pigs became common, such wild game as was plentiful offered an alternative. When we hear of "bread and meat," the "meat" is probably such "heavy" meats as bear and venison as distinct from "bread," which often meant such "light" meats as wild turkey and raccoon. For clothing, the trader or (after about 1720) the settler and his family wore and slept in or on skins or strouds.

A S DIFFICULT AS IT WAS FOR WHITES IN THE NINETEENTH century to believe, life among the Indians had great attractions for many whites. Benjamin Franklin, who was as ready as anyone else to exploit them, said, perhaps rhetorically, that

> when white persons of either sex have been taken prisoners young by the Indians and lived a while among them, tho' ransomed by the Friends, and treated with all imaginable tenderness to prevail with them to stay among the English, yet in a Short time they become disgusted with our manner of life, and the care and pains that are necessary to support it, and take the first good Opportunity of escaping again into the Woods, from whence there is no reclaiming them.

Rhetorically or not, it was a fact that many whites plunged into Indian society voluntarily, and even many white captives had to be forced to return to white society. Each side also kidnapped members of the other: the whites to sell Indians into slavery and the Indians to use whites as hostages or to induct into their communities. There are no statistics on the Indians, but in the French and Indian War (1754–63) more than sixteen hundred whites were abducted in New England alone.

After their victory over the French in 1759, the British authorities thought that the Indians would no longer be able to resist them and pressured those within reach to return the hundreds of captives held by the various Indian communities. Within two years, they had got back 338 captives out of a total they estimated at about twice that many. Americans who have anguished over captives alleged to be in the hands of the Vietnamese will understand the emotions evoked by these figures, but, in fact, the issue was rather more complicated then than now. While many of the captives were harshly treated, others had been adopted into

Indian societies and wished to remain. Some, indeed, had to be dragged, bound and fighting, to their liberation. As Colonel Henry Bouquet observed on October 29, 1764, "These [whites] if not narrowly watched may be apt to make their Escape after they are delivered up: The Guards and Centinels therefore on this duty must be particularly attentive to prevent such accidents happening."

Voluntarily for religious, commercial or other reasons and involuntarily as captives, several hundred English, Scots and Irish people moved into Indian societies in the early years of the eighteenth century. The officials found no effective way to stop them. But the features of Indian life that had attracted them were fast disappearing. As traders and settlers brought in their new products, and particularly their liquor, guns and diseases, Indian societies collapsed. Peoples who had a century before been numbered in the thousands often did not reach a hundred. "We found few Indians there," wrote the Moravian missionary John Martin Mack of one village in 1744, "and those who remained there looked much dejected. They were in number only seven men." By the middle of the eighteenth century, the whole Indian population around the Ohio River had fallen to just 789 warriors.

Having dropped to the point that they could no longer maintain their separate identity, Indians became jumbled in villages where there was no common ground except difference from the whites: the villages were not only polylingual but also polycentric, without clear organization or leadership. While this made the incursion of the whites, both traders and settlers, relatively easy, it also removed most of the restraints on anarchy that come only in organized societies. Like the traders, the Indians had moved into a social wilderness.

Finally concluding that they were doomed unless they fought, the Indian leader Pontiac put together in 1762 a confederation of the remnants of Indian communities from Lake Superior to the lower Mississippi to attempt to expel the whites. The principal objectives were the forts the British had constructed at strategic places to dominate the interior, but the Indians also wanted to burn the settlements and drive out or kill the colonists. Terror was the weapon by which they hoped to prevent future settlement on their lands.

For the first time, the Indians managed to coordinate their actions in a broad strategic plan and captured eight of the twelve British forts; they also won a stunning victory over British and American troops at the Battle of Bloody Run. Warfare reached a new level of savagery: Indians routinely killed prisoners, settlers and traders. In response, the British commander ordered his troops to take no Indian prisoners and instructed his local commander to place smallpox blankets where Indians were likely to find them, "to extirpate this execrable race . . ." William Trent wrote in his journal that when two of the Indians came into Fort Pitt for talks, "we gave them two Blankets and an Handkerchief out of the Smallpox Hospital. I hope it will have the desired effect." It did.

But it was not only the combatants who engaged in vicious acts. The most notorious recorded case was the wanton murder by a group of civilians, known as the Paxton Boys, on December 14, 1763, of

> six peaceable and defenseless Indians at Conestoga, where a remnant of the Susquehannocks with a few other Indians had been living quietly under the protection of the Pennsylvania government. A few days later, on December 27, the Paxton Boys entered Lancaster unopposed and butchered the remaining fourteen members of the Conestoga community, most of them old men, women, and children.

Having tasted blood, the settlers around the Conestoga area began a march on Philadelphia, which they regarded as "soft" on the Indians and where a number of "Moravians" (Indians who had converted to Christianity under the influence of Moravian missionaries) had taken shelter. The panicked governor, William Penn's grandson John, asked Benjamin Franklin to go out to meet them. Franklin bravely did and turned them back, but he was horrified when Governor Penn caved in to at least one of the rebels' demands and began a policy of paying a bounty for Indian scalps. In his *Narrative of the Late Massacres in Lancaster County,* Franklin spoke with a rare voice of reason and empathy, and those who heard it were furious. Governor Penn wrote, incongruously, that "There will never be any prospect of ease and happiness while that villain [Franklin] has the liberty of spreading about the poison of that inveterate malice and ill nature which is deeply implanted in his own black heart."

It should be said that even among the relatively lawless white traders, there were recorded instances of attempts to protect Indians or to punish or restrain those guilty of particularly vicious acts against them. In at least one act, Charles Polk, Jr., the son of Charles the Indian Trader, joined those who sought to create or uphold a degree of law and order: in his capacity as a captain in the militia, he "certified" the murder by a group of settlers of a party of peaceful Indians whom they lured into their midst by the offer of liquor. One of the murdered women was the sister of a Mingo elder, Tah-gah-jute, known by the "white" name of James Logan, who was regarded as "the White Man's Friend." In his widely quoted lament, Logan summed up the tragedy of the frontier. "I appeal to any white man," he said,

> to say if he ever entered Logan's cabin hungry and he gave him not meat, or if he came cold and naked and he clothed him not . . . I had even thought to have lived with you but for the injuries of one man, Colonel Cresap [the man whose house George Washington mentioned], who in cold blood and unprovoked murdered all the relations of Logan, not sparing even my women and children. There runs not a drop of my blood in the veins of any living creature. This has called on me for revenge. I have sought it. I have killed many . . .

This murder precipitated a new round in the bloody confrontations, known as Lord Dunmore's War. As Richard White has icily commented, as a result Kentucky could be settled and Lord Dunmore and the Virginia elite [who were speculating in titles to Indian lands] could now become rich. Dunmore demonstrated how murders occasioned by rum and backcountry settlers could serve the desires of more discreet men to become wealthy.

In their turn, the Indians burned, pillaged and murdered. Both whites and Indians customarily scalped their victims. Who "invented" scalping has been hotly debated for years, but regardless of who is blamed, the practice was eagerly adopted by both whites and Indians. The white governments all along the frontier offered a bounty for Indian scalps. As both whites and Indians became more insecure, frightened and remorseless, the level of often senseless and always appalling violence increased.

FROM THIS VICIOUS PARTISAN WARFARE CAME A DRAMATIC episode celebrated in family history: the capture of Delilah, the daughter-in-law of Charles Polk, by Indians.

By the time of Delilah's capture, during the Revolutionary War, Charles's brother William had long since moved south to western North Carolina, but Charles Jr. had settled in the area where his father had been trading. Settling involved quite a different approach to the Indians than trading; where the father had lived with the Indians, spoken their language and tried to, indeed had to, win their acceptance, his son sought to carve out of their lands a homestead for his family. The father, who left no real record of his life, is known as Charles the Indian Trader, while the son, who did, is known as Charles the Indian Fighter. In this period, the hinterland was designated simply as the Ohio valley, but Charles Jr. lived primarily in what is today Kentucky, where, as a militia captain, he took part in a number of search-and-destroy attacks on Shawnee Indian villages.

These campaigns were commanded by General George Rogers

Clark. Clark's orders from Virginia Governor Thomas Jefferson were that the Shawnee "be driven from their lands or exterminated." Clark took Jefferson at his word and boasted of his "barbarity," slaughtering, scalping or burning alive men, women and children and destroying houses and crops. Throughout the late 1770s and early 1780s, these attacks continued under Clark and various other militia commanders. Charles was not involved in most of them, but he did take part in the almost unending hunt for Indian bands that still hung on around the new white settlements. When caught, Indians were treated as "vermin" to be exterminated. Such operations were by then quite common. Finally, this vicious war came home to the Polks.

In the predawn hours of August 31, 1782, when Charles and most of the men of a rough wooden stockade fort near the modern city of Louisville were away, Charles's young family of four children and a nineteen- or twenty-year-old pregnant wife, Delilah Tyler Polk, were asleep in their little hut. Suddenly, they were awakened by bloodcurdling screams as groups of Indians rushed the stockade, climbed the walls and broke through the roofs.

Delilah, who had her two younger children in bed with her, jumped up when she heard the noise and, taking one child under each arm, tried to rouse her two older children. Before she could do more than stand up, several Indians broke through the door, grabbed her and pushed her out.

The attack happened so fast that no resistance had been made, but in the confusion two men, four women and a young boy had managed to escape. Three others were not so lucky—a man, a woman and a child had been killed. The rest, some thirty people, including Delilah, were taken prisoner. As they watched, numb with terror, the Indians looted the fort, drove them out of the stockade and then burned it.

Fearing pursuit, the Indians rushed the survivors about a mile away to a place where they felt safe enough to pause to take stock of their prisoners. Delilah still had her two infants but could not find the older children. Horrified, she concluded that they had been burned in the fort and bitterly reproached herself for not having managed to get them out.

At about this time, an Indian who was apparently a man of authority arrived. He must have been briefed on the organization of the fort, since he immediately sought out Captain Charles's wife. Obviously hating Charles for what must have been similar, or even worse, attacks on Indian villages, he was delighted to have Delilah and her children as captives. What it meant she could not know, but as her son, also a captive, later reported,

> she could observe a marked difference in the treatment of her children and others taken. On the second morning, they painted her son in Indian style, decorated him in feathers, and some Indian trinkets, and called him "The Young Chief of the Long Knife," the name given the Kentuckians by the Indians of that day.

From the survivors, they selected a few, including Delilah and her children together with another woman, a Mrs. Ash, and her small baby, to take with them either to use as hostages or to adopt into their tribe. After what must have been a horror-filled night, not knowing what the morning would bring or what had happened to those left behind, they awoke at dawn to begin what would be for some a death march.

No sooner had they got fully under way than the Indians took the children away from their mothers. Both Delilah and Mrs. Ash were convinced that the children would be killed. They lost sight of them as they were hurried along through the forest. By sundown, they guessed that they had covered about twelve miles and were exhausted, too numb to be any longer terrified. But to Delilah's amazement, not only did the Indians return the child they had taken from her, but they brought forward the two older children she had thought were burned to death in the fort. What that meant they could not guess. And knowing that prisoners were often tortured to death "to atone" for dead Indians, they did not care to speculate. In fact, by that time, they hardly cared. Delilah and the other prisoners were so fatigued and thirsty

> that she could scarcely breathe. The Indians had brought with them many watermelons from the fort, and while [they were] refreshing themselves with them, she held out her hand as a request for a part to relieve her thirst, which was answered by a general laugh and shout of approbation, and some ten or twelve of them handed her slices which she divided among the prisoners around her.

The Indians obviously thought this was an audacious and brave move befitting the wife of a chief, as they considered Charles. In contrast to Delilah, Mrs. Ash spurned the offer and, shaking her head, whimpered that she would go no farther. Her reaction angered the Indians and convinced them that she would slow their escape. So, a short time later, Delilah "distinctly heard the tomahawk strike her head. She uttered a scream simultaneous with their war-whoop, and all was silent."

Later, when they camped for the night, the Indians apparently discussed killing Delilah also, since she was almost too exhausted and footsore to continue. But one Indian appointed himself her protector and prevented her murder. The next day they trudged on, goaded by the Indians who increasingly feared that they might be overtaken.

Two days later, the party reached the Ohio River, where the Indians had hidden canoes. By this time, Delilah was ready to give up. Her feet were so swollen that she could not even remove the moccasins the Indians had given her. Seeing this, the Indian who had protected her approached, took out his knife and gently cut the moccasins off. He gestured for her to bathe her feet in the river, gave her some oil made from the marrow of buffalo bones to rub on as an ointment and handed her a new, larger pair of moccasins. As her son William later commented, this is an "illustration of the Indian character, to show that even among untutored savages there are traits of benevolence and humanity that are worthy to be preserved.'' He did not say it, but he certainly knew that such a gesture was unthinkable from a white to an Indian.

After they crossed the Ohio, the Indians sat down to decide what to do, and one, Delilah and the remaining white captives thought, harangued the others saying that Delilah ''had lived and traveled so far that he believed the Great Spirit would not permit them to kill her and if they attempted it he would be angry with them and they could not prosper.'' So they pushed her onward.

Finally, on reaching their camp, they separated into small bands. Delilah and one child were assigned to one band and her other children to another. They kept her youngest daughter, as they said, ''to raise as one of their own squaws, which much increased her grief,'' but later traded her to the Shawnees because they feared she would die if they kept her on the move. Delilah learned all of this when the band she was with happened across an Indian trader, a man like her father-in-law, Charles, who was able to move more or less freely among the Indians and knew their language. Then they set off for the little fort that later became Detroit.

Detroit was then held by British forces to whom the Indian war party delivered their captives. There the British held the captive Americans until peace was arranged between the new Republic and Great Britain, at which time Delilah was reunited with her husband. Years later, her son William trained as a lawyer and became a judge but never forgot his days as the Young Chief of the Long Knife.

THE REVOLUTION

"The Colonists are not a Conquered People"

THE BOSTON TEA PARTY OF DECEMBER 16, 1773, STANDS OUT as the most celebrated of the events leading to the American Revolution. While our schoolbooks teach us that it was a unique and daring venture that first focused resentment on the oppressive actions of the British, it was but one of at least half a dozen "tea parties." Others took place up and down the Atlantic seaboard as irate merchants protested against what they regarded as invasion of their liberties (and their purses) by "taxation without representation." More significant, the tea parties were but one stage in a sequence of struggles with the Crown over the colonists' growing sense of capacity for self-rule that began half a century before.

In our selective memory, the Boston Tea Party also ranks as the first of a series of magnificent affirmations of Americans' collective willingness to stand, fight and if necessary die for liberty. That unity is a myth. The realities with which such leaders as George Washington had to cope were indifference, division, hostility, fence-sitting and cowardice among the colonials.

Only by understanding those realities can we see how truly extraordinary was the accomplishment of the leaders of the Revolution. Those realities become clearer if we veer off the well-trod paths of historical study, away from the major urban centers, Boston, New York and Philadelphia, and apart from the handful of well-known leaders, Washington, Hamilton, Franklin and Jefferson. The true character of the Revolution is to be found in the hinterland. This can be seen in the lives of three generations of Polks: William, his son Thomas and Thomas's son Will.

PRIOR TO ABOUT 1750, THE AMERICAN COLONIES WERE JUST "waterfront properties," a fringe of settled areas along the northeastern Atlantic seaboard blocked from the inland forests by the Appalachian mountain barrier. When the brothers William and Charles, the grandsons of Robert Bruce Polk, left their homes on the Chesapeake, they crossed the frontier into the "wilderness" just a few miles north of the present site of Washington, D.C. The Maryland world from which they came would have seemed strange to us, but the Appalachian world into which they plunged would have been utterly alien. For them, traveling those few miles amounted to jumping off the end of the earth.

Other people followed them in the early and middle years of the eighteenth century, so that little pockets of traders and settlers established themselves, usually precariously but always aggressively, on the northern fringes of Maryland and Virginia, in the western parts of Pennsylvania and in the Indian territory that became West Virginia, Kentucky and Ohio.

There the scores of Indian villages and towns were interlaced by a highly articulated network of trails, but travel was arduous, slow and problematical and no markets existed where animals or equipment could be replaced. Indians were often welcoming hosts, but there were limits to their capacity and uncertainties about their hospitality. Consequently, only those drawn by a lust for adventure, land or wealth or those driven by less noble motivations hazarded the enterprise.

The small, isolated cabins of traders first and then later of settlers were always separated by days and often weeks of hard slogging. We can construct a mental map of their positions by taking a handful of coins and tossing them into the air. Where they fall, each coin would represent a "settlement," separated from the others by vast spaces. If we could throw the coins a city block, we would also get a sense of how far they were from the already "tamed" areas of the coastal plain.

Much of the early history of colonial America is made up of the repeated "throwing of the coins" into the Indian areas and of white settlers gradually filling in the spaces among them. So slow was this movement that, in predicting the future of America, Thomas Jefferson thought that America would get established on the Mississippi only about now, the end of the twentieth century, and that the spread across the whole continent would take four or five centuries. That rate of forward movement then seemed a reasonable guess, since the means of communication and transport outside the "waterfront property" were less modern than in the Chinese, Persian and Roman Empires of two thousand years before. Nothing like the giant canal network of China, the rapid postal system of Persia or the Roman military highways was even dreamed of in eighteenth-century America.

While isolation was obvious in the hinterland, separation was a fact of life even in the relatively densely settled coastal areas. Travel between New York and Philadelphia required days of jolting in a stagecoach over rutted trails and fording dangerous rivers or weeks of sailing down the coast. Eighteenth-century Americans hardly knew one another.

Nor did most colonists want to. One of our favorite myths is of the melting pot, in which we all, whatever our provenance, become Americans. But our ancestors did not think in such terms. They settled next to and worked with those with whom they shared religion, language, color, culture, economic status and, often, age. Their neighborhoods were not welcoming to those they regarded as alien by any of these criteria. So, even in the coastal areas, America found its true map in the patchwork quilt so favored by colonial homemakers. Little patches of Dutch, Swedes, Swiss, Huguenot French, Moravian Salzburgers, Palatine Germans, Highland (often Catholic) Scots, Lowland (mainly Presbyterian) Scotch-Irish and (usually Anglican) English set themselves up—and apart—all through the colonies.

And they were rapidly becoming many. In 1700, the entire population of the colonies was only about 250,000. Immigration then speeded up, so that the population almost doubled in a single generation; cumulatively, by the time of the Revolution, the white population was ten times what it had been in 1700. Each year what amounted to the resident population of Boston walked down gangplanks.

The newcomers in this "third wave" of immigrants faced even more formidable problems than those encountered by Robert Bruce Polk and the other members of the second wave. Not only the best lands but also the better jobs were taken and jealously guarded. And such information as exists suggests that the new arrivals were less prepared, less equipped and poorer than the earlier arrivals. Moreover, because the urban economy was not robust enough to absorb them, they were often faced with grim choices. Some few who were desperate and strong enough, particularly among the nearly 100,000 Scots who came direct from Scotland or from Northern Ireland, leapfrogged the settled coast direct into the interior. The vast majority, of course, were unwilling or unable to take such a gamble. Some found relatives or friends to help them, but many, being poor, without relatives and untrained, slipped down into what Karl Marx later termed a *Lumpenproletariat*.

Little empathy for them was evident among those who had already arrived. Not welcome in the established towns, the newcomers were often forced into a seminomadic life rather like modern homeless people. They were seen as a burden by the taxpayers who had accumulated most of the wealth. In New Jersey, for example, the members of the diminutive upper class held about half of all the resources, while about a quarter of the taxable part of the population held no real property. And in Maryland, about a third of the population held assets worth not quite as much as those held by Robert Polk a century earlier, roughly £45. Between the relatively rich and the absolutely poor, fellow-feeling was as rare as between members of different ethnic and religious communities.

Contacts were rare even among the socially and economically privileged men who were to make the Revolution—so rare and so missed, in fact, that new forms of association sprang up. In 1772, as the clouds of civil strife darkened, "committees of correspondence" were set up throughout the colonies so that men could acquaint one another with events in their various areas and could help one another see a commonality in their grievances. In blunt truth, they had to begin just to see one another as something different from Englishmen. Their effort was critical to the success of the unforeseen and unwanted Revolution, but the achievement of a sense of union was a slow and faltering process.

In our celebrations, we like to think of our ancestors as marching to the beat of the fife and drum of liberty. But Patrick Henry, Thomas Jefferson and the other Revolutionary leaders were not romantics. They were almost literally dragged, protesting to the bitter end, into the roles in which we know them. George Washington summed up their reluctance to take the fateful step into revolution, saying, "When I took command of the army [on June 15, 1775], I abhorred the idea of independence." At that time, few if any of the members of the Continental Congress would have disagreed.

Fortunately, some did. But even in the most affected centers, Boston, New York, Philadelphia, the cockpits of the agitation for independence, the records show that very few men (and fewer women) participated in the great events on which history focuses. Of those who did, at least one in three was actively or passively opposed to "liberty." Indeed, so dismayed were they by the coming conflict, even when it was upon them, that, as the chief engineer of the Continental army, the French volunteer Louis Duportail, lamented, "There is a hundred times more enthusiasm for this Revolution in any Paris café than in all the colonies together.'' Many, as astonishing as it may seem to us, appear hardly to have been aware of the events leading to the Revolution. I have told enough of the story of Charles Polk, ''the Indian Fighter,'' in Chapter 3 to show that he spent the years of the Revolution fighting, but fighting local battles over land with Indians, almost totally oblivious to the Revolution. He was not alone. Most Americans kept their eyes on ''practical'' local issues.

Historians swing with the currents of fashion between emphasis on the great patriotic leaders and on their followers. Both can be documented, but both miss much of the drama and meaning of the Revolution. Alongside of this white America from which our national myth has been mined were two large groups of people who were affected—in some cases formed, in others destroyed—by the Revolution: the blacks and the Indians. Only now, two centuries later, are we beginning to understand them and their role in the events. Consider first the blacks.

On the coastal plain, where tobacco, rice and other plantations had been developed, thousands of black slaves were being imported. They were a ''group'' only in the negative sense that they existed apart from the whites. Not only did they come from different African areas, tribes, language groups and religions, but they were divided among the ''outlandish'' (those who came direct from Africa) and ''New Negroes'' (those who had spent time in or been born in the Caribbean and those who were born in the American colonies). While they aggregated about 450,000 people on the eve of the Revolution, they did not live in concentrations sufficient in size to develop into communities. Consciously, as a means of control, whites divided them, even by family members, and isolated them. For the most part, any individual black person would have had intimate contact with fewer than a dozen other blacks and would have been either discouraged from taking part in any church or other gatherings or forbidden to do so. They were not addressed by those who sounded the call for liberty, and probably few would have understood the terms in which it was announced; inevitably, however, they were caught up in the events and played a significant role in the Revolution.

Inland, the Indians presented a mirror image to the blacks. Ruthlessly pushed out of the lands desired by the whites, decimated by diseases against which they had no immunities, tragically debauched by liquor, hunted down and often killed or sold into slavery, and still often bitterly hostile to one another, their societies were imploding and their cultures disintegrating. But enough remained of their spirit and their numbers that they created what amounted to a "second front" during the Revolution.

M ANY STEPS, RELUCTANTLY TAKEN, ALONG DIVERSE PATHS and without a sense of direction, led to 1776. The path of William Polk, born in Maryland about 1700, and his young son Thomas, born in Pennsylvania about 1730, led down the flank of the Appalachian Mountains to the western part of North Carolina about 1754. Why did they and thousands of others take that trail? The common adage that the grass looks greener probably accounts for more than would seem logical, since, at that time, there were almost no maps, no reliable descriptions of territory, no available analysis of dangers and practically no information on climate, possible crops, available markets or anything else that a prudent person today would demand. What there was, was a notion, a general opinion fed by rumor, that somewhere ahead was an empty land with deep rich soil. And behind them was poverty. As their fathers and grandfathers had experienced in the Chesapeake, the better lands were being taken at such a rate that land prices even in the wilds of Pennsylvania shot up. A Pennsylvania Quaker by the name of Robert Parke warned a relative in the old country in 1725 that land "Grows dearer every year by Reason of Vast Quant[it]ies of People that come here yearly from Several Parts of the world . . ." So people who knew well the hardships, the constraints, the dangers of where they were, were drawn ahead, always ahead, like iron filings by a magnet. Chasing some sort of frontier had already become a theme in the American experience; by the mid-1700s, it was irresistible.

What was the land into which they were drawn? The North Carolina we know today was then divided into a coastal plain much like Robert Bruce Polk's Maryland and a backcountry similar to the Indian territory in which Charles Polk had traded. It was to the backcountry that William and Thomas went, but much of their lives there would be shaped by the people of the coast, where the settlements had begun a century before.

Like the Maryland where William was born, the Carolinas—they were divided into North and South only in 1691—were given by the English king to a group of his courtiers to establish a feudal kingdom under the English Crown. As in Maryland, the new settlers inevitably clashed with the Indian inhabitants. Despite a peace treaty with the Chowanoc, the settlers not only took their lands but also kidnapped their children, thus provoking the Clarendon County War, the first of several conflicts that were to punctuate the colony's history. Having won, as they always did, the whites pushed the Indians into the first of a growing list of reservations.

The white population grew slowly at first and then explosively. From a few hundred in the 1670s, it reached 10,000 about 1700 and had doubled twenty years later. By the time William and Thomas arrived, it had reached about 75,000, and on the eve of the Revolution was over 200,000. English, Welsh, French Huguenots, Swiss, Germans and Scots all set up carefully separated communities. After the 1730s, North Carolina had the largest population of Highland Scots in America, and they continued to pour into the country. Fifty-four shiploads of them arrived in the one summer of 1770.

What had been attractive in Virginia and Maryland was also alluring in the Carolinas: tobacco. But the Carolinas additionally fostered two other crops. Rice grew luxuriantly in the swampy lowlands around Cape Fear, and "naval stores" (turpentine and tar) could be harvested from the bountiful pine forests. All three of these crops were highly labor-

intensive; to farm them, the early settlers began to import large numbers of black slaves; over time, by dint of slave labor, planters grew rich.
It was this incipient oligarchy for which John Locke was hired to write a
constitution in 1669. Like all his works, Locke's constitution was built
on a bedrock of landownership. Only those who acquired land acquired
wealth and social status. Wealth was nearly assured, since land was cheap
and the law specified that each "Freeman of Carolina, shall have absolute
power and authority over his negro slaves, of what opinion or religion
soever."

In 1712, the black population of North Carolina was estimated at
only 800, but its growth accelerated with the burgeoning of the plantation system, so that between 1730 and 1767, blacks increased from
6,000 to 39,483. However, since slaves then cost about five or six times
as much as they produced in a year, they were given just enough to
maintain life. Their diet was barely above the starvation level, usually
just a quart of Indian corn daily; only the most humane masters afforded
their slaves occasional meals of meat. And they were provided with virtually no clothing, equipment, utensils or housing. Yet, curiously, at
least some blacks seem to have been allowed to vote in the first election,
since in 1715 the General Assembly passed a law forbidding the practice.
Sexual intercourse between whites and blacks (and whites and Indians)—the word "miscegenation" was not coined until the middle of the
nineteenth century—was made a crime but remained fairly common.
According to a contemporary visitor from Massachusetts, "enjoyment
of a negro or mulatto woman is spoken of as quite a common thing: no
reluctance, delicacy or shame is made about the matter . . ." Thomas
Jefferson complained about the "very strong and disagreeable odour" of
blacks, which he saw as a proof of racial inferiority; but working from
sunrise to after sunset, having no access to bathing or washing facilities
and no change of clothing, that blacks had body odor is hardly surprising. Since few people of either color washed often, the line Jefferson
drew in his writings could hardly have been sharp. As we now know, he
did not actually draw it.

To its credit, the British government made periodic attempts to ameliorate the harsh conditions under which slaves were kept but without much effect. Throughout the eighteenth century, blacks lived under what amounted to martial law, with nightly curfews, prohibitions on gatherings of more than three people and the requirement to carry passes for any movement outside of the plantations on which they worked. Violations were savagely punished with whipping (''well laid on''), having the ears nailed to a post before being cut off, castration or death by hanging or burning. To encourage masters to inflict punishments even when these disabled or killed the slave, the community paid the owner compensation. It was 1774 before it became a crime for a white to kill a black. The penalty even then was relatively light, and the murderer was exonerated if the victim had tried to defend himself.

Manumission was discouraged, and where it occurred, the freedman was ordered to leave the state. If he did not decamp rapidly enough, he could be legally sold back into slavery; always he risked being kidnapped and sold out of state as a runaway slave. When too many freedmen accumulated to be thus handled, shortly after the Revolution, they were required to wear a ''badge of cloth to be fixed on the left shoulder, and to have thereon wrought in legible capital letters the word FREE.''

Given this description, it is sobering to reflect that North Carolina was noted by contemporaries as being far milder in its treatment of black slaves than either South Carolina or Virginia. It was not milder toward the Indians.

Relations with the Indians followed the pattern already common in Virginia, Maryland and Pennsylvania, where traders got them drunk, took their goods and raped their women. By 1710, relations had become so strained that the Tuscarora Indians petitioned Pennsylvania to allow them to move north, saying that they could no longer live or hunt in the Carolinas ''without the constant fear of murder or enslavement.'' When it became clear that they would not be allowed to move, the Tuscarora went to war in 1711; frightened, the Carolinians called on Virginia for its militia and paid the Yamasee Indian enemies of the Tuscarora a bounty

for Tuscarora scalps. Like most of the white-Indian wars, this was literally a war "to the knife," in which about one in every three or four Indians was killed or sold into slavery. Having killed off the Tuscarora, the
colonists fought, one after another, the Yamasee, the I Ye Ye (known to
the colonists as the Catawba) and the Cherokee. By 1763, the remnants
of the Cherokee were the only significant Indian society remaining in
North Carolina.

EXCEPT FOR INDIANS, THE HINTERLAND WAS UNINHABITED AND
separated from the settled, fertile coastal plain by large stretches of
scrub pine and sand across which travel was slow and difficult. So when a
few settlers began to trickle into the backcountry about 1730, they
came southward from Pennsylvania down the Great Wagon Road rather
than from the coastal towns. They were a mixed group. In the earliest
written record, we read names that suggest 140 English, 47 Scots, 7
Germans and 6 French. At first, they were squatters, since the earliest
grants of land can be dated only to 1749, but in the following decade
hundreds of grants were made.

Moving "ahead of the wave," to the western part of North Carolina, William and his son Thomas avoided the mistake made by Robert
when he had moved from Ireland to Maryland. William died shortly after their arrival, but Thomas caught the upsurge in values just at the
right moment. According to family legend, he arrived about 1754 with
nothing but a "knapsack on his back and a goodly share of indomitable
enterprise." Knapsack legend or not, he certainly was to show enterprise.

Thomas was tall, well built and energetic; he soon became recognized as a natural leader, someone other men felt they could trust. And
he combined in his personality those qualities for which the Scots had
become known: hardihood, frugality, pride and ambition. Moderately
well educated for his times, he quickly found an occupation as a surveyor. He could hardly have chosen a better occupation for this frontier

area, since it enabled him to locate choice lands. His first acquisition, some two hundred acres "between Widdow Armor and the Catauba Indian District, joining the Indians line," was registered in November 1764. Subsequently, not only did he acquire more lands easily and cheaply, one prime piece on the Sugar Creek in 1767, for example, at a cost of about 2 shillings an acre, but he identified other rewarding ventures. Recognizing that planks for housing were in great demand, he invested the profits he made as a surveyor and from selling lands in a sawmill and, seeing that the farmers needed to turn their wheat into flour, a gristmill; then, to provide his neighbors cloth and equipment, a store.

So profitable did these ventures become by the time of the Revolution that Thomas was able to sell one piece of land in the new village of Charlotte, to build a school which he and Thomas Spratt (whose daughter Susanna he married in 1755) had founded, for the then huge sum of £920. This one transaction netted him approximately twenty times the total estate of his great-grandfather Robert about seventy years before. And at a critical point in the 1776 British siege of Charleston, he was able to lend the commanding general $6,250 to feed the starving American troops. Later, when he was commissary general for the southern army, he used his own money to buy supplies when the Continental Congress and the North Carolina legislature failed to come through. He had become a wealthy man.

Perhaps the hardest thing for each generation of young people to imagine is frivolity in those who were in their lifetimes serious and aged. But when Thomas Polk was hired to survey the state line between North and South Carolina, in 1772, the line at one point bent erratically (as it still does). The official explanation was that the nearby Catawba Indians wished to remain on the South Carolina side, but according to family legend, the cause was somewhat different: "the surveyors ran across a party with a wagonload of whiskey which they followed . . . [and] even today a whiskey wagon in a vast wilderness would be apt to cause the needle in a surveyor's compass to vary a little."

More acceptably, because more seriously, Thomas had seen how important was even the small amount of education he had, and he began a family tradition, which would be carried on by later generations, of founding schools and colleges. In 1769, he helped to establish the first "academy" in western North Carolina, and while a member of the colonial legislature he sponsored a bill to establish Queens College. It was, in part, British opposition to the founding of these schools that embittered him against the Crown.

NOT EVERYONE BUMPING DOWN THE GREAT WAGON ROAD was so lucky as Thomas in his timing. As hundreds and then thousands arrived, they (like Robert a century before in Maryland) found most of the better land taken and most of the opportunities already snapped up. For them, life was poor, limited and hard. Their land was, as the Quaker naturalist William Bartram found, a scene of desolation with "vast forests, expansive plains, and detached groves [filled with] heaps of white gnawed bones of ancient buffalo, elk, and deer, indiscriminately mixed with those of men, [and] half grown over with moss."

More sensitive to people was an Anglican missionary, an Englishman by the name of Charles Woodmason. In 1766, he found the inhabitants wretchedly poor, "living wholly on Butter, Milk, Clabber and what in England is given to the Hogs and Dogs . . . [They] are reduc'd to the sad Necessity of gathering Apples Peaches & green from the Trees, and boiling them for food." With "No Physician—No Medicines—No Necessaries—Nurses, or Care in Sickness . . . You must lye till Nature gets the better of the Disease, or Death relieves You." Yet, he found, not only did "these Poor People enjoy good Health," they evinced an exuberant spirit. But their attitude toward sex appalled him.

> The Young Women have a most uncommon Practise, which I cannot break them off. They draw their Shift as tight as possible to the Body, and pin it close, to shew the roundness of

their Breasts, and slender Waists (for they are generally finely shaped) and draw their Petticoat close to their Hips to shew the fineness of their Limbs—so that they might as well be in Puri Naturalibus—Indeed Nakedness is not censurable or indecent here, and they expose themselves often quite Naked, without Ceremony—Rubbing themselves and their Hair with Bears Oil and tying it up behind in a Bunch like the Indians . . .

All in all, he found, they lived in the "state of nature," and for Woodmason, that state was worse than even a Thomas Hobbes could have imagined. "They delight in their present low, lazy, sluttish, heathenish, hellish Life, and seem not desirous of changing it."

What Woodmason failed to notice was that North Carolina was one of the fastest growing of the American colonies; its population was doubling each generation and it had become the fourth most populous of the colonies. At the same time, exports of farm products increased dramatically. For him as for other coastal people, the westerners were just "white Indians." Although twice as numerous as the coastal people, they were poorly represented in the state legislature. Rarely having legal title to their homes or farms, they were often treated as the English had treated the Irish a century before. Unable to protect themselves, they were sheep to be shorn by the colonial officials who extorted excessive taxes and pocketed most of what they collected. Thus, long before the Revolution, taxation without representation was a burning political issue in North Carolina.

But, for those like Thomas who lived between the coast and the savage frontier, and had begun to become affluent, other actions by the Crown were equally obnoxious. The most egregious resulted from British mercantilist policies. As fearful of losing their gold and silver as many modern countries are of losing their hard currency, the British drained them away from the colonies. This would probably not have been serious except that the Crown also refused to allow the provincial government to issue paper money. Purchase of needed supplies was so difficult that the colony suffered an almost continuous depression. Then, to add insult to injury, the royal governors and their myrmidons spent public revenues on what appeared to the westerners unnecessary luxuries which only easterners could enjoy. Even before the middle of the eighteenth century, these differences had begun to create the preconditions of the Revolution.

Possibly, they would have come to a head sooner except for the great clash of 1754–63 between France and Britain which the Americans called the French and Indian War. At first, that conflict consumed all the colonists' attentions, but as the French and their Indian allies were pushed farther away from North Carolina, grievances resurfaced.

When peaceful petitions about taxes brought no results, a group of armed men seized a government collector in 1759 and forced him to refund what he had taken illegally. With that action as a precedent, other groups began to take matters into their own hands. In response, the royal governor, Arthur Dobbs, made the worst possible move: he admitted the justice of the protests but also arrested the protesters' leaders. In response, their followers broke into the jail and released the imprisoned men. It would not be wrong to call this the first move toward the Revolution; indeed, that was the opinion of Governor Dobbs, who, with more foresight than anyone then imagined, reported to his superiors in London that he discerned "a republican spirit of Independency rising in this Colony."

In North Carolina as elsewhere, the peace settlement following the French and Indian War dramatically changed the relations between the colonists and the home government in two crucial ways. On the one hand, the colonists no longer thought they needed British protection from the Indians, who, having lost their French ally, were subdued. But on the other hand, the British had seen how costly the war had been and sought to avoid future trouble by stabilizing relations with the Indians. Reckoning that if they could keep the white settlers, whom they regarded as the lawless dregs of Ireland and Scotland, the very scum of the earth, from encroaching on Indian lands, and so provoking Indian wars, they could cut military costs, they drew a line along the ridge of the Appalachian Mountains beyond which there was to be no white incursion (see endpaper map).

The theory was sensible, but the policy contained two fatal weaknesses. First, pressures to settle beyond the Appalachians were too strong and too common to contain. Poorer colonists who had found little or no land available to them on the "English" side of the mountains and who believed that beyond the mountains was a sort of El Dorado of rich, deep soil were determined, at any cost, to get some of it for themselves. Richer members of the coastal elite (including such men as George Washington and Benjamin Franklin) who were speculating in western lands realized that they could profit only if the area was opened to settlement. And, second, just as much as the settlers and speculators, the British intended to take over the Indian lands. They simply wished to do so inexpensively and on their own timetable. So, in practice, they found defining or implementing their policy almost impossible. Tacitly and grudgingly, the British admitted defeat and thus both antagonized the Americans and revealed British vulnerability.

Vulnerability was soon to be shown also in the urgent British desire to pay for the late war. In North Carolina, this came up first in the surveying of areas that had already been taken from the Indians. Seeing this as a preliminary to the imposition of taxes, the squatters set upon the surveyors and severely beat them. They held firmly to the idea that their labor had created such value as the lands had and that, whatever was proclaimed in distant capitals, "possession was nine tenths of the law."

Men who had already taken part in small-scale demonstrations of 1759 came together in the summer of 1766 in a large but amorphous group known as the Regulation. As viewed by the government, the Regulation was an insurrection, and after a period of indecision, the royal governor, William Tryon, decided to "decapitate" the movement by arresting the leaders. His move only furthered their cause. Armed mobs attacked government officials and burned public buildings.

As event followed event, the governor finally got the legislature to declare what amounted to martial law in February 1771. The long delay worked in his favor, since in the meantime he won the support of the more established "near-western" community, including Thomas Polk, who had earlier sided with the insurgents. So when Governor Tryon called out the county militia, in which Thomas was a colonel, it obeyed. With that force, the governor marched to meet the insurgents at a field by the Alamance Creek. There in a short but sharp battle his thousand-man militia defeated the Regulators.

Order had been restored, but the cost of doing so made the collection of taxes even more urgent for the government and even less justified in the eyes of the people. The particular tax that rankled most was one symbolized by a stamp that was to be levied on even domestic transactions. Those who sought to dodge taxes or were critical of how they were to be collected or the amounts to be raised took up the argument that people should pay only those taxes they themselves had authorized. On shaky historical grounds, they maintained that even in England taxation without representation was "unconstitutional"; consequently, since the colonists had no representation in Parliament, taxes levied upon them by Parliament were illegal.

Here, finally, was an issue on which all factions among the colonists could agree, and it was one in which their parochial interests could be elevated above the attempt merely to dodge taxes to the cause of justice and liberty. Many stepped forward to speak of the conflict in these terms. Perhaps the most famous was Patrick Henry in the Virginia House of Burgesses, but in North Carolina, a judge by the name of Maurice Moore produced a pamphlet under one of those fulsome eighteenth-century titles that make the reading of the pamphlet itself superfluous.

The Justice and Policy of taxing the American Colonies, in Great Britain, considered Wherein is shewed, That the Colonists are not a conquered People. That they are constitutionally intitled to be taxed only

by their own Consent:—And that the Imposing a Stamp Duty on the
Colonists is as impolitic as it is inconsistant with their Rights. Non
Sibi Sed Patriae.

British officials were burned, but still only in effigy, and slogans were coined and repeated: the word of the day became "Liberty, Property and No Stamp-Duty." More serious, trade was boycotted, and, more exhilarating, the government seemed at first to give in. The colonists thought they had tasted victory, but the government speedily disabused them by establishing a virtual blockade of the coast. Confused and inexperienced, the colonists had no idea what to do next. They felt themselves still to be good English people, and, precisely because of that belief, they were convinced that the stamp tax was wrong, so they presented a petition affirming their loyalty to the Crown but swearing that "We will at any Risque whatever, and whenever called upon, United, and truly and Faithfully Assist each other, . . . in Preventing entirely the Operation of the Stamp Act."

Their resolve apparently convinced the governor, so he ordered the ships released, and, under threat, the customs officers signed a pledge that they would not reinstate the restrictions. Meanwhile, in Virginia, Patrick Henry had given his famous "treason" speech, inciting the colonists not to comply with the stamp tax, and a Stamp Act Congress had been convened in New York to demand repeal. Finally aware of the gravity of the situation, Parliament passed a new bill, the Declaratory Act, in March 1766 abolishing the stamp duty, but also asserting its undiminished right to tax the colonists; subsequently, the chancellor of the exchequer proposed a series of new duties on many of the manufactured products and commodities being imported in the colonies, including tea.

In Massachusetts and Virginia, parallel events had provoked a similar storm of protest, and leaders in both colonies began to circulate letters to their counterparts in North Carolina and elsewhere, acquainting them with their attitudes and actions. For the first time, there began to be formed an "intercolonial" public opinion that was intended to, and in fact did, encourage the elected leaders in each separate colony in their opposition to British policy. Many of these men formed organizations known as Sons of Liberty to promote their shared objectives.

In an age of sail, when ships took months to make the round-trip across the Atlantic, events moved at a slow pace, but by the spring of 1769, the British government had decided that peace in the colonies was more urgent than revenues and agreed to abolish all duties except that on tea. From the British perspective, this was a major, and hopefully a decisive, concession; from the colonists' perspective, the key feature was not the abolition of most duties but, through tea, the reassertion of Parliament's right to tax as it saw fit. And to this, the North Carolina Assembly, like those in other colonies, expressed adamant opposition. In riposte, the governor dissolved the Assembly. In turn, a majority of the members convoked an illegal, rump session which declared a boycott on all British imports.

Thus, the colonial legislature, having long functioned as a sort of school in which the colony's leaders had learned how to govern themselves, was graduating into rebellion. At the same time, the colonial militia, having long been an instrument of British control, as the war of the Regulation demonstrated, began to function as a center of opposition. Both of these were to prove crucial when war actually broke out. Meanwhile, having integrated themselves into the legislature and militia, the more affluent backcountry men were able to take over local government. One of the foremost of these new leaders was Thomas Polk, of Mecklenburg County, who became a justice of the peace and a delegate to the Colonial Assembly in addition to being a colonel of the militia.

A T THAT TIME, THE LOCAL EQUIVALENT OF THE COLONIAL Assembly was the militia, in which virtually every man served. In Mecklenburg County, the five companies of militia had already begun in the fall of 1774 to select two delegates each to rally in Charlotte, rather like a New England town meeting, to discuss events and to coordinate their response to the growing crisis. Similar Committees of Safety were set up throughout North Carolina in accordance with the articles of American Association, adopted by the Continental Congress in October 1774.

Meanwhile, meetings of Mecklenburg's militia delegates took place periodically until May 1, 1775. At that point, the royal governor, Josiah Martin, acted to prevent the North Carolina Assembly from meeting and sending delegates to the newly called Continental Congress in Philadelphia. Some weeks later, since news traveled very slowly, the Mecklenburg militia gathered to discuss the unfolding events. Then, either on the twenty-first of the month or, more likely, the thirty-first, doubtlessly encouraged by their own oratory and stunned by accounts of the clashes at Lexington and Concord, the Mecklenburg delegates decided to issue a call for independence. They were perhaps the first to do so, but they were not alone. Throughout the colonies, in the year before *the* Declaration was adopted by the Continental Congress, nearly a hundred local groups passed resolutions more or less demanding independence. The last one, the Pine Creek Declaration, was actually proclaimed on July 4, 1776, by a group in the Susquehanna valley who were unaware of the other declaration. But far and away the most famous became known as the Mecklenburg Resolves of May 31, 1775.

The May 31 Resolves began by accepting the charge made by Royal Proclamation that the colonies were in a state of rebellion, and declaring that consequently the Mecklenburg Committee ''conceive[d]'' ''that all laws and commissions confirmed by, or derived from the authority of the King or Parliament, are annulled and vacated, and the former civil constitution of these colonies, for the present, wholly suspended.'' This being the case, the committee proclaimed ''the Provincial Congress of each province, under the direction of the great Continental Congress, is invested with all legislative and executive powers within their respective provinces; and that no other legislative or executive power, does, or can exist, at this time, in any of these colonies." And "That whatever person shall hereafter receive a commission from the Crown, or attempt to exercise any such commission heretofore received, shall be deemed an enemy to his country" to be arrested and dealt with by the committee.

This was certainly a virtual declaration of independence; however, like most revolutionaries, including the members of the Continental Congress, the members of the committee tried to strike a stance both tentative and conciliatory: the new government was to be in effect only "until instructions from the Provincial Congress, regulating the jurisprudence of the province, shall provide otherwise, or the legislative body of Great-Britain, resign its unjust and arbitrary pretentions with respect to America." But the committee was not to be trifled with: in article XX, it directed Colonel Thomas Polk and Dr. Joseph Kenedy "to purchase 300 lb of powder, 600 lb of lead, 1000 flints, for the use of the militia of this county . . ."

With the bit in their teeth, the members of the committee immediately dispatched one of their members, Captain James Jack, to Philadelphia to deliver the Resolves to the delegates of North Carolina to the Continental Congress. There he met a friendly but essentially negative response. At that time, the Continental Congress, and particularly John Adams, was engaged in trying to get the king (with the so-called Olive Branch Petition) "to point out some mode of accommodation" and were not keen to have anyone, probably especially not a group of "white Indians" from the frontier, appear to threaten the British. Consequently, while they were published elsewhere, the Resolves were suppressed in Philadelphia, and word was sent back to North Carolina to sit tight.

It did. When the 3rd North Carolina Provincial Congress met in August 1775, it both set up a committee (of which Colonel Thomas Polk was a member) to prepare a plan "for internal peace, order and safety" and, at the same time, enacted a "test" to be signed by all members, "professing our Allegiance to the King." That cautious stance was general throughout the colonies. One contemporary document put it bluntly:

> We do not want to be independent; we want no revolution, unless a change of Ministry and measures would be deemed such. We are loyal subjects to our present most gracious Sovereign in support of whose crown and dignity we would sacrifice our lives, and willingly launch out every shilling of our property, he only defending our liberties . . .

In effect, the prevailing desire was for a sort of autonomous status within the empire, a status more or less analogous to membership in the later British Commonwealth.

This attitude explains why, when five months later on January 10, 1776, Thomas Paine published his *Common Sense* advocating a separation from Great Britain, the fifty-page pamphlet caused such a furor. It sold more than 500,000 copies within a few months and probably more than any other speech or publication focused attention on the fundamental issue of the dispute with Britain. However, the southern colonies had already made up their minds; indeed, the North Carolina Congress of August 1775 had already set up a Committee of Secrecy to gather and encourage the production of war matériel. Then, on April 12, 1776, the 4th North Carolina Provincial Congress, in the first such act by a colony, authorized its delegates to the Continental Congress to vote for independence. These and scores of other declarations and acts prepared the public for the July 4, 1776, Declaration of Independence.

In fact, the war had already begun before the colonists were pushed into admitting it. Congress had begun to raise an army and appointed George Washington to command it in June of the previous year. Bunker Hill and other battles had already been fought and lost. And in the colonies, several sharp actions had pitted the colonists against one another. In one of the first of these battles of "Whigs" (rebels) against "Tories" (loyalists), Great Canebreak on December 22, 1775, seventeen-year-old

Lieutenant William (Will) Polk, the strapping six-foot-four son of Colonel Thomas, was severely wounded.

BEING WOUNDED IN THOSE CONDITIONS WAS OFTEN FATAL, since medicine, if available at all, was primitive. Will's experience makes this painfully clear. Shot through the left shoulder by a British soldier at point-blank range, he was thrown from his horse. Seeing Will's companions approaching, the soldier fled before he had time to plunge his bayonet into Will. Will then remounted, holding his wounded limb with his right arm, and rode two miles to the encampment of his troop. Since there was no "surgeon" or barber there to dress the wound, his comrades plugged the bullet hole with a ball of tow from their shot bags. There was nothing more they could do for him but make him as comfortable as possible under a blanket—they had no tents—while they waited out a heavy snowstorm. The next day, they lifted him onto a horse, with a soldier seated behind to support him. Slowly and painfully, they made their way ten miles to another encampment, where Will's wound could be roughly dressed. Then, strapped to a litter, he was dragged through the woods 120 miles to Charlotte. He arrived more dead than alive. His was said to have been the first American blood shed south of Lexington. But his ordeal had only just begun: as a contemporary described it,

> large cavities formed from the wound from 4 to 6 inches down the breast back and arm. Compelled to lye on his back for nine months, the consequence was, the back, shoulders and hips were flayed and [had to be] dressed for two months as regular as the wound.

Being powerfully built, young and in good condition, Will survived—else this account could not have been written—but most of the wounded were not so lucky. Often they were simply bayoneted, stripped of boots and coats and left to die by whichever side won the field. That was the fate of Will's brother, Lieutenant Thomas Polk, after the Battle of Eutaw Springs in 1781. His companions sneaked back to the battlefield after their defeat to find him naked and dead.

Those who were able to walk away often had mangled limbs or huge gaping wounds, since muskets then fired lead slugs twice the size of those used in modern infantry weapons. Even the lightly wounded were apt to get gangrene, so that arms or legs would have to be cut off without, of course, any form of anesthetic—biting the bullet was not just a figure of speech. For Will, however, the expression had another meaning as well. In the later Battle of Germantown, as an eighteen-year-old major, he received his second wound; he was shot in the mouth, losing four teeth and suffering a shattered jawbone. There he was lucky. A slightly different angle or a less spent bullet would have been his last. He survived, but the pain would be with him all his life.

Combat was a grim, horrible experience, far from the pageantry we like to imagine. Listen to the words of Charles Stedman on the aftermath of the Battle of Guilford Courthouse, the clash that turned the tide of the Revolution:

> The night was remarkable for its darkness, accompanied with rain which fell in torrents. Near fifty of the wounded, it is said, sinking under their aggravated miseries, expired before the morning. The crys of the wounded and dying, who remained on the field of action during the night exceeded all description. Such a complicated scene of horror and distress, it is hoped, for the sake of humanity, rarely occurs, even in a military life.

Fortunately for them, the rebellious colonists had little conception of the coming horror as they stumbled into revolution in a series of small, hesitant steps. Lexington and Concord gave little hint of the ghastly nature of war but electrified little assemblies all through the colonies. Without much thought of the enormity of the task, and certainly with little coordination, informal groups began the urgent and daunting task of organizing an army, or, more accurately, armies, plural.

How these military bands were composed and how they fought have been subject to much confusion. Americans today cherish the myth of hardy minutemen, deadly marksmen with their long "Kentucky" rifles, hiding, Indian style, behind trees as they gunned down the serried ranks of advancing redcoats. There is just enough truth in this myth to give it longevity, but no more. Informal or pioneer groups of riflemen, drawn mainly from the frontier areas, did play ancillary parts in a number of battles, but they were never the decisive group. Most of the bloody business of slaughter was done by both sides in essentially the same way: by soldiers lining up, firing volleys from inaccurate but relatively rapidly loaded, smoothbore muskets and then having at one another with bayonets. On the colonial side, these troops were known as the Continental Line or national army. They tried to look as much like the British troops as their tattered uniforms would allow, and if they were not so formal as the British, it was because they were not so well trained until the enforced hiatus of winter at Valley Forge. There they first had the opportunity to learn European combat tactics from a sometime Prussian army officer, Baron Friedrich Wilhelm von Steuben. Thereafter, they and the British fought their regular battles in essentially the same parade-ground fashion.

Separate from the Continental Line, each state embodied its own militia. Doing this was a continuous undertaking because men enlisted for only a few weeks or months and had to be lured back into the militia after each hitch. Indeed, even in the midst of battle, to the impotent fury of their officers, militia troops had a habit of running away, occasionally without even firing their weapons. Many enlisted simply to get the bonuses that were held out to lure them into service and once they had pocketed the money, they melted away, then later rejoined to get a second or third bonus or even went over to the British side. When caught, they would often suffer draconian punishment—lashings with as many as five hundred blows or hanging. But even when they stood loyally by their officers, they were despised and often treated as cannon fodder.

Manpower was the worst of the colonial problems, but it was not the only one. Very few of the colonists had any significant military experience. The little that George Washington had as a militia officer under the British and against the Indians was what made him the outstanding American officer. No one else matched even his limited training. Moreover, the country was essentially without military resources. For example, there were few workshops in the colonies capable of producing rifles, muskets or even swords. (Will's sword was made from a reforged scythe, and practically all of the army's muskets were French or British.) Even where equipment or supplies were available, they often could not be conveyed to where they were needed. The only rapid and effective means of moving people and goods among the colonies was by sea, and until near the end of the war when the French intervened, the sea was controlled by the British navy.

Having no navy to pit against the British, the federal government gave out a number of Letters of Marque and Reprisal commissioning American sailing ships to arm themselves as "privateers." Instructions were issued on April 3, 1776, by the Continental Congress, "to the Commanders of Private Ships or Vessels of War, which shall have Commissions of Letters of Marque and Reprisal authorizing them to make Captures of British Vessels and Cargoes . . ."

John Hancock signed the commissions (see illustration for one issued to Captain Robert Polk) and is designated as "President of the Congress of the United Colonies of New-Hampshire, Massachusetts-Bay, Rhode-Island, Connecticut, New-York, New-Jersey, Pennsylvania, and Counties of New Castle, Kent, and Suffex on Delaware, Maryland, Virginia, North Carolina, South-Carolina and Georgia." The term "United States" was not then in use.

Letters of Marque and Reprisal were well recognized in international practice and maritime law to distinguish privateers from pirates, but they could be issued only by a sovereign state, which was not how the British regarded the Revolutionary colonies. So the Continental Congress sought to define exactly the rules of engagement as part of its claim to statehood and also to protect the ships' crews. It feared (with good reason) that the British would treat the ships and their crews as mere pirates. The Letters of Marque and Reprisal specified that

> If you, or any of your Officers or Crew shall, in cold blood, kill or maim, or by Torture or otherwise, cruelly, inhumanly, and contrary to common Usage and the Practice of civilized Nations in War, treat any Person or Persons surprized in the Ship or Vessel you shall take, the Offender shall be severely punished.

Some 224 Letters of Marque and Reprisal were issued to Maryland vessels, but most are confusing or now impossible to trace. Among them, however, were two vessels commanded by Captain Robert ''Bobby'' Polk, the *Montgomery* and the *Black Joke*.

Bobby was a great-grandson of Robert Bruce Polk and a member of the branch of the family that remained in Maryland when William and Charles went west. He was born in Dorchester County in 1744 and became a sailor, engaged primarily before the Revolution in the coastal traffic with the eighteenth-century equivalent of a tramp steamer, buying cargoes, moving them to likely markets and selling or swapping them. From this experience, which was shared by scores of small colonial vessels, he gained an intimate knowledge of the eastern seaboard.

When the Revolution broke out, he accepted the commission to be a privateer. His *Montgomery* was not much of a warship. It had only two cannons and five swivel guns, or falconets, and was manned by a crew of twenty. On it, he was engaged primarily in capturing British ships which he brought into port to sell off the cargoes. The sale of one of these was announced as follows.

By Virtue of a Decree of the Hon. Court of Admiralty of this State, will be sold at public vendue, for ready Money, on Monday the 29th Instant, at Jamestown, on James River, about 7 Miles from the City of Williamsburg, The Brigantine *Sarah* of Great Britain, lately made a Prize of by the *Montgomery* Privateer Capt. [Robert] Polk, of Annapolis, in the State of Maryland, with her Sails, Rigging, and Materials, being 170 Tons Burthen, British built. An Inventory of her Sails, Rigging, and Materials, may be seen on Board the said Ship.——At same Time and Place will be sold her Cargo, consisting of a large Quantity of exceeding good Jamaica Rum, Muscovado Sugars, Coffee, Ginger, Cotton, and sundry other Articles, Shipped on Board the said Ship from Jamaica for the London Market.

Benjamin Powell, Marshall.

Williamsburg, November 1, 1776

Since there were over a hundred similar vessels preying on British shipping at the time, they must have done a great deal of damage and helped to supply the rebels with all manner of commodities. No attempt appears to have been made to turn over either the captured ship or its cargo to the government or to the armed forces. The government was still too disorganized, as the description of John Hancock's office suggests, and probably every attempt was being made to give the ships' captains as much incentive as possible to risk themselves against the larger, more heavily armed and better trained Royal Navy. How important a calculation that was is shown by the fact that, on his next and slightly larger ship, the *Black Joke,* a sloop with twelve carriage guns and twenty-five crew, which was commissioned on June 23, 1777, Bobby was killed in a fight with a British warship off "Martineco" (Martinique) a few months later.

Bobby left a son, Charles Peale Polk, to be adopted by his brother-in-law, the artist of the Revolution, Charles Willson Peale, under whom he would study painting and after whose style he would paint many of the Revolutionary figures.

FINANCIALLY, THE COLONIES WERE EQUALLY WEAK. THE mercantilist policies of the British government had drained them of specie; so to purchase matériel or pay salaries, they resorted to the traditional contrivance of weak governments, printing what quickly became worthless paper money. And the colonies had no significant managerial or production "intellectual capital." Serious as these and other practical problems were, they were dwarfed by the fundamental fact that the population was scattered, distracted by local conflicts or fears and deeply divided.

Throughout the colonial period, regional interests had often put the colonies into conflict with one another; in the Revolution, their disputes expanded to include noncooperation with the Continental Congress and its army. The records are full of desperate pleas by the army commanders, including those of Thomas Polk while he was commissary general of the southern forces, for supplies, reinforcements and money, and the bitter comments of those who received little or none. Each state, often each district, looked to its interests with little consideration for common goals. Even such central figures as Thomas Jefferson emerge badly tarnished in these records.

Almost everyone acted as though all that was required was to *declare* independence. North Carolina did not even elect an executive to replace the British governor until five months after its delegates had signed the Declaration of Independence. In Philadelphia, congressional delegates did not promulgate the Articles of Confederation for a year and a half after they had declared independence. While they delighted in ringing pronouncements, they had little taste for practical problems.

O NE OF THESE PROBLEMS, ALREADY TOUCHED UPON, WAS THE free versus the slave, which by then was white versus black. This was a fundamental division of American society that was immediately obvious to the British, and they sought to take advantage of it. Even before the Declaration of Independence, the royal governor of Virginia, Lord Dunmore, issued a proclamation offering manumission for those slaves who agreed to fight against the American rebels. The colonists, rightly, saw slavery, in the words of James Madison, as their Achilles' heel and "were struck with horror" by Dunmore's pronouncement. The South Carolina Committee of Safety, which was charged with the maintenance of public order, pleaded with the Creek Indians to hunt down runaway slaves; it was cynically hoping not only to show the slaves that they could not escape but also to drive a wedge between these two presumably hostile groups. Meanwhile, Virginia owners warned slaves that even if some escaped or joined the British, their families would pay the price of their defection. Yet, hundreds and eventually thousands did. By the end of the Revolution, perhaps 100,000 in Georgia, South and North Carolina and Virginia had bolted for freedom.

White Americans were baffled by the slavery issue. At one extreme, so frightened of a British-encouraged slave revolt was the government of South Carolina that it offered to abandon the Revolutionary cause if the British would agree not to invade it or to try to liberate its slaves. And at the other, some voices were raised, timidly to be sure, for measures that would win black support. For purely military considerations, George Washington initially thought that the Americans should allow those few free blacks who had already enlisted to continue to serve in the new armed forces. But aware of how acrimonious this question had become in the Continental Congress, he reconsidered. On October 8, 1775, his council of war unanimously decided to reject even free blacks; so those who had joined—probably, like many poor whites, seeing army service as financially attractive—were discharged.

However, two pressures forced a change. The first was Lord Dunmore's proclamation, of which Washington learned only a month after he had begun to discharge blacks; then, as a large-scale slave owner himself, he excoriated Dunmore's "diabolical schemes." But upon sober reflection, he issued orders that recruiting officers should begin "to consider" free black applicants. He feared, he wrote to Congress, that in being spurned, blacks would join the British side. Grudgingly, Congress agreed to allow the reenlistment of those who had already joined the army "but no others."

The British challenge was the first pressure on the Americans; the second came into play almost immediately. Males of any color were required if the war was to be fought. Despite the rhetoric, the white American "common man" proved to be far less willing to serve the cause of liberty than his leaders had hoped. Already in the summer of 1776, twenty-one-year-old Captain Alexander Hamilton worked out a program to enroll slaves, arm them and give them their freedom. It was rejected, but few whites "flocked to the colors," so the policy had to change. Rhode Island led the way in January 1778 by creating a battalion of black slaves who, having been evaluated, would be purchased from their owners and promised their freedom in return for serving as soldiers. Rhode Island was soon followed by other states as their regiments were depleted by sickness, desertion and casualties. As whites became harder and harder to enlist, blacks began to be incorporated into all the Continental regiments, even those of the South.

Some had no choice, since whites who wished to avoid service occasionally sent slaves in their places. In one recorded incident, probably typical of many, a North Carolina white man by the name of William Kitchen deserted his regiment and was caught. To avoid being hanged, sent back or whipped, he made a deal: he sent a slave he owned to take his place. We happen to know about him because he tried to cheat the slave out of the freedom he had been promised.

Overall, an estimated 5,000 blacks served in the Continental forces. Some units were predominantly black. In the Rhode Island contingent, including its all-black battalion, three out of each four soldiers were black former slaves. Even among the 670 men in the North Carolina brigade, at least 42 were black, and of the 7,600 soldiers on duty with Washington's army at Valley Forge in February 1778, about one in ten was black.

However, if necessity drove both the British and the Americans, neither was comfortable with its racial policy. The British almost never armed their blacks and mostly reneged on their promise of freedom. While the Americans did arm many slaves and did grant freedom to perhaps six or seven thousand others, they also used slaves as enlistment bounties. For example, North Carolina in 1780 offered anyone who would join for three years a "prime" black slave between the ages of fifteen and thirty. South Carolina quickly upped the ante, offering three slaves. This practice caused James Madison to ask, admittedly in a rather low voice, whether it would not be more sensible simply to liberate and make soldiers out of the blacks, since, in any event, "It wd. Certainly be more consonant to the principles of liberty which ought never to be lost sight of in a contest for liberty . . ." But even the most determined advocates of the "rights of man," including Madison's close friend Thomas Jefferson, continued to own and exploit slaves throughout and after the Revolution.

THE OTHER MAJOR NONWHITE GROUP WAS COMPOSED OF THE many remnants of Indian societies and the few societies that were both still intact and relatively nearby. Indians had every reason to hate those American whites with whom they were in contact, as the story of Charles Polk, "the Indian Fighter," made clear, but they had also had good reason to distrust the British, against whom they had also often fought. Consequently, they were neither for nor against the Revolution: their aim was simply and logically to maintain their freedom and their lands. Thus, the side on which any given Indian group came down, if it was forced to choose, was probably determined more by location and by the decisions of its Indian neighbors than by British or American threats or inducements. Both the British and the Americans fought, bribed and promised in profusion. Where they could, which was not often, the Indians took advantage of the conflict, but usually they were its victims.

The words of visiting American commissioners who urged the Lenni-Lenape (Delaware) Indians to "Consider us and you as One People" must have rung especially hollow. Particularly so because, while these words were being spoken, large-scale raids by state militias were killing Indians all along the frontier. In one campaign in the summer and fall of 1776, for example, Lieutenant Colonel Ezekiel Polk, a younger brother of Colonel Thomas, and a force of South Carolina militia razed all the Indian settlements east of the Appalachians. For the most part, knowing their cause would stir few Indian hearts and recognizing the limitations on their military power, the Americans mainly tried just to keep the Indians neutral.

The British made a more determined effort to win over Indian supporters: the possible availability of twenty or thirty thousand Indian warriors was as appealing as the effect of their joining the American side was appalling. The British had a propaganda advantage, since, like the Indians, they were fighting white settlers, and they went at "winning the hearts and minds" of the Indians systematically through the actions of several hundred of what later would be called political officers. Some Indians actively aided the British, while others carried out actions—like the attack on a frontier fort that resulted in the kidnap of Delilah Polk— that happened to coincide, at least temporarily, with British strategy.

BOTH THE BRITISH AND THE AMERICANS MADE EVEN MORE determined efforts to hold on to those of their white supporters who fell within the jurisdiction of the other side and to win over waverers. Large numbers of white Americans shifted sides, occasionally more than once, during the conflict. For many, the reasons were not ideological but pecuniary: militiamen were famous for changing sides to claim enlistment bounties, and whole communities offered—as South Carolina did—to abandon the Revolutionary cause or made deals to protect their property. So common was the practice that it was impossible to treat the participants as traitors. The only practical policy was to try to win them back and use them to fight the war. Recognizing this, the first Continental commander in the South, General Horatio Gates, remembered as the victor of the Battle of Saratoga, virtually forced the governors of South Carolina and Georgia to welcome back those who had joined the British side on condition that they join the militia.

On their side, where they had military superiority, the British used the threat of destruction of property to neutralize or win over rebels. In the story of one Polk family member in North Carolina, the process comes clear. Ezekiel Polk, whom we have seen as a militia commander against the Indians in South Carolina, had become a wealthy farmer. Although he was a controversial person locally for having espoused deism, he was elected as a delegate to the Provincial Congress in 1775 and then reentered the militia. At the start of the Revolution, he actively supported the American cause, but in the summer of 1780, the tide of battle turned. After the disastrous defeat of General Gates's Americans at the Battle of Camden, General Charles Cornwallis's victorious troops advanced on Charlottesville, North Carolina, where Ezekiel's most valuable property was located. The danger of losing all he owned was simply too much for him; so, just as Cornwallis moved into his brother Thomas's house, Ezekiel rode into the British lines to promise to seek "protection." That move saved his property, but salvation was only temporary, since the British soon retreated. Ezekiel then managed, adroitly but exactly how we do not know, to get back his old militia commission and again fought for the Revolution. His story was perhaps more spectacular than most, but many thousands of other Americans had similar experiences.

Many Americans were so newly arrived as hardly to think of themselves or to be thought of by others as American. Each year, thousands of immigrants arrived, and many of the thousands walked down the gangplank into the arms of recruiting officers. For most, the issues at stake in the Revolution must have seemed obscure. Which side they joined was partly a matter of where they came from—the Irish arrived with reason to hate the British, the Highland Scots had recently given a pledge to support the British, and the Germans had little affinity with either side. But luck also played a part. Those who landed in areas held by the colonists had little choice but to support them, while those who landed in areas held by the British tended to join them. Both armies were thus composed of what to us would appear as "foreign legions."

Eighteenth-century armies were remarkable for their lack of ethnic uniformity. On the British side in the Revolution, about one soldier in three was German, and roughly the same proportion of the "French" army of 7,500 that arrived on the east coast in 1780 to help the Americans was either German or Swiss. Germans also figured prominently in the American army. Neither army had a common language, much less a common patriotism.

But more significant on the American side was the social division: the officer corps stood apart from and both feared and distrusted the often alien common soldiers. General Charles Lee "openly despised his men and referred to Virginia recruits as 'riff raff—dirty, mutinous and disaffected.' " And General Nathanael Greene described the North Carolina militia as "the worst in the world, for they have neither pride nor principle to bind them to any party, or to a discharge of their duty." Americans were not taken into the army in chains as they had been earlier in Europe, but as already mentioned, some were slaves, which was virtually the same thing. Others were mere children as young as ten, indentured servants, homeless people or vagabonds who were given the choice of service or prison. Some indeed were actually felons paroled on condition of military service. It was not surprising that their officers relied less on patriotism than the lash.

The effects of the composition of the army show up in the very high rate of desertion. About 80 percent of the 3,315 known courts-martial were for desertion or mutiny. Not all of these men were foreigners. Even in General Washington's elite Life Guard, made up of native-born Americans, eight men deserted. Many did not just walk away—they mutinied. The last of the eleven major mutinies was serious enough to force the Continental Congress to flee Philadelphia. Less dramatic than mutiny or desertion, but overall perhaps even more serious, was the constant refusal of troops to serve more than a few months at a time or, even in conditions of the utmost danger, to remain at their posts. At Valley Forge, for example, only forty of one thousand Virginia soldiers stayed in the army while, overall, about three thousand soldiers deserted.

After Valley Forge, Colonel Will Polk, suffering from the wound that had shattered his jaw at the Battle of Germantown, was sent to try to enroll more recruits in North Carolina. He had little success. As he coldly commented,

> the amor patriae and enthusiasm which brought soldiers into the army at the commencement of the War, had very much abated—besides the money had so much depreciated that it was considered next to no consideration as a bounty.

Even toward the very end of the war, in the spring of 1781, in Virginia as many as one-third of the draftees deserted after having received their bounty money.

Almost the only group about whom one reads no complaints from senior officers were the Scots-Irish, who had enlisted in droves and who formed so large a portion of the army that one general described it as a "Mac-ocracy." His appreciation was seconded by King George III, who thought the war was "little more than an uprising of rabble-rousing Presbyterians, largely Scotch-Irish: a sort of latter-day Cromwellian outburst . . ." Virtually all those who left records agreed. A Hessian officer wrote that one should "not call the war an American Rebellion, [for] it is nothing more than an Irish-Scotch Presbyterian Rebellion."

And Captain Frederick MacKenzie of the Royal Welsh Fuzileers was struck by the fact that many of the American regiments "are composed principally of those men."

Formed in the bitter struggles of Scotland and Ireland, the Scots-Irish were famous for always enjoying a fight, but taken as a whole, the common soldiers had more mundane interests. As R. J. Yeatman and W. C. Sellar joked of Napoleon's armies, they "march on their stomachs shouting: *'Vive l'Intérieur!'* " The next meal was probably the most riveting thought in the mind of the Continental soldier. And with good reason. No modern army would have put up with the privation he suffered.

The winter of 1777–78 at Valley Forge, where both Thomas and Will were on duty, was the very worst of the war. One-third of the North Carolina brigade were sick, and many more were "Unfit for Duty for want of Cloathing." Often three men had to share one blanket and many lacked shoes. So cold was the weather, even inside the log huts they had built, that, as General Washington reported to Congress, men were "forced to sit up by the fires all night to keep from freezing to death." As it was, about one man in four died. And the little available food was barely fit even for starving men to eat. "Some of the troops were without bread or meat as long as forty-eight hours, and throughout the camp rose the plaintive cry, 'No bread, no meat, no soldier!' "

Perhaps even worse than the actual physical plight of the army was its psychological distress: it was simply not supported by those in whose cause it was fighting. Although "many farmers in the neighborhood had barns bulging with provisions [they] . . . preferred the hard money paid out by the British in Philadelphia to the paper currency offered by the American commissaries." The only way Washington's troops could get food was by plunder. Far away in London, King George III was told that

though Washington's Patroles and Picquets continually cir-rounded those Lines [around Philadelphia], nor could the severest punishments such as Whipping and Branding some, and putting to Death others deter the people from Supplying the British Troops; and at the same time Washington's Army both Foot and Horse were starving for want of Provisions, the Inhabitants declining to Thrash out their grain or to fatten or kill their Meat, often concealing it . . .

Nor was this just a British view; nor was it just at Valley Forge. As late as 1781, when the British were moving toward the final battle at Yorktown, the North Carolina legislature refused adequate supplies or guns for its desperate troops. In his embarrassment, the governor lamented in a letter to General Greene that "we are a cowardly revengeful set of wretches too contemptible to merit a blessing or exact a damn." And in the same vein, Colonel Henry "Light-Horse Harry" Lee compared the inhabitants of Georgia, unfavorably, to "the Goths and Vandals in their schemes of plunder murder and iniquity. All this under pretence of supporting the virtuous cause of America." As the American historian Hugh Rankin summarized the evidence, "it seems unlikely that soldiers have ever felt so abandoned by the very people they were supposed to be fighting for."

With what we today call hyperinflation, the currency issued by the Congress first declined and finally collapsed. As Thomas, whose thankless task it was to try to cope with this impossible situation as commissioner general in the southern command, wrote on June 4, 1781, Continental money was "of no service" either in paying salaries or in purchasing goods. And the state legislatures were not paying even the nearly worthless money to their troops; in 1781, Virginia was two years behind in its payments to its soldiers. Each state held back, hoping that someone else would foot the bill. The Virginia Board of War and Governor Thomas Jefferson, from whom supplies were desperately requested, were unwilling or unable to help the army in the southern campaign.

Some officers and politicians realized the danger such a lack of responsibility posed. The North Carolina Board of War wrote Thomas

Polk on October 5, 1780, urging him to make greater efforts to procure supplies, warning that "if we do not feed the soldiers they must take care of themselves and will do it at the Point of the Bayonet. This must be avoided if possible." To make up for their lack of support, they authorized Thomas to use force to confiscate locally what the army needed. In a letter to General Greene, Jefferson commented, "I would advise that you make no scruples about property so far as it is wanting for the public; only give orders that the owners be furnished with proper documents that they might be reimbursed." In this climate of irresponsible government and unwilling public, Thomas Polk agonized but decided that he could not carry out a policy of confiscations by force against his neighbors. So, having exhausted his own property and credit on behalf of the army, he asked to be allowed to resume a fighting command. He had a personal as well as a patriotic reason to do so: he wanted to "chase" General Cornwallis out of his house. After one small engagement, he wrote to the North Carolina Board of War from his camp on the Yadkin River, "Glorious affair. In a few days doubt not we shall be in Charlotte, and I will take possession of my house and *his* lordship [Cornwallis will] take [to] the woods." He did and Cornwallis did.

Thomas's replacement as commissioner general was one of the army's most dashing commanders, Colonel William R. Davie. Davie also wanted to fight rather than to become a quartermaster, and in trying to evade the assignment, he told the newly arrived commander of the army of the South, General Nathanael Greene, that he knew nothing of money or record keeping. To his astonishment, Greene replied that "as to *Money* and *Accounts* the Colonel would be troubled with neither, that there was not a single dollar in the military chest nor any prospect of obtaining any . . ."

Worse, Colonel Davie found that he could obtain no credit from civilian merchants, so, as Thomas had realized, "subsistence depended upon compulsory collection and the transportation on the same uncertain and unpleasant means." Frantic for supplies, General Greene pleaded (as Thomas had done) with the nearby states for help. He got some "temporary support" from Virginia, but, he said, "Maryland has done nothing, nor can I hear of any exertions there equal to the emergency of war.—Delaware has not [even] answered my letters.—These states have few men here, and those they have are daily discharged."

GIVEN THEIR MANIFOLD WEAKNESSES, THE AMERICANS IN THE southern theater—where more than 80 percent of the Revolutionary War actions took place—were driven to a strategy that rested on three elements. First, they had to try to prevent a junction between the British and the American loyalists or, as they called them, the Tories, and to prevent the British from raising the blacks and the Indians. Second, they had to avoid major battles when, as they usually were, they were outnumbered and outgunned. When forced into battle, they would "waste" the less reliable militia, preserving at all costs the Continental Line, while doing their best to make each British victory Pyrrhic. Third, they would "hang on," hoping that the British would get tired of the war and/or that the French would come in strongly enough, as they eventually did, to tip the balance in their favor.

The British strategy was, naturally, the reverse on each of these points. First, the British tried to effect junctions with the American loyalists and those who "are tired of the Rebellion" and to enlist blacks and Indians in their cause; second, they sought large-scale battle wherever possible, hoping to destroy the Continental Line troops without whom the American revolt would have collapsed; and third, they sought to use their fleet to prevent the rebels from importing supplies and troops, particularly from the French.

In the first major confrontation in the South, the last royal governor of North Carolina, Josiah Martin, worked out a campaign strategy that involved mustering Highland Scots on the east coast and, in the interior, Regulators, some of whom the last royal governor had won over to the

British side, to form a militia force that would supplement a British army to be landed at either Cape Fear or Charleston. To implement this strategy, the British embarked a large task force under General Cornwallis at Cork to sail to North Carolina.

At all costs, the Americans needed to prevent these forces from coming together. In the South, the key engagement to prevent this was fought at Moore's Creek, in which Colonel Thomas Polk commanded the 4th North Carolina regiment against a force of newly arrived Highlanders. It was a short, sharp action fought, like many of the Revolutionary War engagements, on a scale that sounds almost ridiculously small by modern standards, just a few hundred soldiers, yet the American victory effectively broke the hopes of loyalist supremacy in North Carolina. The loyalists were individually identified and could not return home. Small-scale though it was, this victory gave a tremendous boost to morale throughout the colonies. In far-off New England, one observer enthused, "The Colonels *Moore, Martin, Caswell, Polk, Thackston, Lillington & Long,* have great Merit; any one of these Gent. In this Country would be an over match for a [British general] *Howe, Burgoyne,* or a *Clinton.*"

The second aspect of the American strategy was to wear down the British by small-scale attacks, in many of which young Will Polk fought. To deal with set battles, Colonel Dan Morgan set the preferred strategy succinctly in a letter to General Nathanael Greene.

> I expect Lord Cornwallis will push you till you are obligd to fight him on which much will depend. You'l have from what I see, a great number of militia—if they fight you'l beat Cornwallis if not he will beat you and perhaps cut your regulars to pieces, which will be losing all our hopes. [So] select the riflemen also, and fight them on the flanks under enterprising officers who is aquainted with that kind of fighting and put the remainder of the Militia in the centre with some picked troops in the rear with orders to shoot down the first man that runs, if any succeeds a disposition of this kind will . . .

This became the standard procedure of General Greene throughout his campaign, as Thomas Polk observed in a letter to him on March 1, 1781: ". . . Cartainly [it] is the salvation of our Countrey for you Not to Run any Risque With your armey, for While your safe the British Cannot ocuppy Nor Possess any Part of our Countrey but What is inside their sentreys or Lines."

This third strategy finally won the war: it was, as Greene put it, "We fight, get beat, rise, and fight again." That was the essence of the 1781 battles—the Cowpens of January 17, Guilford Courthouse of March 15, Hobkirk's Hill of April 25 and Eutaw Springs of September 8, where Thomas's youngest son, also called Thomas, was shot in the eye and killed.

Hanging on until the British tired and the French intervened was much harder to implement and was very nearly not accomplished. There were many Americans who tired quickly and sought, like Benedict Arnold, to switch sides. More often, support for the Revolution was grudging and parsimonious. American troops fought, often unwillingly, usually just sporadically, always poorly fed and occasionally with virtually no equipment, while the British fought doggedly for over six years, with well-equipped professional troops who, because they were mostly foreign mercenaries, were expendable.

Meanwhile, far away in Paris, Benjamin Franklin and his little team played the nation's first diplomatic game to a successful conclusion: it was French muskets that American soldiers fired, French troops that turned the tide in the North and the French fleet that made possible the "end game" of the war at Yorktown, where Lord Cornwallis surrendered on October 18, 1781.

THE BRITISH SIGNED THE DRAFT ARTICLES OF PEACE ON November 30, 1782, and began the processes that were to lead to the removal of their forces, the disbanding of the American army, the exchange of prisoners and, finally, the September 3, 1783, Treaty of

Paris, in which Great Britain recognized the independence of the United States.

It had been a stunning achievement, against all odds and in the face of repeated defeats, and is rightly celebrated as the foundation of our country. Without the memory of that victory, the trials that lay ahead might not have been met and overcome. To us, at this distance, the Revolution seems inevitable, but was it? The answer, I believe, is "yes . . . sooner or later."

Consider first the Americans. From at least the end of the seventeenth century, the inhabitants of each colony had managed their own affairs. They believed that their growing prosperity was the result of their own labor, and they elevated this belief into what amounted to a philosophical tenet that economists would later term the labor theory of value. Such economic activity as the colonists along the Atlantic seaboard had with the mother country focused their attention on three issues: restraint of trade (through the Navigation Acts), draining away of specie (as a consequence of mercantilist policies) and taxation ("without representation"). More important in the long run was the colonists' fixation on the acquisition of land. That was why most had come to the New World, and however much they differed on other matters, they all wanted land.

On the British side, many particularly in Parliament wished to let the Americans have their way, but the decisive voice was that of King George III. His analysis of the political problem sounds a very modern note. As he wrote to his principal minister, compromise was not possible. The issue of taxation, he thought, was only a preliminary stage on an escalating path that the colonists were taking to independence; so, to attempt to satisfy individual demands such as revoking the stamp tax would be self-defeating. More pointedly, he felt that parliamentary "hawks" might have impeached him if he had accepted the American demands; even if they did not, a weak response to the American challenge would have set a row of dominoes falling. In his words, whether the laying a Tax was deserving all the Evils that have arisen from it, I should suppose no man could alledge that without being thought more fit for Bedlam than a Seat in the Senate, but step by step the demands of Americans have risen—independence is their object . . . should America succeed in that, the West Indies must follow them, not independence, but must for its own interest be dependent on North America; Ireland would soon follow the same plan and be a separate State, then this Island would be reduced to itself, and soon would be a poor Island indeed, for reduced in Her Trade Merchants would retire with their Wealth to Climates more to their Advantage, and Shoals of Manufacturers would leave this Country . . .

So, each for its own reasons, the British government and the American colonies began and, once having begun, had to fight to the finish the long and terrible war that would give birth to the new Republic.

THE YOUNG REPUBLIC

"That Hydra Democracy"

For General Thomas and Colonel Will Polk, as for most of the officers of the Continental Line, the victory against the superpower of the eighteenth century came so suddenly and so unexpectedly that they were unprepared for peace. Victory should have given the American patriots exactly that tremendous emotional high that we celebrate today in a blaze of fireworks and the strains of the national anthem. But instead they were exhausted from seven years of war, confused about what to do now that the British had been expelled, fearful that the war was only in remission and, above all, desperate to return to the pleasures of daily life.

These sentiments seemed nothing short of subversive to the tiny minority of men who had guided and fought the Revolution. In their eyes, the mass of the people were the same rabble who had so often simply gone home when their enlistments ran out or took to their heels in the midst of battle. If "the people" could not be trusted, the leading veterans decided to perpetuate the only organization they knew and trusted, the officer corps of the Continental Line. They hoped it would continue to function, as it had in the Revolution, as a sort of parallel government to hold together what had been won at so costly a price. In one of their first acts upon the ending of hostilities, on May 13, 1783, just before they disbanded, the officers formed an association to perpetuate their unity under the leadership of General Washington. Fascinated by the classical world as all educated men then were, they named themselves the Cincinnati after the ancient Roman Lucius Cincinnatus, who had left his farm to defend his country in a time of peril. Each of the thirteen states was to have a chapter. The North Carolina chapter was founded by Will Polk.

But this gambit was violently repudiated by "the people," who believed the officer corps to be "an aristocratic junto" engaged in a "barefaced and arrogant" attempt to create a "hereditary Military Nobility." For many of the critics, it was not aspirations of "nobility" that was disturbing but the fact that the Society of the Cincinnati planned to allow foreigners who had fought for the Revolution to join. Even General Nathanael Greene, so brave against the English, shied away from "the current of public prejudice . . . against the Cincinnati." In response to the bitter outcry, a disappointed George Washington forced his colleagues to abort the more overtly political aspects of their association. There would be no extragovernmental flywheel to maintain stability.

STABILITY WOULD BE HARD TO FIND. THE LEGITIMACY OF existing state governments and the national congress was questioned, and they had little real power. The underlying problem was that there was no consensus on what form of government should replace British rule. Political fragmentation derived from the already long tradition of differences among the colonies, differences that had hardly been abated by the Revolution, and by the difficulties of travel and communication; the only effective consensus was the common belief that the Revolution had wiped the political slate clean. The old institutions, even the old laws, were merely "contracts," as John Locke had led Americans to believe, and since these were with the defeated colonial power, Britain, they had no current legitimacy. Thus, relationships of people to one another and to society had to be formed anew. How this might be done was the consuming, passionate debate of the age.

Answers were avidly, hungrily sought. To a degree we today would find impossible to believe, people in that epoch thought and talked about their practical, day-to-day politics in terms of philosophical speculation. As Gordon Wood wrote admiringly, "it was as if all the imaginings of political philosophers for centuries were being lived out in a matter of years . . ." Admittedly, the hundreds of pamphlets and uncounted debates served less as stimulus to thought than as justification for prevailing actions and beliefs, but, nevertheless, it is likely that in no other period of American history did so many people write and talk about public affairs in such intellectual terms. While philosophical works were undoubtedly read only by "the few," their leading ideas became hearsay among "the many."

At first, the popular answers were the exact opposite of what Thomas, Will and other officers of the Continental Line had attempted. From Montesquieu came the prevailing idea that only small, homogeneous communities could preserve liberty, and from the Swiss jurist Emmerich de Vattel came the complementary idea that such small "republics" need not amalgamate; rather they could relate to one another in nonintrusive ways and so form merely a "confederation," or even more loosely, a "council of nations," to whose institutions representatives were, as John Adams called the Massachusetts delegation to the Continental Congress, merely "our embassy." This was, of course, a license for anarchy, as Thomas and Will had feared.

Some of the former officers and leading officials of the Revolutionary governments, however, threw themselves into the state assemblies or the Continental Congress. This was a courageous course; for true believers, these bodies appeared a disheartening, even a disgusting, arena in which many members expressed pride in their ignorance and illiteracy (which they said made them closer to the people) and attacked those with "academical education" or professional skills. Even the more sophisticated representatives were motivated by what James Madison called a "spirit of *locality*" in which there was no room for consideration of the common interests of the new nation. In any event, their role was reduced to little more than messengers; since their constituents tied their hands by detailed instructions, there was no scope for statesmanship. In short, from the perspective of those who had formed the Continental Line, they were merely a continuation, often with the same faces, of the ineffectual, selfish, shortsighted state legislatures that had allowed the army to starve, march barefoot and fight virtually without weapons. As Will wrote of the North Carolina Assembly,

> There are among the members composing the Legislature several very respectable characters; but speaking of them as a Body, I will venture to assert that there never was so much ignorance collected in a Legislative capacity since the days when Laws were enacted prohibiting the frying of Pancakes on Sundays.

That attitude may fairly be ascribed to the elite, but the elite was not alone in its disgust and anger. To the degree that they were effective at all, the assemblies tended to become, themselves, special-interest groups, feathering their own nests and passing patently unjust laws. So, in communities throughout the new states, men continued the old tradition of forming ad hoc committees and associations to manage local affairs, express their opinions or take the "law," if such it could be called, into their own hands. Some of these groups resembled the Regulators of

1767–68. From Massachusetts to South Carolina, violent mobs burned public buildings, closed courts, seized officials and prevented the collection of taxes and imposts. The most famous movement culminated in Shays's Rebellion in 1786 and 1787, but it was only one of dozens. So widespread was anarchy that former radicals began to sound like the old British officials. Those who had guided the Revolution realized that they had loosed a whirlwind.

Some few believed, with John Adams, that the new confederacy could "form us, like separate parcels of metal, into one common mass," but their numbers dwindled. Increasingly, even the most committed walked away in disgust "from the theatre of public action . . ." Among them, Alexander Hamilton, himself a veteran of the Continental Line as an officer on General George Washington's staff, resigned his seat in Congress after eight frustrating and disheartening months in July 1783. James Madison, who had played a significant civilian role in the Revolution, quickly followed. Many, like Thomas and Will Polk, both of whom could have been delegates, stood aloof in anger or disdain and turned to their private affairs. Even those who remained in the legislatures so often abstained that it was difficult to get a quorum on any given day. By the middle 1780s, Congress itself had virtually abdicated, many of the old leaders having come to the conclusion that only if an *effective* union government was created could the Revolution finally give birth to a true Republic. They began to assemble, somewhat like the committee that Thomas Polk had inspired to issue the Mecklenburg Resolves in 1775, to find ways to effect "a more perfect Union."

A fundamental division thus emerged from the experience of the Revolution, a division that was to underlie the myriad events of American politics for at least the next three generations, to erupt in the great Civil War and to continue in different forms down to our times: it was in its simplest, initial form, a split between the Continental Line and the state militias. On one side of the great debate, the officers of the Continental Line, inspired by Alexander Hamilton, formed the Federalist movement to promote strong central government, and on the other were men, many of whom had served in the militias or in the state governments, who found their leader in Thomas Jefferson. They feared government and sought to contain, minimize or even destroy its more intrusive institutions.

The conflict between them was precipitated by the virtual collapse of the Continental government. Whether one takes Karl Marx's notion of the "withering away of the state" seriously or not for later times, there is no doubt that the Continental Congress should have been his prime example. Despite the fact that there was no formal adjournment, it was simply impossible to obtain a quorum after October 10, 1788. At that point, a group of determined leaders of the Revolution decided to meet to find a way out of the impasse.

This was to become the Constitutional Convention, yet there was little indication that a globe-changing document would emerge. The members had no popular mandate, met in secret and disguised their real purpose by announcing that they were meeting "for the sole and express purpose of revising the Articles of Confederation." And although they produced what George Washington called a miracle, it was surely one of the most unpresupposing and unpretentious meetings that such an illustrious group could have had.

There were many distractions: Massachusetts was in open rebellion and its economy was near collapse. Most of the states were deeply divided as liberals struggled to get rid of the colonial legacy of state-established churches. And several of the states were involved in complex diplomatic moves with their neighbors the Indians and with one another. But even granting these distractions, the drafting of the Constitution was hardly a crowd catcher: fifty-five delegates attended for some of the sessions during the late spring and summer of 1787, but only forty stayed to the end, and of these only thirty-eight signed the final document. Of these thirty-eight, fifteen were still in their twenties and thirties. Hardly a representative group—and one deeply distrusted by many of their fellow citizens. A rumor was then being widely circulated that under the guise of revising the Articles of Confederation, this was another ''Aristocratical junto,'' rather like the Cincinnati, and was really planning to invite a European prince to be the American king. Secrecy had not helped.

Other things did. First was the decision to bypass the state legislatures (which could be assumed to be opposed) by calling elections for assemblies specifically convened to approve the document. The second was a sort of sleight of hand in which it was agreed that the Constitution would come into force when nine states (rather than all as required in existing law) approved. Even more important, probably, was the fact that in the new Republic, at least half the adult males were unable to vote—non-Protestants were practically disfranchised in almost every state, and one inhabitant of America in five was a black slave. And many potential voters simply stood aside: of the roughly 640,000 free adult males, some 480,000—three out of four—did not bother to vote. Indeed, had he been in America, Thomas Jefferson would probably not have voted either.

So unlikely was approval and so uninterested was the public that those who favored the Constitution, particularly Alexander Hamilton, John Jay and James Madison, mounted our first and most valuable propaganda campaign, bequeathing to us *The Federalist Papers.* Without their— particularly Hamilton's—enthusiasm, energy and eloquence, we would probably not have a constitution.

As it was, it was a near miss. Of the required nine states, only three (Delaware, New Jersey and Pennsylvania) approved before the end of 1787. The vote in the Pennsylvania convention was 46 to 23. In January 1788, Georgia and Connecticut ratified. Massachusetts was a close call when in February it ratified by 187 to 168. Maryland, South Carolina, New Hampshire, Virginia and New York followed in that order, each with narrow margins. Rhode Island and North Carolina (where, as Will found, Federalism was already unpopular) did not ratify until after the government had actually been formed.

WHILE THROUGHOUT MOST OF UNITED STATES HISTORY, political parties have played major, indeed formative, roles, they were not originally anticipated. In part, no doubt, this was because General Washington was such a towering figure in the young Republic as to cap all latent differences of policy, but it was surely also a result of the shared concern about the fragility, indeed the very survivability, of the Constitution. Organized disagreement was disparaged as "faction." However, before the end of Washington's tenure, splits emerged in the coalition he had put together to "paper over" the disputes that had originated in the Revolution between the Continental Line and the state governments and their militias. In part, these splits were personal (as in political life they nearly always are); in part, they reflected different views of ideal civil life; but in large part they were influenced by different conceptions of the emerging American society. These differences and the "factions" to which they gave rise were mirrored in the Polk family and grew in intensity in the generations to come. They become so general in the larger society and so crucial to an understanding of America that they demand our attention at this point. The easiest way to see them is in terms of two prominent leaders, Thomas Jefferson (with whom the branch of the Polks led by Ezekiel and including the later president, James K. Polk identified) and Alexander Hamilton (with whom Will and his descendants identified).

AS WOULD BE EXPECTED FROM HIS BACKGROUND AS A plantation owner, Jefferson saw an agricultural society as the bedrock of America. For him, the danger was that the virtuous tillers of the soil might be corrupted or their role in society diluted by "artisans." Fortunately, he concluded, this change was not necessary. "While we have land to labour then," he wrote, "let us never wish to see our citizens occupied at a work-bench, or twirling a distaff." Let Europe be

America's factory and keep their workers' "manners and principles" away from our shores.

Hamilton's wartime experience had convinced him that, to survive, America needed to become a very different place. The weakness of central government had nearly defeated America, and, for all Jefferson's delight in the hardy tiller of the soil, Hamilton saw him as the mutinous militiaman. It was well and good to talk, after the war, about the virtues of rural life, but the farmers had refused to sell their crops to Washington's soldiers at Valley Forge except for hard cash. Then, unable to secure funds from state governments or credit from merchants, General Thomas Polk as quartermaster general had used his own money to keep fighting units in the field. And, finally, when the British fleet had blockaded the American ports, soldiers could not procure enough muskets or even swords because few could be manufactured in America. As I mentioned, Will's sword was a scythe hammered into the shape of a sword by a village blacksmith. Only if America overcame these weaknesses, Hamilton believed, could the Republic survive.

Hamilton also saw another danger that must be overcome or, even better, turned into an asset. It arose from the very nature of power. Republics, he had learned in reading history, had often failed not only because they were too weak to protect themselves from foreign enemies but also because they were overthrown from within. Laws alone had not restrained the rich and powerful: thwarted, they would be a mortal danger to the Republic, but integrated, they would be an engine of progress. To win over and involve powerful private interests, he argued, the United States should create a national bank in which both government and financiers participated and encourage, even subsidize, industry.

Will Polk, whom President Washington had appointed supervisor of internal revenue for North Carolina, agreed. Like Hamilton, he had witnessed the ugliness, the dangers and the corruption of weakness and disunity while in the army, and, like Hamilton, he believed that the only way to assure stability to the new nation was to harness those with real power to the public chariot; the means he chose was the one advocated by Hamilton and bitterly opposed by Jefferson: the partly private, partly public bank. He put Hamilton's program into practice in North Carolina.

In 1804, the first part of what would become the State Bank of North Carolina was chartered. After watching the progress of the institution for two years, the state acquired approximately 25 percent of the shares and gave the bank the right to issue paper currency. It was, in fact, formed exactly along the lines and for the purposes advocated by Hamilton—to stimulate industry and commerce and to marry the interests of the rich and powerful to those of the state. Recognizing the source of its inspiration and the purposes to which it was dedicated, it was attacked by the Jeffersonian governor of North Carolina, John Branch, in November 1818. This attack and Will's reply enable us to get at the heart of an issue that virtually convulsed political life throughout the years of the young Republic and sets the scene for a bitter fight in which Presidents Andrew Jackson and James K. Polk were later engaged.

The governor's point of attack was that the private shareholder owners of the bank, having started and run it, were then offering to sell additional subscriptions for more than they had paid for their shares. Today we accept this as the way that venture capitalists operate: they expect to gain from the sale of some of their assets to those who had not taken the initial risk. Since the state owned approximately 25 percent of the capital, it, too, had acted as a venture capitalist. Bravo! said the Hamiltonians; subversive, said the Jeffersonians.

Regardless of ideology, there was an almost desperate need for some form of banking institution. Since before the Revolution, commerce, the payment of taxes and other mundane activities in North Carolina had been stymied by the lack of currency. The first settlers used the paper currency of Virginia and Pennsylvania and a bewildering variety of "hard money" in the form of English, Spanish, German and French coins. A 1775 testament mentions 49 "half Johanneses," $7^1/_2$ guineas, 3 "pistoles," 1 "maidon," 1 "Caroline," 103 dollars, £38 12s

6d, £206 11s of Pennsylvania currency and £698 16s 9d of North Carolina currency. To these were to be added Continental currency, which wildly gyrated in exchange rates. As Will pointed out, it was partly to bring some order into this chaos that the bank had been chartered: *"this* was to be a *specie* Bank," he wrote, "in the midst of a depreciated currency."

That was no easy challenge: "precious metals were scarce, and could be obtained only at a premium [of about 5 percent over paper currency]; It was therefore an experiment; one on which many refused to embark their capitals; and on which, almost all the subscribers ventured with fear and trembling," Will pointed out. Indeed, not all the stock that had been offered was taken up by investors.

But was it fair to the public to profit from attempting to bring order into the currency? Will answered with the question "If the terms of subscription hold out no prospect of gain, or not sufficient gain, who will subscribe?" In any event, he argued, the return, given the risk, was not excessive; it was nearly two years before any dividend could be paid and that was just 2.5 percent. It was only in later years that dividends rose to an average of about 9.25 percent.

And since the Jeffersonians had raised the issue of the role of the state in economic affairs, Will responded with the question for which we still have no simple answer: "Does it belong to the Chair of State to pry into the calculations of Banking Companies?" That the state had a role, he did not deny. The state had chartered the bank and owned the largest (but still a minority) share of its stock; more fundamentally, he explicitly agrees that the bank is for the public benefit. But if the bank operates like a merchant house, with reasonable equity, he argues, "Surely no Court would undertake to prescribe rules for us, or to say that this or that power was sufficient." Finally, with tongue in cheek, he twits the governor for criticizing excessive profits: "we are really at a loss to find an apology for his Excellency, if our profits are really as large as he has claimed, for intimating a wish that the State should be deprived of her share of so large a boon . . ."

ILL AND OTHER FEDERALIST FOLLOWERS OF HAMILTON
differed from the Republican followers of Jefferson not only in
economic affairs but in their view of the role of the citizen in society. I
have suggested that this is partly rooted in and was often expressed by
actions that began in the Revolution. That desperate struggle convinced
Hamilton that anarchy was the poison of liberty and that society must be
held together by strong government: where the people threatened anarchy, the government must exercise its power. In their least attractive activities, the Federalists sought to carry over into peacetime the
techniques of control such as the notorious Sedition Act of 1798, under
which it became a crime to speak or print "any false, scandalous, and
malicious writing or writings against the government of the United
States, or the President of the United States, with intent to defame
. . . or to bring them into contempt or disrepute . . ." Perhaps such
a law was appropriate to the discipline of an army fighting for its life but
not to civilian society protected by the Bill of Rights. Jefferson did not
object to the Sedition Act per se; indeed he wanted it used against the
Federalists! He argued only that it should be enacted and enforced by the
states rather than by the federal government.

But, in general, Jefferson took a rather romantic view of civil strife.
One could imagine a Byron or Goethe rather than a Jefferson writing,
"I like a little rebellion now and then. It is like a storm in the atmosphere." During the 1780s, from his distant vantage point as ambassador
to France, he approved of Shays's Rebellion, on which he coined his famous statement that "The tree of liberty must be refreshed from time
to time with the blood of patriots and tyrants. It is its natural manure."
And when the French Revolution burst around him, he appeared not to
notice it.

As Will watched these opposed doctrines clash in the early years of
the nineteenth century, he grew more apprehensive and tried, in unsuc-
cessful races for the governorship of North Carolina, to halt what he

thought of as the spread of anarchy. As he wrote on December 6, 1832, despairingly, to his younger cousin James K. Polk,* who had been his lawyer and was then a congressman from Tennessee,

> That *Hydra* Democracy is about to devour all order here . . .
> Such is the fruits of the Jeffersonian doctrines of 1798 . . .
> With Lafayette I had hoped not to have long enough lived to
> see the work I had aided in producing broken and the nation
> thrown into convulsion & misery under the government of
> small and impotent Democracies. What is to be done?

He could hardly have chosen a less amenable recipient. James was inspired, as was his grandfather Colonel Ezekiel, a brother of General Thomas, by Thomas Jefferson and would be a lifelong opponent of all that Hamilton had stood for. As a congressman, chairman of the Ways and Means Committee, then as Speaker of the House, but particularly as the friend, supporter and acolyte of Andrew Jackson, he made the Bank his target. To him it embodied all that was evil and dangerous in government and should be restrained to the maximum extent possible.

In their thoughts, words and actions, Will and James focused on the fundamental division on interpretation of the Constitution first laid out succinctly by Jefferson and Hamilton. "I consider," Jefferson wrote, "the foundation of the Constitution as laid on this ground: That 'all powers not delegated to the United States, by the Constitution, not prohibited by it to the States, are reserved to the States or to the people.' " Hamilton, to the contrary, argued what has come to be known as the doctrine of implied powers, contending that certain actions, not specifically spelled out in the Constitution, are appropriate and legal because they are based on "*a general principle* [that] *is inherent in* the very *definition* of Government and *essential* to every step of the progress to be made by that of the United States . . ."

* For the rest of this chapter, I will refer to James K. Polk as "James."

Americans reacted to this debate in two contrary ways: most agreed with Jefferson (and James) that government was a danger to be avoided if possible but with Hamilton (and Will) that making and controlling money was a good thing. Thus, while America was creating itself in the image Hamilton had imagined—with the growth of cities, the relative decline of agriculture, the creation of industry and the vast expansion of arteries of communication—it rejected the political corollary Hamilton had drawn and as embodied in the Federalist administrations of George Washington and John Adams to install, one after another, Thomas Jefferson and his close friends and supporters, James Madison and James Monroe.

But a third vision, more romantic, for a time resolved the pressure of the conflict—westward expansion. Americans were voting with their feet. Both factions wholeheartedly supported the expansion of territory. Jefferson, as I have noted, thought the westward movement would occupy most of their energies for centuries.

THE LURE OF THE FRONTIER WAS NEVER FAR FROM THE thoughts of all Americans of whatever political persuasion. Even those members of the Polk family who had stayed near where they first landed in Maryland and Delaware were captivated by the scent of the vast forests and verdant plains. As population became more dense along the coastal areas, the price of land rose, and it became more and more difficult for each generation to provide its children with that dream of all Americans, a better life than they had enjoyed. The end of the Revolutionary War gave a powerful impetus to these impulses.

Political leaders of North Carolina had already taken advantage of the flight of loyalists to buy up their confiscated lands; then, guided and inspired by that "wheeling and dealing, land speculating, sharp-nosed manipulator, politician, and financier" William Blount, whom President Washington had appointed governor of the western territory that became Tennessee, a number of the political leaders of North Carolina including Thomas Polk arranged for the sale or grant to soldiers of lands on the western frontier. To give a semblance of legality to their project, in 1783 they got the North Carolina legislature unilaterally to repeal a treaty made in 1777 guaranteeing the Cherokees their lands.

Under the 1783 act, land was literally dirt-cheap, but Blount figured out a way to get it cheaper still: he lobbied the North Carolina legislature into issuing more paper money so that it fell in value. Since the state accepted payment in notes at their face value, the hyperinflation gave those who understood currency and had the capital to buy it the chance for the accumulation of vast tracts of land and, ultimately, vast riches. Blount himself was said to have acquired over a million acres. If that land acquisition was at least quasi-legal, speculation in other lands was not, but this did not stop or even significantly slow down its takeover. In what remained of Indian territory, settlement was forbidden by federal law, but as settlers disregarded the distant government and pushed into the hinterland, the Indians were inexorably driven back. Among the whites to profit by this process was Senator Andrew Jackson, who acquired the first of many large tracts that would come his way.

What these men were doing was considered, at least in part, both normal and legal. The practice of awarding lands as a bounty to encourage men to enlist in the military was a traditional British practice in America. It was carried over by Connecticut, Georgia, Maryland, Massachusetts, New York, Pennsylvania, Virginia, South Carolina and North Carolina but not by Delaware, New Jersey, New Hampshire, Rhode Island or Vermont, which had no lands to use for this purpose. Based on service in the Continental Line (no militia duty counted) between 1776 and 1783, or eighty-four months, North Carolina, according to an act in 1780, awarded a lieutenant colonel like William 5,760 acres (nine square miles), while a private got 640 acres (one square mile) and a brigadier general 12,000 acres (almost nineteen square miles). The grateful legislature even awarded the Revolutionary War hero Nathanael Greene 20,000 acres, or thirty-one square miles. The original grants were to be in what became eastern Tennessee, but because many settlers had already taken up lands there, the locus was shifted to middle Tennessee, which became the favored destination of most of the Polks. A total of 6,554 "Revolutionary War bounty land warrants" were issued by North Carolina.

What the veteran received was not a particular plot but a "patent" that gave him the right to claim a given amount of land; he then had to find what he thought suitable or attractive, survey it, make sure that no one else claimed it, mark it—blazing trees was what was then called getting "tomahawk rights"—and enter his claim at a state office that might be days or even weeks of hard travel distant. Obviously, this was an expensive, difficult and often dangerous task which discouraged grantees of small patents and those without much capital and favored those, like Thomas and Will, with the means and incentive to venture. So Thomas set out,

> early in 1786, with his four sons, armed with their rifles, into the wilderness of the Duck River county, in Middle Tennessee, to locate them. [He then] selected the finest lands in that rich valley, ran the line, marked them, and secured the titles, notwithstanding the hostility of the Indians. So when he died in 1793, he left a rich inheritance in lands for his children.

Because one of his grants made on December 26, 1793, was fairly typical of others that disposed of millions of acres of western lands and because such grants did so much to form the new states, it is worth reading in part.

> KNOW YE, THAT WE, pursuant to an Act of the [North Carolina] General Assembly, entitled an act for the relief of the Offices and Soldiers in the Continental line, and in consideration of Signal Bravery and persevering Zeal of Thomas Polk a Colonel in the said Line, have Given and Granted, and by these presents do Give and Grant unto the said Thomas Polk, a

tract of land containing Two thousand one hundred and one acres [three and a quarter square miles], lying and being in our County of Tennessee, on defeated Camp Creeks the North Waters of Duck River . . . together with all waters, mines, minerals, hereditaments and appurtenances, to the said land belong or pertaining to HOLD to the said Thomas Polk his heirs and assigns forever: Yeilding and paying to us the sums of Money, yearly or otherwise, as our General Assembly, for time to time may direct.

Faced with the obstacles of "proving" such a grant, many grantees preferred to sell their patents and stay where they were. A lively market quickly grew for patents which could usually be bought for a modest price. The fact that Thomas, his son Will, his brother, Ezekiel, and others had followed George Washington's lead in becoming surveyors was what gave them a tremendous advantage: they were in a position to pick and choose the best plots. They bought them by the score.

From 1783, when he had been appointed by the legislature of North Carolina to be "Surveyor General of the Middle District," Will had set up his headquarters at French Lick Fort, the site of the modern Nashville. During that period, he was elected to the General Assembly and continued to represent his county until he was appointed by President Washington to be supervisor of internal revenue, which office he held throughout the presidencies of Adams and Jefferson. More than any other members of his family, he was in a position to amass relatively great wealth and to lay the foundations of what became the Old South.

Many of the transactions are difficult to follow, but some stand out. Thus, on February 27, 1796, Will made a profit by selling seventeen patents from the state of North Carolina for plots of land totaling 20,446 acres for "the sum or price of nine Cents, money of the United States per acre." With land at that price, no wonder that a steady stream of people flooded into the hinterland.

The big push into middle Tennessee began a few years later. About

1807, the first of the Polks settled in what became Maury County, south of Nashville, and which ultimately became virtually a Polk county. Indeed, they not only took a leading role in founding Maury County but virtually populated it. Colonel Will's sons all moved there, but the prize went to Colonel Ezekiel Polk, Thomas's younger brother and sometime assistant, who not only became the owner of thousands of acres of rich Tennessee land but could claim to be the father of his county: he fathered at least 14 children, the last of whom was born when he was seventy-one years old, and these children in turn were said to have produced 92 children, who gave him 307 great-grandchildren! One of the grandchildren, James, would become the eleventh president of the United States.

WHILE MOST OF THE POLKS WHO MOVED WEST WERE THE progeny of General Thomas Polk and his brother, Ezekiel, another branch of the family that had stayed behind in Maryland and Delaware struck out on their own. Their incentive was the same but their route was different. They were led by Ephraim Polk 3rd, who had been born in Delaware in 1758 and at eighteen enlisted as a private in a Pennsylvania militia company which, having become the 3rd Pennsylvania Regiment of Foot, fought alongside Will's North Carolina regiment in the Battle of Germantown. In this outfit was Captain Charles Willson Peale, the Revolutionary War portraitist, who would adopt and train Ephraim's cousin Charles Peale Polk. Along with his older brother, Joab, and both Thomas and Will, Ephraim apparently also endured Valley Forge. After the war had ended, Ephraim and Joab returned to Sussex, Delaware. Land there was increasingly expensive, and Delaware had no land to offer them for their services; so Ephraim decided to scout the Ohio valley for a suitable homestead.

In 1785, he passed along the Great Buffalo Road to the Ohio, crossed over and went into what became Kentucky, where he found an area that seemed to him ideal except that the legal status of land ownership was unclear and Indian hostility was clear; so he returned to Delaware. There he married and settled down for a few years. Then, in 1791, his father died and left him enough money so that he could afford to mount an expedition—moving west was an expensive undertaking. Organizing a sizable party of kinsmen and friends, he set out once again, this time with his wife and infant child, in the fall of 1793.

After a long overland trip up through Maryland and Pennsylvania, the party struck the Ohio River at the little frontier post of Mononga-hela near the modern city of Wheeling, West Virginia. There they bought a flat-bottom barge of a kind known as Kentucky broadhorns. Getting their gear, tools and animals aboard must have been quite a chore, and their already large party, including several black slaves, had been augmented by a sizable group of friendly Delaware Indians. When all were ready, they pushed out into the current.

Compared to a wagon, the broadhorn was relatively comfortable and although slow did not require daily and laborious packing and un-packing. But traveling on the river was not safe. Indians along the route watched barges like theirs, filled with white settlers intending to take away their land, with increasing apprehension and bitter hostility. Even at that relatively late date, among them, and sharing their fear of white encroachment, were numerous "white Indians." One of these men, pretending to have just escaped from the "red Indians," signaled the Polks' boat and pled to be taken aboard. As it approached the shore, some members of the party grew apprehensive. They had good rea-son—they floated right into an ambush. Indians hidden behind trees opened fire, but, perhaps fearing that the boat would float past, they fired too soon. Frantically rowing and poling to get the barge back into the middle of the river, the migrants suffered several casualties. From then on, they stayed far from shore as they floated downriver into Ken-tucky. There they founded what eventually became the northern branch of the Polks.

We will meet them again in bizarre circumstances in the Civil War, but what happened to their Delaware Indian companions, who in com-memoration of the trip took on the name Polk, is sadly not recorded.

INDIANS WERE NOT THE ONLY INHIBITION TO THE WESTWARD push of the Polks and other Americans. Hostility toward Britain had not died down after the Revolution. Two years elapsed after the last major battle (when General Cornwallis surrendered at Yorktown) before the Peace of Paris was concluded in 1783, and that treaty left many issues unresolved. The Americans continued to fear that the British were poised on the exposed western and northern frontiers to reassert their power and were angry that they were excluded from trade in British areas. British monopoly, particularly, contributed to the economic depression that marked the years leading up to, and stimulated the desire for, the Constitutional Convention in 1787. Moreover, even ten years after the peace treaty, and as required by it, Britain had still not evacuated various outposts along the frontier and was believed to be arming and inciting its Indian allies to attack American settlers. During this period, the Royal Navy was also impressing American seamen and capturing American merchant ships.

To try to overcome these grievous affronts, Chief Justice John Jay negotiated a second treaty in 1794; it headed off events that appeared likely to lead to war but made little progress toward a real peace and was deeply unpopular in America.

Then as now, most people saw great public events through the lens of private interest. So it was in a letter Will received from a business associate. Reflecting on the impact of the war scare on land sales on April 19, 1794, he wrote that

> I really think there will be no war. The british nation have relaxed their decree of council of the sixth of November last respecting the Capture of all American Vessels bound to French Ports . . . The influential characters in the government of the United States are too interested [in] the funds to wish a war, or not to sacrafice any other object to peace, and a punc-

tual payment of their interest; which hostilities will certainly cut off [and the] mercantile interest of England will not support a war against their own Debtor [which would] disable them to make remittances . . .

For several years at the end of the decade, mutual hostility to Revolutionary and Napoleonic France led to a temporary rapprochement between Britain and America and even to some joint naval activities, but the 1800 election of Jefferson, who had always hated the English, almost immediately soured relations. Jefferson and Secretary of State James Madison were by turns hectoring and inattentive, threatening and weak, undiplomatic and groveling, and the British treated them with contempt. Relations went from bad to worse. Finally, in the spring of 1812, as Bradford Perkins has written, ''with a tiny navy, an unrecruited army, [and] no financial plan, the United States set off to war.'' Billy Philips, a grandfather of Mary Demoville Harding Polk, rode the 860 miles from Washington to Nashville in the remarkable time of just nine days to warn the commander of the southern forces, Andrew Jackson.

Knowing well the strength of Britain and, painfully, the cost of war, Will was dismayed by the war fever that raged in North Carolina. It was led and stimulated by his brother-in-law William Hawkins, a Republican follower of Jefferson, who was the governor from 1811 to 1814. While Hawkins ''zealously led the legislature'' into a prowar policy, Will became a leader of the ''Peace Party.''

Will not only believed that the war was an unnecessary blunder on the part of the administration but was even more dismayed to watch it badly, almost ruinously, conducted. For him, it was the Revolutionary War all over again, but without a George Washington and without a cause. So when President James Monroe offered him a commission as brigadier general (then the second highest rank in the American army) to be head of one of the twelve military districts into which the United States was being divided, he turned it down. However, the country was at war and was being defeated; even the White House in Washington

City was burned. But when he saw the "degrading conditions demanded by the British commissioners from the American government as the price of peace—conditions as new as they are humiliating: inadmissible under circumstances far more perilous than the present, and such as no American ought to succumb to," Will volunteered to serve in any capacity. By then he was not needed. Peace was worked out even before Andrew Jackson won the Battle of New Orleans.

At the end of the war in 1814, Will, at fifty-six, made one last run at the governorship of North Carolina—at that time determined by a vote of the legislature—and lost by three votes. Then, old Federalist that he was, and having long since recognized that "there is no Federal man in the State, however dignified & respectable, that could stand the least chance of being elected," he retired into the political wilderness.

But these years were among the most productive of Will's life. He continued to serve, without pay, as the president of the State Bank of North Carolina while he built his landholdings in the new state of Tennessee. Certainly more important for the future of the country, he continued to play a major role, as president of the board of trustees, in the growth of the University of North Carolina.

Concern with education had been a legacy of his father, Thomas, who had helped to found the first secondary school in western North Carolina and as a member of the legislature had sponsored a bill to create Queens College; it was a legacy Will would pass along to his son Leonidas, who would later found the University of the South at Sewanee.

Will was certainly a hands-on trustee of the university, as we read in a broadsheet of instructions for parents and students he signed on behalf of the board. ". . . sensible of the ill consequences of Students having more money at their disposal than is sufficient to meet their necessary disbursements during the Session," and to avoid "temptation to dissipation, misapplication of time and a relaxation of morals," he recommended that in the first session, students be given no more than $58. Of that, $34 went for board, $12 for tuition and $1 for room rent. With perhaps more realism than encouragement, the schedule allotted $5 for washing and mending but only 50 cents for books. Laws were set forth to govern conduct which specified, among other things, that "A student shall not make horse races, or bet therein, nor shall they keep cocks or fowles of any kind for any purpose." Assemblies for prayer were to be held twice daily. Students were required to study "from the time of morning prayers till eight o'clock, from nine till twelve in the forenoon, and from two till five in the afternoon; and at all other times the Students shall observe a proper silence and a respectful deportment."

There is scant evidence that the rules were observed. Perhaps $34 for half a year's food was not the right proportion, but young James, while a student, walked six miles a day to eat elsewhere. In 1815, when he entered, the university had a faculty of only five professors, but they had very grand pretensions. Entering candidates were subjected to examination on an astonishing range of subjects including Latin and Greek grammar, Caesar's *Commentaries* and works of Sallust and Virgil. James did well and graduated in 1817 at the top of his class, but his brother, William Hawkins Polk, twenty years his junior, would later have considerably more trouble. As James wrote to Will, the boy was a spendthrift, with "a very great disposition to extravagance in dress, in attending theaters—and other places of light amusement" who ran up bills at every store he could reach. So James, the Jeffersonian, turned to Will, the Federalist, to administer discipline; Will did not take the bait. He found young William wild but charming and gave him permission to do as he wished upon his promise that he would study hard. Whether he did or not, he did not gain entry as a regular student. James was angry and, together with his brother-in-law James Walker, wrote young William what amounted to an ultimatum on April 16, 1834, saying,

> . . . it is painful to perceive that your whole mind seems to be ingrossed to effect the object of getting money . . . [But] You have strength of mind and talents to make you an ornament to our family, if your energies and faculties are properly

applied and directed . . . we fear that you are getting into habits that must inevitably destroy you.

His own quest for learning and his worry about his brother put education at the forefront of James's thought as a young congressman in 1828. Aware how difficult it was for people on the frontier to acquire even literacy, he identified what he thought was a major opportunity to help them. He advocated using at least some of the lands taken from the Indians in Tennessee as an endowment "for the promotion of common schools and the education of the poor, under the management of school commissioners in each county." In this proposal, he was bitterly opposed by his fellow Tennessee congressman Colonel David "Davy" Crockett. Having initially supported James's bill, Crockett changed his position and managed to get the bill tabled. As James commented, "We cant trust him an inch." Crockett was less interested in education than in killing Indians.

WHAT TO DO ABOUT THE INDIANS REMAINED A SERIOUS ISSUE throughout the years of the young Republic, but however much they disagreed on other issues, practically every white American agreed on taking their lands. Some, like James, wanted to devote these lands to higher purposes, but most wanted just to have them for themselves. The only serious question was *how* the Indians should be dispossessed—by force or deceit. At the "liberal" extreme, Thomas Jefferson wrote to William Henry Harrison, then governor of the Indian territory, on February 27, 1803, urging him to get Indian chiefs to buy goods "which we have to spare and they want" on credit. Then,

> when these debts get beyond what the individuals can pay, they become willing to lop them off by a cession of lands . . . In this way our settlements will gradually circumscribe and approach the Indians, and they will in time either incorpo-

rate with us as citizens of the United States, or remove beyond the Mississippi.

Since the lands Jefferson sought to have the chiefs sell off to meet their debts were tribal rather than personal, this ploy necessarily turned the leaders into traitors to their peoples. Winning the chiefs over could be and was often accomplished by bribes. There are many examples of which one, in Jefferson's administration, was the "negotiation" with the Sac and Fox Indians in 1805. The goods given to the chiefs were, of course, seen and coveted by other tribesmen, and this opened a secondary aspect of Jefferson's policy. By making goods available through federally owned trading houses, Jefferson hoped to drive out the "Indian traders" like Charles Polk who, he believed rightly, were often a significant cause of frontier violence, particularly through their sale of liquor. But, continued Jefferson, if subtlety did not work, government use of force remained an option:

> . . . our strength and their weakness is now so visible that they must see that we have only to shut our hand to crush them . . . Should any tribe be foolhardy enough to take up the hatchet at any time, the seizing the whole country of that tribe, and driving them across the Mississippi, as the only condition of peace, would be an example to others, and a furtherance of our final consolidation.

Jefferson had established what would be the American government position on the Indians throughout the administrations not only of the Virginia "dynasty" of Madison and Monroe but also the presidencies of Andrew Jackson and James. Americans would not accept Indians into citizenship. Jefferson's protégé, President Monroe, on January 27, 1825, echoed prevailing opinion when he wrote that "Experience has clearly demonstrated that in their present state it is impossible to incorporate them in such masses, in any form whatever, into our system." If they remain where they are, he went on, "their degradation and extermination will be inevitable." Individual settlers, the states and the federal government were united in their unwillingness to accept even the so-called Civilized Tribes, who had adopted the dress, manners and even the names of white society. The brutal fact was that the vast lands they held were too inviting to be left to them. Their very wealth in land condemned them: that was the origin of the removal program that was to be at the center of Jackson's presidency and would spill over into the presidency of James.

The area of ambiguity that remained to be solved after Jefferson's first foray into Indian affairs was the question of what came to be called states' rights. While not exclusively related to Indian matters, it lay at the heart of them because many Indians inhabited lands that "belonged" to the federal government but were located physically within the borders of states, and because the tribes' relationship with Americans was governed by treaties with the federal government rather than with the separate states. The nature of the Indian societies and the question of who had jurisdiction were considered by the Supreme Court in two of the most famous cases it ever decided. In 1831 in *Cherokee Nation v. Georgia,* the Cherokees asked for an

> injunction to restrain the state of Georgia from the execution of certain laws of that state, which, as is alleged, go directly to annihilate the Cherokees as a political society, and to seize, for the use of Georgia, the lands of the nation which have been assured to them by the United States in solemn treaties repeatedly made and still in force.

The background of Georgia's action was an agreement made between it and the United States government in 1802 wherein Georgia gave up its claims to what became Alabama in return for the removal of Indians living in Georgia. In his ruling, denying the Indian request for an injunction, Chief Justice John Marshall (a fellow Federalist colleague of

Will) defined the Cherokee as "not a foreign state in the sense of the constitution" but rather as one of the Indian "dependent domestic nations." However, a year later in *Worcester v. Georgia,* he reasserted the statehood of the tribes as "having territorial boundaries, within which their authority is exclusive, and having a right to all lands within those boundaries, which is not only acknowledged, but guaranteed by the United States."

That position could not be sustained. The pressures were too strong and the position of the Supreme Court was still too weak within the American system. In a famous rebuff to the Court, President Jackson was said to have remarked, "Well: [Chief Justice] John Marshall has made his decision; *now let him enforce it!*"

Indian "removal" was an old policy to which Jackson gave a new implementation. Whereas Jefferson, Madison and Monroe thought and hoped that it would be essentially voluntary or at least not cruel, under Jackson it became coercive and often barbaric. On May 28, 1830, Congress passed the Indian Removal Act. Then, almost immediately and under great coercion, Jackson negotiated separate treaties with the Choctaw and other Civilized Tribes. Under threat of virtual extermination, he forced them to abandon the titles to the vestiges of their ancestral lands. As he laconically expressed it in a letter to James, which he wrote on August 15, 1830, while on his way to "stay one night with my friend Genl. Wm. Polk," "I have had an interview with the Indians and arranged business with them." Shortly thereafter, he again wrote James to say that "I have in the Chikesaw treaty destroyed the serpent."

The "serpent" was condemned to what can only be described as a death march, what the Indians called the Trail of Tears. It almost certainly was not intended to be such, but the imperatives of economy overweighed those of humanity. To make it cheap, the task was entrusted to private contractors, many of whom egregiously cheated on their contracts while others were simply inefficient; in either event, the results were similar. As Alexis de Tocqueville, who witnessed the migration, poignantly wrote,

It is impossible to conceive the frightful sufferings that attend these forced migrations. They are undertaken by a people already exhausted and reduced; and the countries to which the newcomers betake themselves are inhabited by other tribes, which receive them with jealous hostility. Hunger is in the rear, war awaits them, and misery besets them on all sides. To escape from so many enemies, they separate, and each individual endeavors to procure secretly the means of supporting his existence by isolating himself, living in the immensity of the desert like an outcast in civilized society. The social tie, which distress had long since weakened, is then dissolved; they have no longer a country, and soon they will not be a people; their very families are obliterated; their common name is forgotten; their language perishes; and all traces of their origin disappear. Their nation has ceased to exist except in the recollection of the antiquaries of America and a few of the learned of Europe.

Well, nearly but not quite. Despite the massive removals, even those in which Indians were taken in leg irons, many remained. So, on August 8, 1838, James wrote to President Martin Van Buren that

it is extremely desireable, that the emigration of the Cherokees, (who I understand are now assembled in great numbers & supported at great expense to the Government) should not be unnecessarily suspended or delayed. Whist they remain where they are, they must be the cause of continual excitement, among the border inhabitants, and the sooner they can be removed, the better for them and the Government.

And, of course, their removal opened the whole area east of the Mississippi to white settlers. James himself was later to acquire for the United States over 20 million acres of Indian lands.

So DOMINANT WAS THE FIGURE OF ANDREW JACKSON IN THE early nineteenth century that it has been called the Age of Jackson. Jackson and Will had been friends since the Revolution when they were nearly killed together; they had many business dealings together; Will named one of his sons Andrew Jackson Polk; and later Will's son Lucius would marry Jackson's favorite niece in a storybook White House wedding. In 1824, Will expressed lukewarm support for Jackson in his bid for the presidency. The candidates, he wrote, "are all good Democrats I suppose of the Jeffersonian school; and from whom [as a Federalist] I have nothing to hope nor fear . . . yet I have taken Jackson[']s side and will promote his election; not through *thick & thin,* but fairly and honestly." But the two men differed on many issues.

Probably the most important of these was the role of government in finance, and this focused on the Bank of the United States, an issue that dominated Jackson's thought for several crucial years of his presidency, nearly wrecked the Democratic Party and defeated James in his bid for the governorship of Tennessee. The Bank was also a crucial issue for Will, since he had founded, directed and fought for the State Bank of North Carolina, which was a regional clone of the Bank of the United States.

The Bank of the United States had been created by Alexander Hamilton in 1791 for an initial period of twenty years; after that time, it was allowed to die. But in the aftershock of the War of 1812, the lack of a central financial institution proved almost as harmful as the lack of an army. Consequently, in 1816 a very similar organization was rechartered with 80 percent of its equity held by domestic and foreign investors. The government held the remaining 20 percent and elected five of the twenty-five directors. By contract, the Bank was given various privileges including being exempt from state taxes and from paying interest on deposits made by the government; in return it was obligated to pay a bonus and perform fiscal chores for the government without charge.

For a number of years, the Bank functioned well, and the government, many members of which profited from its lobbying and public relations program, raised no objections. Certain key members of the Congress, like Senator Daniel Webster, were on its payroll. With the government virtually in its pocket, it grew so arrogant that James, by then chairman of the House Ways and Means Committee, wrote to President Jackson, that the Bank had suborned the man charged by the Senate to investigate it, even letting the Bank's president prepare his report.

But the critical issue was the nature of the Bank: it was, indeed, the very issue raised by Will in his broadside on the North Carolina Bank. Was the United States Bank merely a private institution, to be run by its own officers and directors? The Bank president's position (like Will's on the North Carolina State Bank) was unequivocal: the Bank was a private company in which the government was merely a minority stockholder. To James's astonishment, the United States Bank officers went much further than Will had done in North Carolina: they refused even to permit government auditors to examine their books.

James and President Jackson took a position exactly the opposite to that of the Bank's president and supporters. And they were backed up not only by a decision of the Supreme Court, which held that it was an instrument of the federal government, but specifically by Alexander Hamilton when he had designed the original institution: ". . . such a bank," he wrote, "is not a mere matter of private property, but a political machine of the greatest importance to the state." As they uncovered more about the Bank's political activities, Jackson and James realized how right Hamilton had been, and they became convinced that the Bank was ready and able to subvert the government. They came out from this assessment exactly opposite to Hamilton and made its destruction an almost blinding priority. So determined were they upon this policy that they either refused to listen to or did not heed the many signs that the Bank was undoubtedly useful, perhaps even vital, to the economy, and that many who were neither Federalists nor bribed to do so supported it. Bringing the issue home to him, James was told that between three-quarters and nine-tenths of the people of his home county favored the rechartering of the Bank.

Will, meanwhile, was interested in investing in the Bank. Writing to a congressional friend on February 1, 1832, he asked if there was a good chance that the Bank would be rechartered and if so whether President Jackson would veto it. He was concerned since, ". . . should the petition be rejected, there is good reason to believe the Stock will fall perhaps below par . . ."

He did not invest. There was no chance that the president would approve. As Jackson wrote to James, "Everyone that knows me, does know, that I have been always opposed to the U. States Bank, nay all Banks." It was not just a matter of his hostility to banks in general but also because the Bank president so overplayed his hand that he frightened the men in Jackson's Democratic Party. When James wrote an anti-Bank report to the Ways and Means Committee of the House in March 1833, the Bank instituted a press campaign against him. During that campaign, James found out that the Bank, covertly, controlled two of the attacking newspapers. A few days later, President Jackson wrote James that he had discovered that the Bank had spent the then great sum of $80,000 on propaganda "to corrupt the people & buy a Recharter of that mamoth of corruption." To both sides, no compromise seemed possible.

Although James was in Congress, not in the cabinet, Jackson regarded him as virtually a part of the administration, and James acted in the same spirit. In a letter to the president, describing the policy he was pursuing in Congress, James came out flatly against rechartering the existing Bank and also against creating any new financial institution to replace it. Unconsciously echoing Hamilton, he wrote that "Any new concern, if not immediately, would very soon pass into the hands of the owners of the present Bank, for the most obvious of reasons—that they are possessed of the wealth and constitute the aristocracy of the country . . ."

Not surprisingly, Jackson's views on banks and on the economy, and also his increasingly dictatorial stance, had disturbed and angered Will and, toward the end of his life, led to a rift between James and Will. Focusing on Jackson's policies, Will's descendants joined the Whig Party (which replaced the Federalists), and after Will's son Brigadier General Thomas Gilchrist Polk described Jackson in a speech in June 1840 as "possessed [of] not one solitary qualification" for the presidency, the two branches of the family virtually stopped all contact with one another. Thomas later supported Henry Clay against his cousin James in the race for the presidency in 1844, and there is no mention of him or his branch of the family in James's correspondence or diary thereafter.

On his own terms, Jackson tried to make peace with and within the Polk family: Lucius, another son of Will, who married Andrew Jackson's favorite niece, had supported Jackson for the presidency in 1828, but then became a Whig and opposed many of the policies Jackson and James were promoting. He and James apparently stopped speaking, and Jackson was saddened by the complexity of the relationships; so on March 14, 1836, he wrote his niece,

I am informed that he [Lucius] has become one of the modern whiggs. Say to him that he is in bad company,—those modern whiggs are the political [Benedict] Arnolds of the day, and differ from those gallant Washington Whiggs of the Revolution, to which his revered father [Will] belonged. *They* could not be bought by the bank as sheep in the shambles, as the modern Whiggs have and are—or for the sake of personal aggrandizment, sell their principles and party, and contest under hypocritical garb of the no party party, which is as much as to say; "we offer ourselves to that party, or any party that will offer us the best offices." I am sure your dear husband does not know these hypocrites as well as I do, or he would never be one of the no party, for he will adhere to principle, and if he does he must abandon them.

"Nothwistanding this advice and warning," his son later wrote, "father was a staunch supporter of the whig party up to and including the year 1860, when he supported the Hon. John Bell for the Presidency. As an indication of his enthusiasm in behalf of the whig platform he voted against James Polk, his kinsman, for the Presidency."

While there were rumblings of discontent, the Bank issue simmered until Jackson left the presidency. Then a financial panic ensued, businesses failed and the government itself became virtually bankrupt. Jackson's party quickly began to fall apart as frightened officeholders attempted to cater to the demands of their even more frightened constituents. James did not. Still clinging to Jackson's bank policy, he watched his best friends and colleagues swept out of office in the elections of 1837, although he, running unopposed, was returned to Congress, was reelected Speaker of the House and became de facto the leader of the party. However, to many it was clear that the rigidity of Jackson's and his position was politically suicidal. James's brother-in-law James Walker put his finger on the problem and outlined a possible solution in a letter to James of August 19, 1837:

> My judgment is that unless the Republican party give the people an institution that will answer all the purposes of a National Bank the Federal party will by their deceptions and a bribed press prevail on the people to allow them to make a bank monopoly for themselves and their British allies. My view then is that it is true patriotism to discard prejudices, and at once make a controuling Bank, in which the states shall be the exclusive stockholders, and that cannot by possibility come under individual irresponsible controul, that cannot be made a political machine, nor be liable to sudden contractions & expansions, nor the pro[du]cer of panics . . . I may be mis-

taken in the remedies proposed by our leading men but if I am
not, I tremble for the consequences.

But neither Jackson nor Polk could be dissuaded: for them, the Bank was
not a financial institution but a political force, outside of electoral control, which unless stopped, would dominate the government and destroy
the very security and well-being that had been Hamilton's original
quest.

THE BANK WAS NOT JACKSON'S ONLY ENEMY—INDEED, HE
made enemies quickly and easily throughout his life. The other issue that aroused his passion fueled the bitter conflict that was to lead to
the Civil War. That was the constitutional balance between the imperatives of the federal Union and states' rights, which is surely one of the
most complex matters in American politics. The matter was purposely
left vague in the Constitution. It had to be, because there the clash between current reality of an impotent and forlorn central government
and future hopes of the Federalists could not be resolved or, if resolved,
would have been the death of the project to create a new basis for government. The Constitution emerged from the Philadelphia convention
as a document of inspired vagueness, allowing each generation to shape
its meaning as growth and change demanded. In Jackson's time, the
choice between states' rights and union—which I have suggested partly
grew out of and were mainly exemplified by the Revolutionary War contrast between the militia and the Continental Line—was particularly
acute. It is still not, and probably can never be, resolved to everyone's
satisfaction.

Despite earlier episodes when his pride, ambition or avariciousness
led him close to treason, as it frequently and colorfully did, Jackson
came down firmly on the side of the Union and against those who
thought that each state could "nullify" federal laws it disliked. Over this
issue he broke with his vice president, John Calhoun, and fastened the

task of preserving the Union firmly on James. In Jackson's eyes, the nullifiers (whom he called nullies) were a major danger to the Union. As he wrote to James on May 3, 1835,

> the nullifiers, I mean [by them former Vice President] Calhoun & Co . . . mean to build up a Southern confederacy, and divide the union . . . You and [Senator Felix] Grundy . . . are looked to, to take a firm and open stand in favour of the republican principles . . . & preserve Tennessee from the disgrace of uniting with the piebald opposition to put down my *administration and my fame* . . .''

Not only James but his wife and his brother, William H. Polk, who later ran for governor of Tennessee on a pro-Union ticket, would do what they could to carry out Jackson's command.

THE JACKSON LEGACY WAS ALMOST THE RUIN OF JAMES AND the Democratic Party. Meanwhile, like all political figures, James carried out the ''meat and potatoes'' functions of his office. Much of his correspondence as a member of Congress is filled with letters concerning the appointments of postmasters, cadets for West Point, military officers, getting applications for pensions processed and even taking out subscriptions to newspapers for his constituents back in Tennessee.

Jackson's administration has gone down in American history for its use of political office to punish rivals and reward supporters. The spoils system existed long before the Jackson administration, but it was undoubtedly carried to an extreme then. As a young theology student, fresh out of West Point, Will's son Leonidas was disturbed by the vengeance of the Jackson administration: he used the word ''proscriptions''—the Roman expression for the authorized killing of political opponents—for Jackson's actions. ''His descending to the removal of petty postmasters in obscure parts of the country,'' he wrote, ''seems hardly suitable employment for the head of so great a nation, whose very station must furnish ample business of a more elevated and altogether more useful character. Were I a politician, I fear that I would find in the administration thus far enough to shake my Jackson principles.''

Use of political office to promote the interests of supporters is, fortunately or unfortunately, a timeless feature of representative government and saddles the representatives with continual problems. As James wrote to Andrew Jackson on August 31, 1830, he like other congressmen ''cannot personally know the thousand applicants who present themselves with their vouchers and letters.'' Consequently, he said,

> it is but seldom that I recommend anyone for office. The commendatory letters for office are ordinarily easy to obtain, and persons giving them without intending to mislead or deceive the appointing powers, but too often act more from a spirit of accommodation to the applicant, and a want of real courage to refuse, than from any personal knowledge of him themselves.

But some must have been irresistible. Consider this one James received:

> Dear Sir,
>
> After my compliments to you I will inform you that I wante you to try and see if you cant have something don for me when you go to Congress in giting me a pention. I have under stood you was a perticular frnd to the old Soldiers. I have maid all the proof that is nessary and the papers is in the office of the Ware departemente and if you can git me a pention you can pay your self out of it for you trobl. I am in a very low situation my self. I have note been able to [do] any work for the last four or five years.
>
> I went in the survis in the year 1782 August 25th and was Discharged in year 1783 July 5th.
>
> Andrew Derryberry

Whereas Andrew Jackson treated political office like a military command and, in letters to James, wrote as though he were positioning subordinate commanders for a battle—"do not permit yourself to be out generalled"—James was a consensus-builder. That is not to say that James adhered any less resolutely to his chosen positions—his letters ring with conviction and are replete with such tags for the positions of his political enemies as "unholy," and in his eyes his supporters were always "the real people." Even where he echoed Jackson's sentiments, as he did on the issue of the Bank of the United States, he wrote in a reasoning rather than in a preemptive style.

James's style, undoubtedly, was set in large part by his personality, which was less assertive, less dogmatic and less violent than Jackson's. James's pragmatism was also undoubtedly reenforced by his experience after having been elected Speaker of the House on December 7, 1835. There he had to contend, on a daily, even an hourly, basis with men of skill and conviction who often disagreed with him. As one of his congressional colleagues, Archibald Yell, wrote to him, "I am getting to believe that you are possessed of a rare quality, which I heretofore somewhat doubted, that of *Modesty* . . ." That was a quality he showed a few years later in the way he conducted his office as governor of Tennessee: he ran the state government with only five officials: a secretary of state, controller, treasurer, attorney general and school superintendent.

In one of those unintended jokes of history, James had as early as 1827 acquired the nickname "the Black Pony." The nickname had nothing to do with the later sobriquet "dark horse candidate" but was fastened upon him by Davy Crockett in commenting on his speed and diligence in making the rounds of his electoral district.

James was to a degree unmatched before or since in the Polk family a political man; his career spanned most of the elective offices then available to him. From the state legislature of Tennessee, he moved to the United States Congress, where he served on a number of committees and was chairman of the even-then-powerful Ways and Means Committee and twice Speaker of the House. Returning to Tennessee, in the aftermath of the Bank crisis, where the policies pursued by Jackson, Van Buren and him had resulted in a political catastrophe for their party, he was elected governor; it seemed to many, and apparently also to him, that his political career might, with luck, bow out with nomination to the relatively insignificant position of vice president. A better one would come.

Looming over the young Republic's horizon during these years was the dark storm cloud of slavery. The cloud would soon engulf the whole nation and with it the entire Polk family, so we need to get an idea of its complex nature.

Perhaps the hardest task a historian faces is to recapture the emotions or sense of right and wrong of previous times. Often it is a disagreeable task, because our ancestors were frequently indifferent to actions and thoughts we find morally repugnant. So it was about slavery. Slavery had long been a fact of life throughout America, not just in the South, and slaves were discussed in terms as casual as might have been used for cattle. Prices were the major topic. In North Carolina, "a likely man [then sold for] from 400 to 500 Dollars—stout Boys from 350 to 400 Dollars—and Women from 300 to 375 Dollars," wrote one of Will's neighbors, but Will, "being good at a bargain," might do better.

As horrible as we find slavery to have been, it was not a homogeneous institution. The common characteristic was lack of freedom, but there were gradations of deprivation. Some slaves were worked in mines as inhumanly as the ancient Romans had "wasted" theirs. Others worked in the fields like domesticated animals. Some managed to practice trades or professions with a degree of autonomy and even wealth. Others worked in white households where some formed close attachments to their owners. Overall, their diet was probably not worse on average than that of most European peasants, but they had no protection from the lust, anger or sadism of masters. At best, even for the artisans and craftsmen, liberty was restricted. Few were allowed off the premises of their workplace and were discouraged from meeting slaves from other areas. When a slave was entrusted with an errand, he or she had to carry a pass that specified his name, the name of his owner and the exact route he was to follow.

This "peculiar institution"—the phrase was already in common use as shown by a letter written by Lucius's daughter Mary in June 1864—had changed little since early colonial times, except by spreading into new areas as the Indians were pushed out. And those men who set up the Constitution were not anxious to change it; not only did most of them profit from it, but it seemed a part of the "classical" heritage of the Old Testament Hebrews, Greece and Rome. It is in this light that Jefferson's draft of the Declaration of Independence must be read by the historian if not by the jurist. While eloquently proclaiming that "all men are created equal; that they are endowed by their Creator with certain unalienable rights; that among these are life, liberty, and the pursuit of happiness," Jefferson did not mean by "men," as we have come to interpret his document, "human beings"; he meant free, white males. He linked slaves with "other moveables."

At the time the Constitution was being debated, there was little thought of the rights of slaves or of the right of slavery. The issue that was uppermost was the effect of slaveholding on representation in the Congress: were slaves to be considered as "men" for purposes of allocating seats or only as property for the allocation of taxes? The Constitution ducked the question by setting both representation and taxes according to "the aggregate number of inhabitants" but referring the "qualifications on which the right of suffrage depends" to each state. In *The Federalist,* number 42, James Madison held out the hope that the *traffic* in slaves was to be banned after 1808. This was perhaps as far as he wished to go, since he was a slaveholder, but if he and his colleagues hoped to get the Constitution approved, it was as far as they *could* go.

Slavery was so much a part of the American scene that no definition of it seemed needed. The most complete definition was given some years later in a case before the North Carolina Supreme Court. In *State v. Mann,* the court held that the services of a slave

> can only be expected from one *who has no will of his own, who surrenders his will* in implicit obedience to that of another. Such obedience is the consequence only of uncontrolled authority over the body. The power of the master must be absolute to render the submission of the slave perfect . . . The slave, to remain a slave, must be made sensible that there is no appeal from his master . . .

The judge made clear the moral repugnance of the verdict, saying, "As a principle of moral rights, every person . . . must repudiate it [and recognize that] it constitutes the curse of slavery to both the bond and the free portions of our population. But it is inherent in the relation of masters and slaves."

"Inherent" is probably the key word in the view of most southern whites: they took refuge in the fact that they had not created slavery but were born at a time when it had been in existence for centuries. They were outraged by what they regarded as northern hypocrisy and were fond of pointing out that the slaves had been imported from Africa on ships owned and manned by northerners who, having been paid for the slaves, then wanted the southerners to give them up. They also recognized that their way of life rested on a largely agrarian economy that, in an age with very little machinery and inanimate power, was dependent upon slavery.

Finding an alternative to slavery baffled even the most humane and liberal. On an individual basis, the granting of freedom was possible if often costly and difficult. Will Polk freed his "Carriage Driver Henry" in his will and left him the then considerable sum of $100 to start a new life, but usually the manumitting owner had also to send the former slave out of the state. Few statesmen or politicians in the North or the South even contemplated addressing the massive problems that would arise in freeing all the slaves. Jefferson, as usual, had led the way. He was in favor of expelling even free Negroes (as well as blacks convicted of crimes and slaves) to Africa, believing that it would be impossible for whites and blacks to mingle in the society of the new Republic. Blacks, he wrote, were inherently inferior and always alien.

His ideas were embodied in the American Colonization Society, which was founded in 1817, with a number of notable Americans including Henry Clay (who later ran against James for the presidency in 1844) among its members. Monrovia, named for President James Monroe (who also owned slaves), was the destination to which they planned to send liberated and expelled blacks.

Attending a meeting of the society on January 21, 1829, was Leonidas Polk, who had recently graduated from West Point and was in training for the Episcopal ministry. As he wrote to his father, Will, when about six hundred free blacks had been sent to Africa,

> All that is wanting to remove not only the blacks that are free, but those that are enslaved also, is the consent of their owners and funds to transport them. There is land sufficient and productive to support them; and as to climate, fortunately, the great body of blacks are in that part of the Union from which they experience least inconvenience in Africa. Now I believe in the course of not many years one State after another will be willing to abolish slavery. This is proved by the state of things in Maryland and Virginia, the slave States farthest north, and from a variety of motives funds enough will be raised to gradually transport them.

To our generation, this seems not the moral position of a young man in the grip of a religious fever, as Leonidas certainly was, but a severe form of apartheid. Years later, Leonidas would turn against the expulsion of blacks to Africa as cruel and unjust. But within the context of the 1820s and 1830s, the Colonization Society had taken a relatively progressive although wholly impractical step. At that time, there were approximately 200,000 freed blacks, of whom about a quarter were still living in the South. While legally free, they were rarely given anything like minimal civil rights. In North Carolina, they were required to wear identifying patches indicating their status. Elsewhere, even in the North, their situation was not only bad but declining: after a brief period in which they could vote, free blacks were disfranchised in New Jersey, Maryland, Connecticut, Rhode Island and New York.

The Missouri Compromise—specifying that slavery was to be legal in Missouri but would be banned in the new northern territories—was worked out in Congress in March 1820 after violent disagreement between antislavery and proslavery whites. Even Thomas Jefferson had weighed into the fight urging that Congress avoid taking a stand against slavery lest whites abandon the southern plantation states. But Congress could not duck the issue when Missouri stood on the brink of entry into the Union; the compromise satisfied almost no one; Jefferson considered it "the knell of the Union." Although he was premature, he was nearly right.

Most blacks were neither free nor living in the North or the new West; so I turn to the correspondence of James to get closer to what was the more common experience. James was personally removed from contact with slaves, but he was regularly informed of happenings on his plantations, which were run by two apparently fairly typical overseers; their reports on the slaves under their control make ugly reading, dealing not only with crops but with runaway and disobedient slaves, and we have to assume that James read them. Probably most absentee owners received similar reports, but few have been preserved.

James's overseer Ephraim Beanland wrote James on December 1, 1833, that "Jack and Ben has wrun away on Friday last [after] I corected him . . . I have not heard of them since. And Sir your boys has traded so much with white people and bin let run so loose reined that I am compeled to not let won of them of one [off of] the plantation with out he askes my leave . . ."

About three weeks later, Ben turned up in Tennessee at the house of James's brother-in-law James Walker, who immediately wrote that "Your man *Little Ben* has made his appearance here last night . . . His back, I am informed bears evidence of severe whipping. Whether Beenland has acted with too much severity or not I cannot say, but I am fearful he has not judgement enough to keep the negroes in proper subjection. I wrote to him yesterday requesting him to moderate, and expressing fears that he had been too cruel . . . It seems useless to send him [Ben] back [to the plantation] unless it is in chains."

Beanland wrote James with a report on the plantation before James had time to get Walker's letter. In his first sentence, he shows the attitude of the overseer, relating the condition of two slave women and the mule: "We'r ar all well and Lisabeth and Mriah has both fine living children and Garisan and the mule has cum long since." Then he repeated that "I corected him [the slave Jack] and I corected him for teling em 5 or 6 positif lyes and whilste I sent to diner they boath left the field and I have not heard of them since . . . I want them boath brought back. If they aint they rest will leave me also."

Adlai O. Harris, another brother-in-law, reported that "Jack was very badly whip'd indeed, that Beanland salted him four or five times during the whipping, that Ben was also whipd but not so badly . . . I am very much afriad that he [Beanland] will not treat your negroes as you would wish."

The clash in attitudes between the absentee owner and the overseer comes out in a letter Beanland wrote on February 1, 1834, with veiled criticism of James's "soft" attitude toward Ben, saying, "Ben ought to be brought back to the plantation for he is a grand scoundrell and I do not think that he ought to be befriended in any such an maner. Now if I corect any of the others any they are shore to leave me thinking if they can get back to that will do for they must be youmered [humored] to as well as Ben and Sir I do not think any such foolishness as this write for I caime hear to make a crop and I am determined on doing of it."

So evil a reputation had the overseers as a group—ironically, a large proportion of them were northern—that some owners refused to hire them. But the overseers had a final trump card: if the owner did not do what they recommended, the crop might fail. Beanland was constantly urging James to buy more slaves and was "glad to hear of you a byinge 5 negroes. My cotton is a goinge to turn out well I thinke if I can get it out but I do ashore you that I cant get it out in time if donte get more hands than I nowe have got."

There must have been a good deal of local trading among landowners and overseers in the rural areas of the South. Beanland recommended the purchase of a boy who was described as "a rite smarte blacksmith and A good shumaker and a hood huar," who was owned by a Parson Reaves, who "says that if his boy Fill wold not run away he wold not take $1000 for him . . . at $600 and I thinke he is verry cheape boy . . . he can be broke from runninge a way."

Despite ample proof that Beanland was cruel to the slaves, James and his partners sent him to open and manage a new plantation in Mississippi. He made a financial failure of it, and because of that, as James's brother-in-law Silas M. Caldwell wrote to James on January 31, 1836, "I[t] would have [been] well for us that we never had any thing to do with *Beanland*."

But other overseers were no better, at least in their handling of the slaves. Caldwell wrote again to James on July 23, 1841, that "Your Boy Addison has run away from your farm and is at my house. From the wounds that are on his neck & arms it appears that the Overseer intended to kill Him. The wounds are well. He says the overseer says he will kill him and is afraid to stay there. You will please write to me what to do with him." There is no extant reply, but the overseer, Isaac M. Dismukes, wrote on September 1,

Adderson and gilburt got hear a fiew dais since . . . and hea stade there [Tennessee, to which he had fled] three dais and was sent back with adderson . . . I should of whip them as soon as the landed had it not of bin your request that mr bobit

[William Bobbitt] should bin preasant though I think that if I had of taken them and of whip them as soon as the got hear that gilburt would not of run away again soon which I should of dun if I had not thought that you would of thought that I would whip them too much though that is what I neaver had dun since I have bin dooing of bisness and it is what I would not doo as to disenable them from work one our. My fealinges would not suffer mea to gone as fair as that . . . If hea getes back thane have him iron and send him to mea if you please. I wil not inger him by whiping him. I beleave that they balieve that tennessee is a place of parridise and the all want to gow back to tennessee.

The editors of James's papers comment that "Polk probably agreed to the correction [a euphemism for whipping] of his runaway slaves, for his agent William Bobbitt wrote on August 29, 1841, that he approved of Polk's 'determination to put a stop to it, by making examples of the offenders in every instance, that is by correcting instead of selling.' " Being sold "downriver," as the saying on the Mississippi went, to a "negro trader" was, if anything, a more fearful prospect than being whipped.

We must ask, was cruel treatment typical? For many years, southerners would have said no. But we know that even Thomas Jefferson had his slaves whipped, and he sold recalcitrant slaves to "negro traders." He, like James, probably never personally witnessed a whipping, but he certainly knew of it. And I believe we can be fairly certain that given the notion that slaves were merely a form of property, to be used rather like draft animals, and that lashing was also still standard punishment for white prisoners, it was probably common among the 385,000 owners of slaves. In some areas and at some times, it was undoubtedly worse. At least this is what former slaves have said, and while it is rare that southern slave owners detailed such treatment, it is not surprising that they did not. Most have been anxious to cultivate the image of happy servants, loyal to their masters, living under their benign guidance. And for the "house" slaves, like those enumerated in Will's testament, there is probably much truth in this, but the field hands were an entirely different matter, and the way they are casually discussed in letters to and from James, it is clear that little sentiment was wasted on them. On their experience would hang the future of the nation.

THE PRESIDENCY

"Mr. Polk's War"

Who is Polk?" That was the taunt of the Whig Party when news came that James had been nominated for the presidency by the Democratic Party. Today the taunt falls flat as James, the "dark horse candidate," has come, slowly to be sure, to be recognized as one of America's greatest presidents, but in the spring of 1844 it seemed an adroit campaign thrust.

Despite the jape, James was then almost as well known nationally as in his home state of Tennessee. He had served seven terms in the U.S. Congress and had twice been elected Speaker of the House of Representatives. But after having served one term as governor of Tennessee, he had been defeated for reelection in 1841 and 1843; so, on the eve of the Democratic Party convention, James was a politician whose drive seemed to have petered out. As the quest for political office has been described, it can be like climbing up a well-greased flagpole: easy at first, it gets harder and harder to reach the top, and as the candidate frantically struggles upward, he is apt, through no fault of his own, to slip and slide so that the golden knob on the top remains ever beyond his reach. That must have been how his life looked to James in the months before the convention.

FROM AT LEAST HIS COLLEGE DAYS, JAMES WAS A POLITICAL man. At the University of North Carolina at Chapel Hill, he spent as much time in the debating society as on his studies. Being in poor health because of a gallbladder disorder, he avoided the rough-and-tumble rustic student sports and their horse-racing and cockfighting entertainments. Except for horseback riding, which was then more a means of transportation than an exercise, he never seems to have shown any interest in strenuous physical activity. Politics was an all-consuming passion.

Paradoxically, like many men who live intensely public lives, he was a private person. His letters, even to close family members, are formal in address and distant in content. His closest friend and political supporter once complained that despite receiving many letters, he was unsure exactly what James really thought. With his brother, William, for whom he acted as guardian and foster father, there was little show of affection or even of warmth, and with his wife, Sarah, such letters as survive deal mainly with political or business affairs. Friends he had but most were, in his phrase, more "political friends" than "personal friends."

Throughout his adult life, James would be, as we would say today, a workaholic. His approach to the law, his profession, was like his approach to politics. He won his battles not because he swept people along with his charisma but because he awed them with his thorough knowledge of each issue and wore them down by his persistence. Associates and enemies alike agreed that he was always the best prepared man in every debate. And throughout his career, he exhibited a tenacity in pursuing his clearly announced objectives that was rare in his age and has seldom been surpassed by politicians in ours.

T HE FIRST TASK OF THE POLITICIAN, OF COURSE, IS TO GET elected. James's campaigns not only tell us a good deal about the man but also place him clearly in the context of his times. It takes a considerable leap in imagination to understand and feel those events, so crucial to a grasp of our national traditions, but James's experiences give us an almost unique insight. To appreciate them, we must bear in mind that in the 1830s and 1840s America was still a small society. The population had grown by 1840 to only a little over 17 million. Of these, about two persons out of three were of either English or Scots descent; so the society was, by our standards, amazingly homogeneous. (About one of every six persons was black, but of course they were denied the franchise.) The population lived in societies that were hardly more than neighborhoods. Only about one American in nine or ten lived in a community larger than 2,500. In many areas, roads were still little more than trails; so movement was always uncomfortable and often restricted to horseback. The telegraph had not yet come into use and the mails were slow, infrequent and often inaccessible. To publicize their opinions or to spread information, citizens engaged local printers to turn out broadsheets, since newspapers, in our sense of the word, existed only in a few urban centers.

James's twelve campaigns reflect the society in which he lived. Each grew progressively more complex and covered more territory than the one before, so taken together they give us views of broader and broader sections of the country. The first, for a position in the Tennessee legislature in 1823 when he was a twenty-eight-year-old lawyer, was relatively simple, since James canvassed only his kinsmen, friends, clients and acquaintances in the middle Tennessee area around his hometown of Columbia. It was a campaign involving little more than making social calls and mentioning his family name. Running for the U.S. Congress as he began to do in 1825 and did seven times until 1837 was more intense, since it involved not only taking a stand on national issues but facing, for the first time, determined opposition from an organized political party, the Whig successors to the Federalists. Still, since it was to represent only a single district, it remained a sort of neighborhood affair. But when he campaigned for the governorship of Tennessee, as he did three times, James's task became far different.

In a letter to Martin Van Buren of New York, the leader of his political party, known then as the Democracy, on December 8, 1842, James recounted the problems of campaigning in Tennessee.

> The labour of canvassing a State like this of more than six hundred miles in extent, and reaching from the mountains of Virginia & Carolina to the Swamps of the Mississippi, and of visiting and addressing the people in more than eighty Counties, is greater than can be estimated by any one who has not performed it. It requires four months of unceasing [horseback] riding and speaking. I have twice performed it, and standing in the relation which I do to the Democracy of the State, I must undertake it again.

He did, and on this next campaign, as he wrote on August 18, 1843, he "laboriously canvassed the State for near five months, and made more than *ninety* speeches to popular assemblies of the people." Those popular assemblies have given us the term "stump." What the candidate did was to climb upon a tree stump and harangue everyone he could reach. He often got them together by promising some food and a lot of drink. And by appearing nearly always with his rival—it then being the custom for the rival candidates to travel together and speak one after the other—he could usually promise a boisterous, sometimes funny and often violent afternoon's entertainment for people who seldom had much distraction. It was James's failure to recognize, or at least to admit, that politics was a form of popular entertainment that led to his first defeat in 1841.

Knowing James to be a sober and serious man, not noted for his delight in "pressing the flesh," and one wont to run an "issues campaign," the Whigs in 1841 nominated a folksy, backslapping, humorous candidate for governor known as "Lean Jimmy" Jones. Parading as a "man of the people"—"the miserable farce about log cabins" had already begun in American politics, as one of James's correspondents wrote—Lean Jimmy avoided the abstract and often boring great issues to amuse the little gatherings by his jokes and to discomfit James by his sallies.

James's pain in trying to meet his adversary on this unfamiliar turf is palpable. In desperation, he drummed up a single, not-very-funny joke, and like some well-known modern politicians, he told it at meeting after meeting. He could get away with that because each new audience knew nothing of his previous speech. But doing so, he fell down to Jimmy's level and into his hands. What went wrong was not only that his joke was not very clever and that his adversary was better at jesting than he but that Lean Jimmy sometimes had the last word. So one day when James told his joke, comparing the Whigs to "neighing and whinnying young colts" scrambling to get hold of their mother's teat—which James thought spoke to a farmer audience—he got caught. Lean Jimmy had finally thought up a suitable retort. One can imagine him raising his arm to quiet the homespun crowd and then, almost convulsed with laughter and pointing at James, shouting, "That's right, folks. Time to wean 'em. This here 'young colt' has been at the public teat for fifteen years. Let's wean *him* on election day."

James didn't try his joke again. And Lean Jimmy swept him out of office.

It wasn't only campaigning that was burdensome to politicians. Getting elected was beginning to be expensive. Of course nothing then compared to the vast outlays of money spent on campaigns today, but neither was there then any public or party support for candidates. They had not only to continue to support their families while not earning a salary but also to pay their campaign expenses out of their own pockets. The Whigs were better organized and spent proportionally more on their campaigns, but "the Democracy" gave its candidates virtually no help. We see this in a reply James received from one of his closest friends and supporters whom he had urged to run for a sixth term in Congress: Cave Johnson wrote to James on January 4 and February 17, 1843,

> I do not see how I am to run under any circumstances—a wife & two & prospects for a third—poor & sickly & getting old. I cant upon my pay support them here if I could get them along safely & to leave them, I had as well be divorced. After being here 20 mo[nths]. Out of 24 how can I spend all my time traversing hills & dales only again to be absent nearly all the time & make nothing . . . It will be very unfortunate if I am again nominated.

Having constantly been running for office or serving in Congress or the governorship since 1823, James had earned practically no money and had gradually run through the legacy left by his father and grandfather. He was particularly pressed by debts accumulated during the failed 1841 gubernatorial campaign, but when he tried to borrow money in Cincinnati, Washington, Philadelphia and New York and through friends in Congress, he got no support. He then tried to sell his last possession, farmlands he had inherited from his father, but in the midst of a depression, he found no buyers. Like his friend Cave Johnson and even more like his inspiration, Thomas Jefferson, he failed financially everywhere. So bad had his finances become that less than a year before he was elected president, he had trouble raising $50. Needing that amount to give to a nephew, he had written to his wife from Mississippi on October 26, 1843, "See Knox & ask him to raise for me if he can $50 and give it to *Lucius* to bear little *Marshall's* expenses out. *Lucius* says he will be hard run for money. Tell *Knox* I will raise the money some-how on my return & repay it to him." Public life was the highway to the poorhouse.

Reading such letters, one is struck by how little James was influenced in his political philosophy by his own experience. For a man as concerned as he with running an issues campaign, he made little or no attempt to relate issues not only to what the general public wanted or needed but to the financial pressures he experienced. He was from the beginning and remained an old-fashioned Jeffersonian at a time when the public was turning away from Jefferson's legacy. The "independent yeoman farmers," on whom Jefferson placed his bet for democracy, were as eager as Alexander Hamilton's artisans and financiers to sup at the public trough. And in the midst of a painful and incomprehensible depression that lowered the prices they could get for their produce and made money scarce, farmers wanted a government that would help them and pay for "internal improvements" such as roads, canals and railways. James's program promised only rigid adherence to constitutional issues about which few in his audiences had even heard and austerity. He was opposed to economic relief proposals (such as a more protective tariff, a federal bankruptcy act and a new national bank). Hamilton would probably have been as uncomfortable as James on that stump with Lean Jimmy, but it was Hamilton's program for which the farmers voted.

James put a brave face on defeat. "Though *beaten* in the late contest in the State, and in the Union I hope our friends will not for a moment despond. Our defeat must be but temporary. We battle for the ancient & long cherished Republican principles of our fathers, and must ultimately succeed. For myself I am in the field for re-election undismayed & unterrified and with a perfect confidence . . ." But as one of his friends replied, "It seems that we have met the enemy and we are theirs."

Ruins of Carlaverock Castle, Dumfriesshire, Scotland, the seat of the Earl of Maxwell, the head of the Maxwell/Pollok clan. (*Courtesy of the National Monuments Record of Scotland*)

Cavanacor House, the house in Ballindrait, Lifford, county Donegal, Ireland, in which Magdalen, the wife of Robert Pollock/Polk, lived before her trip to America. (*Photograph: Milbry C. Polk*)

The sycamore tree from which Robert Pollock/Polk would probably have been hanged had he not fled Northern Ireland. (*Photograph: Milbry C. Polk*)

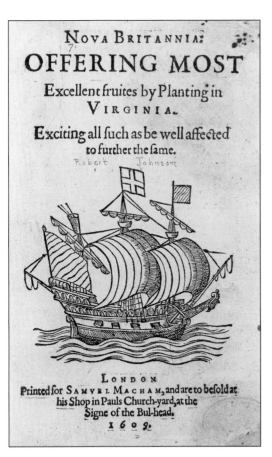

Pamphlet cover inviting emigrants to the New World. Real estate scams were known even then. (*Courtesy of the Library of Congress*)

Dutch *fluyt,* or "fly-boat," as portrayed in an engraving by the Dutch artist Salomon Saverij dated c. 1650, now in the Nederlandsch Historisch Scheepvaart Museum, Amsterdam. It was on a boat much like this that Robert, Magdalen and their children sailed to America in 1680. (*Courtesy of the Nederlandsch Historisch Scheepvaart Museum, Amsterdam*)

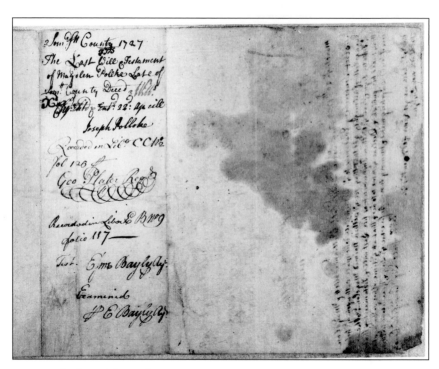

Will of Magdalen Polk. A rare, very early will of a woman in the colonies.

The courthouse where in 1775 the Mecklenburg Declaration of Independence was proclaimed by Colonel Thomas Polk. It was the first of nearly a hundred read out by irate colonists in the year before the Continental Congress passed the draft prepared by Thomas Jefferson and Sam Adams.

By the KING,

A PROCLAMATION,

For suppressing Rebellion and Sedition.

GEORGE R.

 HEREAS many of Our Subjects in divers Parts of Our Colonies and Plantations in *North America*, misled by dangerous and ill-designing Men, and forgetting the Allegiance which they owe to the Power that has protected and sustained them, after various disorderly Acts committed in Disturbance of the Publick Peace, to the Obstruction of lawful Commerce, and to the Oppression of Our loyal Subjects carrying on the same, have at length proceeded to an open and avowed Rebellion, by arraying themselves in hostile Manner to withstand the Execution of the Law, and traitorously preparing, ordering, and levying War against Us. And whereas there is Reason to apprehend that such Rebellion hath been much promoted and encouraged by the traitorous Correspondence, Counsels, and Comfort of divers wicked and desperate Persons within this Realm: To the End therefore that none of Our Subjects may neglect or violate their Duty through Ignorance thereof, or through any Doubt of the Protection which the Law will afford to their Loyalty and Zeal; We have thought fit, by and with the Advice of Our Privy Council, to issue this Our Royal Proclamation, hereby declaring that not only all Our Officers Civil and Military are obliged to exert their utmost Endeavours to suppress such Rebellion, and to bring the Traitors to Justice; but that all Our Subjects of this Realm and the Dominions thereunto belonging are bound by Law to be aiding and assisting in the Suppression of such Rebellion, and to disclose and make known all traitorous Conspiracies and Attempts against Us, Our Crown and Dignity; And We do accordingly strictly charge and command all Our Officers as well Civil as Military, and all other Our obedient and loyal Subjects, to use their utmost Endeavours to withstand and suppress such Rebellion, and to disclose and make known all Treasons and traitorous Conspiracies which they shall know to be against Us, Our Crown and Dignity; and for that Purpose, that they transmit to One of Our Principal Secretaries of State, or other proper Officer, due and full Information of all Persons who shall be found carrying on Correspondence with, or in any Manner or Degree aiding or abetting the Persons now in open Arms and Rebellion against Our Government within any of Our Colonies and Plantations in *North America*, in order to bring to condign Punishment the Authors, Perpetrators, and Abettors of such traitorous Designs.

Given at Our Court at St. *James's*, the Twenty-third Day of *August*, One thousand seven hundred and seventy-five, in the Fifteenth Year of Our Reign.

God save the King.

LONDON:

Printed by *Charles Eyre* and *William Strahan*, Printers to the King's most Excellent Majesty. 1775.

King George III replies to the Mecklenburg Resolves and other declarations of independence in the American colonies. (*Courtesy of the Emmet Collection of The New York Public Library*)

IN CONGRESS.

The D E L E G A T E S of the U N I T E D C O L O N I E S of *New-Hampshire, Massachusetts-Bay, Rhode-Island, Connecticut, New-York, New-Jersey, Pennsylvania*, the Counties of *New-Castle, Kent* and *Sussex* on *Delaware, Maryland, Virginia, North-Carolina, South-Carolina*, and *Georgia*, TO All unto whom these Presents shall come, send GREETING: KNOW YE,

THAT we have granted, and by these Presents do grant Licence and Authority to *Robert Polk* Mariner, Commander of the *John* called the *Montgomery* of the Burthen of *twenty five* Tons, or thereabouts, belonging to *Gilbert Middleton*, in the Colony of *Maryland* mounting *two* Carriage Guns, and navigated by *Men*, to fit out and set forth the said *Schooner* in a warlike Manner, and by and with the said *Schooner* and the Crew thereof, by Force of Arms, to attack, seize, and take the Ships and other Vessels belonging to the Inhabitants of Great-Britain, or any of them, with their Tackle, Apparel, Furniture and Ladings, on the High Seas, or between high-water and low-water Marks, and to bring the same to some convenient Ports in the said Colonies, in Order that the Courts, which are or shall be there appointed to hear and determine Causes civil and maritime, may proceed in due Form to condemn the said Captures, if they be adjudged lawful Prize; the said *Robert Polk* having given Bond, with sufficient Sureties, that Nothing be done by the said *Robert Polk* or any of the Officers, Mariners or Company thereof contrary to, or inconsistent with the Usages and Customs of Nations, and the Instructions, a Copy of which is herewith delivered to him. And we will and require all our Officers whatsoever to give Succour and Assistance to the said *Robert Polk* in the Premises. This Commission shall continue in Force until the Congress shall issue Orders to the Contrary.

By Order of the Congress,

John Hancock PRESIDENT.

Dated at *Annapolis, in Maryland*,

this *fifth* Day of *September* 1775.

Letter of Marque and Reprisal issued to Captain Robert Polk by John Hancock.

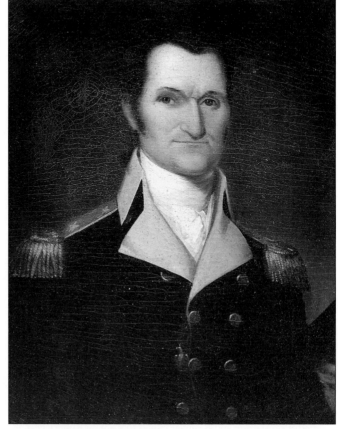

A typical bill for surveying. This was for the survey of two plots aggregating about three square miles in Tennessee in 1806 by Will Polk for $14.75.

Colonel William "Will" Mecklenburg Polk. (*Painting in the possession of Milbry C. Polk*)

Early American political hype: the campaign poster of James K. Polk and George M. Dallas as Democratic Party candidates for the presidency and the vice presidency. Their slogan was "Press Onward." (*Collection of the author*)

One of the surviving plates given
by Jean Lafitte, the pirate,
to the grandfather of Molly
Demoville Polk, c. 1815.

James K. Polk as the
youngest man to become
president. (*Courtesy of the
Library of Congress*)

President James K. Polk

The White House as it was in the presidency of James K. Polk.

James K. Polk and his cabinet in an early photograph in the White House State Dining Room, 1846. (*Courtesy of the James K. Polk Memorial Association*)

President James K. Polk, worn by four years of incessant labor, shortly before leaving office. (*Courtesy of the Amon Carter Museum, Fort Worth, Texas*)

Rattle & Snap plantation in Maury County, Tennessee, built by George Washington Polk, where James H. Polk was born and grew up.

Ashwood Hall, built by Leonidas Polk and lived in by Andrew Jackson Polk.

Portrait of George and Sallie Polk's children at Rattle & Snap. *(Original was burned in 1938; copy in possession of the author)*

Sallie Hilliard Polk, mistress of Rattle & Snap, wife of George Washington Polk and mother of James H. Polk. *(Original was burned in 1938; copy in possession of the author)*

St. John's Church, Ashwood, the Polk family
church built by Bishop Leonidas Polk.
(*Photograph by Milbry C. Polk*)

Belle Meade plantation, the home of Mary Demoville Harding Polk.

General Leonidas Polk, CSA, c. 1863. (*Courtesy of the Library of Congress*)

General Lucius Eugene Polk. (*Courtesy of the Library of Congress*)

Captain James H. Polk, said to have been the
youngest captain in the Confederate army.

Antoinette Polk, daughter of Andrew Jackson Polk, and later Baroness de Charette de la Contrie. (*Courtesy of General R. R. Van Stockum, USMC*)

Uncle Bob Polk, messenger for James H. Polk.

Mary "Molly" Demoville
Harding Polk as a
young woman, c. 1880.

Esther Winder Polk Lowe,
c. 1850, who was married
to the governor of
Maryland and on whose
account of the aftermath
of the Civil War the author
draws. (*Courtesy of the
Maryland Historical Society*)

The second time around in his defeat for the governorship in 1842, he reacted far more strongly. With that defeat, his hopes to be nominated for the vice presidency in 1844 dimmed, and as Paul Bergeron has written, this "second setback was almost more than Polk could cope with; he went into seclusion for days." But like so many politicians in our age, he had a relatively open way to return to normal life: he was a lawyer. By then lawyers already dominated elected positions in American politics; then as today, they were able to do so in no small part because, more easily than men of any other profession or trade, they could pick up the threads of civil life after leaving government service. James made that jump handily. As he wrote, "I have gone to my profession in earnest, & think I will *now* make some money."

But James never for a minute lost sight of his real love, politics. He even managed to find a silver lining in the dark cloud of defeat: he had received a larger number of votes than ever before, 54,000 out of a total of just over 110,000. "Though temporarily defeated the Democracy of the State are neither conquered nor subdued, but are ready and willing to renew the contest as they will do in the Presidential canvass of 1844," he wrote to the man he assumed would be the presidential candidate, Martin Van Buren. In this letter, he was both bolstering his own flagging spirits and preparing the way for a bid to become vice president.

BRAVE TALK ASIDE, THE MONTHS THAT FOLLOWED WERE THE worst period in James's political career; he seemed almost crushed by the defeat. So sure was he that he was on the side of right and reason, he simply could not accept the fact that the voters of Tennessee would not share his vision. After all, as he wrote all his correspondents, what he stood for was all according to the Constitution, while the measures advocated by his Whig opponents—causing the government to tax the many to help the few, intervening in spheres allocated to the states, even to create "domestic improvements," and threatening the stability of the Union—were simply unconstitutional. All through his correspondence run phrases that equate "the Democracy" with right, reason, constitutionality, morality, while the beliefs and actions of the Whigs are set off as not only wrong but evil. For example, having described a senator as "a managing, tricky man in whom no reliance is to be placed [with] . . . his own personal and sinister purposes to effect," James goes on to say, "I consider him little better than a Whig." That rigid mind-set would typify all of his actions in public affairs throughout the rest of his career.

James was similarly stubborn in his allegiance to his mentor. Throughout his career, he almost blindly associated himself with Andrew Jackson, took on Jackson's enemies, befriended his supporters and fought for his major issues. He gives no evidence that he ever calculated the benefits or the costs of this stance; rather, he seems completely to have believed in "Jacksonianism." To this position, he remained true even when the voters turned against it, as they did in 1840 and 1842.

The purity of his almost filial relationship to Jackson stands out in contrast to his attitude toward other political figures, to whom he had no personal ties of loyalty. For example, in his successful race for governor in 1839, he shrewdly distanced himself from the party leader, New York's Martin Van Buren. He urged that Van Buren, who had offered to come to Tennessee to help him get elected, not come and endorse him. "Our opponents," he wrote, "have already falsely charged that I was the Government candidate, selected and sent out, on a mission to revolutionize the state . . . But Mr. Van Buren's appearance in the state, pinding the elections, would be immediately seized upon, and heralded forth, in every corner of the state, to give colour to the charge." Van Buren was not pleased.

But with Jackson, as his correspondence and diary make clear, James had a relationship that was embedded in politics but rose far above it. Jackson was, at base, emotionally congenial to James, since James had inherited from his grandfather Ezekiel a passionate belief in Jeffersonianism. He grew up in an atmosphere in which the "consolidating" tendencies of the Federalist or Whig followers of Alexander Hamilton were anathema. Jackson was an old family friend, a fellow Scots-Irish frontiersman, a neighbor and, insofar as either was religious, a Presbyterian. To say that they saw eye-to-eye is an understatement. Jackson would look upon James as virtually a son. As Jackson had become known as Old Hickory, James was quickly dubbed the Young Hickory.

A man of strong, even bitter, opinions, Jackson saw the world in terms of a sort of political Manichaeanism: there were *our* forces of right, justice and honor—with particular emphasis on honor—who necessarily (and with relish) battled *their* dark forces of evil. Jackson's (and Polk's) definitions of these categories were not always or even often those familiar to us, but that did not diminish the power of their influence on Americans in the 1830s and 1840s.

The Jacksonian persuasion was a continuation of the Jeffersonian legacy in which the proper arena of American political life was the state, and the federal government, while of crucial and growing importance, was constrained by the Constitution to be mindful of that fact. If either intruded into the proper sphere of the other, the Union was endangered.

It followed that the federal government must be of a proportion suitable to the carrying out of its modest tasks—the executive branch numbered fewer than five hundred people in Jackson's administration— and the office of the president, even in James's administration in the 1840s, was comprised of only two people, the president and his private secretary. Modesty was not only a feature of government; it was a major part of the very justification for the federal government. This was the bedrock of James's political philosophy, and to it he was to devote his entire life.

JAMES'S HOPE WAS TO GET THE VICE PRESIDENTIAL NOMINATION on a Van Buren ticket. There had been a move to get him nominated for that post in 1840, but James had suspected that he was being used merely to swing some southern states over to the New York ticket, so he had bowed out. But as the convention of 1844 approached, he actively sought the vice presidency; and this time he was determined that ''my name will in no event be voluntarily withdrawn'' despite suggestions from his friends that, being a young man, he could afford to wait four or even eight years for a better chance.

The issue then at the forefront of public opinion was the admission of the recently proclaimed Republic of Texas as a state. Texas was believed to be under threat of attack by Mexico, which had never accepted its independence. Reports from Texas were full of bluster and sounded to James more like panic than bravado. One letter he received typified the lot: on April 10, 1843, John J. Goodman wrote,

> We have had some fears of mutch hard fighting but we now believe all the treats of that black Hartet Despot Santaana [Santa Anna] is a Hoax; he has long since bin satisfied that Anglo saxons were thorns in Texas and it was Truly remarked by that despot in '36 that Texas was to Mexico as a fractured limb to the human boddy, that it was only calculated to destroy the hole body, and that Texas was only a bead of Thorns. Well a bed of Thorns it is to him and I am of opinion if he ever tryes the Experiment again of reconquering Texas again he will be taught to believe that Texas valor is a perfect Toronado . . .

''Perhaps,'' the Americans thought. But this time, they were aware that the British and the French were identifying themselves with the Mexicans and suggesting that the leaders of the young and weak republic (even, it was alleged, bribing them) work out a deal with Mexico.

James, strongly pressed by Andrew Jackson, was in favor of immediate annexation. Van Buren was cool to the idea and shortly before the convention came out against annexation. For Jackson that was heresy, and he immediately called James to the Hermitage to give him his marching orders. Reporting on his visit to Andrew Jackson, James wrote to Cave Johnson on May 13, 1844,

He urges immediate annexation as not only important but indispensible. He speaks most affectionately of *Mr. Van Buren,* but is compelled to separate from him upon this great question, and says both he and *Mr. Benton* have by their letters [opposing annexation] cut their own throats politically. He has no idea that *Mr. V.B.* can be nominated or if nominated that he can receive any Southern support. He is not excited but is cool and collected and speaks in terms of deep regret at the fatal error which *Mr. V.B.* has committed. He says however that it is done and that the convention must select some other as the candidate.

Van Buren's disavowal of annexation split the party and brought Michigan's Lewis Cass to the fore as a rival candidate. He received a majority of the votes on the first ballot, but he could not satisfy the so-called Jackson rule of 1832, which required that nomination to the presidency be supported by two-thirds of the delegates. Each ballot gave Cass more votes but not the required two-thirds.

As excitement and frustration mounted, General Gideon J. Pillow, who functioned rather like a campaign manager (since by tradition candidates did not attend conventions), wrote James on May 24 to say that "The breache between the V's & anti-V's has become impassible." At that point, a move was made to bring in Silas Wright of New York as a compromise candidate, but he immediately declined, making one of the first uses of the revolutionary new device Congress had paid for, "Mr. Morse's Electric magnetic telegraph," and Pillow wrote to James the next day that he was "satisfied you are the choice of 2/3 of the convention for the Vice, & almost every one of your friends say they would prefer you for the Presidency. Things may take that turn yet." At the end of six ballots, the convention was completely stymied. As Pillow reported almost breathlessly,

We have been all day engaged balloting for Candidate for President. We commenced at 149 for Van & 82 for Cass. After 6

Ballotings we now stand 99 for Van & 116 for Cass, 32 for [Richard M.] Johnson & 35 for Buckhannon [James Buchanan]. We have for 2 hours past had the most extraordinary excitement in convention. The whole convention had well-nigh got into a general pell-mell fight. The Ohio Delegation produced it all. At this moment the excitement is still wholly ungovernable by the chair. If the balloting continu[e]s the chances will be for the nomination of Cass judging from the present vote. The V.B. men will not go for Cass and the Buckhannon men say they must. I doubt very much if Cass can ever get 2/3 of the votes. I have within the last few minutes received a proposition from a leading Delegate of the Pennsylvania & of Massachusetts to bring your name before the convention for President.

At that point, James was nominated, and on the ninth ballot he was selected unanimously. He has left no written record of his thoughts, but we can imagine that for the week it took for him to receive the news—''Mr. Morse's Electric magnetic telegraph'' ran only between Washington and Baltimore—the anxiety must have been almost unbearable.

At forty-nine, he was the youngest man ever to run for the presidency; he was deeply conscious not only of that fact, then considered a disability, but was determined not to be regarded as merely a southern candidate. Painfully and recently aware of the costs of disunity and weakness, he strove, above all, to attempt to heal the evident split in the party. It was clear that his nomination, although *pro forma* unanimous, had done little to unify it. And whatever his thoughts may have been, his friends and advisers urged that unless he managed to find some way to bring unity to the feuding factions, he would be defeated in the election. His answer was the most remarked-upon feature of his candidacy: in his acceptance on June 12, 1844, he pledged not to seek a second term. It was a tactically wise but strategically disastrous move.

Just as it was considered improper for James to have attended the convention, so it was improper for him to campaign for the presidency personally. Given the terrible ordeal he had so often endured in the past, James must have welcomed this custom. In an age before photo ops and sound bites, candidates had less possibility of being seen or heard, and James, at least, was delighted that this was so. As he wrote to John Kane on June 19, "I desire to avoid appearing before the public as far as I can do so with propriety." He "attended no rallies, made no speeches, and wrote but one public letter throughout the entire course of the campaign." He was following the advice of one of the few journalists he knew and trusted, J. George Harris, who wrote to him on September 24, 1844, "Your *friends* throughout the Union would be glad to see you *absolutely silent* until the day of election. That is *their* feeling. [The Whig nominee Henry] Clay is killing himself by writing on all subjects and even to the editors of newspapers without being called on."

So, to answer the question "Who is Polk?" the general public had to refer to his public record. This is exactly as James had demanded they do: "a public man's public declarations & acts," he wrote in his one campaign sally,

> furnish the best means of learning his opinions . . . When I
> accepted the nomination . . . I fully approved and ratified
> the political creed, which was laid down by the nominating
> convention in the Resolutions which were unanimously passed
> by that body . . . The Doctrines therein, set forth, were
> such as I had entertained long before they were re-declared by
> that body.

The campaign itself was hard fought, and although James ostensibly stood aloof from it, he wrote detailed suggestions (they would take no more) to his allies throughout the nation. Local issues predominated.

One particularly ugly issue arose in New York, where a recent up-surge of European, mainly Catholic, immigration had resulted in a back-lash of "nativism." The self-proclaimed "native Americans," by which was meant those who had been born in America, engaged in attacks on those who had immigrated. Some of these attacks became bloody affairs. Justice John Catron, an old Democrat who had been appointed by Jack-son to the Supreme Court, wrote James on June 8, 1844, with sound advice: don't get involved.

> A good-deal is said about the Native American question. I think it is a very delicate one, not to be touched if to be avoided by you. Keep your [news]paper free from it, if you think with me. The Catholics are with us, & the other side will keep them so, no fear of that.

More serious because of wider import was the growing split be-tween the North and the South. James was, of course, a southerner, as were most of his close advisers and friends. Like Andrew Jackson, he watched with growing anxiety the machinations of such people as for-mer vice president John Calhoun of South Carolina who were already flirting with a states' rights position so extreme that they were willing to disband the Union. The current issue was largely one of political balance but was already given an emotional charge by the issue of slavery.

Just after his acceptance of the nomination, James's closest politi-cal friend, Cave Johnson, urged him to adopt a conciliatory posture toward the North. This was the same message, linked this time with the incorporation of Texas, he was getting from Andrew Jackson. At the time of his break with John Calhoun and the "nullifiers," Jackson had made a toast that would echo through the nation for years—"Our Fed-eral Union—it must be preserved"—and this toast was thrown back at him and at James as an argument against incorporating Texas. So on June 29, 1844, Jackson wrote to James that to preserve the Union "ef-fectually & permanently, Texas must be reannexed to the United States, the laws of the Union extended forthwith over the Oregon, which would place this Federal Union on as permanent bassis as the Rockey Mountains . . .''

Another aspect of the North-South split harkened back to an issue that had divided Jefferson and Hamilton at the beginning of the Republic: the North wanted a high tariff in order to protect its ''infant'' industries from cheap imports, while the South wanted free trade in order to exchange its produce on the most favorable terms for imports. James and the other Jacksonians saw this split not only in geographical but also in social terms: it was the rich industrialists taking money from the poor farmers. A clear stand on this issue was urgent, but it must not alienate the North, as Robert J. Walker, who later became James's secretary of the treasury, warned just a few days after the party convention. ''. . . there is but one question,'' he wrote, ''which can by any possibility defeat your election. It is the tariff.'' Walker recommended supporting a tariff that would ''supply the wants of the Government economically administered'' and protecting both industry and agriculture. James adopted the gist of Walker's proposal, what came to be called ''the Jefferson, Jackson, Van Buren and Polk doctrine,'' thereby negating its potential to split the election along regional lines.

M EANWHILE, THE WHIGS HAD NOT FORGOTTEN LEAN JIMMY, and while they also addressed these major issues—Clay took a very similar position on the tariff—they hit on various campaign ploys. First, they used their relative wealth and better organization to buy actual ownership or at least cooperation of the nearly always venal press; second, as Clay came out firmly on both sides of the ''nativism'' issue, vice presidential candidate George Dallas reported to Polk that Clay, who was a large slaveholder, was said to have pledged that if the abolitionists would vote for him and he won, ''he will emancipate all his slaves the day after his inauguration!'' Dallas was bemused by the naiveté of the public to such ploys.

In times of extreme excitement like the present, poor human nature seems capable of any absurdity; otherwise, I should not conceive it possible that such wretched tricks and stratagems could work beneficially—otherwise indeed than injuriously— for the party who resorts to them. If they are measures necessary to election, God grant that you and I may never be elected!

At another point, a rather unlikely dirty trick was also tried, accusing James's long-dead grandfather Ezekiel of treasonous conduct during the Revolution. While it may not have made much difference to the public, it hurt James deeply.

The next attack was more serious because it contained an important element of truth. It was the charge that James was "an *ultra* slaveholder," "cruel, hardhearted, and tyrannical to his slaves." James *was* a slave owner, as previous presidents from Washington through Jefferson, Madison, Monroe and Jackson had been—and as some of those who followed would be up to the Civil War. And naturally, this fact figured in the campaign. Slavery was an issue from which James could not escape. By our standards, although not those of most of his contemporaries, this was a grave offense against humanity. But the attack did not raise what we would regard as the serious issue; rather, it rested on a clever but not convincing forgery known as *Roorback's Tour*. On his tour, "Roorback" claimed to have met a slave trader who had in tow forty of James's ragged, pathetic, starving slaves with James's initials branded on their shoulders. There was no Roorback, and James never owned (or branded) forty slaves. The book had been plagiarized (with this part added) from a travel memoir by G. W. Featherstonhaugh. The account was widely quoted by the Whig press but, having been exposed as a fraud, probably redounded to James's favor and served to cover up the really serious issue of his actually owning and working slaves.

To try to jostle James into a good laugh when the electoral situation seemed unpromising, his friend Adam Huntsman, who had indirectly done James a favor in 1836 by beating Davy Crockett for a congressional seat, ended his letter of October 7, 1844, by saying, "There is a pretty strong objection to you which is well founded, as Washington, Madison & Jackson had no children. If you succeed the world will believe that the qualifications for an American President lies *all* in his head, and *none* in his Breeches."

T HE ELECTION WAS CLOSE, AND TO HIS CHAGRIN, JAMES CAR-ried neither his natal state, North Carolina, nor the state he had so long and so often represented, Tennessee. When all the votes had been counted, he had won, but the campaign nearly ruined him financially. At the end, triumphant as president-elect, he could hardly afford to rent the hotel rooms he needed in Washington before he could move into the White House. As he wrote to Cave Johnson on December 21, 1844, "You know I have no money to spend unnecessarily, and to avoid being subjected to an extravagant or enormous charge, it is necessary that a *distinct bargain* shall be made in advance." The deal he got was for "1 Public parlour, 1 Dining room. 1 Chamber. 1 office room." This was to house James and his wife, his private secretary and one other person. The arrangement also stipulated that "He is to pay no Corkage for any wines of his own he sees proper to drink." The rate was $140 for the first week and $100 for each additional week. Accommodation was also to be provided for the two servants he and Sarah took with them, William Goff, a black freedman, and his also free mulatto wife, Disley. And to get to Washington, he sought to make a virtue out of necessity by traveling ". . . in the usual mode in which other citizens do . . ." Modestly.

There is not a lot of humor in the letters James wrote and received during this period, but perhaps one lightened his mood somewhat as he set off short of cash and full of uncertainty on his awesome task. It was from a black slave who belonged to his nephew. Hired out, as was then fairly common, to work for another man as a skilled artisan, Blacksmith

Harry lived in that twilight zone between the agonies of draft-animal drudgery in the fields and the flawed freedom of the emancipated southern blacks. Making use of what little liberties as he had, Blacksmith Harry had placed bets on James's election, even though, as he couldn't help reminding James, James's record during the past four years was not good and he had lost heavily betting on him. So as he wrote on November 28, 1844,

> I have been so over Joyed at the newse of your Elevation that I have hardly . . . Eate drank slep or worked any since I heared the Glorous newse . . . I have ben betting and lousing on you for the last several years but I have made it all up now. I must tell you whate I have won on your Election & I have got near all in hand cash $25 and 11 Par Boots 40 Gallons Whiskey 1 Barrel flower & Lotts of tobacco but you must not think that I will drink the whiskey my self. No sir for I have Treated it all out in Electionaring for you through my friends who stood by me in [your past] Electionaring troble.

Every successful candidate soon learns that everyone seeks in one way or another to profit from his success. Before he had even moved in, James was warned that the White House was "the most uncomfortable barrack . . . impossible to keep it warm in cold weather" and was urged to turn it into a warehouse to store the collection that would become the Smithsonian Institution. That advice he did not accept.

But the White House had other uses. There is nothing like winning the presidency for discovering relatives! It beats even having a house on the French Riviera, as James discovered when he received a letter from Mary and Robert Atherton on November 29, 1844.

> I was Married in 1827 and now we are in possession of five Children 2 daughters and 3 Sons. My husband has always been employed in the Cotton Manfactureing as A Maneger. He is

getting tired of it. His friends and your friends has been ad-
viseing him to apply to you for An Office and we hope that you
will grant it . . . if you are A Relation of mine I intind on
going to the Big white house to see you next Summer If I live.

Whether the Athertons descended upon the White House is not recorded, but if they did not, they were practically the only visitors James
and Sarah managed to keep out.

THE INAUGURAL ADDRESS WAS ALREADY THE CEREMONIAL AND
customary way in which a president-elect announced his program,
set forth his philosophy of office and made the transition from candidate
to chief executive. James worked hard to make his an eloquent statement in which he sought to raise the sights of his audience above contemporary divisive issues to the overarching principles of the
Constitution. To his rain-drenched small audience, he emphasized that
the Constitution was "the offspring of concession and compromise,
binding together in the bonds of peace and union this great and increasing family of free and independent States." And, consistent with his lifelong beliefs, he pledged himself "to assume no powers not expressly
granted or clearly implied in its terms." Pointedly, he said, the federal
government "does not force reform on the States." But he also declared, in a statement based on an already questioned view of the white-
Protestant-only definition of humanity, that "All distinctions of birth or
of rank have been abolished. All citizens, whether native or adopted, are
placed upon terms of precise equality. All are entitled to equal rights
and equal protection."

And with another bow to Andrew Jackson, he repeated Jackson's
toast, "Our Federal Union—it must be preserved." His program was
simple—frugality in spending, compromise in politics and westward expansion.

On Texas, he came out flatly for annexation and warned third parties not to meddle in the issue but offered them the "carrot" of increased trade.

> Our Union is a confederation of independent States, whose policy is peace with each other and all the world . . . the annexation of Texas to the United States [should be seen] not as the conquest of a nation seeking to extend her dominions by arms and violence, but as the peaceful acquisition of a territory once her own . . .

And Texas was not alone.

> Our title to the country of the Oregon is "clear and unquestionable," and already are our people preparing to perfect that title by occupying it with their wives and children. But eighty years ago our population was confined on the west by the ridge of the Alleghanies. Within that period—within the lifetime, I might say, of some of my hearers—our people, increasing to many millions, have filled the eastern valley of the Mississippi, adventurously ascended the Missouri to its headsprings, and are already engaged in establishing the blessings of self-government in valleys of which the rivers flow to the Pacific.

As they stood in the pouring rain, not all his audience was pleased by his remarks. The ambassadors of Britain, France and Mexico may be excused for being dubious about James's assertion that "The world has nothing to fear from military ambition in our Government." Later, reading the text, at least one listener pointed out the painful disparity between rhetoric and reality in race relations. John N. Mars of the New York Conference of African Methodist Episcopal Zion Church wrote to say that

In looking over your Inaugural Address I find it contains two or three Sentences that I must confess that I do not understand . . . the first is, You Say, All distinctions of Birth or rank have Been Abolished . . . Did you mispeake, or did you speake what you ment? . . . The Second is, you say, that All Citizens whether native or adopted, are placed upon terms of precise Equlity. Now Sir as a candid man Bound to the Bar of God I ask is this so? You Sir will confer a greate favour on me if you will just explain this point also. The third is, you Say that, All are intitled to Equal rights and Equal protection. Sir is this a fact? If so, why Sir will you not proove it By letting my Brother and my Sister come out of your own prison house of Bondage to injoy the rights that God has given them? And this is done, then and not untill then, can I believe that you ment what you there asserted.

Forming his cabinet was the first task James faced. Because of the nature of his nomination and the way the election was conducted, he felt, as he stated to his close friend and prospective postmaster general Cave Johnson on December 21, 1844, that "I am under no pledges or commitments . . . My object will be to do my duty to the country, and I do not intend if I can avoid it, that my counsels shall be distracted by the supposed or not conflicting intents of those cliques [in the Democratic Party]." This was, at best, an idealistic assumption for which his long career in politics offered no basis. Practically everyone in the party had either a claim on office for himself or a favorite candidate to propose. They soon would press those claims relentlessly.

The disappointed presidential aspirant Martin Van Buren led the pack. Zeroing in on the highest-ranking and most prestigious appointment in the cabinet, he wrote on January 18, 1845, "For Secy of State you want, above all others consideration, a man of bland manners, good temper, great quickness of perception, industry and high personal character." Naturally, the only place to find such a man was among Van Buren's close associates in New York.

Van Buren was not alone with such helpful advice; each local political faction wished to place its aspirant for the next presidential election in a high-profile position, and in an age before the mass media, the best place to do this was in the cabinet. Recognizing this and attempting to avoid constant politicking by men who should be administering the government, James made all cabinet appointees pledge to resign if they conceived presidential or vice presidential ambitions. Probably from his days as governor, James was aware of that truism of American politics that when a president assembles his cabinet, he has all of his political rivals in one room.

Only a part of the cabinet was formed by the time he actually assumed office, but once formed, it surprisingly proved to be a hardworking, generally harmonious set of counselors upon whom James was able to, and did, depend far more than any president in our own times.

But, already in the choice of the cabinet, it became clear that he had made a serious strategic mistake in announcing that he would not seek a second term; he had done so in the hope that by promising to stand aside after 1845, the various factions in "the Democracy" would unite at least for his term of office. In fact, by removing himself from future contention, he immediately liberated them to fight one another for position in anticipation of the spoils of future victory. So, from his first day in office, he had become a lame duck.

THE CABINET WAS ONLY A SMALL PART OF JAMES'S APPOINT-ment headache. Immediately after his election and long before his inauguration, he was beset by office seekers. As he wrote in near desperation to Martin Van Buren,

The City is crowded with strangers, a large majority of whom have their own personal & selfish ends in view. After the 4th of

March [inauguration day] I will cause it to be made known that I will make no appointments whilst they remain in the City. In this way I hope to disperse the crowd, when I can act deliberately, and understandingly, upon their applications.

The deluge of office seekers was an inevitable consequence of the Jacksonian spoils system and would drive James to distraction throughout his term of office. The White House was unfenced and unguarded, James's office door was required by custom to be open and there was no one who could or would stop any intruder. Those too far away to barge into his office to plead in person wrote. In every mail came floods of letters as men staked out their own claims or warned against those of their enemies.

Today a president has a staff larger than the entire executive branch of the government in the 1840s that is charged just with vetting applications for jobs. Back then it all fell on the president's shoulders. "I have been occupied three or four hours every day," he wrote at one point, "in hearing the speeches and representations of the office seekers and their friends who pressed their claims . . ." The flood would not diminish until the very last day of his administration.

Out of the vast mass of importuning or condemning letters, one must have offered some comic relief. On hearing that "the notorious Isaiah Rhynders" was said to have been received at the White House, a clerk in Troy, New York, wrote to warn James.

Rhynders, I have known from a boy—but a few years since, he was *Cook* on board one [of] our river Sloops . . . He *purposely* got deeply in debt, failed, did not pay his creditors a farthing, removed to New York, became a *Bully* to a *Brothel* . . . His Mother is a prostitute and his Sisters *no better than they Should be.*

Appointments were not easy.

To UNDERSTAND THE PRESIDENT'S JOB, JAMES HAS LEFT US with one of the most remarkable documents of any holder of that lonely and august position, his diary. It gives almost hour-by-hour accounts of his four years of administration, and since he did not intend it for publication, it is a frank and accurate presentation of his thoughts and opinions on almost every issue and every personality he encountered. But perhaps the strongest impression one gets from reading it is that he must have had no privacy. Meals were interrupted, callers arrived without appointments at all hours of the day and until nearly midnight; during confidential conferences with senators, congressmen and even with his cabinet, casual acquaintances marched into the room, sat down and began to chat. Delegations of schoolchildren swarmed in, uninvited and unannounced, to perform little concerts or give speeches while he was trying to prepare messages for Congress. Even during the planning of the Mexican War, office seekers, people asking for alms or contributions, old friends and complete strangers, some of whom were not even American citizens, thought nothing of barging into his office and settling down to watch him work or announce and plead for their concerns. He had one butler or "messenger" whose job it was to announce people—but not to screen them or to protect him. He so infrequently closed his door that when he did, he made a special mention of the event in his diary.

And in an age with limited means of transport and communication, his only way to reach his cabinet members, with whom he met in council at least once a week and often nearly every day, was to send his private secretary (his nephew J. Knox Walker) to ask them to join him. Long delays were partially avoided because most of the cabinet were housed in virtually adjoining buildings. He had no staff other than his private secretary and, of course, no means of duplicating or processing handwritten messages except by having them laboriously written out by pen by his secretary or, in emergencies, by the confidential clerks of the departments.

Added to these problems was the need to host not only open nights when any passerby had to be welcomed in the White House but frequent dinner parties for congressmen, diplomats, the judiciary, visiting state governors, relatives and friends. He tried to keep his Sundays free for his family and church, but often he could not even do this. So his working days ran from 6:00 or 7:00 A.M. to nearly midnight at least six days a week. Even Christmas was a working day.

There were, of course, no photo opportunities, although James was the first president to be photographed. Such preservations of events or personages were laborious affairs, however, taking hours out of his daily routine, and often not succeeding. On June 16, 1846, James noted in his diary that

> Mr. Healey, the artist, requested the cabinet & myself to go into the parlour and suffer him to take a degguerryotype likeness of the whole of us in a groupe. We gratified him. We found Mrs. Madison [widow of President James Madison] in the parlour with the ladies. Three attempts were made to take the likeness of myself, the Cabinet, & the ladies in a group, all of which failed.

It was the custom that his portrait was to be painted, and miniatures had to be made for the striking of medals to be presented on ceremonial occasions, particularly to visiting Indian chiefs. He bitterly complained of these distractions, which always took several sessions of several hours each, but perhaps for vanity and certainly for custom he went along with them.

For relaxation, he mentions daily walks around the square in front of the White House, but he also recalls that during many if not most of these, which dwindled as the pressure of work mounted, he became a walking target for beggars, job seekers and congressmen with confidential concerns. Rarely, he managed a horseback or carriage ride to "take the air," such as it was in the swamps around the rather miserable village that Washington then was. He remarks in his diary entry of June 1, 1846, that "Being much wearied by my long confinement [in my office] for many months, I took a ride on horseback with my Private Secretary in the evening." Apparently, he found this relaxing and tried it again three days later, using it to call on one of the cabinet members who was sick in bed so he could consult him. In his first year in the White House, he records having gone out to dinner with a friend, a "political friend" at that, only once. On August 15, 1846, James took a carriage ride six miles into the Maryland countryside with the secretary of the navy. As he wrote in his diary, "It was the second time I had been without the District of Columbia since I came to Washington in February, 1845. In May, 1845, I visited Mount Vernon and viewed the tomb of Washington."

As he was beginning to realize, his work habits were killing him.

> My long confinement to my office has considerably enfeebled me & rendered some recreation necessary. After having looked into the laws passed by the last Session of Congress and given the necessary directions for carrying them into effect, no public interest will, I think, suffer by my absence for a few [days]. All the members of the Cabinet agreed to remain at their posts, except Judge Mason, the Atto. Gen'l, who at my request accompanied me.

Whether or not he "learned" the lesson of needing rest, he could not apply it. As late as August 15, 1848, he confided in his diary that he had not been three miles from the White House in the previous thirteen months.

James must be faulted for his inability to delegate. No competent modern executive would take it upon himself to look into the reappointment of a junior naval officer who had been convicted by court-martial and cashiered or to determine who would be postmaster of a city or town or which candidates should be accepted as cadets at West Point. James seems to have realized that his almost microscopic administration was a fault, but he didn't know what to do about it. He had no competent staff to which to delegate, but even if he had, he believed that dispensing patronage was the way to create and maintain party unity. So he simply worked longer hours and took no vacations. On December 29, 1848, a weary James wrote in his diary that

> No President who performs his duty faithfully and conscientiously can have any leisure. If he entrusts the details and smaller matters to subordinates constant errors will occur. I prefer to supervise the whole operations of the Government myself rather than entrust the public business to subordinates, and this makes my duties very great.

As with modern presidents, James had to lobby congressmen and senators for support for the bills proposed by his administration. Dozens of examples are recorded, but this one may be taken as typical. Pennsylvania senators were opposed to James's tariff bill that reduced the rate on imported iron. James asked Senator William H. Haywood of Pennsylvania to come to the White House on July 23, 1846, where for two hours he explained to him the rationale behind the bill, listened to his complaints and suggestions and then said to Haywood that

> I regarded it as the most important domestic measure of my administration, and that from all I had learned its fate would depend on his vote . . . I told him if he voted against it he would strike a severe blow upon my administration, inflict great injury on the country, and as a friend I must say to him that I thought he would ruin himself. I begged him for his own sake, for the sake of the country, and for the success of my ad-

ministration to consider well before he voted against it. He was manifestly deeply impressed with the appeal which I made to him, and left saying that he would think of it to the last moment before he voted.

The effect must have been stronger than James had realized, since two days later, Haywood resigned his Senate seat.

As James confided in his diary right after the passage of his administration's revised tariff bill on July 29, 1846,

> This great measure of reform . . . has given rise to an immense struggle between the two great political parties of the country. The capitalists & monopolists have not surrendered the immense advantages which they possessed, and the enormous profits which they derived under the tariff of 1842, until after a fierce and mighty struggle. This City has swarmed with them for weeks. They have spared no effort within their power to sway and controll Congress . . .

James had to keep close tabs on all the rumors and actions of the congressmen and senators, to attempt to win them over or defeat their apparently constant machinations, and to pass judgment on their importunities for rewards and offices. That in itself was virtually a full-time job. And unlike presidents in our times who maintain not only in the White House but in every government department and agency staffs of "congressional relations" officers, he had no one to whom to delegate such matters. The very idea of offices dealing with such matters would have then been regarded as sinister, almost "un-American."

Moral standards, if not "loose" by modern practice, were certainly different. Sexual scandals had figured in most American administrations from Washington's onward. They were not a feature of James's, but there were occasional attempts to bribe congressmen, and the executive had no way to counter the attempts except by exposure. Just after Senator Haywood resigned over the tariff issue, James was informed that "a manufacturer" had visited a senator whose vote might defeat the tariff bill (Haywood's name was not mentioned) and offered that "if it did not pass he could loan to him . . . any amount of money which he might want . . . in other words an attempt to bribe . . . I was shocked at the story, and said nothing but to express my astonishment." That was, in actual fact, about all he could have done.

How, given these diverse, all-consuming and exhausting duties, James managed to write by hand and under candlelight a daily diary— one entry of which (July 31, 1848) is approximately three thousand words—amounting in all to the equivalent of about two thousand printed pages almost surpasses belief.

M R. POLK'S WAR'' WAS ACTUALLY TWO—THE ''COLD'' war with Great Britain over Oregon and the shooting war with Mexico—and magnified all of the problems already faced by the administration, as well as raising additional ones. They were not fully understood at the time and have long since faded from the memory of most Americans, but they were of enormous importance in the growth of the country.

Essentially, the issues involved were simple: they were a continuation of the westward push that had typified American history since the beginning of the seventeenth century. Great Britain had established control (partly through its Hudson Bay Company) over an area in the far Northwest into which American settlers had moved. American settlers had also moved (by Mexican government invitation) into Mexico, which had broken away from Spain. The Americans had revolted and declared Texas an independent republic in 1836. For nearly a decade, they had maintained their independence, although Mexico had not recognized it. During that decade, the British government, eager to acquire an alternative source of cotton for its expanding mills, had been working to bring about Mexican recognition in order to prevent Texas from being absorbed into the United States. Not very much was then known about events or conditions in either the Pacific Northwest or Texas, but James and his colleagues saw the hand of Great Britain behind both.

On the "Oregon territory," James had asserted in his election campaign and in his inaugural address that the United States had a "clear and unquestionable" title. The American public agreed; even former president John Quincy Adams passed word to James that he would support him on the Oregon question.

When the British rejected out of hand the American offer of a compromise, James withdrew the offer and declined to negotiate further, telling the cabinet that

> the only way to treat John Bull was to look him straight in the eye; that I considered a bold & firm course on our part the pacific one; that if Congress faultered or hesitated in their course, John Bull would immediately become arrogant and more grasping in his demands; & that such had been the history of the British Nation in all their contests with other Powers for the last two hundred years.

The Oregon issue was quickly overtaken by the annexation of Texas. As one reads James's diary and the various state papers, it becomes clear that whatever was happening in Mexico or even in Texas (and in the unlikely event that it was accurately reported), it was "history" by the time news of it was carried to Washington.

This much was known: Texas had gained its independence in 1836, and no Mexican government had been strong enough to deal with that reality; indeed government after government was overthrown when it was accused of being soft on Texas. Beyond those two facts, everything was conjecture. The most important conjecture was that Texas was believed (we now know correctly) to be working with Great Britain to get Mexico to recognize it. The British government was represented by an active and intelligent agent who regularly moved between Texas and

Mexico. James Hamilton, Jr., a former governor of South Carolina and then a commercial agent for the Republic of Texas, wrote to James on February 23, 1845, that if Texas was not annexed by autumn, Britain would certainly arrange Mexico's recognition. Although the people of Texas wanted to be annexed, Hamilton commented, "the officers of Govt. and the ambitious Men who look to distinction beyond that which a subordinate State Govt can confer, are inimical to it."

Meanwhile, the belief was growing that Mexico would intervene militarily with results, given the lack of American military preparedness, probably similar to the disasters of 1812. Jacob L. Martin, then secretary of the American legation in Paris, wrote to James on May 17, 1845, that the "boldness of the British govt. [on the conflicts over Texas and the Oregon territory] proceeds chiefly from its confidence in its formidable means of offence, especially its steam-navy, greater than that of the world besides." He went on to comment that

> it makes me indignant to see our government accused in the English papers of a rapacious desire to rob Mexico, of one of her fairest provinces, at the very time when it is admitted that England & perhaps France, are willing to gurantee the independence of Texas, provided she consents to maintain her separate existence, which would certainly be robbing Mexico just as effectually of Texas, as the annexation. The true objection is not to taking Texas from Mexico, but adding it to the U.States.

To counter the British moves, James sent Andrew Jackson Donelson, who had been President Jackson's private secretary, to Texas to work out terms for annexation. At that point, it was rumored that Mexico was gathering a force, armed and partly paid for by the British, to invade Texas. James was keen to act to defend the outnumbered and ill-equipped Texans—he saw the annexation of Texas as *"the* great question of the times"—but until the Texas "convention" accepted the American offer of annexation, he could take no direct action. However, as he wrote Donelson on June 15, 1845, "The moment they do this, I shall regard Texas as a part of our Union . . . and not permit an invading enemy, to occupy a foot of the soil East of the *Rio Grande.*" On June 21, 1845, the Texas Congress adopted joint resolutions accepting the United States offer of annexation and calling for a constitutional convention.

James then moved in American troops under General Zachary Taylor to within striking distance of the disputed frontier. Months of relative quiet followed, but finally on May 9, 1846,

> About 6 o'clock P.M. Gen'l R. Jones, the Adjutant General of the army, called and handed to me despatches received from Gen'l Taylor by the Southern mail which had just arrived, giving information that a part of [the] Mexican army had cross to the Del Norte [i.e., crossed over the Rio Grande River], and attacked and killed and captured two companies of dragoons of Gen'l Taylor's army consisting of 63 officers & men . . . I immediately summoned the Cabinet to meet at $7^{1}/_{2}$ O'Clock this evening . . . The Cabinet were unanimously of [the] opinion, and it was so agreed, that a message should be sent to Congress on Monday laying all the information in my possession before them and recommending vigorous & prompt measure[s] to enable the Executive to prosecute the war.

The impression I get from the diary is that James wanted a war and that the Mexicans obliged him; without their attack on Taylor, it would have been hard or perhaps impossible for him to have acted. Having decided to act, James and the cabinet had to determine what the objectives were. Secretary of State James Buchanan wanted to issue a declaration that "in going to war we did not do so with a view to acquire either California or New Mexico or any other portion of the Mexican territory." James wrote in his diary on May 13, 1846,

I told Mr. Buchanan that I thought such a declaration to Foreign Governments unnecessary and improper; that the causes of the war as set forth in my message to Congress and the accompanying documents were altogether satisfactory. I told him that though we had not gone to war for conquest, yet it was clear that in making peace we would if practicable obtain California and such other portion of the Mexican territory as would be sufficient to indemnify our claimants on Mexico, and to defray the expenses of the war which that power by her long continued wrongs and injuries had forced us to wage. I told him it was well known that the Mexican Government had no other means of indemnifying us.

Baldly put, James had sanctioned America's first imperial war.

In response to his message, the House took only two hours to declare war, of which, James was told, "$1^1/_2$ was spent in reading the documents." The declaration passed the Senate by a vote of 42 to 2. But while the Congress was willing to sanction the war and congressmen were eager to obtain commissions for their friends and relatives, they were not keen to give the executive branch any more authority than absolutely necessary to prosecute it or to negotiate its end. James constantly complained in his diary that time after time his hands were tied when he might have ended the war through negotiation or with more effective military action.

AS WE HAVE PAINFULLY SEEN IN OUR OWN ERA, THERE IS A built-in tension in the American government between the civilian executive and the military; the Constitution makes clear the paramountcy of the civilians, but occasionally in our history a tension has arisen or differences of opinion have come about that have led to insubordination or even disloyalty. Up to that point in our history, the civilians had won, but all sophisticated Americans in the nineteenth century had before them the lessons of classical Rome where the civilians lost. James became convinced that such a challenge to the authority of the presidency had arisen. He believed not only that his two senior military commanders, General Winfield Scott and General Zachary Taylor, were limited and inefficient but also that they were disloyal and were conniving for the presidency. As he wrote of the one, "Gen'l Scott did not impress me favourably as a military man. He has had experience in his profession, but I thought was rather scientific and visionary in his views." As frequently in the jockeying for position between the civilian and military sides of our government, the issue focused on the "tools" the military demanded as necessary to do its job. Like all generals, Scott asked for far more than the executive was willing to give. "I did not think," James continued, "that so many as 20,000 volunteers besides the regular army was necessary, but I did not express this opinion, not being willing to take the responsibility of any failure of the campaign by refusing to grant to Gen'l Scott all he asked."

To James's consternation, Scott then decided not to go to the battlefront and wrote an insulting letter saying that the reason he decided to stay in Washington, essentially out of touch with the actual war, was that "I do not desire to place myself in the most perilous of all positions, a fire upon my rear from Washington and the fire in front from the Mexicans." Furious both at this insubordination and at the insult, James told the secretary of war to order Scott to go or he "would supersede him in command." James believed that Scott had shown that "his partisan feelings are such that he is unfit to be intrusted with the command." Scott made a sort of apology on May 26, 1846, but as James remarked, "it is too late to recal what has been done."

Logically, James should have turned to the other general officers to replace Scott, but this was not an attractive option. Scott had powerful political friends (and ambitions), and the other available general, Zachary Taylor, while a brave soldier, was, James thought, "not fit for a higher command than that of a Regiment."

Not only the generals worried him.

I find it impossible to give much attention to the details in conducting the war, and still it is necessary that I should give some attention to them. There is entirely too much delay and too much want of energy & promptness in execution on the part of many of the subordinate officers, which must be corrected.

His orders were slowly if at all carried into effect. "I find," he lamented on September 22, 1846, "that I am compelled to give some attention to these details or the movements of the army will be delayed and embarrassed."

He uncovered a strong hint of corruption in the supply department and clear evidence of inefficiency; worse, he was baffled by what seemed to him gross stupidity and wastefulness. He was told that the quartermaster general was purchasing "an immense train of baggage wagons" to carry supplies to the troops. Although neither he nor the cabinet knew much about Mexico, it was common knowledge that northern Mexico was a dry, rugged country almost devoid of roads, wholly unsuitable for wagons. Astonished, James called in the quartermaster general and suggested that, to a nonmilitary man, such an organization of supply made no sense. Was it not true, James asked, that "in all the wars in Mexico which had preceded the present, the baggage and munitions of war had . . . been transported on mules"? Yes, the general agreed, that made much more sense, but he was just doing as he was told: General Taylor had requisitioned the wagons so he was buying them. James decided to send the quartermaster general to the front.

That did little good. On March 20, 1847, he learned that the order he thought he had stopped of "the purchase & employment of thousands of wagons" was not only going ahead but that contracts had been put out to buy one thousand horses and mules to drag them. Worse, the animals were to be purchased far away north in Ohio.

> . . . this was great folly, as well as involving the country in a vast expense. I asked them why horses & mules in Mexico,

which were to be had in great numbers & which were accustomed to the climate & which could be had at one-fourth the
price which must be paid in the U.S. were not procured . . .
The truth is that the old army officers have become so in the
habit of enjoying their ease, sitting in parlours and on carpeted
floors, that most of them have no energy, and are content to
jog on in a regular routine without knowing whether they are
taking care of the public interest or not.

The military deeply resented civilian interference. General Scott
lashed out at James, referring to him in front of the army staff officers as
"Little Jimmy Polk of Duck River [Tennessee]."

Undeterred, James kept digging into all aspects of the war and took
a greater and greater role in managing it. His low opinion of the army
chiefs appeared to be confirmed when General Taylor, unauthorized, allowed a trapped Mexican army to escape with their weapons under a flag
of truce at Monterey. James was in despair: "It was a great mistake in
Gen'l Taylor to agree to an armistice," he wrote on October 11, 1846.
"It will only enable the Mexican army to reorganize and recruit so as to
make another stand." They did and the war dragged on with increasing
casualties. "I shall find it to be necessary," he wrote despairingly in his
diary, "to give more of my attention to these matters of detail than I
have heretofore had it in my power to do."

Intelligence, even of a basic kind, was also severely lacking.

Great embarrassments exist in directing the movements of our
forces, for want of reliable information of the topography of
the country, the character of the roads, the supplies which can
probably be drawn from the country, and the facilities or ob-
structions which may exist in prosecuting the campaign into
the interior of the country. Gen'l Taylor though in the country
gives but little information on these points.

So James called in everyone he heard of who had ever been in Mexico and "debriefed" them, often in front of the whole cabinet.

James personally began to set out the routes of march, numbers of troops, commanders and tactical objectives of the entire campaign. For this he has often been criticized, both by Generals Scott and Taylor and by later writers. Such controversies over logistics, tactics and strategy, as we have learned in more recent wars, are never-ending. But wars do end, and this one did, by an overwhelming thrust into the very heartland of Mexico. Following battles at Veracruz, Chapultepec and a number of now nearly forgotten sites, in which the president's younger brother, William Hawkins Polk, took part as a major of dragoons, the Americans captured Mexico City. On February 2, 1848, a treaty was signed just north of the capital, and six months later the last of the troops embarked for the United States. The United States had almost doubled in size.

GOING FAR BEYOND THE WAR ITSELF WAS THE ISSUE OF THE relationship of the Mexican War to the delicate balance of power among the states and between the states on the one hand and the federal government on the other. This issue was brought into focus and suffused by increasingly emotional opinions on black slavery. Like many of his contemporaries, James found himself caught in the dilemma, but he could not see, or refused to admit, the relationship of the issue of slavery to the Mexican War. In his diary of January 5, 1847, he had confided his opinion that

> Slavery has no possible connection with the Mexican War, and with making peace with that country. Should any territory be acquired by a Treaty with Mexico, Congress will have the full power to raise the question of slavery in it upon the organization of a territorial Government in it, or upon its admission as a state of the Union. Its introduction in connection with the Mexican War is not only mischievous but wicked. It is, more-

over, practically an abstract question. There is no probability
that any territory will ever be acquired from Mexico in which
slavery could ever exist.

But a few weeks later, on June 30, Secretary of State Buchanan
came out in opposition to the acquisition of any territory below the 32°
parallel (roughly on a line from just north of Austin westward) because
the Northern states would be unwilling "to acquire so large a country
that would probably become a slave-holding country if attached to the
U.S." In reply, James indicated that "I preferred the 26° [the parallel
running from roughly Brownsville to just north of Monterey and extending west to include most of Baja California] to any boundary North
of it, that if it was found that that boundary could not be obtained I was
willing to take 32°, but that in any event we must obtain Upper California and New Mexico . . ."

The Mexican War pinpointed the issue, but slavery increasingly divided both the general population and the political leadership. James did
not see this as an urgent moral and legal issue as we today view it; for
him and many of his contemporaries, it was an issue to be avoided. It had
already been settled in the Constitution, and doing anything to disrupt
the delicate balance there achieved, regardless of humanitarian considerations, risked destroying the Union. He deplored the willingness of both
pro- and antislavery politicians to take that risk. As he wrote in his diary
on April 6, 1847,

> The truth is there is no patriotism in either faction of the
> [Democratic] party. Both desire to mount slavery as a
> hobby[horse], and hope to secure the election of their favour-
> ite upon it . . . I now entertain a worse opinion of Mr. Cal-
> houn than I have ever done before. He is wholly selfish, & I am
> satisfied has no patriotism. A few years ago he was the author
> of Nullification & threatened to dissolve the Union on account
> of the tariff. During my administration the reduction of duties

which he desired has been obtained, and he can no longer complain. No sooner is this done than he selects slavery upon which to agitate the country, and blindly mounts that topic as a hobby[horse]. Gov. [Silas] Wright's friends in Congress as unpatriotically have shown by their course that they desire to mount the same hobby[horse] in the North and hope to be successful by their opposition to slavery. They both forget that the Constitution settles [these] questions which were the subjects of mutual concessions between the North and the South. I am utterly disgusted at such intriguing of men in high places . . .

The man who is sometimes taken to be the champion of freedom for the slaves, Congressman David Wilmot, sought to attach a rider (the so-called Wilmot Proviso, which the Republican Party would adopt in its foundation in 1854) to an appropriations bill, using the language of Thomas Jefferson in the Northwest Ordinance to prevent slavery from being introduced—Mexico had already abolished slavery—to any territories taken from Mexico, while James, a slaveholder, is often portrayed as slavery's defender. The reality is more nuanced.

James met with Wilmot and told him that he did not desire to extend slavery. For Wilmot's part, as he declared in Congress,

> I have no squeamish sensitiveness upon the subject of slavery, nor morbid sympathy for the slave. I plead the cause of the rights of white freemen. I would preserve for free white labor a fair country, a rich inheritance, where the sons of toil, of my own race and own color, can live without the disgrace which association with negro slavery brings upon free labor.

Put baldly, James was concerned with the interstate politics of the Union and Wilmot with the working conditions of whites. Both stood aloof from what we would consider the central issues of slavery, the fate of the blacks. That issue was only beginning to capture the imagination of the white population. From our perspective, we are right to condemn their moral indifference to the fate of their fellow human beings, but to understand them, we must tread warily with our moral judgments on an age that did not share them. Yet, we can also see that the Mexican War played an important role, as James feared, in events leading to the Civil War: it released the winds that "blew, and beat upon that house; and it fell: and great was the fall of it."

BESIDE THE TRAGIC ISSUE OF SLAVERY, THE QUESTION OF RELIgion increasingly gripped the American public. "Mrs. Polk being a member of the Presbyterian Church I generally attend that Church with her," James wrote in his diary, "though my opinions and predilections are in favour of the Methodist Church." But having grown up in a religiously permissive environment—one set by his grandfather Ezekiel, who was a deist—he was not baptized and joined no church officially; his diary mentions his attendance of the Dutch Reformed, Unitarian, Episcopal and Congregational as well as the Methodist and Presbyterian Churches.

When he was petitioned by the Mormons, who had been persecuted in Illinois, for permission to migrate westward, James wrote in his diary of June 3, 1846, "I told [the Mormon representative] Mr. Little that by our constitution the mormons would be treated as all other American citizens were, without regard to the sect to which they belonged or the religious creed which they professed . . . ."

James was revolted by religious intolerance from whatever source.

On October 14, 1846, a Presbyterian clergyman, "Rev'd Wm. L. McCalla," called on James to censure the administration for appointing Catholics as chaplains in the army in Mexico. James was furious.

I found him to be a fanatic, proscriptive in his religious opinions, and most unreasonable . . . I felt great contempt for

Mr. McCalla and for his religion and gave him my mind freely. I told him that, thank God, under our constitution there was no connection between Church and State, and that in my action as President of the U.S. I recognized no distinction of creeds in my appointments to office . . . I consider him either a knave without vital religion or a fanatic without reason. I have met with no man during my administration, among the numerous office-seekers who have beset me, for whom I have so profound a contempt . . . I have a great veneration and regard for Religion & sincere piety, but a hypocrite or a bigotted fanatic without reason I cannot bear.

James is best known for having added enormously to the territory of the United States by defeating Mexico and facing down Great Britain, but in some of the lesser issues he met, James left a legacy almost as important. His administration founded the Smithsonian Institution, surely one of the great cultural endowments of our society, as well as the U.S. Naval Academy at Annapolis, thus carrying forward the family's commitment over the generations to the foundation of educational institutions. On July 4, 1848, he laid the cornerstone to that towering symbol of the capital city, the Washington Monument. Having seen how difficult was communication in America, he took part in founding the United States Postal Service. And in the last act of his administration, he signed the bill, though with misgivings, creating the U.S. Department of the Interior.

Increasingly, however, he was weary of office and aware that his health was declining. At the last, he was aware that he was also losing such political power as he had exercised. In one telling entry into his diary, he described himself as "a setting sun." When an official of the State Department comptroller's office did not answer an inquiry,

although it had been more than six weeks since it had been referred to him [and] . . . was about to make some other remarks, when, feeling indignant at his conduct, I told him that I thought it probable, as I was to retire from office shortly, he regarded me as a *setting sun,* and did not deem it necessary to obey my orders.

But there were personal, even philosophical, intimations of more than political mortality. In his diary for November 2, 1847, James wrote, "I am fifty-two years old today, this being my birthday. I have now passed through two-thirds of my Presidential term, & most heartily wish that the remaining third was over, for I am sincerely desirous to have the enjoyment of retirement in private life." He tried to scotch rumors that he might run for a second term despite attempts to convince him to do so. And on the following year, he struck a somber philosophical note.

> Upon each recurrence of my birthday I am solemnly impressed with the vanity & emptiness of worldly honors and worldly enjoyments, and of [the wisdom of] preparing for a future estate. In four months I shall retire from public life forever. I have lived three fourths of the period ordinarily allotted to man on earth. I have been highly honoured by my fellow-men and have filled the highest station on earth, but I will soon go the way of all the earth. I pray God to prepare me to meet the great event.

By February 1849, he was absolutely exhausted ("worn out" would be a more accurate description, as one can see from the "degguerryotype" [see illustration] of him at this time) by

> four years of incessant labour and anxiety and of great responsibility. I am heartily rejoiced that my term is so near its close. I will soon cease to be a servant and will become a sovereign. As a private citizen I will have no one but myself to serve, and will exercise a part of the sovereign power of my country. I am

sure I will be happier in this condition than in the exalted station I now hold.

His term ended on March 3, 1848.

G OING HOME TO NASHVILLE, JAMES WAS WEARY AND WORN, and while the trip was triumphal it was also long and exhausting. Finally after an unending sequence of dinners, rallies and congregations, he virtually collapsed. Out of affection, interest and curiosity, his people thronged in upon him at every opportunity. He was both delighted and fearful.

> I have been much honoured by my countrymen and am deeply grateful to them. I may say that I regard the distinguished marks of respect everywhere shown me by the people, without distinction of political party, on my journey homeward, as the most gratifying and highest honour ever paid me by any portion of my fellow-citizens. Though fatigued & feeble . . .

Worse, it forced him to go to parts of the country then in the grip of a great epidemic of cholera. In New Orleans, along the Mississippi and even in Nashville, cholera was rampant. In the cities and towns he passed and on the riverboats and trains in which he was traveling, a number of people died in close proximity to him.

Cholera was an especially terrible disease in the nineteenth century. Little was known of the cause and nothing of a possible cure. The infected quickly became dizzy and nauseous, got violent cramps in the stomach and soon were afflicted by both vomiting and diarrhea. Unable to contain any liquid in his stomach, the victim would expel up to two gallons until completely dehydrated. Death could occur within a day of contracting the disease.

For James, this terrible end came on June 15, 1849, less than four months after he had left the White House.

THE OLD SOUTH

"We build forever"

"THE PAST IS A FOREIGN COUNTRY: THEY DO THINGS DIFFER-
ently there." That remark of L. P. Hartley is especially true of the
Old South. We would find the physical environment unfamiliar and the
society organized on principles alien to our notions of political correct-
ness. Even more distancing, the era has passed from reality into myth.

For those who looked back across the great divide of the Civil War,
as Molly Harding Polk, George Washington Polk and other Polks did,
the Old South was one of those classical epochs that transcend history. It
had not lasted just a couple of generations but an epoch. Chronology had
little meaning. Life was remembered as an unending sequence of gay and
romantic balls interspersed by grand and formal receptions. Horse
races, hunts and other demonstrations of the manly arts took up the
slack. There was no conscious imitation, but the Old South, at least in

that memory, was like the Russia and England of the same period. Great houses spaced by vast woodlands and smaller fields marched across the map. The grandeur of the Polk plantations—Rattle & Snap, Ashwood Hall, Hamilton Place, Willsgrove—was magnified when added to them was the residence of cousin James K. Polk, the White House. Cousins flocked to festivities, showed off prize horses and prided themselves on their horsemanship and gallantry. The frontier was quickly veneered by a code among the gentry. Feudalism had been re-created and chivalry flourished. Not surprisingly, the works of Sir Walter Scott were the favorite reading. Mark Twain wrote after the dreadful Civil War that Scott's popularization of knight errantry among the Southern aristocracy was "in great measure responsible for the War."

So in attempting to see and understand the Old South, we are like hikers standing on an isolated hill surveying a vast, mist-shrouded panorama. Clearly, we need guides. But even taking advantage of the eyes and actions of those of the Polk family who lived then to get a sense of the concrete, it takes a jump of imagination to relate. The faded "degguerryotyped" faces that stare out at us from albums look unlike living relatives and figures in the often charming portraits seem dressed for costumed balls; their writings sound with spelling and punctuation we no longer consider ours; diaries, letters and newspaper articles recount activities and concerns from which we have long since turned; their enjoyments amuse in ways they did not intend; and their beliefs are often the very prejudices that we have struggled to overcome. A foreign country, yes, yet in the inhabitants we find the seedbed from which we have sprung. So let us listen with a sympathetic ear even when the message is not always to our liking and look with an imaginative eye even when the mist of time is hard to penetrate.

PERHAPS THE MOST STRIKING FEATURE OF LIFE IN THE OLD South was the prevalence of sickness. The warm climate operated on stagnant or near-stagnant waters in rivers, lakes and wetlands to spread "fevers" and a variety of lethal but then unidentified pathogens. The letters of family members to one another are full of references to yellow jack, cholera, measles, smallpox and other often deadly killers. People understood as little of the causes and the cures as when the Polks first settled in the Maryland Chesapeake two hundred years earlier. As Leonidas wrote to his mother from Tennessee on July 15, 1841, "Truly in the midst of life we are in death."

"Bilious Cholera" was perhaps the most terrifying ravage, striking suddenly and horribly killing the patient, as it killed James K. Polk shortly after he had left the White House. But other, often unidentified epidemics were frequent. As Will Polk wrote to his daughter Mary on September 22, 1822, from Raleigh, "never has there been so much sickness known here & indeed it is not confined to the town, but pervades the whole upper country [killing] from 30 to 40 at least White & Black . . . Your Brothers, Hamilton, Rufus & Washington were all very sick." Smallpox was still a dread killer, although, as Mary B. Polk wrote her mother, Sarah, from Philadelphia on November 22, 1823, the use of vaccines was becoming more common. Even relatively minor illnesses for which we now have a variety of over-the-counter medicines were baffling. Sicknesses seemed to contemporaries to transmute themselves from one cause to another. As Leonidas, then a young student, wrote to his father, Will, on July 31, 1822 from Chapel Hill, "Henry Potter was taken sick soon after he came to this place with the Billious Fever from eating too much fruit it was thought, it has turned to the Typhus fever, and . . . they have nearly given him out several times . . ."

And, bad as disease was, it was often the doctor whom we would find most frightening. In attacking what he thought was the ailment, he often weakened and sometimes killed the patient. Listen to Leonidas again on the common remedy for nearly everything—bleeding. "Jim was taken sick on Friday last with pains in his head, side and back, and with slight fevers . . . [I] got Barr to bleed him, but he continued to get worse . . ."

The "Upper" South was, relatively speaking, healthy; it was in the

"Deep" South, and particularly in Louisiana, that death seemed often to lurk in the verdant gardens just beyond the spacious verandas. What shape it would take seemed almost whimsical, but rarely was it far away. And no sooner was one ravage apparently beaten back than another appeared. On July 9, 1849, the by-then-bishop Leonidas wrote his sister Susan from Bayou Lafourche, Louisiana,

> during the presence of the disease [we were] absolutely so occupied as hardly to have a moment for anything but attention to the sick and dying . . . such a visitation must be seen in order to be realized. Of all the population on my place white and black amounted to between 360 or 70 I suppose not more than say 50 who did not have the disease. Of this number we lost 70 of all ages, 25 children, 29 men and 16 women . . . I had also two or three slight attacks at home after the attack I had in N[ew] O[rleans].

Then came what they called the black vomit. On October 2, 1855, Leonidas wrote from New Orleans—then regarded as the most unhealthy city in America—about the "presence and ravages of our Southern Epidemic. The character of the fever this year," he wrote,

> has been full as bad as in '53, and the mortality would have been as great had their been material. The number of cases of black vomit has been unusually large. But three years in succession has left comparatively few unacclimated. The opinion used to prevail that our creole population was exempt, but not so with this later form of fever. Nativity is no longer a protection. I heard the other day of a child only 18 hours old which died of black vomit. Indeed the season has been remarkable for the number of cases among children. Two of my city clergy— the only two not acclimated—have been down with it and have recovered, and the wife of another also. Four of my ser-

vants, and two of my daughters have been ill of it, and have escaped, and my wife has just had a very violent attack but is
now out of danger.

The wealthier people preferred to live in the countryside. For
many, it was only an aesthetic preference, but it worked to their advantage in terms of health, even though the causes of the various "plagues"
were not identified. Rural living was far cleaner than city living simply
because people were farther apart. As people were packed closer and
closer together, privies (from *privé,* the French word for "private")
ceased to deserve the name. There was no available means to prevent the
contamination of the water supply by sewage; so diseases, especially
cholera, were endemic and chronic. Where a river ran through or by a
town, as usually was the case, it was indiscriminately used as a source of
drinking water and a means to dispose of filth. New Orleans was the
worst because its hot, humid climate fostered the luxuriant growth of
pathogens in stagnant pools and languid streams, but even relatively tem-
perate cities like Philadelphia and New York suffered devastating on-
slaughts of cholera and other epidemics.

Because horse-drawn vehicles were common, city streets were
often covered with layers of manure. What the horses did not contribute
the people did. Trash and even ordure were routinely thrown out of
windows and doors because there was often no other way to get rid of
them. And scattered throughout most cities and towns were all sorts
of small workshops, many of which billowed soot and smoke and some
of which, particularly slaughterhouses and tanneries, gave off noisome
odors and sent forth squadrons of flies. With little concern paid to any
public service, especially sanitation, such cleaning as was done was the
role of feral pigs. On his tour of America, Charles Dickens was fascinated by "these ugly brutes" who roamed freely, eating refuse and also
occasional dead, dying or just drunk citizens. At least one city, Charleston, was tidied by flocks of buzzards.

Partly for health, no doubt, towns grew slowly and sparsely. Leonidas Polk was surprised in 1839 to find the then frontier town of Little Rock "much in advance of my expectations. There is a population of 1500 or 2000." Its growth was exceptional. Even a generation later, in 1860, fewer than eight people of each one hundred southerners lived in towns of more than four thousand, and five of the southern states had not a single town with as many as ten thousand people.

It wasn't only city living that constituted a health hazard. Few people bathed often. The poorer people wore the same clothes until they literally fell off their backs. In the South, slaves were usually provided with two outfits yearly and had few facilities for bathing or for washing their clothes. Among free whites, soap, when used at all, was so harsh that its use was usually restricted to clothes rather than bodies. Even for babies, it was common for diapers to be merely dried before being put on again. In the warm climate, the result can be imagined.

Without running water, there could be no inside toilets. Chamber pots were standard equipment in all living quarters, and borrowing from European custom, they spread to the dining rooms of the great houses. On her return in 1859 from a grand honeymoon trip to Paris, Mary Polk Yeatman (a granddaughter of General Will Polk) shocked her family's sense of decorum when she unpacked a French china dinner set: it was found to contain "twelve small, individual chamber pots for the gentlemen's use after the ladies had retired from the table." The custom of women retiring from the dining room after dinner (which seems to us today so stilted and "sexist") and the now unfashionable massive sideboards both had utilitarian purposes in an age without indoor toilets.

Although indoor toilets were almost unknown, some of the great houses like Rattle & Snap, the house of Will's son George Washington Polk, had rudimentary indoor plumbing for bathing. That was a prerogative of the rich, but it did not effectively set them apart from the less privileged. Indeed, one of the many ironies of what we now refer to as segregation was that the wealthiest of the whites were in constant and intimate contact with black slaves who prepared their food, nursed their babies, often slept in their rooms and, evidently, often gave birth to their mulatto children but who had little or no access to modern bathing or toilet facilities.

Finally, beyond wealth, race, social status and manner of living, flies and mosquitoes made all men equal. Because food was prepared in the open or in cookhouses without screens, flies acted as ambassadors from the manure piles and privies to kitchens, and mosquitoes brought the swamps into every bedroom however elegant. But compared to living in towns, country living was pure pleasure.

That is, except when one had an accident. Then, there was no advantage to country living. Today we would regard as nearly criminal anyone being forced to undergo the pain experienced by Molly Harding Polk's Aunt Patsy, her grandfather Harding's sister, when as a result of a broken leg she suffered amputation without anesthetics. As she laconically wrote in her "Reminiscences of a Pioneer in Louisiana," "my suffering was only known to my God and myself." And in his youth, about the same time, James K. Polk underwent a gallbladder operation, also of course without anesthetics. Faced with these and other terrors, our ancestors showed a numb fortitude or silent resignation that is almost beyond our ken. Resignation was often the only practical approach to the accidents and tribulations of life. As Leonidas wrote a fellow clergyman on being faced with yet another epidemic, "We have . . . put our trust in God, and face the danger at once."

Less lethal but more constant and painful was the tooth and gum disease that afflicted practically all nineteenth-century Americans. As one social historian has remarked, "Hundreds of thousands of Americans had at least some of their teeth badly rotted, a source of chronic pain and foul breath to many, with extraction its only cure." Consequently, hollow-jawed faces peer out at us from the early daguerreotypes, looking almost as drawn and as alien to us as Third World famine victims in modern photographs. Even young people, like Will's daughter Mary, endured "operations" to relieve the pain. Will wrote Mary on July 27, 1822, sending her "money to pay the Dentist for the operation made on your teeth; tho' I think you had better be careful not to make a very free use of the powder." One wonders what that powder could have been, perhaps opium to cut down on the pain. There wasn't much else.

Teeth could be pulled, but for really serious diseases, it was the patient who had to be extracted. Kipling echoed the advice of many American doctors when in one of his poems on India, he had an English soldier speak of being "safe out 'ere." Knowing the dangers of their own localities, doctors were apt to suggest travel to some other area as the most likely cure for almost any sickness. As a young man, Leonidas was sent off first to Kentucky to overcome some Tennessee malady and then, when he was thought to have another undiagnosed but serious malady (which may have been "consumption," or tuberculosis), his doctor urged him to drop everything and immediately take ship for Europe. Believing he had only a few months to live, he rushed to New York, from which on August 1, 1831, he sailed.

The journey could hardly be described as medicinal: for nineteen of the stormy twenty days he spent on the ship to Le Havre, he was violently seasick; then he entered a Paris in the midst of revolution; after a trip through Holland, Switzerland and Italy, he returned to Paris, where he, along with thousands of French people, caught the cholera.

Paris was considered, as James K. Polk, then a congressman, was informed, "the great reservoir of science of Europe and I might say of the world . . . [and] There are at this present time between two & three hundred Americans in Paris, the majority of whom are students of medicine." But neither the young Americans nor the more august French medical men treated Leonidas. Almost a year after he had left, he returned to America, chastened by what he had seen and thinking no more about the mysterious illness (or diagnosis) that had sent him on his wanderings. There may have been something to travel, after all.

EDUCATION WAS ANOTHER MAJOR REASON FOR TRAVEL. DE-spite the rigors of voyaging on the Atlantic, many southern families sent their children to study in England or France. One group of in-laws of the Polks offers a common example. As soon as he could afford to do so, Colonel Philemon Hawkins devoted himself to the task of educating his sons but found that "the patrons of literature were so few and seminaries of learning so scarce, that there was not a classical school in all this country, to which he would send his first two sons . . . Under such circumstances, he concluded to send them to Scotland." The boys, perhaps hearing of the delights of ocean passage in sailing ships, were unwilling; so "he sent them to Princeton College, which seminary was at that time, owing to the great want of intercourse, such as is now in use, by stages and steamboats, almost as difficult of access as many of the European Colleges."

The lack of suitable local institutions pushed generation after generation of Polks into the creation of educational institutions. General Thomas set the pace by founding a small school just before the American Revolution. Will took up the cause with another school and the University of North Carolina, and Leonidas would later found a girls' seminary and the University of the South at Sewanee, Tennessee. In between, while in Congress James struggled for the creation of a free public school system supported by federally controlled lands and, as president, founded the U.S. Naval Academy at Annapolis. Their efforts were outstanding, but the quest for education was an unending struggle for all southerners.

Culturally, the Old South lagged behind the rest of the nation. The 1850 census shows that only eight out of ten native whites were literate, whereas in the North practically everyone could read and write. By digging into such figures, we get another picture of the split between the small farmers and the gentry. The 46,274 "planters," defined in the census of 1860 as those who owned twenty or more slaves, were completely literate and more likely to have attended college than men of any other part of the country. But men of the South were less likely to study science or technology than their northern counterparts and more apt to focus their intellectual interests on the classical world.

The image of the classical world gripped the imagination of most educated Americans in the century between the Revolution and the Civil War. We see this in the political dimension in the discussions that surround the framing of the Constitution and, later, in reading tastes and literary allusions. Perhaps the most extreme example is provided by Governor Charles Polk of Delaware.

A member of the branch of the family that had never left the Chesapeake, he was the son of Judge Charles Polk of Sussex. He was born in 1788 and was twice governor of Delaware, from 1826 to 1828 and 1836 to 1838. A Federalist, he was particularly ''classical'' or ''Roman'' in his tastes and interests; when he died, one of his obituaries pointed out that

> His power of memory was remarkable . . . . He could repeat
> by rote nearly the whole of Virgil, Horace and Livy, in Latin,
> and Xenophon's ''Anabasis'' and ''Memorabilia'' and ''Thu-
> cydides'' in Greek. A few weeks before his death he repeated
> without error, either in Latin or English, Cicero's first oration
> against Cataline.

Charles was a prodigy, but many men of the privileged class not only read Greek, Latin and Hebrew but had a familiarity with the classics that is rare in our time.

In contrast, little was done to educate women, and less to educate the slave population. Indeed, as Charles Dickens noted during his trip to America, ''there are laws against instructing slaves, of which the pains and penalties greatly exceed in their amount the fines imposed on those who maim and torture them . . .'' It was the rare slave who, before the end of the Civil War, was literate. Yet, as European visitors noted, it was not uncommon for a black or mulatto "mammy" to teach the white children in her care to read.

Much instruction took place at home, where it was common to find an imported governess or tutor, as in contemporary English, European and Russian aristocratic houses. George Washington Polk got his first education at Hamilton Place in this manner from a Mrs. Turnbull, a severe woman who claimed Huguenot ancestry and from whose strict attentions and demands for memorizing and reciting poetry George would flee to the loving arms of his black mammy. Many of the governesses were, as Sir Charles Lyell found on his visits to the Old South, either from England or from the North.

Women were given opportunities for education, but the offering was generally meager. "Female academies," like the ones to which many of the Polk women went, focused the attention of their pupils on the "practical" arts of homecraft and entertainment with not much more emphasis on literacy than was required to read the Bible and the then wildly popular romantic novels. For example, Will sent his daughter Mary to what would later be called a finishing school in Philadelphia run by a lady of considerable pretensions but rudimentary attainments. Mary's task was to acquire only what would make her a suitable wife and mother. Will made that clear in a letter to her on July 1, 1823.

> I have come to the conclusion that the study of Phylosiphy, astronomy & chemistry by young ladies is really nothing more than [word unclear] waste of time; and wish you not to loose any of your time in acquiring a further knowledge of them or any of them; but that you fill the space that they would occupy in the study of gramor, Geography, Mathmatic, Belllettre & Historical reading with French . . . By doing [word lost] you will be enabled to give more time to the [word lost] painted to make yourself a greater proficient in them all, as well as in Musick.

A limited role was laid out for women, and for that, they needed only limited skills. Mary was expected to learn to play the harp and piano, to do embroidery and to carry on an interesting conversation but certainly not to cross the line into serious affairs. It was a relatively rare young woman who, like the daughter, also called Mary, of Mary's brother Lucius, discovered a talent—in her case painting—and pursued it into what amounted virtually to an academic career. After marrying Henry Clay Yeatman, that Mary went off on the Grand Tour of museums, palaces and antiquities sites not only in Europe but also in the eastern Mediterranean, becoming in her day perhaps the best-traveled American woman.

The cultural horizon of most southern men and virtually all women was far more constricted. Books remained relatively rare, and most newspapers were little more than collections of public announcements interspersed by occasional political tracts. With travel difficult, tedious and occasionally dangerous, intellectual and social intercourse remained local.

VAST EMPTY AREAS SEPARATED PLANTATIONS AND TOWNS. Even after most of the fertile bottomlands in western areas had been settled for a generation or more, the hill country and much of the wetlands along the rivers remained vacant; so the cultivated land resembled islands in a wider sea. Throughout the Old South, separation was a major fact of life. Even neighbors were often several hours or a daylong carriage or horseback ride away; family members in neighboring states were rarely seen and were virtually out of contact for months or even years. The mails were slow, unpredictable and expensive. Correspondents often complain of missing letters. Usually it was just annoying, but occasionally was more serious. When George Washington Polk decided to get married in Tennessee, he had to profusely apologize in a letter dated November 26, 1840, to his mother, then in North Carolina, for being unable to communicate in time to get her approval.

As the frontier was pushed westward, the new lands were even more lightly settled than those farther east. Although much of Louisiana had long been settled by the French and Spanish, much of the Mississippi valley hinterland remained under Indian control until shortly before the Civil War. Molly Harding Polk's Aunt Patsy took eight weeks to go down the river from Tennessee. As she remarked in her diary,

> We were frequently annoyed by the Indians when landing at evening, which we were always compelled to do [to avoid running aground]. All on the left of the Mississippi was owned by the Chickasaw and Choctaw Indians. Where Memphis and Vicksburg [now] are was then Chickasaw Bluff and Walnut Hills . . . We had considerable trouble, after leaving the Mississippi, passing through bayous and lakes. Many places [in Louisiana] looked as if a boat had never been there before . . .

A few years later, Leonidas was made "missionary bishop" of the areas that would become Alabama, Mississippi, Louisiana and Arkansas. The area was not only vast; it was largely inaccessible or accessible only on horseback. As he lamented to a fellow churchman on August 10, 1840, it

> would require *two years of incessant active labour* to *visit* as a Bishop ought to visit the field assigned him, without one day of rest intervening. It is in extent about equal to all of France, the surface exceedingly rough and the facilities of communication off the river wretched. I have often felt strongly, that a Miss[ionary]. B[isho]p ought not to have a family. He should be literally married to the church.

His first foray, a five-thousand-mile venture on horseback, foot and riverboat, was not only dangerous and exhausting but dispiriting: the settlers were hostile. "We have never had any preaching here, and we don't want any," said one man, while a more modest Texan urged Leonidas to "go back, go back; we are not worth saving!"

Faced with the challenge of space, as they moved west from the Atlantic coast, settlers set up that distinctive feature of southern and frontier societies, plantations. Many of these were simply small homesteads farmed and maintained by only one family, occasionally aided by one or more black slaves, while others, like medieval English manors, were huge and comprised autarkic societies in which scores or even hundreds of slaves labored and lived. Big or small, they were, indeed at first had to be, virtually completely self-sufficient, since they had little access to outside sources of supply. Only from cities could specialists be imported to make clothes, process food, shoe animals, construct buildings and make and repair tools; in the rural areas, all these and many other functions had to be done on the spot. Small farmers had to be jacks-of-all-trades, but on the larger plantations, specialized skills were fostered among the slaves. Some men proved to be better at blacksmithing and some women sewed better than others. The prudent owner encouraged the growth of skills. In his will of August 1833, Will Polk bequeathed several slaves, indicating their professions: Jordan, Jim, Joe, Charles, Stephen and Austin were listed as carpenters, Humphrey as a weaver and shoemaker, Harry a mason and Parlom a blacksmith.

Sometimes the owners allowed their more skilled slaves to set up virtually independent businesses, as Andrew Jackson Polk did with his skilled blacksmith, "Uncle" Josh. But, often, since the owners of nearby or neighboring plantations were kinsmen, they easily fell into the habit of borrowing the skilled labor of one another's slaves, as Will's sons did in building and running their plantations.

It would be a mistake to think of plantations in primarily economic terms. True, they were supported by the growing of crops and the raising of animals; they even manufactured clothing, tools and other goods, mainly for support of the inhabitants, and some even engaged in fairly sophisticated industry or mining. But particularly in the area of Tennes-

see where most of the Polks lived, owning a plantation was a social imperative, the embodiment of worldly success. So important was this
imperative that even when agriculture ceased to be economically viable,
the landed gentry refused, at ruinous cost to themselves, to give up their
lifestyle. This lifestyle may be taken as fixed between roughly 1820,
when Will and Ezekiel moved their sons and daughters to Tennessee,
and 1861, when the Civil War began the process of destruction. The
high point was reached in the 1850s. Thus, the entire era of what I have
called the Old South, one of the two mythic periods—seconded by the
Wild West—of the American experience, lasted only about two generations.

Three plantations held in the Polk family or by close relatives may
be taken as typical of the great estates. They not only give us something
of a picture of the Old South but are important in two other respects.
One is parochial: each generation of Polks was afflicted with an "edifice
complex." When names of the members of each generation tended to
be forgotten or confused, the names of their houses remained. They began with White Hall on the Chesapeake, ran through the White House
in North Carolina and would continue in Tennessee and elsewhere down
into the twentieth century. Nor was this just a Polk family endeavor: it is
impossible to think of George Washington away from Mount Vernon or
Thomas Jefferson apart from Monticello. Aspiring and wealthy Americans of their times built themselves into the landscape on as grand a scale
as they could afford, or, indeed, far beyond it. The houses dominated
the people, so that each generation overspent itself in creating or recapturing the memory and image of a grand lifestyle. They all anticipated
and took to heart the admonition of the great English art critic John
Ruskin, who wrote, "When we build, let us think that we build for
ever."

The building of Rattle & Snap was begun in 1845 about seven miles
outside of Columbia, Tennessee, on a tract of land given to George W.
Polk by his father, Will. The name has a curious history. According to
family legend, Will won some 5,648 acres from the governor of North

Carolina in a "bean" (dice) game, so he called it after the throwing of the dice. Will then divided the land among four of his sons; George got about fifteen hundred acres and called his plantation by the name of the whole plot. The house was built on an elevation, a quarter of a mile from the main carriage road in a park of oak, elm and walnut trees. The architect is unknown, but construction was carried on almost entirely by black laborers, and the brick, stone and lumber were made, quarried or cut and shaped on the plantation.

The front facade of the house is dominated by ten Corinthian columns. They were the major imported items, being brought in sections by boat from Cincinnati to Nashville and from there by ox wagons to Columbia. In the architectural taste of the period, the columns were a statement of the notability or pretension of the owner. Their importance is attested by the fact that they cost the then almost astronomical sum of $40,000, or roughly as much as all the rest of the house. Resting on huge stone pillows, they rise twenty-six feet to wooden capitals decorated with cast-iron acanthus leaves. And they massively contribute to the view of the house from the highway, which is one of the most dramatic in the Old South. It is fitting that Rattle & Snap is now a National Historic Landmark (see illustration).

The interior was made for gracious living and lavish entertaining. Beyond the spacious entrance hall were large drawing and dining rooms and a library. The main part of the house aims at the classical proportion of six-to-five and aggregates 3,564 square feet (an ell adds an additional 1,080 square feet). The second floor of the same proportions contained not only four bedrooms but a ballroom and the great innovation of the period, an inside bathroom. One bathtub that survived into the 1930s was fashioned from a huge wooden block lined with lead into which water was conveyed from the outside in lead pipes. Perhaps the most interesting feature of the house was a miniature railway used to bring supplies into the vast cellar.

Said to have been even more elaborate than Rattle & Snap was the neighboring plantation of Ashwood Hall, which was built by Leonidas in

1836 and later bought by his brother Andrew Jackson Polk. The main house, set in a two-hundred-acre park, was roughly handled during the Civil War and then, after having been unoccupied for many years, was destroyed by fire in 1874 (see illustration).

Closer to Nashville, Belle Meade was the pride of the Harding clan. Like the Polks, with whom they intermarried—Molly Demoville Harding married James H. Polk—they were already an old "American" family, having settled in Virginia about 1650. The first Hardings arrived in Tennessee just after the Revolution, and, like the Polks, they arrived in force. Five brothers settled in the area around Nashville of whom John Harding, like Will Polk, was an avid land purchaser. In some twenty-nine transactions carried out before 1842, he added to his original plot of 250 acres to create a farm of 3,500 acres, and from a "double log cabin" he went on about 1810 to build the great house of Belle Meade.

Molly Harding Polk was the granddaughter of the youngest son, Thomas. She spent a part of her childhood at Belle Meade. For her, it was the embodiment of the myth of the Old South. As she remembered her days there, she was proud that "Five presidents were entertained there besides congressmen, judges, generals, artists, actors and actresses, historians and the Grand Duke Alexis . . . with whom I ate breakfast."

The Hardings vied with the Polks for the title to the best horse stud in America; to cap their claim to the accolade, they also created a deer park of several hundred acres on which, in 1859, there were some two hundred deer, twenty buffalo and a number of elk. By all accounts, particularly by its numerous foreign visitors, Belle Meade was one of the great showplaces of America.

St. John's Church was the inspiration of Leonidas Polk. When he moved to Tennessee, he carved out a plantation from lands given him by his father, Will, but he was ordained as an Episcopal minister in 1831. Thereafter, he held religious services regularly in his house, Ashwood

Hall, for the members of his family, his neighbors and the resident black communities. When the congregation grew too large for his house, he determined to build a church. He got his brothers and his mother to contribute land, money, supplies and equipment. Then, as he wrote to his mother in 1839, "We put all in hands [of the slaves] to make brick, put them up, do the carpentry, plastering etc. etc." Clay for the bricks and wood for the beams and furniture came from the plantations. Skills grew in the performance of the tasks: a mason learned on the spot or, as Leonidas thought, was guided by a vision. The result was the family church, which was consecrated in 1842. In 1849, perhaps a typical year, forty-seven blacks and ten whites were baptized, while nine whites and three blacks were buried in the adjoining graveyard, in which generations of the family and friends, white and black, have been laid to rest.

PRIMITIVE COMMUNICATIONS AND THE LACK OF PUBLIC FACILI-ties emphasized the already ingrained heritage of the frontier to give rise to "southern hospitality." Sometimes with curious consequences, as appears in another of Molly Harding Polk's stories—of Jean Lafitte, the pirate. She heard it from her Aunt Patsy. The story began on a very stormy night when Aunt Patsy's brother, Molly's grandfather, was having a family party at their plantation in Louisiana. As Molly wrote,

> The young people . . . were having a good time dancing and playing cards when suddenly the knocker at the front door sounded. Everything stopped, for a visitor on such a night was a great surprise since it had been raining all the evening and the roads were almost impassable . . .
>
> Uncle Martin went immediately to the door to find a stranger dripping and cold seeking shelter from the storm, saying he was lost. He was taken in and given dry clothing. After which Uncle Martin viewed him and talked to him for a

few minutes. Finding him interesting he concluded to invite him into the drawing room since he did not know what else to do with him.

When he entered the door he said, "Ladies, this is our friend . . ." The man added, "Mr. Smith." He was perfectly at home having all the society airs and graces, so the evening was all the more enjoyable for the novelty.

Of course, he was discussed at bedtime for all realized there was a secret that he was hiding. When morning came and the man servant took him his cup of black coffee, the stranger was gone; but there was a note of thanks for the wonderful hospitality.

After a time he was forgotten, but the after years revealed his identity. Uncle Martin was sailing for South America (possibly Cuba), and his ship was overtaken by pirates. All on board were made to walk the plank except himself. My uncle thought his time had come, but instead a sailor touched him on the arm and said, "The captain would have you to come to his cabin."

He was waved to a seat by the captain and after a moment was asked, "Did you ever see me before?" My uncle replied, "I think not." "Yes you have; look well. I am the man you took into your home the stormy night and was treated so royally some years ago in Louisiana. You saved my life, and I am saving yours." He landed him in a small boat in New Orleans while his ship weighed anchor further out.

After two or three years there was a note saying, "I am sending you and your noble wife a box of china; the history will follow." Laffitte went to Cuba on a filibustering expedition under General Lapazz. He was captured and sent to Spain in chains, so I suppose he was executed or died in prison. We never heard the history of the plate, but I have it.

Reading George Washington Polk's "Reflections and Reminiscences" on life in the Old South conjures a whiff of what are, perhaps curiously, the better-known contemporary Russian stories and novels because in the Old South as in Russia the rural life was centered on plantations farmed by servile populations. George might, indeed, have been writing notes for Turgenev to use in *A Sportsman's Sketches*.

George's mother, like so many women of that era, died in childbirth; so he was raised by a mammy named Jinny who is buried beside several of George's brothers and sisters and his father and mother in the family graveyard at St. John's Church in Ashwood.

Like all the young men of that period, George's life centered on the delights of country living, horseback riding, hunting, fishing and walking in the woods that then abounded in middle Tennessee.

As he grew older—he was just fourteen when the Civil War began—he began first to observe and then to take part in the activities of the older people. In visiting one another to gossip, play whist in front of the fire on long winter evenings and dance, friends, relatives and neighbors became so entangled in a skein of "kissing cousins" that telling them apart became itself a parlor game. As George wrote, "It was rare indeed during the summer months, for the house to be without its capacity of refined, charming and attractive guests. The tables were always supplied with all the luxuries obtainable, and in abundance, most of the fare being produced on the plantation, and prepared by excellent cooks . . ."

For all the Polks, it was the family—what sociologists would call the extended family—that was important. And the children were never made to feel apart. Unlike children in contemporary English great houses, they were included in all activities. So George's account draws on personal observation.

Among the Polks, singing was a favorite pastime in which, with few distractions and, of course, no radio or television, everyone joined. Often it was spontaneous and casual, but on Sundays at church it was the black people who were outstanding; they were already justly famous for their performances of spirituals. Music did not stop there. Dancing parties, with quadrilles, cotillions, lancers, contra dances (originally known in England as country-dances) and the Old Virginia Reel, were favorites. The music was furnished by black musicians, often playing only a violin, triangle, tambourine and flute, but playing with great gusto and no little skill as they "prompted" the dancers in a loud voice.

Pleasures were simple and without much variation, so all the more anticipated were the frequent fairs. "First Monday" was held at the neighboring town of Columbia, and to it people flocked in carriages, buggies, on horseback and on foot from all over the state to trade animals, swap news and amuse themselves. As George wrote,

> The "Square" which surrounds the Court-House is thronged, also the four streets leading into it for a distance of about two hundred feet. Here is the place where everybody meets everybody else, and is the rallying ground for all of them, for the transaction of business, discussion of crop prospects, local gossip, local and national politics, bargaining, selling and buying; groups of men gather here and there, now separating, now forming new ones. The political office seeker avails himself of the crowds to announce his candidacy for the office to which he aspires, or wage a friendly campaign, confident of a respectful hearing. The merchants are overwhelmed with business, their shops are crowded with customers, and extra clerks have their hands full.

In the early autumn, First Monday gave way to a far grander event: the weeklong county fair, which was a combination of social gathering, trade fair, music festival, stock show and amusement park. George was thrilled by "the usual side-shows, among which I recall the Siamese Twins, the two-headed girl, and other monstrocities, revolving swings the forerunner of the modern Ferris wheel, quack Doctors, patent medicine vendors, great barrels of drinking water, restaurants, lemonade, ginger cake and cider stands and many other catch penny schemes.''

They were exciting, but for each family an even greater day came with the wedding of a favorite daughter. George lovingly describes several, but, for the Polks, the biggest of all was the one of his mother and father at the White House when Andrew Jackson gave away the bride.

Mary Eastin, the granddaughter of Rachel Jackson's brother, Colonel John Donelson, was the favorite niece of Andrew Jackson and as his hostess went with him to the White House. There, on April 10, 1832, after a whirlwind courtship, in which she was literally snatched away from her then fiancé, she married Will's thirty-year-old son, Lucius.

Andrew Jackson was absolutely delighted at the prospect of her marriage, and although by that time in somewhat straitened circumstances, due to his heavy expenditures on the campaign and running the White House, he went all out to make the event spectacular. First, he sent Mary off on a shopping spree for her trousseau. She really splurged: $11 went for a white satin hat (with an additional $1 for the box to put it in) and $2 for a wreath of orange blossoms to cap it.

But what really astonished even him was the program he undertook to beautify the dilapidated White House. First, he virtually reversed the building by erecting the north portico on Pennsylvania Avenue, which then became the main entrance (as it is today; before then the main entrance was on the south). To remind himself and his guests of Tennessee, he planted the magnolia trees that still bloom in the garden. Then, to provide a suitable interior setting, he spent the then enormous sum of $10,000 just to decorate the room in which the wedding was to take place, buying five hundred square yards of carpet and fixing above the entrance door twenty-four gilded stars representing the members of the Union.

Knowing his people well, he must have worried about what they would do to the carpet, so he also bought twenty spittoons to be placed within easy range of the guests. That was a prudent investment because at that time practically every American male chewed tobacco and spat streams of tobacco juice. Chewing tobacco was a national addiction that astonished (and revolted) European visitors. On his tour of the United States, Charles Dickens was particularly dismayed.

> As Washington may be called the head-quarters of tobacco-tinctured saliva . . . the prevalence of those two odious practices of chewing and expectorating . . . soon became most offensive and sickening. In all the public places of America, this filthy custom is recognized. In the courts of law, the judge has his spittoon, the crier his, the witness his, and the prisoner his; while the jurymen and spectators are provided for, as so many men who in the course of nature must desire to spit incessantly. In the hospitals, the students of medicine are requested, by notices upon the wall, to eject their tobacco juice into the boxes provided for that purpose, and not to discolour the stairs . . . I was surprised to observe that even steady old chewers of great experience, are not always good marksmen, which has rather inclined me to doubt that general proficiency with the rifle, of which we have heard so much in England. Several gentlemen called upon me who, in the course of conversation, frequently missed the spittoon at five paces . . .

How much damage was done to the new rugs we are not told, but the affair ended on a high note: it was a very proud President Jackson who accompanied his niece down the aisle. Mary and Lucius then returned to Tennessee and moved into Hamilton Place. There they had twelve children (including two sets of twins), and, perhaps not surprisingly, Mary died in childbirth in 1847.

ABOUT A MILE AWAY FROM HAMILTON PLACE WAS A "WIDE place in the road" where the post office, country store, doctor's office, blacksmith shop and tollgate were located. The tollgate, which repaid the association that built the highway, was attached to the front porch of the keeper, who doubled as the postman. This is where the big event of the day happened—the arrival of a four-horse stagecoach that brought the mail. Not much mail arrived, but all the neighbors sat around to hear the latest gossip. It was a welcome break in the routine, but, at least in memory, it was the lush countryside in which everyone took delight. Listen to the words of George Washington Polk.

> How well I recall the ever welcome days of spring-time, the most attractive season of the year, when the air is ladened with the fragrance from the blossoming fruit trees, when the leaves on the forest trees are budding, the flowers in the old garden unfolding their leaves, and the evening chirp of the Katydid is heard on every hand, all heralded by the songs of the birds returning from their winter flights . . . The great pear tree which stood in the old garden was most popular with the youngsters. I do not think I have anywhere eaten fruit of such delicious flavor as this tree produced.

It is a shibboleth of our times that "development" equates to industrialization. At least some people in the early-nineteenth-century South thought so too. One of the most remarkable was Sarah, the wife of Will Polk. I say remarkable not only because she foresaw the importance of a revolution in transportation and communication but especially because such foresight and the actions that followed it were not then expected in a woman.

Women in the South have been termed "steel magnolias." Sarah Hawkins Polk may be taken as a good example of these two apparently contradictory qualities. Famous as a gracious hostess, devoted wife and attentive mother, she was trained like all aristocratic young women to play the harp, converse in French and discuss "feminine" subjects. That was the "magnolia" in her. The "steel" was almost literally that, since she was also a promoter of the first railway in North Carolina.

Like many of the small leaps into the dark that began the Industrial Revolution, the building of the railway came about not only almost accidentally but in response to what seemed a disaster: in 1833, the capitol building in Raleigh was destroyed by fire. The legislature refused to consider rebuilding in any material that might burn again but was reluctant to pay the great cost to cart stone from the only available quarry. So Sarah pushed the construction of a railway between the building site and the quarry. In truth it wasn't much of a railway—being only a cheap strap-iron tramway, costing $2,250 a mile, pulled by a horse and running just two miles—but it was the precursor of greater things.

Significantly, the Raleigh line was called the Experimental Railway. This was a period of great experimentation in railed transport. The early attempts were, like Raleigh's, to transport building materials and ran on what was then termed "railed pavement." In Raleigh, the rails were made of wood. Later wooden rails were capped by a thin strip of iron, but it was not until nearly a generation later that what we know as the railroad "T" iron rail came into general use.

Steam locomotives, inspired by an English design, first came into use in 1829; so the horse-drawn line in Raleigh was obsolescent even before it was built. But that did not deter Sarah. When enough stone had been transported, in 1833 the company put a passenger car upon the track "for the accommodation," as the announcement read, "of such ladies and gentlemen as desired to take the exercise of a railroad airing." As her line earned 300 percent on the original investment, Sarah proved herself a "railroad baron[ess]" on a small scale. So profitable was the Experimental Railway that others were encouraged, and, arguably, it was the progenitor of the entire network of southern railways that would come into existence twenty years later.

Sarah's example and the challenges her son Leonidas faced as he performed his duties as a missionary bishop along the western frontiers inspired him to a vision of the future. For him, it was not profit that counted but the possibility that the railway would prove a means to unify the country. As the rapidly rising population spread out over the vast spaces of the West and South, Leonidas foresaw the rise of conflicts of interest and style that might tear the Union apart. He told an old West Point friend that "the true preventive of such a calamity would be found in the creation of a complete railway system which would so unite all parts of the country in the bonds of a common interest as to make a disintegration of the Union difficult, if not impossible." As he did as a missionary bishop, so he did as a missionary railwayman, going on what amounted to a lecture tour—the concept had not yet been formulated—and distributed some five thousand copies of an address advocating the building of local railway spurs.

One group that listened was made up of Charleston businessmen who were alarmed at the decline of commerce in their area; so following Sarah's lead, they undertook the wildly ambitious project of building a 136-mile line, then the longest railroad in the world. Exciting times they were for transportation, but much of the South paid little attention. Even nearly thirty years later, Louisiana, Arkansas, Texas and southern Missouri had almost no railroads.

It wasn't only railways that caught Leonidas's attention. When he was farming in Tennessee, he imported machinery to make bagging and set up a steam mill to grind flour. In what has been called in our times "moving downstream," men like Leonidas were trying to find ways to convert their primary products—cotton, jute, wheat and corn—into more finished goods and to find ways to get them more cheaply and more quickly to markets. They were already aware that if they did not make this transition, the South would remain economically little more than a "third world" colony of northern factors and bankers. Some already claimed that almost half of the profit of southern agriculture found its way into northern pockets.

But there was great opposition to their efforts. Many southern leaders, including James K. Polk, doggedly opposed the protective tariff—then also demanded by northern states to defend their industry against cheap English imports—which might have enabled the South's nascent industries to thrive. Andrew Jackson and James K. Polk also opposed federal government support to "internal improvements" (or what we call infrastructure projects, such as roads, bridges, canals and railroads), and so they unwittingly accentuated the slide of the South toward a relatively backward status.

Nevertheless, as Sarah demonstrated in Raleigh, a few small-scale projects would be successfully pushed ahead. The most colorful was without doubt the growth of the Mississippi steamboat. The first of these, the *New Orleans,* went into service in 1812, and within a few years, New Orleans was linked to Louisville and even Pittsburgh, making possible the move of several members of the Polk family into the new areas of the Deep South and the new West.

Such movement toward industrialization and infrastructure development that was achieved came about less by positive moves than by the threat of impoverishment as the price of the major primary product, cotton, fell.

Cotton was as important to the Old South as tobacco had been in early colonial America. Like tobacco, it exhausted the soil and so stimulated another thrust outward to virgin lands. Westward movement was further encouraged by the desire of the new states to "catch up" with the older states. Georgia, for example, encouraged migration by offering without charge to new white settlers some 30 million acres of lands it got from the dispossessed Cherokee and Creek Indians. That created what might be termed a "cotton rush." Nearly 100,000 Virginians took advantage of the offer. Caught up in similar moves into Mississippi, Arkansas and Texas were a number of members of the Polk family, including James K., his brother, William H., and several of the sons of Will who acquired plantations in these new areas.

Not only did cotton exhaust the eastern areas of the South and encourage the opening of the western areas, but it was a determining factor in the way people lived and worked in both. First, even with the cotton gin Eli Whitney had invented in 1793, cotton was a crop that in the technology of the time virtually required slavery. In practice, less than 10 percent of the cotton was produced by nonslaveholders. Second, the whole southern society was fixated on cotton. On the eve of the Civil War, the southern states produced about 4.5 million bales (each of which weighed about five hundred pounds), which constituted well over half of the total value of American exports. But, third, it is surprising how marginal a crop it was. Cotton prices were the roller coaster on which the Polk family—and indeed the whole southern planter society on some 74,031 plantations—rode. The price (per pound) rose and fell from year to year by as much as 50 percent, but the trend was steadily downward during the period of the Old South. Sadly, very few of the Polks were sensitive to this trend, which, in the larger sense, doomed the Old South.

An acute contemporary analysis of the failure of the plantation system was provided by a well-informed economist long before the Civil War. J. D. B. De Bow set up a "best case" plantation, capitalized at $100,000, and calculated that it would earn a gross yearly income of $7,000, but after deducting the major items of expenditure, the owner would receive a net return of only $1,700. A very poor rate of return, and, he points out, even that is illusory, since it does not provide for hundreds of small annual purchases, breakage, contingencies, amortization or even the upkeep of the planter and his family. When these things are taken into account, he wrote, "It would require an extraordinary coincidence of favorable circumstances to leave the smallest margin of profit to the planters."

Bluntly put, agriculture in the Old South was an economic failure. The basis of wealth was neither agriculture nor industry; it was the rise in the value of land taken from the Indians. General Thomas, Colonel Ezekiel, Colonel Will and their contemporaries endowed the next generation with the capital that made the Old South possible. Lands that they got for pennies an acre were selling by 1850 for an average of nearly

258 ‎ POLK'S FOLLY

$5.50 an acre. When southern society was thrown back on existing resources, it became impoverished. But still it clung to the only system it knew, plantation agriculture based on slavery.

T HE WHITE-BLACK RELATIONSHIP WAS VASTLY MORE COMPLEX and fluid than is generally appreciated. Between the Revolution and about 1830, leading southerners appeared to be growing ashamed of slavery. George Washington freed his in his will; so did John Randolph. Patrick Henry, Thomas Jefferson and James Madison, even when enjoying individual slaves, condemned the institution. Led mainly by the Quakers, there were more antislavery societies in the South than in the North, including some fifty just in Virginia. In the early years of the nineteenth century, a society was formed (of which Leonidas originally approved) to collect and return slaves to Africa; some fifteen thousand blacks were actually returned. The society's sponsors soon realized that their efforts could never be more than a token, since during the years of its existence, the American black population increased by 3 million.

The conservative reaction came after 1830 in part because of fears of slave rebellion. Every slave-owning society from at least ancient Greece onward has feared it. The Old South was no exception. The black revolt of Haiti was luridly publicized, and memory of it was refreshed by frequent rumors of local incidents and "plots." In 1856, a rumor spread throughout the South that a revolt had been set for Christmas. Everyone, black and white, was on edge, and the sudden appearance of a comet lent a sense of awe and mystery. As George Washington Polk wrote, the comet "blazed across that fair summer sky, and in the minds of the superstitious portended dreadful calamities . . . and when we night after night never tired of viewing it, a feeling of awe and mystery enveloped us . . . its flaming tail stretched fully half the arch of the heavens."

News accounts of the Indian Sepoy Rebellion against the British seemed to confirm the cosmic message and were taken as a model of the pillage and rapine that might happen at home. As fears rose, militia-appointed patrols to catch runaways became more common. It seemed logical, to both southerners and northerners, that blacks would revolt. Yet in 1859, when the abolitionist John Brown raided Harpers Ferry and brought weapons to distribute among them, not a single slave or freed-man rose to help him.

Manumission may be taken as the litmus test of the southern atti-tude. In 1782, Virginia passed a liberal manumission law but in 1805 made it very difficult by requiring the immediate removal of the freed person; other states followed, and in 1851 Kentucky passed a law re-quiring freedmen to leave the state. In Virginia, if the freedman did not leave the state within twelve months, he could be sold back into slavery.

Whatever their motivation, some masters evaded the law by al-lowing their slaves to live as virtually free persons. Molly Harding Polk's Uncle John of Belle Meade left a testament in 1842 for the care of two of his slaves after his death. They were to be allowed to live wherever they wished, on the plantation or off, given a generous pension and "be well taken chearee of as one of the famley as long as theay live."

One of the arguments against manumission was that owners might free the old and infirm, who would then become a burden on the com-munity; so a major, if not always intended, part of the process of gaining freedom was preparing the person with a skill by which he or she could earn a living.

Particularly in middle Tennessee and particularly in the Polk houses, "the practice of importing workmen from the east was discon-tinued in favor of teaching one's slaves to handle the construction and ornamentation" of the plantation houses.

Having acquired rudimentary skills, slaves began to be either hired out or allowed to set up on their own in villages and towns to ply their trades for their masters' or their own benefit. Use of their services was one of the early and important means by which the little separate com-munities began to form a larger society. As significant, a new tier formed among blacks, those who lived midway between slavery and freedom.

Only certain trades were generally open to such people. In 1830, North Carolina, Georgia and Louisiana passed laws prohibiting the teaching of literacy to slaves. So, as much as possible, freedmen were to be kept to lesser occupations. Barbers were mostly freedmen, and in Virginia there were 4,224 blacksmiths and 3,728 shoemakers reported in the 1860 census.

Particularly in Louisiana, where a more thorough mixing of the races was a heritage of French and Spanish times, some free blacks not only owned plantations but also black slaves. And there is one curious example recorded of a black church buying its minister to keep him when he was on the point of being sold elsewhere.

Many freedmen were mulattoes. And among them were increasing numbers who were physically indistinguishable from those who were legally white. "I sometimes discover," wrote Sir Charles Lyell in 1846, "that my American companions cannot tell me, without inquiry, to which race certain coloured individuals belong." In short, as white southerners had long recognized, there were not two races, white and black, or two social conditions, free and slave, but two continuums with many intermediate positions among which evolution was thought to take place not only by "nature" but also by "nurture."

Whether identifiable as blacks or not, those who gained their freedom often found themselves in a legal and social limbo. While gaining what was theoretically equal status before the law, they lived under many restrictions and, most significantly, had lost their white protectors. Moreover, they joined a tiny, marginal group. The most numerous were, naturally, along the border with the free states; Maryland, for example, had about 84,000, while Mississippi had only 773 and Arkansas 144.

But despite attempts at manumission, the vast majority of the southern blacks were and remained slaves. Like most southern property owners, Will and his sons took slavery of blacks as a natural or at least a legal given. Without slaves, land in the amounts the early settlers acquired could not have been worked given the technology then available. That there was a sizable and growing population that stood between black slavery and white freedom was considered unexceptionable and useful. And that there were areas of the United States that operated on a different system was considered normal even when people in those areas occasionally pressed their ideas on southerners.

The Missouri Compromise was worked out in Congress in March 1820 after violent disagreement between antislavery and proslavery whites. Even Thomas Jefferson had weighed into the fight, urging that Congress avoid taking a stand against slavery lest whites abandon the southern plantation states. But Congress could not duck the issue when Missouri stood on the brink of entry into the Union; the compromise was that slavery was to be legal in Missouri but would be banned in the new northern territories. The compromise satisfied almost no one; Jefferson considered it "the knell of the Union." Although he was premature, he was nearly right.

SLAVERY MAY BE SEEN AT THE ROOT OF THE DISTINCTIVE SOUTHern way of life. Only because blacks worked the fields could whites aspire to a more elegant and refined society. But since this society rested upon what whites assumed to be a latent revolution, they developed a Spartan code of militarism into which they blended values they imagined to be something like the medieval code of chivalry. Men thought of themselves as knights errant and their ladies as their sacred charge. That colorful son of the South, Sam Houston, summed up the passions of the southern chivalry in a letter to Lucius J. Polk. "There are five things on earth which I love," he wrote. "A fine woman, a fine horse—a fine Dog. A Game Cock and fine arms."

In the modern form of chivalry, dueling took the place of the medieval tournament. Men were encouraged to be "hot-blooded" and prided themselves on never accepting an insult or tolerating what they regarded as cowardice. Many duels, of course, were not recorded, but quite a few were. And many were by eminent men. The most famous is actually in the North, where Aaron Burr killed Alexander Hamilton, but Andrew Jackson was known to have participated in many. Sam Houston shot General William A. White in the groin. White lived and a grand jury indicted Houston, but like most cases involving feuds, the action failed and Houston was let off. James K. Polk's younger brother, William H. Polk, shot and killed a man in what was less a duel than a street fight; he was not only let off by a grand jury but went on to occupy high office in Tennessee and in the federal government. As John B. Hays described the events in a letter to James K. Polk,

> On Saturday, December 1, 1838, William got into an argument with Richard Hays over the possibility of a fancy dress ball in Columbia, Tennessee. William said that Hays "would be a proper person to interest himself with the ladies." Hays made an insulting rejoinder and William then threw a glass of wine in Hays' face. Hays threw one in Wms face. Wm then got a hold of Hays & beat him, Hays not much resisting. It there ended, they making peace.

Unfortunately, Hays spread the story that he had won the fight. William then demanded that Hays admit the truth. When he did not, William "gave Hays a horse-whipping. I presume from the accounts of those who saw it, a severe one, Hays not resisting at all." Through an intermediary, William tried to apologize, but Hays would not accept it and rounded up his friends and armed himself. He spent the next day practicing with the guns and announcing that he would kill William. The next morning, Hays went into the main street, drew his gun and called on William to defend himself. "Hays fired and missed. Wm. Fired [and] . . . struck him a little above the right eye, between the hair and eye. He died this morning [September 4] and has been taken to Davidson for interment. No one was drunk."

On January 12, 1839, a grand jury rejected the charge of murder and indicted William for assault and battery, for which he was found guilty. It was a slap on the wrist. Almost no duel ever drew more punishment.

Not all southerners, of course, approved of dueling. Andrew Jackson feared that James K. Polk's opponents in the House of Representatives might force him into a duel and advised him not to allow himself to be so trapped. For Jackson, that represented a major change in lifestyle, but James had no intention of being forced into a duel, since he regarded dueling as "this unchristian object . . . the immoral, unchristian, and savage practice of dueling."

Lethal affairs duels were, but almost as lethal, at least socially, was to turn down a duel. Indeed, right in the middle of the Civil War, when one would have thought there was enough death, Marshall "Marsh" Tate Polk, who lost a leg at Shiloh, challenged Pollock B. Lee, accusing him of cowardice in battle. According to James Hilliard Polk, Lee "refused Marsh's challenge on the ground that he [Marsh] was a cripple, I acted for Marsh in the matter and when lee would not meet him, I of course offered to take his place . . . Lee would not meet me and that evening in the presence of a large gathering of officers Marsh denounced him as a liar and coward, shaking his finger at him and telling him that the ball which carried away his leg, had spared his right arm and trigger finger—Lee slunk out of the Hotel and we saw no more of him."

THE CIVIL WAR

"This hideous carnival of Death"

". . . THE FEDERAL BATTERIES ON THE HILL TURNED LOOSE WITH solid shot, and rocks [from the wall in front of us] were flying in every direction," wrote James Monroe Polk—then twenty-five years old and one of the many great-grandsons of Colonel Ezekiel—of the first day of the Gettysburg battle.

> . . . so great was the confusion that I have no recollection of passing over . . . When we reached the battery at the top of the hill, the men had all left. Some dead were lying around, I don't remember how many. Harris of our company was in front of me. He put his hand on the cannon and was looking over the hill. The cannon was lying on a rock, I think, and the wheels behind the rock. I could hear the minnie balls going

over our heads. I said to him, "Hold on, Harris, we are by ourselves; wait till the balance come up." "Oh, I want to see where they have gone," replied Harris, "they are not far off." About that time a shell burst in front of us and a piece of it went through his breast, and it seemed to me that I could run my arm through that man's body. His face turned as white as cotton, and strange to say, he turned around and tried to walk in that condition, but fell over and was dead in less than five minutes. His people lived somewhere in Virginia, but I don't know their address. Now I could see the Third Arkansas to our left, and could hear Colonel Manning's voice; then I saw three or four hundred Federals throw down their guns and surrender to them. I saw General [John B.] Hood walking down the hill holding his arm. I understood that his arm was broken above the elbow and four inches of the bone taken out.

That was one man's view of Gettysburg, where on July 2, 1863, eleven thousand Federal and Confederate troops lost their lives.

When he thought over the experience, as he did night after night for years after the horror of that day, James Monroe Polk reflected that "if all the leaders and men who make war speeches and excite the people knew that in case of war they would have to pick up their gun and help to fight the battles and take their chances along with the men, there would not be many wars."

How astonished he would have been to find that not only did that terrible war go on to its logical conclusion but, since it ended, generation after generation of Americans in the hundreds of thousands has refought and sought to relive its battles in full-dress simulations. Each year, millions of Americans visit the battle sites. Many more millions have avidly followed its course in films and TV documentaries. Thousands of books and tens of thousands of articles have delved into the minutiae of every event and the personalities and actions of every general and many privates. Replicas of weapons, uniforms and battle flags are produced for Civil War "buffs" by an industry on a scale that would nearly have turned the course of the war had it then existed. As a nation, we are truly obsessed with the Civil War.

And with good reason. One cannot imagine the United States today without the cataclysmic changes wrought by the Civil War. The emancipation of black slaves would certainly have been delayed, perhaps for half a century, and in some areas slavery might have lingered even longer. And had the South not been defeated, America would have been balkanized socially, economically and politically. Moreover, while change is a continual process, it usually occurs slowly, silently and unobtrusively; in the Civil War, it came about violently, in tumult and in ways that left no one untouched.

Did it happen just because, as James Monroe Polk suggested, a group of leaders, safe in their homes and offices, could view warfare abstractly, careless of the terrible tragedies of combat; or accidentally, because they "miscalculated," as politico-military analysts today would say, the odds of victory; or ignorantly, because those in power had no personal knowledge of the horror it would involve, or impotently, because they felt caught in a process over which they had lost control? Ever since the time of the Civil War, scholars have debated the causes. Clearly, there can be no one answer: contemporaries give evidence for all positions.

On one issue, there can be little ambiguity: capacity. Southern leaders knew from the 1860 census how inferior they were to the North in power: of the 27 million free white Americans, 21.5 million were living in the North, that is, the North contained over four times the effective population of the South (since the South benefited only in limited ways from its 3.5 million blacks). Moreover, the population of the North was growing about 20 percent faster than that of the South. In other ways, the disadvantage of the South was even more evident. Three-quarters of the railroad mileage, practically all of the nearly four thousand miles of canals and more than 80 percent of the manufacturing capacity were in the North.

These statistics, as persuasive as they are, do not give a full picture of the South's disadvantages, since in such critical fields as iron, ammunition and weapons production, the North had virtually a monopoly. Such arsenals as were located in the South were mainly just depots for equipment manufactured in the North. And what was recorded in these depots shows that the resources of the South were farcical. In Tennessee, the "keeper of public arms" reported in January 1861 that the state contained only 350 carbines, all of which were unserviceable, 8,761 muskets, over half of which were badly damaged and almost all of which were obsolete flintlocks, and four cannons, of which two were unusable.

In nearby Lexington, Virginia, Captain William Stewart Polk of the Maryland branch of the family had turned the Virginia Military Institute (VMI) into a workshop. The countryside had been scoured to find every kind of new or antique firearm, and William's twin tasks were to convert flintlock muskets into more serviceable percussion locks and to manufacture cartridges.

On October 1, 1861, the Military and Financial Board reported to the General Assembly that "At the time of the organization of this board there was not a cap factory in the whole South, nor a powder mill in operation, nor a manufactory of small arms to any extent, and but one cannon foundry." Even when the Confederates captured northern rifles, particularly the more sophisticated Spencer or Henry rifles, they could use them only so long as the ammunition they captured lasted, since they did not have the capacity to manufacture it. Contrariwise, the U.S. government was able to purchase over 146,000 Colt revolvers, since Colt, which was nearly bankrupt at the time of the Mexican War, had become a pioneer multinational arms producer.

But statesmen drew differing conclusions from these statistics. Some thought it better to join the winning team by staying in the Union. Holding the Union together at all costs had been the position of Presidents Andrew Jackson and James K. Polk and would be the unflinching commitment of James's brother, William Hawkins Polk, who ran for governor of Tennessee on a pro-Union ticket, and Andrew Johnson, who was the wartime military governor of Tennessee and would be Lincoln's successor as president.

Others reacted to the current situation and trend in exactly the opposite way: they thought it was better to end the relationship before the South was overwhelmed. This was to be the position of most of the contemporary Polks. The judgment was summed up for them, melodramatically to be sure, by James Hammond of South Carolina, who wrote that the trend toward the creation of new western states would enable the northern-western antislavery coalition to "ride over us rough shod . . . and reduce us to the condition of Hayti . . . If we do not act now, we deliberately consign our children, not our posterity, but our *children* to the flames." In short, what such men feared was that the South would be, in fact was being, transformed into a domestic "third world" country.

What was clear to pro- and anti-Unionists alike was that it would be impossible to stand aside. There could be no neutral ground: not only did the country split apart but so did states, communities and even families. Antiwar sentiment reached virtually to rebellion in parts of the North, while in the South, Virginia was split so that the new state of West Virginia was created; the eastern part of Tennessee was the scene of a guerrilla war; and regiments were formed for both the Union and the Confederacy in Kentucky and Missouri. In many battles, brothers fought one another. And while this did not happen among the Polks, cousins were frequently recorded on opposite sides, indeed occasionally in positions of command. Famously, the widow of President James K. Polk insisted on flying the Union flag outside her house in Nashville even as she sheltered some of the possessions of her Confederate relatives.

The cost of decision was also hotly debated. Few had personal knowledge of combat. It had been almost half a century since America had suffered the consequences of a general war with a major power. Neither the War of 1812 with Britain nor the Mexican War had touched most Americans painfully, and the struggles with the Indians hardly ranked as wars. Moreover, during the years between roughly 1815 and

1860, about 5 million Europeans arrived who knew little of warfare in America and had no personal experience with it. So, with minor but important exceptions, particularly in the officer corps, few Americans of military age in 1860 had any idea of what war was like or what lay ahead. To this extent, we may say, as we nearly always can about the beginning of wars, that ignorance played a crucial part in decision making.

Ignorance—and excitement—affected people in different ways. The easiest to see and to document is the more mature versus the younger.

Leonidas Polk, who in his middle fifties was Episcopal bishop of Louisiana, did not have personal experience of combat, but he knew of it vicariously from his father, Will, who had been twice severely wounded in combat during the American Revolution. And as a student in West Point, Leonidas had closely studied the Napoleonic wars. So, at least vicariously, the horror of war was in his mind when on December 26, 1860, he made his eleventh-hour appeal to President James Buchanan to try to avert the war.

"At a time like this," he wrote to the president, "it is the duty of every citizen to aid in clearing away the difficulties by which we are surrounded, and to prevent, if possible, further complications. It is under a sense of duty that I take the liberty of addressing you." He feared, he wrote, that "the want of accurate and reliable information as to the true state of feeling and determination of the southern States might cause you to interpret your obligations to your oath of office differently from what you would if you were in full possession of the facts as they are."

He knew the facts, Leonidas asserted, because in his Episcopal duties, he traveled widely and talked with all the southern leaders. The essential fact was that the southern state had "deliberately and inflexibly" determined to leave the Union. "This feeling is deepening and widening every day, and no difference exists except as to the mode of effecting it. To attempt to prevent it by force of arms would instantly extinguish that difference and unite the whole population as one man."

President Buchanan was in the final days of his presidency and could hardly have seriously considered, much less implemented, the program of conciliation Leonidas advocated, particularly in the face of the mandate given President-elect Lincoln and the Republican Party in the elections the month before. But as torn as most Americans, Buchanan waffled on the central issue: he did not believe, as he told Congress in his final message, that a state had the right to withdraw from the Union, but at the same time, he asserted, the federal government did not have the right to compel it to remain. On both of these issues, President-elect Lincoln had no doubts. And so it was that Leonidas's appeal amounted to mere whistling into the gathering storm.

Contrasting with Leonidas and his generation were thousands of younger men. For many of them, war appeared as romance, almost like a tournament of knights, a chance to prove valor. Leonidas's younger brother, Andrew Jackson Polk, on the lawn of his elegant plantation, Ashwood, excitedly gathered his cousins and friends together on July 5, 1861, to form the "Maury County Braves," Company F, 1st Tennessee Cavalry.

All over the South young men rushed to sign up for "honor." They wasted few words on abstract notions such as the possible constitutional justification of secession or protection of property or the economics of slavery. For them, the war was a fever, burning in their imaginations with notions of glory. Not pomp and circumstance but dash and derring-do. Battle would be exciting, and every young man was a brave. What could be better? That question would soon be answered, as it was for thirty-six-year-old Captain Andrew Jackson Polk. Less than a year after he had ridden to war in a beautiful carriage with the finely matched horses driven by his groom, he limped back to Ashwood, shattered in body.

But what the young men sought spilled over to the infirm. Andrew Jackson Polk's brother, forty-three-year-old George Washington Polk, wrote to his son in December 1861, "I should like to take a turn at those rascally Lincolnites by the side of my boys. Save me a horse and a sword if you can. I will try to get a pair of pistols in Nashville. I have a

splendid sword but I do not think it quite long enough for cavalry.''
With more sense, his wife wrote a few months later, in February 1862,
''Your Pa has been suffering greatly from Rheumatism . . . [he] feels
like getting up a company of 100 men—I can not object another time if
he wishes and thinks it right, but I do *fear* for him . . .''

D URING THE TIME HE WAS WRITING HIS APPEAL TO PRESIDENT
Buchanan for peace and reconciliation, and during the early
months of 1861, Leonidas was engaged in organizing and raising funds
for the creation of a new university, the University of the South, to be
built at Sewanee. To our ears, it is both bizarre and yet curiously familiar
to hear how tenaciously such men as Leonidas sought to go forward with
their already announced programs in such times. Despite the portents
that were certainly clear to him by the end of 1860 that war was virtually inevitable, we find him in Tennessee promoting his university project. He even kept on after the attack on Fort Sumter when war had
become a reality. Throughout the country, men shared this propensity
to stick to the close and familiar when all about was losing the semblance
of normality and coherence.

The reality of war soon overtook them all. While Leonidas was
meeting with officials and potential donors on the Sewanee university
project in the spring of 1861, Governor Isham Harris asked him to call
on President Jefferson Davis in the provisional Confederate capital,
Richmond, Virginia, to impress upon him the need for an adequate defense of the Mississippi valley. Leonidas, who had known Davis at West
Point, wrote him outlining the vulnerability of the West and urging that
Davis not be so carried away by his desire to protect Virginia from a Federal attack that he left the West unprotected. In his reply of May 22, Davis asked Leonidas to come to meet with him in Richmond.

Leonidas did, and during a long discussion of affairs in the West,
Davis startled Leonidas by asking him to enter the Confederate army and
assume command of the Mississippi area. Immediately and firmly, Leon-

idas refused. It must have seemed almost a jest to him: his whole life had been devoted to the church since he had left West Point thirty-four years before. And during that time, he had apparently never even read a book on military tactics or logistics and, having resigned his commission to enter the ministry immediately upon graduation, had never served even a day in the army.

As incredible as it would seem today for such an appointment to be made, it should be weighed in the contemporary scale. Not only was Jefferson Davis primarily concerned with the psychological impact Leonidas's appointment would have in the West, where there was much opposition to secession, but, as he knew, none of the generals, North or South, had experience in handling formations larger than regiments. Armies as such did not then exist in America, and military professionalism was still a rudimentary concept. There was no such organization as a general staff as yet; that function had been conceived in Prussia but had not yet spread to America, and the closest that general officers had come to training in the use of armies was whatever they had managed to read, mainly in the rudimentary French they had been taught at West Point, about Napoleon's campaigns. If Leonidas was unprepared, so were all the rest. Then-Captain U. S. Grant was a "mustering officer" on the Illinois governor's staff and was engaged only in trying to whip a group of short-term volunteers (including a descendant of the northern branch of the Polks, William Harrison Polk) into the 21st Illinois Infantry, and Major Stonewall Jackson was just a "tac" at VMI, teaching tactics to young men like Leonidas's son William Mecklenburg Polk.

What Leonidas found in Richmond was a collection of his West Point acquaintances, led by Davis and General Robert E. Lee. Already joining them were others who were to be the leading generals of the South: Albert Sydney Johnston (Leonidas's West Point roommate), Joseph E. Johnston, John Magruder, Pierre Gustave Beauregard, Robert S. Garnett and Henry A. Wise. Leonidas felt right at home. But he declined to join them.

Davis wrote him a warm personal note asking him to change his mind and then sent an official appointment; still Leonidas resisted. So Davis arranged that a visiting delegation from Mississippi urge him to accept. As he wrote his wife on June 22,

> . . . they have been after me again. I have now had this matter before me a week, and have thought and prayed over it, and taken counsel of the most judicious of my friends, and I find my mind unable to say No to this call, for it seems to be a call of Providence. I shall, therefore, looking to God for his guidance and blessing, say to President Davis that I will do what I can for my country, our hearth-stones, and our altars, and he may appoint me to the office he proposed. And may the Lord have mercy upon me, and help me to be wise, to be sagacious, to be firm, to be merciful, and to be filled with all the knowledge and all the graces necessary to qualify me to fill the office to his glory and the good of men.

His reluctance is still evident when, in his assumption of command, he issued General Order No. 1. In it, he wrote, "In assuming this very grave responsibility, the general in command is constrained to declare his deep and long-settled conviction that the war in which we are engaged is one not warranted by reason or any necessity . . ." The sole aim the Confederacy pursued, he continued, "is to be let alone, to repose in quietness under our own vine and under our own fig tree. We have sought and only seek the undisturbed enjoyment of the inherent and indefeasible right of self-government, a right which freemen can never relinquish, and which none but tyrants could ever seek to wrest from us . . ." The future was not bright. The contest would be one of "unparalleled atrocity." There should be no false optimism, but neither should there be dumb despair. "Numbers may be against us, but the battle is not always to the strong . . . In God is our trust."

S HORTLY AFTER ASSUMING COMMAND OF THE FAR WESTERN SEC-
tion of the Confederate frontier, Major General Leonidas Polk was
faced with an invasion of Federal troops. It was clear to him and to the
Federal commanders that this frontier was the most vulnerable part of
the southern defense. In addition to the Mississippi itself, on which the
great advantages of the rapidly growing Federal river fleet would prove
decisive, the Ohio River offered an easy and rapid means of transport by
steamboat from the northeast to the west for Federal troops and heavy
equipment. Other rivers, particularly the Cumberland and the Tennessee, plunged southward into the Confederate heartland. Linking them
together was the already sophisticated railroad net that had grown in the
previous decade.

By employing rivers and rails, the Federal forces gained enormous
advantages of speed and surprise to achieve local superiority. Conversely, the Confederate command had to rely primarily on "foot
power" to shift troops along their frontier. Worse for them, their new
industries, particularly those engaged in weapons production, grew up
in Nashville; there, located as they were on one of the major transportation hubs and near the Kentucky border, they were a major objective of
Federal forces and were particularly vulnerable to attack from the
North. Consequently, interdicting the rivers or at least minimizing their
use had to be the essence of Confederate strategy. It could be successful
only if fortifications were created and held on the Mississippi and if Kentucky, which was trying to remain neutral in the war, could be denied to
Federal forces. These were the challenges that Leonidas had to address in
the fall of 1861.

By this time, Ulysses S. Grant had advanced from the rank of captain on the staff of the governor of Illinois to brigadier general in the
United States Volunteer Army in command of one of the columns invading southward into Tennessee.

General Grant had moved a powerful force of about twelve thousand men down the Mississippi with the aim of knocking out the various forts the Confederates had established to prevent the Federal forces from cutting off Tennessee from New Orleans. Leonidas had a somewhat smaller force under his command and was much weaker in artillery; he did, however, have the advantage of defending rather than attacking. Neither side had what modern commanders regard as absolutely essential, close observation and background intelligence. Consequently, the as-yet-inexperienced commanders were often unable to distinguish a feint from a main objective and, unsure of their still untested troops, were extremely cautious. Leonidas was particularly worried about committing his troops because Grant's river flotilla gave him far more mobility than the rebel forces.

Belmont, where they met, was little more than a location on the map, initially so little prized that it had been abandoned by Federal forces. It derived such importance as it had from the fact that it was directly across the river from the Confederate base and railhead at Columbus and because it offered a means of access to pro-Confederacy forces in Missouri.

By nature an aggressive commander, Grant also sensed in Belmont a major personal opportunity. He knew that President Lincoln was distressed and angry over a recent defeat in Missouri where a Federal force of about three thousand men had been forced to surrender. And caught in a bitter rivalry with other Federal commanders, Grant knew that a good performance would solidify his command. Finally, although he did not often talk of this, he was still suffering from neglect bordering on oblivion during precisely those years when his military career should have flowered. Grant needed a victory. Belmont could be it. So on personal as well as strategic grounds, it assumed an importance that related little to its physical appearance.

From his experience in the Mexican War, where he served as a quartermaster to one of the regiments, Grant had learned that supply was the key to victory, and at his disposal was a fleet of river transports and gunboats. They were his great advantage. Contemporaries report that he spent much of the fall of 1861 thinking about and planning how to use them against either or both Belmont and Columbus. He even dreamed up a novel form of military transport, coal barges fitted out like floating barracks. Finally, on November 6, he loaded his still-green Illinois infantry regiments with all their supporting artillery and cavalry on his transports and began moving them downriver. After lying up overnight near Cairo at the junction of the Ohio and Mississippi Rivers, he issued them rations and ammunition and prepared them for their first big test.

He had prepared well. Landing on the morning of the eighth, he launched an attack that drove the Rebels right to the edge of the river and captured their camp. Up to that moment, the Federals were victorious, but, inexperienced soldiers that they were, the Illinois infantry, whooping with delight, turned their attention to looting the Confederate camp. All discipline disappeared, units became scattered and even the officers joined in the mirth and song as a brass band pounded out "Dixie" in satire of the Confederates.

At that point, Leonidas, who had known that Grant was coming but did not know where he would strike, decided that the Federal force was fully committed, that the attack was not a feint, and himself committed the bulk of his forces from across the river at Columbus. After moving them as far upstream as he dared, he began attacking the Federals in the flank and rear, driving them steadily back. Victory turned quickly into rout, so that the Federals were saved only because of the presence of their gunboats and transports. Grant himself was spotted by Leonidas and narrowly missed being captured or shot as he hastily boarded one of his transports. In his *Memoirs and Selected Letters,* Grant later wrote,

> I mentioned to an officer, whom I had known both at West Point and in the Mexican war, that I was in the cornfield near their [the Confederate] troops when they passed; that I had been on horseback and had worn a soldier's overcoat at the time. This officer was on General Polk's staff. He said both he

and the general had seen me and that Polk had said to his men, "There is a Yankee; you may try your marksmanship on him if you wish," but nobody fired at me.

Psychologically, the battle was important to both sides. Despite their near disaster, the Federals learned that they could fight and survive, and the Confederates believed they had won a substantial victory. Commanders on both sides congratulated their troops. Grant began the march that would take him to command of the Federal forces and ultimately to the presidency. Most important for the southerners, the Federal troops left behind about a thousand usable muskets and rifles.

BELMONT WAS A HARD-FOUGHT, BLOODY AND EXHAUSTING BAPtism for both armies, with each suffering about six hundred casualties, or about one man in each five who had actually fought. It was a harbinger of many tragedies to come. What to do about the prisoners became the critical question for each commander. It was quickly addressed by Grant and Polk.

"After the Battle of Belmont," wrote then-Lieutenant E. W. Rucker many years later,

General Grant came down the river in a boat under a flag of truce. General Polk got on the 'Grampus,' a boat that was used for running about, and went up and met him. Through his courtesy, I was allowed to go along on the trip. The two boats got together, and after shaking hands pleasantly, for they seemed to have known each other before, they had some wine (furnished by General Grant). We were all standing, and when they filled their glasses, General Grant said: "Here's to George Washington!", and General Polk quickly responded, "Good! The first Rebel!"

Cordial they were, under flag of truce, but privately it was a different matter. "I think him rather second rate," Leonidas wrote to his wife, "though I dare say a good man enough." But the purpose of their meeting was the somber tasks of burying the dead, caring for the wounded and exchanging prisoners.

On prisoners, the federal government had no consistent policy. Initially, President Lincoln wanted to treat them as traitors, outlaws or pirates without any of the (admittedly meager) protection of the customs of war. That meant they would be, or could legally be, hanged or shot. Indeed, that was Lincoln's original intent. However, when Jefferson Davis threatened to treat Federal soldiers exactly as the Union treated Confederates, Lincoln ordered his generals to back down.

HUMANITARIAN TREATMENT OF PRISONERS WAS OFTEN DIFFIcult to achieve, but sometimes, as in another exchange between Grant and Polk, the attempt to accomplish it could be almost whimsical. On November 10, using for the first time Leonidas's name and title, Grant wrote,

It grieves me to have to trouble you again with a flag of truce, but Mrs. Colonel Dougherty, whose husband is a prisoner with you, is very anxious to join him under such restrictions as you may impose . . . I will be most happy to reciprocate in a similar manner at any time you may request it.

I am, general, very respectfully,

Your obedient servant,
U.S. Grant,
Brigadier-General, U.S.A.

Leonidas replied,

Sir: I am in receipt of your letter under cover of your flag of truce, asking for Mrs. Dougherty the privilege of joining her husband, who was unfortunately wounded in the affair of the 7th.

It gives me great pleasure to grant her the opportunity of rendering such grateful service, and I hope through her attentions the colonel may speedily be restored to such a condition of health as is compatible with the loss he is obliged to sustain.

Reciprocating your expressions of readiness to interchange kind offices, I remain, very respectfully,

Your obedient servant,

L. Polk

Major-General Commanding

Such courtly behavior could not survive long in the conditions of deadly combat. It was perhaps inevitable that a fratricidal war would produce atrocities, but the nature of the strategy adopted by both sides, and particularly by the Federal armies, greatly extended their range and intensity. Witness the travails of James H. Polk,* who at nineteen commanded Company E of James T. Wheeler's 6th Tennessee Cavalry.

A grandson of Will Polk, James H. was said to have been the youngest captain in the Confederate army. Like many of his cousins, he grew up on a plantation in Maury County, Tennessee, where horseback riding was the favorite sport. Under Generals John Hunt Morgan and Nathan Bedford Forrest, the cavalry—or, as it was often employed as highly mobile, mounted infantry or "dragoons"—became perhaps the most successful of the Confederate forces. It "hampered and bewildered the Federals to such a point as almost to paralyze them . . ." Raiding deep into Federal-controlled territory, often covering as much as fifty miles a day, Forrest and Morgan cut rail links, destroyed supplies and trapped, captured or killed thousands of Federal troops. Perhaps not since the great Mongol invasions of Asia had cavalry proved so successful a military force or been used with more drama and dash. But there was a price to be paid, and young James H. paid it.

---

* Hereafter called "James H." to distinguish him from James K. (the president) and James Monroe Polk (who fought at Gettysburg).

He had written to his father on November 19, 1861, "Buy Sam Jones' horse [because] we are going to have hot—hot—times. I want a gentle horse—my colt will do fine in a month or two. Be sure to do this . . ." As he later told his wife, he loved that horse, Skedaddle, which must have been excellent, since it was evaluated by the army at the then great sum of $200. But on a raid behind Federal lines, his horse went lame. He thought he could ride to safety if he rested it, but he was surprised by a Federal patrol as it was being reshod. So on January 3, 1864, at twenty-one years of age, he was captured in Hickman County, Tennessee, northwest of Nashville. Unfortunately for him, General Grant and other Federal commanders had convinced President Lincoln that exchanging prisoners worked to Confederate advantage; so exchanges had temporarily stopped. Thus James H. began a tour through Federal prisons. His first stop was in Nashville; then he was sent to a military prison in Louisville and on to Camp Chase, Ohio; next, two months later, to Fort Delaware, an island in Delaware Bay.

Writing to his mother from Fort Delaware on April 22, 1864, James H. complimented his guards, no doubt knowing that his letters were being read, saying that "Genl Schoepf has command of the island and does everything in his power to render our condition more pleasant [so] Cheer up and be rejoiced that nothing worse than a prison life for a few months was allotted to me." The reality, of course, was quite different. Fevers and other illnesses raged in the camp; practically no medicines were made available in retaliation because the Confederacy, under blockade, did not supply—because it did not have—medicines to the equally miserable troops at Andersonville and other prisons); and rations were barely "enough to sustain life." As he later told his wife and his sons,

> they ate dogs and rats [when they were lucky enough to catch any] with mush made of meal that was black with age and spoiled. Often there were as many as 15 worms taken out of their ½ pint. For that was the amount [of gruel] given them

for breakfast. The rations consisted of four hard tack crackers often rotten and green with mold and 1 ounce of meat for dinner. They had beans or rice soup, and [for] supper all the wind that they could inhale.

But, of course, he could not then write such things.

In his next letter, on June 8, he hit a more dejected note: "I have despaired leaving here soon as Genl. Grant still knocks away at the gates of Richmond and until he gives up the campaign the exchange of prisoners will not be resume[d]." At that point, events about which he probably was not even aware took control of his life. Far away to the South, where the war had begun, Fort Sumter was still in Confederate hands. Both it and the nearby town of Charleston across the bay were under daily bombardment from the Federal bases on Morris Island. Hearing that there were Union officers imprisoned in Charleston, the federal government decided to retaliate by placing Confederate officers on Morris Island where they would come under fire from the Confederate forces. (Retaliation was a feature of the approach to prisoners on both sides and, as in all feuds, fed upon itself, so that regardless of whether the original action was purposeful or not, each side escalated the vengeance.) Along with a large contingent of his fellow prisoners at Fort Delaware, James H. was transported on a prison ship down to South Carolina to act as a human shield.

From Morris Island, he wrote to his father on October 15 to say about all he could say to reassure his family and pass censorship: that the rations he received "are almost such as the prisoners furnished with at Delaware—enough to sustain life . . . Give my warmest love to all the family. I have to be concise being allowed to write but one page. May God bless you is the prayer of your devoted son."

Near death from starvation, James H. was lucky. Twenty prisoners had been marked for exchange, but he was slipped in as the twenty-first, since it was thought he would not live long. He survived and immediately rejoined his army.

IN ADDITION TO ITS EMPHASIS ON EXCHANGE, HUMANITARIAN treatment of prisoners and the legality of retaliation, the code of military conduct adopted by the Union forces in Article 22 of General Orders 100, the so-called Lieber Code, enjoined protection of the lives and property of civilians. This was, in practice, hardly even a faint hope. War is by its nature destructive, and in a "popular" war, it is often impossible to distinguish between soldiers and those who shelter them. As General William T. Sherman wrote, "There is not a garrison in Tennessee where a man can go beyond the sight of the flagstaff without being shot or captured." Northern commanders went much further, however, than attempting just to prevent this cooperation. They embarked upon a program of deliberate destruction. For the most part, this approach to total war is identified with Sherman, but, in fact, it was a common practice. A war correspondent for a northern newspaper, the *Cincinnati Commercial,* was stunned by the "gloomy pall of smoke . . . [that] hovered over the scorched and blistered face of nature in dismal clouds . . ."

At that time, the woman who would marry Captain James H. was a child. Living with her family, the Hardings, at Belle Meade plantation just outside of Nashville, Molly witnessed the policy of destruction firsthand. As she later wrote,

> An officer who was in charge of the soldiers camped on the place told me it was a principality, and he never hated to destroy things as much as he did on that occasion. This officer I met at West Point years after. He was the father of Mrs. General Scott. Her husband will be remembered as the chief of staff; I think under [President Woodrow] Wilson. They left not one tree standing on the plantation. Besides, they burned 20 miles of cedar rail fencing and destroyed 20 miles of rock fencing used in fortifying Nashville. My grandfather lost over a million dollars [worth of property] by the war . . .

With Nashville occupied by Federal troops and besieged by the Confederate cavalry and with supplies short and a black market flourishing, it was inevitable that the city would attract a horde of racketeers, opportunists and desperate men. The pro-Confederate citizens were, of course, disarmed and were still assumed, as Molly had said of her Harding grandfather, to be rich. Rumors spread of buried treasure. So houses were routinely searched and the residents threatened by looters.

In the palmy days before the war, Molly later recounted, her grandfather had hidden a small keg of gold coins somewhere in the house; although his own daughter, Molly's mother, Betsy, did not believe it, the story inevitably became the gossip of the whole area. So soldiers and their camp followers searched the house time after time as Molly's mother stood by helpless. Meanwhile, the family grew more and more desperate simply for food, since virtually everything they had, had been looted. Just after one of the many searchers was leaving, cursing and threatening to burn down the house, Molly's mother angrily turned on her father and said, "Do you see what this silly story has done to us?" Then, pausing, she looked closely at her father and, somewhat mocking his great age and infirmity, asked, "Father, what would you have done if that ruffian had found the gold?" The old man steadied himself on his cane, then stood upright and pulled out of the cane a sword. "Why, I would have run him through with this," he said sternly.

Molly's grandfather soon took to his bed, and as he lay dying, he called Betsy to his side. Barely able to speak, he began to tell her where to find the keg of gold. Of course, Betsy did not believe there was a keg and was trying to calm her father in his last moments. He grew angry and, using almost his last reserve of strength, commanded her to be silent and listen. With parched lips, he whispered, "In the attic . . . behind the chimney . . . there is a crevice . . . in the crevice is the . . ." Then he fell silent. Betsy saw that he was dead. "Poor Father. An old man's fantasy. I know he wanted so much to help us," she sighed to little Molly through her tears.

Weeks passed and the plight of the household grew more and more desperate. Finally, they had eaten every scrap of food and sold everything in the house the looters had missed. They were on the brink of starvation. Betsy herself must have been hallucinating in her weakness and she recalled the pathetic last words of her father. "I wonder," she said aloud, but then laughed, as Molly remembered, and said, "But no, it cannot be." "What, Mommie?" Molly asked. Without another word, her mother turned and walked upstairs and climbed into the attic. There, indeed, she found the crevice and, gingerly climbing into it, bumped into the keg. With a loose brick, she broke open the top and thrust her hand inside. Pulling it out, she clutched a few quarter eagles in gold.

Desperate not to confirm the rumor, she kept only one and rushed off to town to buy some food. Over the ensuing years, one by one the coins kept the family alive. As Molly wrote, "I have handled that same gold on birthdays and at Christmas . . ."

AS THE FIGHTING SEESAWED BACK AND FORTH IN MIDDLE TEN-nessee, discipline among the soldiers often broke down. At first, there was little looting of property or molesting of civilians, but beginning in 1863, looting and foraging became more common.

Fearing for the safety of the family silverware, Will's son George Washington Polk hid the silver of Rattle & Snap in a hollow section of one of the ten tall Corinthian columns on the front facade. His brother Lucius had his silver "sown up in a stout sack and hidden underneath his house"; then fearing that this hiding place was compromised, he sunk it at the bottom of a well. Neither was found during the war.

IN THE CENSUS OF 1860, THERE WERE 668,956 BLACK SLAVES OF military age (along with 21,667 free "men of color"). As areas of the South fell under occupation, slave owners tried to evacuate or hide their slaves. Some areas loyal to the Union, most notably Maryland, were also slaveholding. Federal authorities had to decide what to do with the blacks, many of whom, naturally, ran away from the plantations on which they had been working. At the beginning of the war, the federal answer was legally clear if morally ambiguous: they were the rightful property of their owners and must be returned. This was routinely done in Maryland and in the District of Columbia, but in rebel areas, the situation was more complex and varied. In August 1861, the Congress passed a law authorizing the seizure of property used "in aid of the rebellion." Property was taken to include slaves, and runaway slaves in increasing numbers presented themselves to federal authorities as "contrabands."

President Lincoln was initially opposed to arming the slaves, sharing as he did the racist attitudes of the people in his home state of Illinois, but he issued instructions that they were to be impressed into labor corps and used by the army "as you may deem most beneficial . . ." At first numbering in the tens of thousands, they rapidly grew to over 200,000 by the time of the Emancipation Proclamation. So beneficial was this addition of labor that some historians believe that they "tipped the balance in favor of Union victory."

Regarding these people, the Confederate position was quite simple: runaway slaves were still the property of their original owners wherever they might be found. If they remained in territory controlled by the Confederacy, which most did, they could be apprehended. They usually were until about the beginning of 1864 when they became too numerous. In this action, the Confederates continued a practice that dated back over two hundred years. Indentured servants and slaves, both black and Indian, had been running away whenever they could since the beginning of the seventeenth century. The fact that many had done so in wartime was also not new: tens of thousands had sought freedom during the Revolution. And if the black became a soldier? The Confederate position remained the same as that on which George Washington and other Revolutionary generals had acted: he had not gained freedom by becoming a soldier unless by the action of the side from which he came. Thus, in the

Revolution, blacks who had been given their freedom to fight for the Revolution were "soldiers"; those who had been given their freedom to fight for the British were still treated (when they could be caught) as slaves. George Washington did everything he could after the British surrender to be sure that as few as possible got away with the retreating British.

Right up to the outbreak of the Civil War, practices in some northern states were virtually as restrictive as those in the South. Indiana, Iowa and Illinois passed laws banning all blacks, slave or free, from entering their territory in the 1850s; Ohio, which had previously had a similar law, still remained hostile to runaway slaves, and Kansas promulgated a proslavery constitution in 1857. Even the language of the Wilmot Proviso, which had been issued during the administration of President James K. Polk, made clear that much antislavery sentiment was based on racist motives and aimed not to improve the condition of blacks but to protect whites.

But while disabling prejudice against blacks lingered in many northern areas for a century, the mood in respect to the treatment of slaves was dramatically changed in the decade before the Civil War. As many writers aver, the new sympathy for runaway slaves derived in part from the disparity between the emotional treatment of the flight of slaves in Harriet Beecher Stowe's 1852 runaway best-seller, *Uncle Tom's Cabin,* and the stern legalism of the Supreme Court decisions upholding the right of recapturing "property."

Meanwhile, opinion in the South was undergoing a slower and less dramatic transformation. Many southerners conceded that slavery was not just a "peculiar institution" but, in the words of General Robert E. Lee, "a moral and political evil." However, except for private cases of manumission, always on a small scale, southerners did little to end slavery. The reason was partly economic. Probably typical of the "plantation class," approximately one-quarter of the estate of George W. Polk was made up of the slaves he owned. Even if he wished to, manumitting slaves was not a simple act: it often required both providing that they not be a public burden by giving them a sum of money, a sort of severance pay, and also arranging that they leave the state. Additionally, slavery was intermittently profitable, and as the price of cotton rose in the years just before the Civil War, owners realized an incentive to keep their slaves, as Leonidas had pointed out in his letter to President Buchanan.

President Lincoln also moved slowly on the slavery issue. His central aim, as he proclaimed repeatedly, was the same as that of James K. Polk and Andrew Jackson: to save the Union. To save the Union, he was willing to compromise on slavery, willing as he put it to preserve or destroy it or destroy part and keep part. Indeed, he went further and offered to condone slavery to win the rebelling states back for the Union. Following the Battle of Antietam on September 17, 1862, he implied that slavery had a chance when he warned the Confederate states that he would free their slaves if they did not return to allegiance. They did not, and three months later, on January 1, 1863, he issued the Emancipation Proclamation.

In the Proclamation, Lincoln did not include Tennessee. So when blacks drifted into Nashville from the rural areas farther to the south, many were seized by the Union army and forcibly impressed into labor corps. Ironically, the Federal army of occupation initially paid wages for the labor of many runaways not to them, but to those southern whites who still legally owned them.

Northerners were also hostile to the idea of using freedmen as soldiers. Following Lincoln's orders, the federal government rejected the idea of using black soldiers: the secretary of war declared that "this Department has no intention to call into the service of the Government any colored soldiers" and ordered that existing black militias be immediately disbanded or face arrest as "disorderly gatherings." There was so much popular opposition to black soldiers that they "had to drill out of sight to avoid a white backlash." But as casualties mounted and public support grew, Congress authorized the formation of black military units. Among them were at least three hundred blacks who joined the Federal forces under the name Polk and so, presumably, had been slaves of the members of the Polk family.

Not all blacks were opposed to the Confederacy. And not all whites were opposed to liberation and recruitment. In the South, too, the exigencies of the war were changing attitudes and actions. In many areas, free "men of color" contributed their labor and occasional supplies toward the Confederate war effort, and, particularly in Louisiana, blacks became soldiers. Some, men of "mixed blood," mulattoes, passing as white, even served as officers. Toward the end of the Civil War, the severe shortage of manpower drove even advocates of racial segregation to urge the freeing of the slaves to turn them into soldiers.

In January 1864, General Patrick R. Cleburne, arguably the most distinguished general in the Army of Tennessee and known as "the Stonewall Jackson of the West," who was the immediate superior and closest friend of General Lucius Eugene Polk (another grandson of Will), wrote a proposal which Lucius Eugene countersigned, advocating slave emancipation and black enlistment. After pointing out that he had never owned a slave, Cleburne analyzed the costs of slavery to the South: it had prevented English assistance to the Confederacy, made possible the Union's enlistment of (by then) 100,000 blacks in the Federal forces and gave what he considered a moral cover to "a brutal and unholy war . . . in violation of the Constitution . . ." Further, as he pointed out, the South was losing the war, having "spilled much of our best blood, and lost, consumed, or thrown into the flames an amount of property equal in value to the specie currency of the world [and being] hemmed in today into less than two-thirds" of its territory. "Our soldiers can see no end to this state of affairs except in our own exhaustion; hence, instead of rising to the occasion, they are sinking into a fatal apathy, growing weary of hardships and slaughters which promise no results . . ." And, he said, whereas the South had only one source of manpower, those of its white citizens who were still fit and not yet in

Parole pass during Federal occupation of Nashville.

Leonidas LaFayette Polk, the agrarian crusader, who almost became the second Polk president.

The letterhead of the Polk Brothers Stockyards in Fort Worth, Texas, during the 1880s.

The Polk Brothers Stockyards, from which James H. provided horses for the British army.

The Polk Brothers Stockyards in the great days of Texas ranching.

Mary "Molly" Demoville Harding Polk, the author's grandmother, whose stories began the search for this book.

Colonel William Dudley Gale, staff officer (and son-in-law) to General Leonidas Polk, whose graphic account of the rout of the Confederate army is quoted in Chapter 8.

ROY BEAN'S JERSEY LILLY, ICE COLD BEER & LAW WEST OF THE PECOS (FEBR. 21ST 1893)
LEFT TO RIGHT: SAM HENSHAW, TEXAS RANGER; J.T. BOND, R.R. PUMPER; SAM BEAN, SON OF JUDGE BEAN; JOE McCARTHY, R.R. BRIDGE EMPLOYEE;
JOHNNY WELCH, JUDGE BEAN'S GUN MAN; JACK ADAMS, R.R. EMPL; JUDGE ROY BEAN "LAW WEST OF THE PECOS"; LON TATUM AND BABY;
RANCHMAN; JIM KING, R.R. EMPL.; CHARLIE MILLER, R.R. EMPL.; JACK KOON, R.R. EMPL.; ARCHIE BOND, R.R. EMPL.; (CLEVELAND) H. HOWELL, R.R. EMPL.;
MAHONY FROM JERSEY R.R. EMPL.; 2 BOYS — ELWOOD & LELAND BOND; JOSE CANTU; RAMON CANTU; JOSE SANCHEZ; NEXT 2 MEXICANS UNKNOWN
GUADALUPE TORRES; LAST MEXICAN UNKNOWN.

"Judge" Roy Bean, "the Law West of the Pecos," and his bunch of desperadoes, gunmen, rangers and drinking companions in front of his saloon-courthouse. Bean maintained that he always gave a man a fair trial before he hanged him. He had a crush on the beautiful actress Lillie Langtry and named his headquarters at Dead Man's Canyon the "Jersey Lilly." (*Courtesy of the Library of Congress*)

Pancho Villa, the great Mexican guerrilla leader, whose raid on a border town started the Mexican "punitive campaign" and who defied the armed might of the United States for years.

The 11th Cavalry musters on parade in Mexico. (*Courtesy of the Library of Congress*)

The old and the new: the awkward, underpowered motor vehicles mire in the mud after a sudden flash flood, whereas the horse cavalry pulls through. Mexico, 1916. (*Courtesy of the Library of Congress*)

The Mexican punitive campaign was the first American war in which the airplane was extensively used (mainly to carry mail). This plane could achieve the then remarkable speed of 70 miles per hour. (*Courtesy of the Library of Congress*)

General John J. "Black Jack" Pershing led the American raid into Mexico and went on to command the American Expeditionary Force in France and Germany in World War I. Mexico, 1916. (*Courtesy of the Library of Congress*)

Frank Polk as acting secretary of state in 1918. (*Courtesy of the Library of Congress*)

The contribution of Sam Colt to democracy in America:
"he made all men equal." This is the pistol with which James
H. Polk is said to have shot the sheriff of Laredo, Texas.

The Martin MB-1, or GMB, which in 1919 was the first aircraft to fly around the entire frontier of the United States. The flight took 114 hours and 45 minutes at an average speed of about 65 miles per hour. Jack Harding was copilot in the crew of four. (*Courtesy of the United States Air Force Museum, Wright Patterson Field*)

The *New Orleans*, the first plane to circumnavigate the world,
on which Jack Harding flew as copilot.

Betty Lawson in court dress at the coronation
of George VI in London, 1937.

George W. Polk as a
U.S. Navy pilot on
Guadalcanal, 1942.

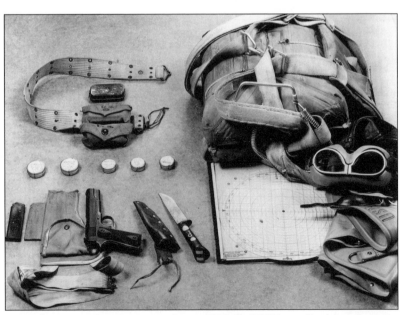

Survival gear issued to Lieutenant George W. Polk, USNR, on Guadalcanal, 1942.

Lieutenant George Polk, called "Mr. America" by his native rescuer, "Schemuel" (wearing George's equipment), on Malaita, the Solomon Islands, in 1942 after George's plane went down on a rescue mission. He was missing eight days in Japanese-held territory.

The "SOC" scout plane in which George W. Polk was shot down on Guadalcanal in 1942.

General George Patton, commander of the 3rd Army, and Colonel James H. Polk, commander of the 3rd U.S. Cavalry, confer at a roadside near the Moselle River in France during the drive into Germany in September 1944. *(Photograph courtesy of James H. Polk III)*

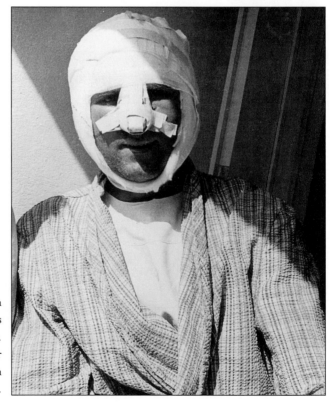

The life of a foreign correspondent was never easy. George W. Polk after a plane crash in Lebanon in 1947.

General James H. Polk with President John F. Kennedy and the U.S. ambassador to Germany, George McGhee, in Berlin in 1963. (*Photograph courtesy of James H. Polk III*)

George W. Polk broadcasting for CBS from the Church of the Nativity, Bethlehem, on Christmas Eve, 1946, with the help of John Donovan of NBC. *(Photograph taken by William R. Polk)*

John Donovan of NBC broadcasting from the Church of the Nativity, Bethlehem, on Christmas Eve, 1946, with the help of George W. Polk of CBS. *(Photograph taken by William R. Polk)*

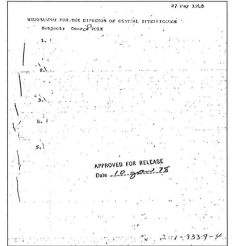

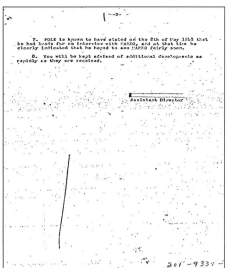

CIA document released (almost totally blanked out) under the Freedom of Information Act over thirty years after George Polk's murder.

George W. Polk broadcasting for CBS from Cairo in November 1946.
(Photograph taken by William R. Polk)

Lucius Burch of
Memphis, Tennessee.

Telegram of appoint-
ment of Lucius Burch
to represent Martin
Luther King, Jr., just
before his assassination.

uniform, the North had three: its own "motley" population, "our slaves" and Europeans who joined to fight slavery.

Finally, it was irrational and stupid to believe, he said, arguing against racial prejudices, that the blacks were not soldier material.

> For many years, ever since the agitation of the subject of slavery commenced, the negro has been dreaming of freedom . . . to attain it he will tempt dangers and difficulties not exceeded by the bravest soldier in the field . . . The slaves are dangerous now, but armed, trained, and collected in an army they would be a thousand fold more dangerous; therefore when we make soldiers of them we must make free men of them . . .

Southerners were not convinced. Part of the reason was that they expected blacks to harbor sentiments like those expressed by a slave in Tennessee known only as Tom. ". . . one ting's sartin," he said, "dey don't dar to try us. Jess put de guns into our hands, and you'll see that we not only know *how* to shoot, but *who* to shoot. My master wouldn't be wuff much ef I was a soldier."

It was not until March 13, 1865, that blacks could be enrolled in the Confederate army. A few days later, on March 27, Will Polk, the son of Lucius and nephew of Leonidas, petitioned the Confederate adjutant general to be allowed to raise a regiment of black troops. He had enlisted as a private and had risen to the rank of lieutenant and served as adjutant of the 48th Tennessee Infantry. His proposal was endorsed by two generals but was not acted upon. The last endorsement was affixed to the petition the day Richmond fell. Instead, perhaps as a sort of consolation prize, Will was promoted to major and sent back to fight in the Army of Tennessee.

Even when blacks were allowed to enlist, they were rarely given their freedom. Partly this was because many southerners believed the "good" blacks were content with their lot. With those closest to them, the "house slaves," they had reason for this belief. Many southern officers even took their "body slaves" with them as they went to war. Leonidas had his Altimore, and his nephew James H. had his Bob. James H.'s letters to his mother and father were carried back to Columbia by Bob (who could easily have run away or crossed into Union territory); not only his conduct but also the letters evince the affection between the two men. That this was not unusual is attested by foreign visitors, like the Englishman Lieutenant Colonel James Arthur Lyon Fremantle, who remarks time after time that "Their slaves . . . [despite the privation and danger of the war] generally remain true to them."

IN BOTH THE EASTERN AND THE WESTERN THEATERS, THE CONfederate armies aimed primarily to defend their territories. The underlying strategy was similar to that of the American armies in the Revolution: to outlast the superior forces of the attacker, hoping that northern public opinion would sour on the war and demand a peace settlement and that Britain, and perhaps France, cut off by northern blockade from the cotton that was vital to their growing industry, would intervene to help the South. From the beginning, however, the southern generals realized that the existing frontiers were essentially indefensible and adopted the adage that "the best defense is a good offense." In the West, this meant pushing far enough up the river systems to prevent easy access to Tennessee and to prevent closure of the Mississippi River. In pursuit of this objective, Leonidas felt compelled to invade the ostensibly neutral state of Kentucky. When he moved, President Davis was horrified, thinking that this action would unify the then deeply divided public opinion in Kentucky against the Confederacy. Davis was right, although, as Leonidas pointed out, whatever the public might have thought about the issue, the government of Kentucky had already become at least an ally if not a full member of the Union.

A similar evaluation drove General Robert E. Lee into campaigns in the East which the Confederacy could not afford and which, ultimately, doomed it. Lee had, in effect, violated exactly the strategic decision that had won American independence: while winning his battles he lost his armies, suffering larger casualties proportionally than any other Confederate or Federal commander. Consequently, he failed in his strategic objective, which had to be to bring the federal government to a peace settlement. So brilliant, however, were his tactics that he came close to succeeding in the summer of 1863 and August of 1864. During that period, the Union will to fight faded, and many politicians and soldiers felt with Captain (later Supreme Court Justice) Oliver Wendell Holmes, Jr., that "the Army is tired with its hard and terrible experience [and] I've pretty much made up my mind that the South have achieved their independence."

The correct Union strategy was the opposite of the Confederate's: to seek battle and to use its overwhelming resources to achieve a speedy victory. It was the merit of Grant to realize this, but in the East the Union commanders were slow to understand. Whereas it should have been General Lee who was carefully hoarding his soldiers and equipment, it was General George B. McClellan who did. Where Lee attacked, McClellan evaded.

Generals commonly have a terrible time making the right choice between tactics and strategy; it is in the nature of the profession to seek actions that will win fame. So rather the grand theater of heroic combat than the marketplace of small transactions. In the Revolution, General Nathanael Greene, by necessity, made the right choice but hated every minute he did it. He knew he would never rank as a great general by retreating, but it was his strategy of judicious retreat, avoidance of major battles and engagement only in selected small-scale ambuscades that won the Revolution. In the Civil War, the South had no Greene.

It was in the West, as James M. McPherson has written, that the Confederacy "really lost the war." There General Braxton Bragg was in overall command during the crucial phases. A methodical organizer, Bragg was an erratic campaigner, throwing men heedlessly into battle but then, having suffered heavy casualties, failing to follow up when victory was at hand. In the midst of battle, he lost attention, becoming lethargic, unable to concentrate and shying away from decisive action. Feared by the soldiers whose lives he so easily jeopardized, he also lost the confidence of all his subordinate commanders, among whom he constantly sought scapegoats for his own mistakes.

Leonidas, as the commander of one of the two corps that usually made up Bragg's army, was often Bragg's target. Leonidas advised, argued and suffered but carried out orders until, after the failure of Bragg's campaign into Kentucky, he wrote, on behalf of all the other generals in Bragg's command, to President Davis urging his removal. The move was perhaps necessary, but it was not judicious. It merely annoyed Davis, who was a close personal friend of Bragg's and was unwilling to credit serious criticism of him. He summoned Leonidas to Richmond and grilled him on his relations with Bragg. Leonidas was blunt in his replies and summed up by saying that, while Bragg was a good organizer, he was "wanting in the higher elements of generalship." Like many political leaders when faced with an unpleasant task, Davis temporized, leaving Bragg in command and promoting Leonidas to lieutenant general. That, of course, solved nothing but left Bragg furious with Leonidas.

Bragg's opportunity to act against Leonidas came after the Battle of Chickamauga, a little "wide place in the road" a dozen miles south of Chattanooga, Tennessee, on September 19 and 20, 1863. There, Bragg had again failed to follow up on a hard-fought victory, and again he sought scapegoats. He turned on Leonidas and accused him of not launching an attack as promptly as he was ordered to do and relieved Leonidas and two other generals of their commands. Leonidas then requested a court of inquiry. Bragg refused and got rid of Leonidas by sending him off to Mississippi to command Confederate forces there.

The result was far more serious for the Confederate command than the personal feud between Bragg and Leonidas. Virtually all of the senior officers in Bragg's army petitioned President Davis, saying,

> Two weeks ago this army, elated by a great victory which promised to prove the most fruitful of the war, was in readiness to pursue its defeated enemy. That enemy, driven in confusion from the field, was fleeing in disorder and panic-stricken across the Tennessee River . . . Whatever may have been accomplished heretofore, it is certain that the fruits of victory of Chickamauga have now escaped our grasps . . . The Army of Tennessee, stricken with a complete paralysis, will in a few days' time be thrown strictly on the defensive, and may deem itself fortunate if it escapes from its present position without disaster.

The prophecy proved all too true.

Both Leonidas and Ulysses S. Grant, linked together at the first significant battle, also shared such serious problems with their superiors that both were threatened with arrest and courts-martial. Opposed to Bragg in the West and then Lee in the East, Grant was the general who understood the fundamental advantage of the North in manpower and supplies. He sought battle under almost all circumstances, knowing that he could afford to lose more soldiers than his opponents, that victory could be achieved only by "wasting" the rebel army. And for this reason also, he always opposed, as he did at the beginning of the war in his correspondence with Leonidas, the exchange of prisoners. As he wrote to President Lincoln, as difficult as it was to guard, care for and feed prisoners, doing so was far easier than fighting the Confederate soldiers they would again become when released. He and all the Union commanders knew that whereas released Federal prisoners tended not to reenlist but just to go home, and so were lost to the army, Confederate prisoners usually rejoined—as young Captain James H. had done immediately upon his release. Grant's strategy thus emphasized killing or capturing and imprisoning Confederates regardless of cost in men and treasure.

P REVENTING THE DEATH OF THEIR SOLDIERS BECAME ONE OF the great tasks of southern civilians. Men did most of the fighting and dying, but women not only helped to feed, clothe and feed them but also gave them moral support. As James H.'s mother, Sallie Polk, wrote her son on February 26, 1862,

> I go nearly every day or two to the Hospital—and carry some-
> thing to our sick and wounded Soldiers—poor fellow[s]—
> what a life—but they are so well cared for in Columbia [Ten-
> nessee], the ladies have devoted themselves to them—Your
> dear old Aunt Mary is there every day of her life—Heaven will
> bless her—for her works . . .

These were common activities, but there were others that were less common. As Federal Provost Judge John Fitch wrote,

> Nashville was a rebel city, occupied as conquered territory,
> and swarming with traitors, smugglers and spies. Of its male
> inhabitants a large number were in the rebel army; and its
> women, arrogant and defiant, were alike outspoken in their
> treason and indefatigable in their efforts to aid that cause for
> which their brothers, sons and husbands were fighting. The
> city, in fact, was one vast "Southern Aid Society," whose sole
> aim was to plot secret treason and furnish information to the
> rebel leaders.

Often in such occupied areas as Nashville, the usual roles of men and women in war were reversed. Men who were aged, sick or wounded stayed at home and passively suffered the privation of war or the rigors of military occupation. Conversely, women sometimes acted as spies and occasionally, as in the escapade of Antoinette Polk, they went considerably further, helping Confederate soldiers to avoid capture. As Mary Polk Branch, her cousin, described Antoinette's famous ride,

> She was visiting me when I saw in front of my house, on the Hampshire pike, Major Hunter Nicholson dashing down the pike, pursued by cavalry in blue coats. I knew at once that Columbia had been taken possession of by the Federals and I called to Antoinette Polk. She came down the steps, the gauntlets in her hand, and her hat with its long ostrich plume in the other, ran for her horse in the stable, dashed through the woods, to reach Mount Pleasant pike, where Ashwood Hall [the plantation of her father, Andrew Jackson Polk], and the homes of her two uncles, each a mile apart, were situated. They were filled with [Confederate] soldiers who would be taken by surprise and captured, unless she reached them in time.
>
> She gained the gate, which opened upon the pike, and as she did so, she saw approaching her three Federal soldiers, fast riders thrown out to capture prisoners, and then commenced a wonderful race. The horse [she rode] was a young thoroughbred, and seemed to realize her peril. The last she saw of the cavalrymen they were digging their spurs into their horses' sides with their heads almost on a level with those of their horses. She gained the woods and was lost to their sight. On reaching Ashwood she roused the Confederate soldiers, and was taken almost fainting from her horse; the horse's mouth covered with blood and foam from its bit. The [pursuing federal] soldiers picked up a trophy, her long ostrich plume, which dropped from her hat, and returning showed it to the colonel, who said, ''Why did you not shoot her in the back?''

One of the most remarkable characteristics of the Civil War was how close the combatants were to one another. Not only did they speak the same language and share experience and even family ties, but they were physically often right on top of one another. The primitive photographs of the period show the dead and wounded stretched out side by side, and drawings depict the soldiers just a few feet apart blazing into one another's faces with rifles and pistols or plunging their bayonets into one another's bodies. As Sam Watkins, a private in a Tennessee regiment, saw in battle after battle, "The dead, dying, and wounded of both armies, Confederate and Federal, were blended in inextricable confusion. Now and then a cluster of dead Yankees and close by a cluster of dead Rebels. It was like the Englishman's grog—'alf and 'alf."

Casualties were horrendous. Of one battle, Watkins wrote,

> . . . on this memorable day, every man in our regiment killed from one score to four score, yea, five score men. I mean from twenty to one hundred each. All that was necessary was to load and shoot. In fact, I will ever think that the reason they [the federal troops] did not capture our works was the impossibility of their living men passing over the bodies of the dead. The ground was piled up with one solid mass of dead and wounded Yankees. I learned afterwards from the burying squad that in some places they were piled up like cord wood, twelve deep.

Overall in the war, one out of four white American males of military age was killed or wounded. Officers were in the thick of the fighting too. Indeed, probably more generals were killed in the Civil War than in any war before or since. Maps were virtually nonexistent, communications were slow and rudimentary and units became almost inextricably mixed in the whirling melee. Soldiers just behind the next wall or around the bend of a path might be friend or foe. From days of marching and fighting, men were exhausted, hungry and terrified. As they became separated and command broke down, each man judged that any shape or shadow might mean death. Often soldiers opened fire in numb reaction to unseen or unidentified dangers, sometimes shooting their comrades. It was in this way that General Stonewall Jackson was shot by his own troops. "Friendly fire" was one of the most dreaded of combat experiences because it often provoked a return fire and so did not only pointless but double damage. And it was virtually impossible to stop once it became general.

At the Battle of Perryville in the first half of October 1862, several Federal and Confederate generals and a larger number of regimental and company commanders had already been killed. Virtually all order disappeared. Just at twilight, when there was enough light to shoot but not enough to identify, one of Leonidas's brigades moved into a new position. From his command post, he watched with horror as it came under fire from a nearby regiment. Casualties were already almost unbearable, and this accident was one catastrophe too much. In those days when communication depended upon a fast-riding aide, he would normally have sent one of his young men galloping to warn the two regiments to cease firing, but in the confusion of the battle, Leonidas found himself temporarily alone. Without a minute to spare, knowing that the firing would soon become deadly, he put his spurs to his horse and dashed toward the nearest regiment.

By that time, it was too dark to see more than shapes, and as he galloped up, he shouted angrily for the commanding officer. When that man appeared, Leonidas ordered him to stop shooting immediately. The colonel stammered out, "Why, sir, I thought they were enemies." "Enemies!" retorted the general. "Why, I have only just left them myself! Cease firing this instant!" Then, thinking to ensure compliance, he demanded the name of the colonel.

By this time, nonplussed and somewhat suspicious, the colonel returned the question: who was this strange figure who had ridden out of the dark with such preemptory orders? In a flash, Leonidas realized that the regiment was not one of his. Probably the Indiana accent alerted him. But alone and surrounded by Federal soldiers, he could only hope to bluff. "I'll soon show you who I am, sir," he shouted in now pretended fury. "Cease firing, sir, at once!" And wheeling his horse, he began a slow canter back to his own lines, yelling as he went, "Cease firing . . . cease firing . . . cease firing!" Then, reaching the protection of some trees, he raced as fast as his horse would carry him. Telling the story later, he was able to laughingly claim that "I have reconnoitered those fellows pretty closely."

Guarding the Mississippi River was one of the most critical tasks of Leonidas's troops. The Federal forces deployed a strong force of riverboats, many of which mounted heavy artillery, and the Confederates created a series of strongpoints to try to block them. While the South did not have the industrial capacity to manufacture many cannons, priority was given to a few very large guns for use in such forts as Columbus. One of these was named Lady Polk either as a joke on Leonidas or in compliment to his wife—no one dared ask too closely—and just after the Battle of Belmont Leonidas came to inspect it. As the officer in charge, Lieutenant E. W. Rucker, recounted,

We had gotten the gun mounted and all right for inspection and trial . . . when Captain Keiter and his men, about fifteen as I remember, came up and saluted General Polk and said he was ready, and asked the General if he would not step to the windward a little in order to better observe the effect of the shot, which was intended to go up the river, and we were to see about where it would fall in the water . . . Captain Keiter stepped to the rear, and gave the command "Fire!" The gunner pulling the laniard, the gun immediately exploded and was broken all the pieces. At the same time, almost at the same instant, a magazine which was built in the parapet on the right side exploded also. There were several hundred pounds of powder,—yes, a thousand or more,—which exploded. General Polk and I were hurled about twenty-five or thirty feet back, and fell together . . . As I picked myself up, I felt someone by my side. I touched him, and inquired, "Who is this?", and the answer came "General Polk." It was dark as midnight, or appeared so, the smoke and dust having gotten into our eyes and hair and clothes . . . I said "General isn't this Hell?" . . . and he answered that it smelled [like brimstone].

Battle followed battle, skirmish followed skirmish, countermarch followed march in numbing sequence. We remember at least some of the names of the great events—Gettysburg, Shiloh, Antietam, Perryville, Chattanooga, Chickamauga, Bull Run—but for the soldiers there was little to distinguish the great events from the exhausting daily routine of death. On September 28, 1863, Leonidas's son-in-law and aide, Lieutenant William Dudley Gale, wrote to his wife, Leonidas's daughter Katherine, about a night that was becoming almost typical.

The moon was shining as clear as possible and gave a most unearthly appearance to this horrid scene. Wounded, dying, and dead men and horses were strewn around me & under me everywhere for the field was yet hot & smoking from the last charge, and thousands were lying insensible, or in agony, where a few short moments [before] they stood in battle array. I can never forget the horrid indecency of death that was pictured on their agonized faces upturned in the pale moonlight as I spurred my mare over and around their prostate forms. Ten thousand fires lit up the scene and revealed still more vividly this hideous carnival of Death.

But occasionally in the midst of bleak military dispatches comes a spark of humor and happiness at being alive. Another of Leonidas's aides, Lieutenant W. B. Richards, wrote in his diary on September 8,

Clear and Warm . . . The Army marching in the very best
of spirits under the conviction that we are to have a fight. The
dust terrible and very warm. Reached Scotts on Chickmauga
Creek About 5 P.M. . . . went in bathing with [young staff
officers] Yeatman, Williams, Meck [Polk], Murphy, Morgan,
Wheeler and Gale. Delightful. Wagons and the Army late getting into camp, sleeping in the orchard on the straw.

On May 11, 1864, Lieutenant Gale stood with Leonidas while he
reverted to his role as a bishop and baptized Lieutenant General John
Bell Hood. "The rite was administered by Lt. Gen'l Polk," Gale wrote,
"with two or three witnesses & by the light of a dim tallow candle. Lt.
Gen'l H. seemed much impressed. He is a fine looking man, 6 feet 2
inches high, thin narrow face, bright and intelligent, & beard, changing
into white nearly in the moustache. He is much impeded by the loss of
his limb." (Hood had lost his right leg at the Battle of Chickamauga.)

Two weeks of heavy skirmishing, attacks and retreats followed as
the heavily outnumbered southern troops fell back. At one point on May
27, they determined to hold a line and, in Gale's words,

At 3 P.M. a vigorous assault was made on our extreme right
which was held by Gen'l Granberry's Brigade and Gen'l
Govan's. The object evidently was to turn our right. The enemy approached suddenly and in 3 or more lines of Battle and
were repulsed with such havoc as I have never seen on any
field. They were under our fire for 3 and ¹/₂ hours but were
protected a good deal by dense woods, but when he made the
assault on Granberry, he got within 20 yds. of our line, and
here their track was marked by a line of dead that were in
many places so close to each other that one could not walk
among them. Some of them were horribly mutilated and all
nearly were shot in the head or neck. I saw one man who had

11 balls in his head. Oh the horrid sight! Were it not to defend our soil & families I should fear the curse of God would come upon us for such horrible butchery. Every principle of my nature revolts at the practice & institutions of war. God grant that we may soon have an end of this dreadful carnage. Gen'l Cleburne [commanding the brigade of Brigadier General Lucius Eugene Polk] estimates that he killed and wounded at least 3,500 men.

Lucius Eugene Polk fought, perhaps, the hardest war of all the Polk family. Born in 1833, the son of Will's second son, Dr. William Julius, he enlisted at twenty-seven years of age as a private in Yell's Rifles of Arkansas. Promoted to third lieutenant (or ensign), he commanded the company at the Battle of Shiloh, where he was wounded in the face. As most of the officers had been killed, the regiment elected him colonel. He was wounded again at the Battle of Richmond on August 30, 1862, and again at the Battle of Perryville on October 8, 1862. In December of that year, he was promoted to brigadier general. Engaged in almost every battle, Lucius was repeatedly mentioned in dispatches for outstanding bravery. At Kennesaw Mountain, Georgia, in June of 1864, he received his fourth wound (being struck by a cannonball) and, crippled, was forced to retire from the army.

(That branch of the family suffered terribly: Lucius's brother Cadwalader had his horse shot out from under him and was left for dead on the battlefield but recovered and finally made his way home. Another brother, Rufus, having been wounded and captured, spent his seventeenth birthday in a prison on Johnson's Island. An uncle, General Laurence Branch, was killed at Sharpsburg.)

Returning on crutches to his home at Columbia, Tennessee, Lucius lived quietly almost to the end of the century. In 1887, restored to his civil rights, Lucius was elected to the Tennessee Senate. We will meet him again.

LEONIDAS WAS DESCRIBED BY HIS ENGLISH VISITOR COLONEL Fremantle as "a good-looking, gentleman-like man with all the manners and affability of a 'grand seigneur.' He is fifty-seven years of age—tall, upright, and looks much more the soldier than the clergyman . . . He is much beloved by the soldiers on account of his great personal courage and agreeable manners." His staff officers adored him. As Gale wrote to his wife (Leonidas's daughter) on Sunday May 12, 1864,

Rain all night and continuing this morning, promising another bad day. The condition of the troops is bad indeed. For twelve days they have been wet to the skin each day and all the time covered with mud. The only consolation being that our enemy is suffering in the same degree, and that it is all for the cause [for] which we have left home and friends and all. Today we were all gratified to hear the Gen'l read the morning Service. This is the first time since the war began has he done so. I am more than gratified to find his military life has not impaired his Church manner at all but that he possesses as much of the truth and beauty of a true devotional manner as he ever did. God grant the influence of the example of our beloved General & Bishop may not be lost on any of us . . ."

Then came a profound shock. Two days later, Gale wrote again.

Tuesday 14th . . . Oh day of gloom! Oh black eclipse. Oh day of agony and deep distress for today has fallen one of Earth's noblest and best, the bravest & truest of all our brave . . .

It had been agreed that this morning Gen'l [Joseph E.] Johnston should call by for Gen'l Polk & that they should proceed to the Hdqrs. of Gen'l [William J.] Hardee and taking him along, go to the hill held by Major Gen'l [William B.] Bate and reconnoitre the enemy's line. This hill called Pine Mountain, is a round hill rising, detached, out of the plain and about one mile & a quarter from our line of battle and in front of Gen'l Hardee's right & Gen'l Polk's left. Arriving at the hill all dismounted and went cautiously to the crest where Slocum's battery was in position. We had a good view of the enemy's line in front & below, could see his working parties and his flag not more than $5/8$ of a mile distant. We were continually warned by the cannoniers to keep out of sight or we should be shot, but emboldened by the silence that reigned everywhere the Gen'ls walked about and examined the enemy's line to their satisfaction, and had, as by common resolution begun to separate and get away, when the report of a rifled cannon was born upon the air and at the same instant almost the whistling shell buried itself in the parapet near us. We all separated instantly and sought safety by retiring, I with Gen'l Hardee a little to the right & Gen'l Polk & Gen'l Johnston, who were engaged in conversation, to the left. In a few moments I saw them turn and start in the direction of where I was, which was the way to our horses. Just at this time the second shot came and as soon as the report was over a man said to me, one of the Gen'ls was killed. I asked what Gen'l (Gen'l Jackson of the Cavalry was there too) when he said Gen'l Polk. I started in the direction where I last saw the Gen'l and met Lt. Hopkins, pale and excited, calling to me that the Gen'l was killed by a shell in [his] side. I ran up at once and found him lying on his back, nervously working his under jaw. I saw, Oh God, the dreadful hole in his side, his broken arms, his grey head & streaming beard, but I was too late to catch a word. He was already gone, he was dead . . .

It appears that after he and Gen'l Johnston had finished their observation on the left, they started back and later

turned away to the right, thus placing the point of the hill between himself and danger, while Gen'l Polk walked directly
forward and when he gained the apex, paused for a second to
take a last look when the fatal shot came and he fell. He was
hit evidently by a 3 inch rifled shell, unexploded, which struck
him just above the point of the right elbow and a little behind,
passing squarely through his chest and coming out just above
the left shoulder & a little behind. He received the shot within
a few minutes of 12 on Tuesday, the 14th of June, 1864, at
Pine Mountain, about 6 miles N West of Marietta.

By what must have been one of the remarkable coincidences of the
war, William Harrison Polk, a soldier in the Federal army and a descendant of Ephraim Polk, who had migrated down the Ohio River to Kentucky, was just a few yards from the cannon that fired the fatal shot. He
later wrote Leonidas's son a graphic account of what happened on the
Union side.

A young deserter came into our lines, and the three generals
being clearly observed on the cleared space of Pine Mountain
[he] was handed a powerful field glass and asked to name who
the officers were. [Orders were given to fire.] The first shot
went high, skipping over the top, when two of the officers
walked away. [Then the gunnery commander said,] "Let me
sight that gun," which he did very carefully, the[n] gave the
word "fire." That shot proved the fatal one, at once your signal corps on top of the mountain wig-wagged the news to the
rear. Captain Thayer, Division signal officer, who had deci-
phered your code a few days before spoke up and said: "That
shot killed General Polk . . ."

The continuing tragedy of the war was brought out by William Harrison
Polk's next remarks: the gunnery commander said, "Thank God! They

killed my brother yesterday and I have killed a Lieut. General.'' A few days later, the gunnery commander went forward ''between the lines of fire of two guns, to watch where the shots struck and to pass back word to Elevate or depress the guns. One of your sharpshooters evidently saw him peep from behind a tree and then turn his head to speak to the gunner. While his head was so turned, a bullet entered the back of his head, coming out from [the front of] his head.'' The two events were, in the grand scheme of things, just two more deaths.

Meanwhile on the Confederate side, legends rapidly grew. Private Sam Watkins, who happened to be on the spot when Leonidas was killed, later wrote,

> I saw him while the infirmary corps were bringing him off the field. He was as white as a piece of marble, and a most remarkable thing about him was, that not a drop of blood was ever seen to come out of the place through the cannon ball had passed. My pen and ability is inadequate to the task of doing his memory justice. Every private soldier loved him. Second to Stonewall Jackson, his loss was the greatest the South ever sustained. When I saw him there dead, I felt that I had lost a friend whom I have ever loved and respected, and that the South had lost one of her best and greatest generals.

General William T. Sherman, reporting the death of Leonidas to Federal commander General Henry W. Halleck, wrote laconically, ''We killed Bishop Polk yesterday and today the fighting goes well.''

AND SO IT DID. THE FEDERAL JUGGERNAUT ROLLED INEXORAbly forward. In December 1864, the end was near, and again Gale graphically paints the breakup of the Confederate army in a letter to his wife, this time from Tupelo, Mississippi.

As our men fell back before the advancing yankees Mary Bradford ran out under heavy fire and did all she could to induce
the men to stop and fight, appealing to them and begging
them, but in vain . . . Gen Hood told me yesterday he intended to mention her courageous conduct in his report,
which will immortalize her. The men seemed utterly lethargic
and without interest in battle. I never witnessed such a want of
enthusiasm, and began to fear for tomorrow, hoping that Gen
Hood would retreat during the night, cross Duck River, and
then stop and fight; but he would not give up. However, he
sent all his [supply] wagons to Franklin, which prepared the
men still more for the stampede of the next day. The enemy
adapted their line to ours, and about 9 a.m. began the attack
on [General Benjamin] Cheatham, trying all day to turn him
and [get] in his rear. They succeeded about 2 or 3 P.M. in
gaining the pike behind the gap, and in crossing got in the rear
of Gen [Alexander P.] Stewarts headquarters, which on the
side of the knob [a hill near Columbia] looking toward Nashville. We could see the whole line in our front—every move
attack and retreat. It was magnificent. What a grand sight it
was! I could see the Capitol all day, and the churches. The
yanks had three lines of battle everwhere I could see, and parks
of artillery playing upon us and raining shot and shell for eight
mortal hours. I could see nearly every piece in our front, even
the gunners at work. They made several heavy assaults upon
Gen [Robert E. Lee's son General G. W. C.] Lee's line near
John Thompson's, and one in front of Mrs. Mullin's. At length
having gained our rear, about 4 P.M. they made a vigorous assault upon the whole right line and left. Bate gave way, and
they poured over in clouds behind Walthall, which, of course
forced him to give way, and then by brigades the whole line
from left to right. Lee held on bravely a while longer than the
centre and left.

Here was a scene which I shall not attempt to describe, for it is impossible to give you any idea of an army frightened and routed. Some brave effort was made to rally the men and make a stand, but all control over them was gone, and they flatly refused to stop, throwing down their guns, and indeed, everything that impeded their flight, and every man fled for himself.

Reynold's brigade was ordered to the right just before the rout began, and got to which [where] I was when I halted it and got the General to form it in line across the point of the knob just in the path of the flying mass, hoping to rally some men on this and save the rest by gaining time for all to come out of the valley. NOT A MAN WOULD STOP! The First Tennessee came by, and its Colonel House, was the only man who would stop with us, and finding none of his men willing to stand, he too went on his way. As soon as I found all was lost, and the enemy closing in around us, I sent a Courier to Gen Stewart, who had gone to Gen Hood's quarters in the rear of Lea's house, to inform him of the fact, that he might save himself. This courier was mortally wounded, and left at Franklin. Finding the enemy closing in around us, and all indeed gone, I ordered the couriers and clerks who were there to follow me, and we rode as fast as I could to where I thought Gen Stewart and Gen Hood were. They were gone, and in their places were the yankees. I turned my horses head toward the steep knobs and spurred away. It was the only chance of escape left. The first place I struck the hill was too steep for any horse to climb, and I skirted along the hills hoping to find some place easier of ascent, but none seemed to exist. Finally I reached a place not so steep, and in the midst of thousands of retreating soldiers I turned my horse's head for the ascent, resolved to try it. The bullets begun to come thick and fast. Now, I found my saddle nearly off, and was forced to get down, but on I went on foot. All along the poor, frightened fellows were crying out to me, "Let me hold on to your stirrup, for God's sake." "Give me your hand and help me, if you please." Some were wounded, and many exhausted from anxiety and over-exertion. On I struggled until, I too, became exhausted and unable to move. By this time the enemy had gotten to the foot of the hill and were firing at us freely. What was I to do? I twisted my hand in my horses mane and was borne to the top of the hill by the noble animal, more dead than alive. I was safe, though, and so were my men. We descended the Southern slope and entered the deep valley whose shadows were darkened by approaching night. The woods were filled with retreating men. I joined the crowd and finally made my way to the Franklin Pike, where I found Gen Stewart who was much relieved, for I had been reported as certainly killed or captured. All night long we fled . . . On we marched, through ice and rain and snow, sleeping on the wet ground at night. Many thousands were barefooted, actually leaving the prints of blood upon the ground, as the enemy pressed us in the rear . . .

The fate of the whole Confederate army was summed up by the experience of the regiment in which so many Polks had served and died, the 1st Tennessee. When it left Nashville on May 10, 1861, it numbered 1,250; during the war, approximately 3,200 men had served in it; and at its surrender on April 26, 1865, it numbered just 65. Only 7 of the original group were still there.

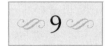

REVOLUTION
AND DIASPORA

"When things go wrong, go west"

WHEN HE MADE HIS WAY BACK TO HIS FATHER'S HOUSE IN rural Tennessee, James H.'s ragged clothes and emaciated body seemed mocked by the serene white columns that loomed before Rattle & Snap. But as he walked slowly up the long drive through the park, he began to see that the house and the very land had been almost as battered as he. Fences had been torn down for firewood, untended fields were overgrown with weeds and brush and a stillness had fallen upon the land. Horses and cattle were no more and the throngs of field hands had departed. As he reached the front porch, he could see grimmer reminders of war: broken windows and the marks of bullets.

But the greeting he received was warm. His father, George, who was crippled by arthritis, limped more than James remembered, and his face was lined by care and worry. His embrace was still strong but less with bodily strength than with emotion: in the last bitter months of the war, all communication between father and son had been replaced by lurid rumor. Each thought the other had been killed, and James, walking back along the trail of General William Sherman's March to the Sea, had imagined that Rattle & Snap, like dozens of plantations he had passed, would be only a smoking ruin. He was astonished to find that it was not. As his eyes wandered over the familiar rooms, he noticed that almost no furniture remained.

From behind the house, the voice of his mother, Sallie, suddenly sounded. Sallie came running into the room, brushing her hair out of her face. Tears streamed down her cheeks as she embraced James, and her hands cautiously checked his face, shoulders and back for the wounds she had feared.

Sensing her fear, James laughed and said that he had been lucky, that nothing was wrong that a few good meals could not mend. Then, in his turn, James noticed not only the telltale marks of grief and worry on Sallie's face but the unfamiliar bend of her back and the roughness of her hands. He had seen such signs before. Of necessity and hunger, she had turned from crocheting to hoeing. There would be few good meals there.

Barely able to tear themselves physically apart, they began to catch up on recent events. Each wanted to know what had happened to the other. James brushed aside all questions on the last, bitter days of the army's rout and surrender and his long walk home. What remained of his shoes spoke eloquently to that. But he demanded to know all about them, about relatives, about houses and about the blacks. The story was not a pleasant one.

The best news was that none of the family's houses had been burned. One was on the point of being torched when the Federal officer who had orders to demolish it saw a portrait of the owner wearing a Masonic key and, being a Mason himself, took his men away without carrying out the order. But bands of soldiers, often acting on their own, helped themselves not only to all the farm animals and grain but to anything that caught their eye in the house or outbuildings. Sometimes if they didn't find what they wanted, they just smashed or burned whatever was handy. There was no way for George to stop them, but Sallie sometimes appealed to their sense of shame.

As for the nearly one hundred blacks whom James remembered, most had left. Some were earlier taken away by the Federal troops to use as laborers to work on fortifications; only a few of them returned. Then, when the Confederate forces pushed back into the county, other blacks ran away, fearing that the Confederates would impress them as laborers or even evacuate them into the Deep South. In any event, since there was no seed to plant, no tools to till the soil and no draft animals, most of the field hands had drifted off. Some had made their way into Nashville but had come back after a particularly vicious riot in which Federal white soldiers killed a number of former slaves. Finally, only the household staff, including James's boyhood companion, Bob, remained.

NOT MANY MILES AWAY, SIX-YEAR-OLD MARY DEMOVILLE "Molly" Harding, whom James would later marry, was also beginning to sort out the memories of her own wartime tragedies. Two years earlier her father and mother had decided to flee embattled Nashville for the illusory safety of Atlanta. It was a terrible mistake. The country through which they had to pass had been picked clean by the armies of both sides, and as all semblance of law and order disappeared, the roads were filled with desperate men. On crossing the Appalachians, Molly's mother contracted first typhoid and then pneumonia and died. Dispirited, nearly starving and himself sick, Molly's father turned his wagon around to take his four children, including the baby who had been born on the road, back to Nashville. That was as dangerous a move as the decision to flee. On the road, they were repeatedly accosted by bandit gangs and stripped of the little they had left, but in an unusual act of pity for the little children, the usually vicious robbers left them their wagon.

Nashville was no safe haven either. As a prominent Confederate and member of the Harding family, one of whose leading members was already in prison, Molly's father risked arrest and imprisonment; in fact, when the family reached Nashville, Federal troops immediately surrounded the house in which they had taken refuge, but, by a fortunate coincidence, the wife of the Federal commanding general came to the house and saw the condition of the little children. Due to her intervention, Molly's father was paroled and given a pass to get out of the city.

Others were not so fortunate. Military officers, naturally, were treated with great suspicion even when badly wounded. When Marshall "Marsh" Tate Polk, the nephew (and as a young man the ward) of James K. Polk, was captured after he lost a leg at the Battle of Shiloh, the president's widow, Sarah, fearing that he would die in prison, went to General Philip Sheridan to ask for his release. Sheridan refused, saying that he had known Marsh at West Point years before and was sure that he "would come back to fight them strapped to his saddle if he let him go." Sheridan was right. Once he got free, Marsh did return to battle, strapped to his saddle.

The willingness to continue the fight, indeed the lust for battle, that the Federals ascribed to Confederate officers was one of the several causes of the treatment the Confederates feared they would receive at the end of the war. They had good reason to fear. Examples were made of a number of officers. One of the most famous was the commander of the Confederate raider *Alabama,* who, when captured, was charged with piracy, a hanging offense. Both officers and civilians feared what amounted to war crimes trials. Right after the fall of Richmond, Vice President Andrew Johnson publicly called for the "traitors, at least the leading ones, [to] be executed." A few hours later, when President Lincoln was shot, Johnson was heard to repeat time after time, "They shall suffer for this. They shall suffer for this." It was in this mood that, shortly after assuming the presidency, he forced General Sherman to withdraw the terms of an armistice (including a universal amnesty) he had concluded with Confederate General Joseph E. Johnston. What would have happened is unknown, since General Grant intervened and threatened to resign if the parole Sherman had granted was not honored. Johnston at least partially backed down, while Sherman, himself no friend of the South, was outraged and wrote to James E. Yeatman, brother-in-law of Lucius Polk,

> I confess without shame that I am tired and sick of war. It's glory is all moonshine. Even success the most brilliant, is over dead and mangled bodies, the anguish and the lamentations of distant families, appealing to me for missing sons, husbands and fathers. You too, have seen these things and I know you also are tired of war; and are willing to let the civil tribunals resume their place; and as far as I know, all the fighting men of our army want peace. It is only those who had not heard a shot, nor heard the shrieks and groans of the wounded and lacerated (friend or foe) that cry aloud for more blood, more vengeance, more desolation and so help me God, as a man and a soldier I will not strike a foe, who stands unarmed and submissively before me, but will say, "Go and sin no more."

Whether those were the sentiments of the fighting men, Sherman was right that they were not those of the politicians in Washington. Congressmen wanted blood, and if thwarted from vengeance on paroled soldiers, they would hunt down the civilian leaders. The prime fugitive, of course, was Confederate President Jefferson Davis, who was captured on May 10, imprisoned and even put in chains. Two members of his cabinet, Robert Toombs and the only Jewish member, Judah P. Benjamin, decided not to test the issue and escaped to Europe.

Although by no means a prominent figure, Andrew Jackson Polk, who had early been invalided out of military service and spent most of the war trading in cotton as a civilian, also prudently made his way to the safety of Switzerland. Fearing reprisals and having a fortune to protect, he never returned, and his daughter, the gallant and glamorous Antoinette, married into the French aristocracy to begin a new branch of the family.

It wasn't just the government that came down hard on the Rebels. Hatred was a common emotion. More than other conflicts, civil wars leave residues of enmity that last for generations; scattered throughout the border states and the North were thousands of families who had lost relatives, husbands or friends. Vengeance was in the air. And, disarmed, the demobilized Confederates feared for their lives from the attacks of those against whom they had fought. In some areas, there were more sordid motivations. As had happened in the Revolutionary War, abandoned property had acquired new owners who were unwilling to give it up and so opposed the return of the former owners. These sentiments were particularly strong in such disputed border areas as eastern Tennessee, Kentucky, Missouri, West Virginia and Maryland. There returnees were quickly turned away, as Esther Polk recounts.

In 1861, Esther's husband, Maryland former governor Enoch Lowe, who was known to be pro-Confederate, had fled to Virginia. Then in 1863, when the Union army had approached Richmond, the Lowes fled farther south to Georgia, where they stayed with former governor James Johnson, whose wife was Esther's aunt. After the Confederacy surrendered, they returned to Maryland but were quickly forced to leave again. Not only did they meet with public hostility, but Enoch could no longer practice as a lawyer and his house had been seized.

At that time, the states that were farther from the front were believed to be less hostile to returning Confederates than those on the border. Cosmopolitan New York was thought to be the most tolerant of the lot; so, as Esther later wrote in a memoir for her daughter, former Confederates "from all ranks in life were to be found in New York, occupied in menial services trying to make a living." Thus,

> In April 1866 we journeyed into New York with our nine children and there your father at the age of 45 years entered again into the battle of life. I have often thought how courageous to

go into a strange land, in an unsympathetic community . . . Truly it was courage engendered in a transcendent sense of duty to his children. The burden was heavy—seemed over-powering—but manfully he shouldered it and marched on though staggering under its weight.

Not so prominent as former governor Lowe, and probably benefiting from the tendency to treat soldiers as honorable exceptions, William Mecklenburg (Meck) Polk, son of Leonidas, also set out for the North. Having ended his military service as inspector general in the Army of Tennessee, and with little education except for two years at Virginia Military Institute, he decided in 1865 to become a doctor.

After a brief period in the University of Louisiana, Meck enrolled in the medical department—as it then was—of Columbia University. He could hardly have sought a safer haven, and he made good use of the opportunity. Less than four years after the end of the war, he graduated and got a position as an intern in Bellevue Hospital. Having got his feet firmly on this professional ladder, he never took them off. In 1880, he became professor of obstetrics and gynecology at New York University and in 1898 became dean of the medical department of Cornell. But throughout those years, he must often have cast his eyes back to the stirring days of the war, since, in addition to over a hundred medical papers, he wrote a laudatory biography of his father, the bishop and general. His nostalgia was assuaged by the public recognition he received in generous amounts for his medical accomplishments, which culminated in his being elected president of the New York Academy of Medicine. And far beyond the other members of his generation, he left an estate of nearly a million dollars and a son who had risen to high government office.

Meck was a prime example of a group of men who have been termed Confederate carpetbaggers. Less well known than the northern carpetbaggers and scalawags who went south, they were surprisingly numerous. The historian Daniel Sutherland believes that as many as sixteen thousand southerners moved north at about the same time as Meck did. To illustrate them, Sutherland picked out the fictional character Ashley in the popular novel *Gone With the Wind* as a sort of archetype.

> Had Ashley gone north, he would have been a fairly typical Confederate carpetbagger . . . Ashley never denounced the Confederacy or regretted his defense of southern honor. He laid down his sword willingly but not in shame. He simply understood that, whatever its merits, the Confederate cause had died at Appomattox . . . Ashley's reason for wanting to go north was characteristic too. "I want to stand on my own feet for what I'm worth," he tells Scarlett . . . "This is my last chance. I'll go North. If I go to Atlanta and work for you, I'm lost forever."

Many others fled to Mexico, and at least one Polk, Captain James Monroe, whom we met at the Battle of Gettysburg, moved to Brazil. So many left that one young woman from Georgia wrote just after Robert E. Lee's surrender, "The men [here] are all talking about going to Mexico and Brazil, [and] if all emigrate who say they are going to, we shall have a nation made up of women, negroes, and Yankees."

Well, not quite. The majority stayed in place. And there they tried to take up their lives where they had left off. One unfinished project of Leonidas Polk immediately claimed the attention of his friends and Episcopal followers: the creation of a university. The place he chose was called Sewanee, which is the Creek Indian word for "southern"; that is precisely what Leonidas had in mind, a *southern* university. His project was interrupted by the Civil War and by his death, but by 1868 his friends and followers had realized his dream. The first nine students arrived to be instructed by the institution's first four teachers. It wasn't much of a place in which they gathered. Leonidas had hoped to more or less duplicate the building of All Souls College, Oxford, but in the aftermath of the war, a few clapboard and log huts were the best that could be managed.

Hardly could auguries have been less promising. Episcopalians were a tiny minority in the South, but that fact had not deterred Leonidas, who had asserted that his church's mission was "to all, as well to those who differ from us as those who agree with us." Money was almost nonexistent, so fund-raising was exceedingly difficult. Moreover, the record of the Episcopalians in education was dismal. Whereas other Protestant churches, especially the Presbyterians, Methodists and Baptists, had been successful in founding and running colleges, the Episcopalians suffered one defeat after another. At least ten of their ventures either failed to get under way or closed after a few years, while their flagship institution, William and Mary College in Virginia, cut itself loose from the church. If it had taken uncommon vision and determination for Leonidas to found Sewanee in the relatively prosperous days before the Civil War, his successors must have been endowed with blind audacity to launch it in the war's grim and impoverished aftermath. Yet his dream was realized, and Sewanee is today recognized as one of the premier universities of the South.

Other activities were not so benign. In the aftermath of the surrender, many southern whites felt that the war had not so much ended as assumed a different shape. And having lost the "first phase," they were determined not to lose the second.

At first, like James's mother and father, they could only suffer in silent resignation or, like Molly's father, throw themselves on the mercy of the Federals. Such defenses were intrinsically weak and rapidly became even weaker. It seems to be a general fact of wars that the fighting soldiers treat their defeated foes with more compassion than those who replace them. So the letters and diaries of the Polks affirm after the Civil War. They all emphasize the importance of the military code of honor. But behind the armies came adventurers who sought only to profit from the weakness of the defeated. Many were simply thieves, but some were motivated by a genuine hatred of white southerners.

Being relatively few in number, these scalawags or carpetbaggers, as the white southerners called them, allied themselves with the recently liberated blacks. Federal officials were ambivalent about them. On the one hand, the officials sought to keep order and found it easier to do so by cooperating with such governments as remained in place. On many occasions, they were willing even to take the side of the whites against the blacks and the carpetbaggers, and they did so. But on the other hand, it was Union policy to foster the contemporary version of affirmative action by encouraging former slaves to assert their newly proclaimed rights. They created an agency to accomplish this in the Freedmen's Bureau but found the carpetbaggers also to be useful allies. So southerners assumed that the carpetbaggers were supported by the army of occupation. This made them irresistible to such people as George and Sallie.

The area in which all the conflicts occurred was race relations. And a murky area it then was. Each party saw different dimensions and disagreed, often violently, over the ways to reconstitute some sort of society. As fairly typical plantation owners, George and Sallie believed that their relationship with "their" blacks was warm and affectionate and that if the agitators would leave them alone, peace, stability and prosperity could be reestablished easily. Although Union policy varied not only over time but from area to area, it was still committed to some degree of emancipation and identified as its opponents the southern plantation owners. Blacks were also divided in their degree of sophistication and in the degree of risk they were willing to assume, but practically uniformly, they saw the old system as tyranny. Slavery in Tennessee was, as Stephen Ash has written, "first and last a system of brutal exploitation of black people by white people, and the fruit it bore was ugly and bitter." Ash recounts one of the worst among many that civilized white people could hardly believe but that, for blacks, were all too believable:

Annie Young, a slave on a Sumner County farm, watched as an overseer one day "staked a [slave] man down with two forked sticks 'cross his wrist nailed in de ground and beat him half to death with a hand saw 'til it drawed blisters. Den he mopped his back wid vinegar, salt and pepper. Sometimes dey'd drop dat hot rosin from pine knots on dose blisters.''

Such stories would have horrified George and Sallie as much as they do us. They may not have been typical; indeed, they were probably lurid exceptions, although hundreds have been collected. But they were apparently the staple news that was passed through the black community, which for the first time really was a community in which large groups were in touch with one another. Hatred ran much deeper in the black community than most whites could have imagined. As the Federal army plunged into the South, blacks not only sacked and burned plantation after plantation but in one well-publicized riot even dug up graves, scattering the bones of the former owners. It appeared to southern whites that their nightmare of slave rebellion was finally coming to pass.

Thus, clashes between those asserting new rights, those bent on taking over property and those trying to defend their positions and property were inevitable.

As THEY MADE THEIR WAY HOME AFTER THE SURRENDER, CONfederate soldiers like James thus found a world vastly different from the one they had left. Although they could not have known, they returned to a lull in the storm that was engulfing the South. In 1865 and 1866 the full impact of ''reconstruction'' had not yet arrived. They could not know that, of course, and believed that the worst was over. Emboldened, they focused their annoyance and anger on the little ways in which the freedmen demonstrated their liberation—by violating such previously forbidden actions as refusing to move off sidewalks to allow whites to pass, traveling without passports, acquiring guns and insisting on being called ''mister.'' These were petty signs, but in the making was a real social revolution.

That revolution had already been announced in the fall of 1864 by

General Sherman, who, in his Special Field Order No. 15, created what amounted to a separate black state along the Georgia and Carolina coast. Each black settler was to receive a plot of confiscated land and could borrow mules from the army to plow it. Sherman had a limited aim: he hoped to disencumber his army of the horde of black camp followers he had picked up as he marched across the South, but his action acquired massive proportions as some forty thousand blacks took up his offer. Terrified whites feared it would set a precedent.

In most areas it did not. Particularly in rural areas like the Maury County to which James H. Polk returned, the existing governments were allowed to remain more or less intact. While slavery no longer existed as a legal category, no property was confiscated. The white oligarchy became warily optimistic.

Southerners concluded that there was little northern support for actions like Sherman had taken. Their long-term belief that northerners neither understood nor liked blacks seemed to them borne out by the report that in July 1863 New York had experienced a "riot [that] degenerated into a virtual racial pogrom, with uncounted numbers of blacks murdered on the streets." Closer to home, they heard that Union soldiers stationed in Nashville frequently clashed with blacks and had also engaged in a large-scale race riot. They were well aware that in a number of northern states, blacks were still denied voting rights or even excluded from residence. Southerners believed that their attitudes toward blacks were by no means unique.

At first in Tennessee, the military rulers made little attempt to enforce emancipation. As military governor, Andrew Johnson did not favor it. Such remarks of his as "I believe slaves should be in subordination and I will live and die so believing" were widely quoted. Himself a slave owner, he repeated in a number of speeches his support for "this Government with slavery under the Constitution as it is . . . Before I would see this Government destroyed, I would send every negro back to Africa, disintegrated and blotted out of space . . ." As his biographer laconically comments, "he certainly had no great interest in the future of the freedmen."

More significant, when he became president, Johnson attempted to extend throughout the South the program he had pushed as military governor of Tennessee. Provided the states retroactively voided their secession, repudiated the Confederate debt and formally abolished slavery, Johnson sought in a series of proclamations to return virtually to the *status quo ante*. He stopped General Sherman's "revolution" dead in its tracks. Moreover, while he was regarded as being hostile to the "plantation class which had looked down on him" and vaguely talked about trying prominent Confederates for treason, he began to grant exemptions, amnesties and pardons on so generous a scale that a covert business grew up in his entourage to broker special deals.

The old southern ruling class read these signs as a license to reorganize. Particularly in rural areas, governments that had existed in Confederate times were still functioning. So, throughout the South, beginning in Mississippi and South Carolina, they began toward the end of 1865 to pass what came to be known as Black Laws, which reimposed upon the recently emancipated blacks all those laws of slavery that had not been specifically abrogated and even some that had been. Desperate for labor to cultivate their fields, they required blacks to be employed or face arrest with punishments of whipping or being "sold" as laborers. And they made even "insulting language" a crime.

But what appeared clear to the southern whites about northern attitudes was, in fact, not so. There were strong opposing forces. They made themselves felt at first in the presence of northern troops among whom a number of former black slaves served. As the army was being withdrawn, Union officials in the Freedmen's Bureau moved in to help southern blacks make the transition to freedom. In part of its activities, the Freedmen's Bureau resembled CARE in the days after the Second World War, distributing food, clothing and other necessities, but it went beyond CARE in taking on a sort of social engineering role. In addition to attempting to help blacks learn how to manage their personal economies, it redistributed abandoned or confiscated lands. Indeed, some of its supporters had intended that it go much further, managing plantations for which freed blacks would work for wages, like northern white industrial laborers, but in the final analysis most blacks were constrained to accept sharecropping, since few whites had any means to pay wages.

To say the least, the signals received in the South were mixed. Meanwhile in Washington, the policies of the White House and the Congress diverged sharply. Whereas Johnson aimed to reunify the country regardless of the fate of the black community, Republican radicals in Congress wished both to punish the South for the war and to foster the rise of blacks. The contemporary influential journalist Charles A. Dana opined that northerners didn't really care very much about the blacks (except that the Republicans wanted to win their votes), but they were uniformly unwilling to forget the rebellion. Thus, it was partly as a result of the resurgence of southern white power, but also because of the clash between the White House and the Congress, particularly after the 1866 elections returned a radical majority that could override Johnson's vetoes, that the policy of the government moved toward what came to be called Radical Reconstruction.

The Reconstruction Act of 1867 divided the eleven Confederate states (except Tennessee) into five military districts in which no attempt to retain purely white power was to be tolerated. The point of attack was precisely on such plantation owners as George. Tax rates were increased and payment in American specie, which they did not have, was required. So plantations began to be auctioned off at mere fractions of their worth. It was in this way that Rattle & Snap was sold in 1867. Its former owner, George, took refuge in the rectory of the family church, where he lived out the rest of his life "in genteel poverty." At the same time, efforts were made to uplift and empower the poor, ill-educated, politically emasculated black population. This constituted a revolution and one that was to be carried out almost literally overnight.

Arguably, had the Radical Reconstruction policy been implemented immediately after the Confederate surrender, when the fact of defeat was uppermost in everyone's mind, it would have been accepted more readily. When it was implemented, two years after the surrender and after a period in which southern leaders thought they were back in charge, it was the more opposed and the more resented. Under the best of circumstances, bringing about a modicum of tolerance and creating a minimally acceptable degree of social peace among black former slaves and white former masters would have required not only great goodwill but also constructive leadership and firm organization; in the mood of sullen defeat, unrealistic expectations and opportunism, and the lack of a consensus on what constituted legitimate public authority, it is remarkable that clashes were not worse than they were. But they were bad enough.

Being firmly opposed to Reconstruction and unable to use government, from which most of the active males were excluded, the white community turned to terrorism. Its best-known organization was the Ku Klux Klan.

For what must rank as one of America's most vicious, and certainly most weird, organizations, the origins of the Ku Klux Klan are surprisingly prosaic. Begun in Tennessee in 1866 as a sort of social club, it was apparently patterned on one of the first college "Greek letter" fraternities, the Kuklos Adelphon (or Kappa Alpha), which had been founded at the University of North Carolina in 1812. According to its founders, it originally had no political motivation or aspiration.

However, in the context of post–Civil War dislocation, when governments seemed impotent to enforce order and when armed bands roamed more or less at will, robbing, raping and killing, whites liked the idea of an occult vigilante group. Since the perceived threat was primarily from the black community, which whites believed to be governed by superstition, they also found the bizarre costume and fantastic titles of the Ku Klux Klan ideal. And they had a precedent for their use of violence in the patrols that in slave times had ranged over the countryside at night. Thus it was that in 1867 the little social club was taken over by "generals, politicians, and vigilantes." As it was transformed, at least one of its founders deemed it perverted and repugnant and urged that it be condemned and dissolved.

The Union-imposed governor of Tennessee rightly saw it as a guerrilla army, made up of former Confederate soldiers and led by the great Confederate cavalry general Nathan Bedford Forrest. It is not known for sure whether or not James H. became a member, but if he did not, he was an exception. When the United States Congress removed the civil rights of former Confederates, young men like James were turned, literally, into outlaws.

Maury County, Tennessee, was in late 1867 the major center for the Ku Klux Klan, and its ghostly beginnings are set out in a letter, written many years later in 1910, by Leonidas's daughter Susan Polk Jones to her brother Meck,

> The political state of this part of the country was in a very perilous condition, and toward Christmas failing the justice that would have been accorded by the Courts of Law, a secret organization had been formed among the better class of young men (who having served in the Confederate Army were debarred from political rights) for the protection of the safety and honor of the community. A day came when a murder was committed, near Columbia, under the most atrocious circumstances of a highly respectable and unoffending citizen; his death was quickly avenged by a body of men disguised both they and their horses beyond all recognition.
>
> At twilight they assembled as if by magic, at the grave of the victim, and mutely with mystic signs paid a last tribute to the dead. Leaving the cemetery, the mysterious band, numbering about forty, with solemn and muffled tread wended its way up the hill to the residence of Mrs. Polk [widow of Leoni-

das] . . . with bowed heads the strange company filed before her, and the waning light vividly silouetting their figures against the faintly glowing West, the red robed riders followed their white clad Captain—the original Ku-Klux-Klan passed swiftly out into the dusky night.

Southerners have liked that sort of image of the Ku Klux Klan— mysterious, mystical, solemn and chivalric—but the organization soon began to engage in barbaric practices. These caused many of the original members to oppose it as cowardly, brutal and perverse. One former officer who did was Lucius Eugene Polk. Having become known as one of the bravest and most stalwart of the Confederate commanders, he returned on crutches to Columbia, Tennessee, where he hoped to live out his life in peace. But he was to fight one more battle. As his sister Mary described the episode,

> on my brother Lucius' plantation, one night he was aroused by negroes from the quarter, calling at his window, begging him to get up; that there was "A company of Kuklux at the quarter." He went at once, and demanded what they wanted. They said: "One of the negroes on the place has done a great deal of mischief, and we have come to whip him." My brother said: "I know him to be a good negro, and you can not whip him." "But we must!" "You can not," said my brother; "if you do it will be over my dead body, for I am his natural protector." "Well, General, your life is too valuable to be given for this negro's, so as we do not wish to kill you, we will go."

By that time, as Stephen V. Ash has written, the Ku Klux Klan had "degenerated from disciplined and obeisant (though brutal) instruments of white society's will into gangs of larcenous and ungovernable holligans without social purpose or sanction."

A FTER HIS FATHER LOST RATTLE & SNAP, JAMES MOVED DOWN to a small piece of land the family still owned on the Mississippi about forty miles south of Memphis where he tried to begin a new life by planting cotton. As his wife later wrote, "His life was hard for he encountered overflows [that is floods from the Mississippi], boll weevils, droughts, etc. but he found it bearable for sometimes he made money. The people of the south had nothing but land, and [he realized that] they must make an effort."

Cotton was nearly the death of the South in the nineteenth century, as tobacco was in the eighteenth. It exhausted the land and so played a major role in pushing settlers ever westward. Causing erosion, it contributed to the "overflows" of rivers and particularly of the Mississippi, and it was generally unprofitable. It had steadily declined in value for nearly a century: from about 36 cents a pound in 1800, it hit a low of 7.7 cents a pound in the 1840s. It fell further in the years after the Civil War. Seven cents a pound was the break-even figure for a typical plantation. It was a rare year that even a well-run plantation on "rich bottomland" made money. Worse was to come. In the immediate aftermath of the Civil War, farm property in the southern states declined drastically, so that properties that "had sold for $150,000 fell in value to $10,000. Meanwhile, the cost of borrowing money rose steadily. At nearly every county seat, mortgage sales were monthly events through almost the entire reconstruction period." That is how James H.'s father lost Rattle & Snap in 1867, and James H. would learn these things in years of hard labor before giving up and acting on the current admonition, "When things go wrong, go west."

J AMES H.'S YOUNGER FIRST COUSIN WHO WAS NAMED FOR James's father, George Washington Polk, had gone ahead. Too young to fight in the Civil War, just a few years after the war had ended he had gone to work surveying the route of the Missouri Pacific. The West he encountered was not much more civilized than the Pennsylvania wilderness in which Charles and William had lived over a century before. Out in Kit Carson, Colorado, George had the misfortune to fall ill and spent two months recovering in what went under the name of hotel. It was, he wrote, "a large two-story building, the inside partitioned with canvas, so that one could without difficulty hear every noise from one end to the other, and there was plenty of noise. Gambling and dance houses were in full blast all over town, lawlessness prevailed and murders [were] frequent."

Young George was the odd man out. Having been raised in the genteel beauty of Hamilton Place, just across the road from Rattle & Snap, and not having been hardened by the fury of the Civil War, as James was, he was stunned by the "roughs, cut-throats, thieves, gamblers and low women." But after exposure to such able teachers, George was as ready as James to resort to the current supreme court of the West. When a group of thieves put in a claim to his horse, he turned out his railway crew as a well-armed jury. The claimants speedily withdrew both the claim and themselves.

Following the railway's progress, George turned south and west into Texas. Texas in those days, as vividly described by the sister-in-law of George's cousin and another namesake, was a state of

> unfenced stretches of wide open plains and broad prairies, its thousand miles of grazing land for the enormous herds of long-horns, made cattle rustling possible. Rolling prairie land, green in spring, golden brown in the summer because of so few rains, and near the river, either the Rio Grande or the smaller Trinity, the country heavily eroded. Dirt roads, dusty in summer, and in the winter when the black gumbo (mud) made it impassable at times, the deep ruts which the wagons cut into the mud, caused the horses to stumble . . . all this was Texas in those early days. Not much cultivation. It was

purely a cattle country. The Johnson Grass grew as high as a horse's head.

When the southern transcontinental line was painfully sledged into place across the vast plains, George reached the Pecos River where a few tents and shacks gathered around a saloon, on the facade of which "in large letters were the words 'Hell in Texas' . . . In less than a week after this saloon was opened for business, a man was shot and killed, it being the first of other killings later on."

With more accuracy in describing its citizens than the word "town" did the place, it took the name Vinegaroon from one of its most formidable inhabitants, a large whip scorpion, "which, when disturbed, emits a volatile fluid having a vinegary odor." As George noted, it was, like the town, "very repulsive in appearance, and reputed to be very poisonous."

One of George's first visitors was a Mr. Stevens, who had the dangerous task of carrying to this godforsaken camp a little black bag with $300,000 in fifty-dollar bills to pay off the railway workers. Arriving in a hail of bullets, he rushed to George's tent where the safe was kept. He probably felt like getting inside and leaving the cash outside because, "While we were conversing, someone came over from the dance hall and reported that two women had been shot. One of them had been killed outright. The other was badly wounded. The shooting was in the midst of a quadrille set. The dance was only stopped long enough to drag out the corpse of the dead woman and carry the wounded one to a neighboring tent."

Thrust to the fore of a population of "gamblers, cappers, saloon-keepers, abandoned women, thieves and their satellites," whose "regular routine of business was gambling, dancing, drinking and fighting" was "Judge" Roy Bean, who administered "the law west of the Pecos." The local estimation of his title, judge, was summed up in the saying that "west of the Pecos there is no law and west of El Paso there is no God." That was unfair, Bean defended himself: he claimed always to give a man a fair trial before hanging him. But he had a certain claim to judicial grandeur. It was derived from the railroad.

The railroad had not yet reached El Paso, so few men worried about the divinity, but at least the officials of the railroad were anxious to have some sort of law, any law, at their railhead because few railway laborers managed to pass by the town without being robbed. Asked how life in his town was, Roy Bean was heard to say, "Everything is perfectly peaceful here . . . There hasn't been a man killed for four hours."

The railroad got the state to assign some rangers to try, if not exactly to keep order, at least to minimize the robberies and murders. The rangers were not delicate in their application of justice, but in those cases too marginal to justify immediate hanging, they would have to take their prisoners before some sort of court. And there was no court closer than Fort Stockton, which was a grueling three-hundred-mile horseback ride away. So at the request of the railroad, Roy Bean entered the western legend.

Payment for judges fell far short of what Bean thought proper, so he padded his wages by running a saloon, and in his mind, the two establishments were mutually supporting. As George found, one of Bean's favorite lesser penalties for convicted felons was the obligation to buy a couple of dozen bottles of "hooch," which given the short expectations of life had to be "paid for on the spot." George did not record who enjoyed the drink, but with the shadow of the noose falling on the floor in front of him, the prisoner probably gratefully treated both judge and jury.

Most of the defendants were alive at least when they entered the courtroom, but that fine distinction did not trouble Judge Bean. In a rare case of accidental death, a railway workman fell off a bridge and was killed. Going somewhat beyond what a judge normally did, Bean examined the body and instructed the group acting as a jury that the man had died accidentally. That seemed to settle the matter for the jury but not for Bean, who pronounced a slightly different verdict.

The deceased came to his death by accident, but there is another matter to be attended to. I find upon the body a revolver and forty dollars. Now it is contrary to the laws of Texas, and to the peace and dignity of this state, to carry concealed weapons. I therefore confiscate the pistol and fine the deceased forty dollars for this breach of law.

Then, as George noted, "he coolly pocketed the proceeds."

T EXAS WAS TRULY A FOREIGN COUNTRY TO MARY DEMOVILLE "Molly" Harding when she married James Hilliard Polk on November 24, 1885. She had spent much of her youth in Belle Meade plantation, which was still owned by her cousins. Much of its grandeur had faded in the Civil War and during the period of Reconstruction, but there was still enough of the finery stored away in trunks that the young people could re-create former times in their dress-up games. As Molly wrote,

The house was a large brick surrounded by immense porches, very beautiful. The floors were of white ash seasoned until they were hard as stone for my head often tried them. They were waxed until you could almost see yourself in them. There were fourteen grandchildren and a happy lot we were . . . We used my grandmother Harding's finest togs, velvet capes, bonnets bedecked with plumes and black lace shawls. Priceless treasures they would be now. We never tired of telling [of] some imaginary party we had attended. Those were great days and will live in memory as long as life lasts, in fact I treasure them with tears.

Living a life partly in fantasy was probably part of what protected her. But the other part was equally important. Like many apparently fragile southern women, Molly called on inner strength. With pride, she related how as a young woman, upon being asked to her first ball in Nashville, she wore "the most artistic dress in the room." Proudly, she later wrote that she had bought the silk material at a fire sale and "shut myself in a room alone for two or three days and made every stitch of it myself."

In later years, she looked back nostalgically.

> It seems I am engrossed in the images of my memory, but all these things are mingled with the dust of yesterday. I suppose I am old so to speak for my path is growing a little steep, but I cherish in my heart the wish that some day I may go back to my old home and spend a few hours among the things where life casts its gentle shadow.

She was not to have those hours. In fact, just three hours after she was married, she and James left for Texas. It was to be an experience far from gentle. After staying for several months in a wretched little hotel, rather like the one that George described, a "hotel" that doubled as a saloon, gambling den and, perhaps, whorehouse, they moved into "a four room shack of long standing near Captain Polk's business"—that is, right next to the stockyard. Despite what must have been a nearly overpowering smell, Molly was not discouraged. There was little she could do about the smell, but she set to work to try to cover the realities of the shack with paint and paper, "and with my dainty belongings the inside was very sweet," but neither she nor James had checked the roof.

> We were treated the second night to a perfect downpour, and it kept us busy moving ourselves and our belongings to keep dry. Then came a northern, the worst ever; and I was kept in bed for two days waiting for the flues to be fixed. This was the real West . . . The front steps were three logs with bark on them.

Molly's home was a far cry from the Belle Meade in which she was born or the Rattle & Snap in which her husband had lived. Americans were generally proud of having come *out* of a log cabin background, but no one was proud to go back *into* one, yet I suppose Molly took some solace in the fact that all this had, more or less, happened before. She remembered that her great-grandmother was said to be the first white child born west of the Allegheny Mountains, lived inside of a log fort and for childhood games had molded lead bullets for her father to fire against Indians. As Molly wrote, "So life goes on."

Life did indeed go on, and often must have seemed to her to go on in cycles. If she was in the trough of a down cycle, in her mind's eye she saw hope ahead. She was rather proud that "many charming men enjoyed our hospitality . . . German noblemen and English earls and lawyers and our friends who drifted from our old homes . . . as well as most of the outlaws of the day (Frank and Jessie James, Harper who served with [General] John Morgan and so on) . . ."

OUTLAWS THERE WERE IN ABUNDANCE, SINCE JAMES AND HIS brother Rufus had established the Polk Brothers Stockyards in Fort Worth, where they bought and sold cattle and horses. It was a magnet for the men who then ranged through the West. Many were of dubious reputation. Indeed, the line between legitimate cattlemen and rustlers largely depended on where you were. James bought many of his cattle and horses in Mexico. Both were much cheaper along the frontier, in part, no doubt, because their origin was shrouded in mystery. Other than brands, there was no way to tell where they had come from or how they had been acquired. Questions were better left unasked.

In the last decades of the nineteenth century, the Texas-Mexican frontier, as James's cousin George had discovered, was one of the most lawless areas on the planet. Judge Roy Bean was perhaps the most colorful of the lawless lawmen, but he was by no means unique. Having little understanding of the law as anything more than a license to hang, sheriffs were also given to supplementing their meager salaries at the point of their guns. They could nearly always find a reason to arrest a man, and those arrested often got shot "trying to escape." Both the law and lawmen were better avoided. That was often not difficult as their writ ran about as far as the range of a Winchester. But exposing one's back was often a terminal mistake.

Even more dangerous than exposing the back was exposing a wallet. Then whatever line that might have been drawn between lawmen and outlaws became fatally smudged. What James made of the smudge was my favorite of Molly's stories.

The story was set in Laredo. Then as now, it was a double town: Laredo itself was in the United States, while just across the Rio Grande, Nuevo Laredo was in Mexico. The river was shallow enough to wade across without getting a Colt six-shooter wet, but it was an important barrier, since anyone in trouble with what was euphemistically called the law on one side had only to cross to the other side to escape retribution. That gave the two towns an air of freedom congenial to a certain class of men. They robbed, fought, whored, gambled and murdered at will. Even by Texas standards, the town was considered "unhealthy." About all this, Molly probably knew more than she let on to the little boy sitting at her feet, but for her (and him) it was what happened there that counted.

According to Molly, James was in an angry mood. Apparently, the men who were to have delivered him a herd of cattle did not show up. Why they didn't was not part of Molly's tale, but it is not unlikely that the way they had planned to acquire the herd was not regarded with favor by those whose brands the cattle wore. Even in rural Mexico in those wild times, cattle rustling tended to be frowned upon, and when no trees sufficiently tall for hanging were to be found, the winning team (that is, those with the most guns) often simply dragged the culprits (that is, the losers) to death through the rocks and cactus. So there were probably extenuating circumstances for the failure of James's suppliers to arrive in Laredo, but they did not cool James's annoyance. He carried throughout his life a goodly store of annoyance acquired during his days as a prisoner of war. And having ridden all the way down to that godforsaken town to buy cattle, he had been let down. Molly was right—he was in a foul mood.

Laredo was full of men in foul moods. The whole town was built to cater to their moods. So James did what everyone in Laredo did: he wandered into one of the town's two thriving institutions, the saloon. (Grandmother, of course, would not have mentioned the other one.) There, bellying up to the bar, he ordered a whiskey. The lethal liquid that went under that name in Laredo bore little resemblance to the one more familiar today. But it did have one virtue: a tumbler of it cost a nickel.

Still sour, James gazed over the scurvy clientele sitting at little round tables, playing cards, drinking and getting ready for some trouble to break the boredom. He had seen their kind many times before. Turning back to the bar, he reached into his vest and drew out the sack of gold coins he had planned to spend on the herd of cattle, poured them on the bar and began to fish around among the glittering array for a humble nickel. He took his time.

Meanwhile, the saloon fell silent. Such a sight was not often seen in Laredo, and it provoked wishes that were even more lethal than the bartender's whiskey. Those too wise to believe they could outdraw the others shook their heads in astonishment and mumbled that they had just looked upon a man who would never see the sun rise again. Several made for the door to spread word up and down the dusty street. There would surely be some fireworks, and everyone wanted to witness the excitement.

James at last found the nickel, paid, scooped his gold coins back into the leather pouch and shoved it back in his vest. Then he did something even more unbelievable. He asked if he could get a bed for the night. He might just as well have asked where he could crawl into a rattlesnake hole. A bleary-eyed old man standing near him shook his head and mumbled, "Be careful, friend . . . the sheriff here . . ." Then he broke off what would surely have been an indiscreet, perhaps fatal, remark. In silent reply, James pushed the whiskey bottle over to him.

Not a sound was to be heard in the saloon as the bartender, dumbfounded, almost whispered, "A bed . . . why, sure, pardner, right up those stairs . . . third door down on the right. They's a cot and blanket right inside." Then recovering himself, he boomed out, "That'll be a dollar . . . in advance."

James went through the ritual again, found a gold dollar and pushed it across the bar, turned around, nonchalantly walked among the tables, not apparently noticing anyone, climbed the stairs and disappeared behind the third door.

There he immediately changed his demeanor. Pulling the cot into the middle of the room, he wadded up the blanket so that it looked like he was under it. Then he put his hat on the cot where his head would have been. Crossing the room, he took off his coat and, folding it behind his back, sat down in a corner facing the door. Pulling out his Colt single-action .45, he whirled the cylinder to check that it was fully loaded and cocked the hammer. Then balancing it on his knees, he aimed at the door.

He didn't have a long wait. After just a few minutes, the hinges creaked as the door was stealthily pushed open and a figure was silhouetted by the faint light of lanterns in the saloon. The pistol in his hand caught a flicker of light. James pulled the trigger. There was a deafening explosion, and the acrid smell of the smoke of black powder filled the little room.

Shouts rang out below and men came running with lanterns. There, stretched out across the doorjamb, was . . . the sheriff. Cold, stone dead. As they pulled the body out, James got up, made his first and only comment—"greedy fellow"—closed the door and climbed onto the cot. It was hard to get a good night's rest in Laredo.

During the 1899–1902 Boer War, James furnished horses for the British army. This was the beginning of what would grow into a large business. Fifteen years later, during the First World War, Fort Worth would ship to Europe about 100,000 horses, valued at $11 million, so that it was then the largest market of its kind in the world.

James's contract with the British army during the Boer War required that all the horses be ridden at least once. None had been. To keep the price down, they were mustangs from the prairies or even feral horses from the badlands along the Mexican border. Wherever they came from, they were completely wild, had never carried saddles or worn bridles and were dangerous. So James assembled a group of devil-may-care cowhands, described as being only slightly less wild than the horses and, particularly when drunk as they often were, far more dangerous. In relays, these men lassoed the horses, manhandled them into narrow corrals or otherwise immobilized them, cinched on saddles, forced bits into their mouths and climbed on.

Those who have seen a rodeo may think they can imagine what happened then. They cannot. In a rodeo, otherwise reasonably tame horses are goaded into bucking by having a second girth tightened around their stomachs, but no rodeo display could possibly compare with the bucking, whirling, screaming outburst of fear and fury that exploded when a truly wild horse felt the weight of the rider. The cowboy was lucky if he lasted more than a few seconds and even more lucky—and with a better chance to be alive—if the horse did not roll over on top of him or manage to get its teeth into him.

There was no extra payment for broken bones. Cowboys were cheap and plentiful. But after watching this melee, James often remarked to Molly that he had unintentionally struck a blow for the freedom of South Africa—he was sure that these horses would kill half the British army.

Oddly, it didn't work out like that. On the way to South Africa, the transports carrying the horses ran into severe storms, and when they were finally unloaded, the grateful horses were as tame as saddle mares.

So it was that both James and his cousin George participated in the two great myths of the American experience, the Old South and the Wild West.

A WALL OF SILENCE SURROUNDS MARSHALL TATE ''MARSH'' Polk in family papers. Not one single mention of his sad and ignominious end occurs in any correspondence. Family members were probably not trying to protect him but were shocked and humiliated.

Marsh was a grandson of Samuel and a great-grandson of Ezekiel; his father was one of President James K. Polk's brothers. Born at Charlotte, North Carolina, in 1831, he graduated from West Point in 1852 and entered the army as a young lieutenant. In 1855, he took part in the Sioux Expedition as a member of the staff of General William Harney (who was known to the Indians as Mad Bear). This brutal campaign of expulsion or extermination began a generation of wars against the Great Plains Indians in which Crazy Horse and Sitting Bull came to the fore as leaders.

Marsh then resigned from the army, possibly horrified by the brutality of that campaign, and returned to Tennessee. But he could not escape war. When the Civil War began, he immediately enlisted and served as a captain of artillery in the Confederate forces where, in the ferocious Battle of Shiloh, he was badly wounded and had a leg amputated. Captured by the Federal forces, he was imprisoned until President Polk's widow, Sarah, who thought of herself as virtually his foster mother and fearing that he would die in prison, secured his exchange. Undaunted by the loss of his leg, he returned to fight as a colonel and chief of artillery for the Army of Tennessee.

After the general amnesty of 1869 had restored the franchise to

Confederate soldiers, he entered state politics. In 1877, he was elected to the first of three terms as treasurer of Tennessee. Family accounts of his life end there, but, sadly, Marsh's life did not.

While I have found no family letters that recount the next events, they were fully (and surprisingly sympathetically) reported from January 1883 in a series of articles appearing in the *Nashville Daily American* and the *Daily World*. In brief, Marsh was caught short in speculating. Sadly, everything he touched went sour. When he bought Tennessee bonds, they lost value as the result of an adverse Supreme Court ruling; he made large personal loans to friends who defaulted; and he got involved in a scheme, which was at the least beyond his capacity and may have been bogus, to develop silver mines in Mexico. Then, having lost far more money than he could afford, he began to cover his losses with state funds.

Early in 1883, a committee of the Tennessee Senate discovered a deficit of $400,000 in the accounts of the state Treasury, and when the report was delivered, Marsh had disappeared. He was apprehended, together with his cousin Van Leer Polk, by detectives in San Antonio on January 11, but the agents apparently accepted a bribe to release them, and once released, they headed for Mexico.

Marsh was arrested about eighteen miles from the Rio Grande by a U.S. deputy marshal to whom Marsh offered $8,000 if the marshal would allow him to escape to Mexico. When he refused, Marsh said philosophically, "Well, this settles it; I cannot deny it longer." He agreed to return to Tennessee without attempting to raise legal delays.

It was a travel-worn and crestfallen Marsh who was met by his son, James Knox Polk II, at Little Rock, Arkansas. There, as one of his captors told a reporter, "Polk evidently feels the disgrace he has brought upon his name very keenly." When the party reached Nashville, he was taken off to jail. Almost as unhappy as he were his captors, since the state defaulted on the reward promised them, and one commented that "he had become attached to the Colonel [on the trip back to Nashville]

. . . and if he had it to go over again, would not arrest him for any reward."

The *Daily World* reporter wrote sentimentally on January 14
that

> Amongst the crowd who gathered together to see the stricken
> treasurer as he returned to the city and scenes of his former
> greatness were those who came out of curiosity, those who
> came out of respect, and many who came with no other feel-
> ing than to gratify a morbid appetite to see suffering of any
> sort. There was an individual, however, an humble colored
> man, whose countenance dark and expressive suffused with
> the noble glow of genuine sympathy. His hair whitened by age
> and his form bent in the ravages of time, made him conspicu-
> ous as he struggled to maintain a place in the surging crowd,
> and he peered curiously, almost piteously around into the
> strangely unsympathizing faces about him. As Col. Polk was
> taken from the train in the charge of police and detectives, the
> old man's limbs trembled and his lips fell apart, while his
> whole face was filled with the expression of intense affection
> and sorrow. Raising his hands as he saw Col. Polk taken he said
> with a sigh, "I nursed Marse Marsh. He is the best man in the
> world. I don't believe he has done anything wrong and I am
> going to stand by him in the trouble."
>
> It was "Reuben," the old servant of the Polk family, who
> came from Columbia to see his old master.

Marsh was indicted by the attorney general of Tennessee and was
brought to trial in July, when the *Daily World* reported "an excited, eager throng [gathered] and the utmost attention was paid to the argument." The trial was, indeed, the most exciting event in Nashville for
many a year. His lawyer's defense was that Marsh may have been guilty
of a "default of pay" but not of embezzlement. The jury did not agree;

they found him guilty as charged. He was sentenced to twenty years in the very penitentiary on which he had recently served as a state inspector and was fined $366,540.10. He appealed, but before the case came before the court, he died, on February 28, 1884, of what was called "paralysis of the heart." Some thought it was suicide.

THE LIFE OF MARSH'S COUSIN LEONIDAS LaFAYETTE POLK could hardly have been more different. His branch of the family had remained in North Carolina when Thomas, Ezekiel and Will moved their families west to Tennessee. He got his cumbersome name from the chance visit of his cousin Bishop Leonidas at the time of his birth in 1837 and from the family's relationship with the French hero of the American Revolution, Lafayette.

Like most of the Polks at that time, Leonidas LaFayette's family were farmers but on a more modest scale than the Tennessee Polks. They were the sort of people on whom Jefferson had pinned his hopes for America. As he wrote,

> Those who labour in the earth are the chosen people of God, if ever he had a chosen people, whose breasts he has made his peculiar deposit for substantial and genuine virtue. It is the focus in which he keeps alive that sacred fire, which otherwise might escape from the face of the earth . . . the proportion which the aggregate of the other classes of citizens bears in any state to that of its husbandmen, is the proportion of its unsound to its healthy parts, and is a good-enough barometer whereby to measure its degree of corruption.

But strong and bright as the farming life appeared in Jefferson's time, it quickly narrowed and dimmed in the nineteenth century. As we would say in modern economic terms, the "primary products" produced by farmers lost value in comparison to the "value added" products of the industrial, financial and service sectors of the economy. Even with such great innovations as the cotton gin and such apparent cost reductions as cheap land and slave labor, farmers lost wealth and, as they did so, lost both political power and social position. This trend was already apparent well before the Civil War when many went bankrupt, and it was greatly speeded up and intensified by that war.

Much of it was the farmers' fault. Partly for social reasons, they devoted much of their best land to ruinous crops, first tobacco and then cotton, and failed to replenish the land by rotation and adequate use of fertilizers. So long as land in the West remained cheap, there was insufficient incentive to improve agricultural methods. But even after cheap land was no longer so available, farmers stuck to their old methods and uneconomic crops. It was the rare man who, like James or Meck, left farming for a new profession, and even James, to the end of his life, called himself a planter.

By the 1880s, a general sense of malaise had spread through rural America. It was particularly strong in the South but was evident throughout the Middle West. The problems faced by farmers were similar, but farmers were widely scattered and politically divided. Local issues predominated, and the divisions left by the Civil War made farmers in different areas of the country seem more like enemies to one another than sharers in a common plight. Few read more than the Bible or local broadsheets. Certainly no publications either brought them together or spread information on their common concerns. Each little group of farmers, one might almost say each individual farmer, was isolated from his fellows. It is hard for us today to fathom that isolation: there were, of course, none of the media on which we rely, and having to walk or ride buggies or horseback made a trip to town where one might swap information a rare event. Rarer still was a visit to a city or to other states. And in neither crossroads village town nor city was there any recognized meeting place for farmers. It was into this group of related problems that Leonidas LaFayette plunged to create the first specialized agricultural publications and the first mass movement of farmers, the Alliance.

At the bedrock of their dilemma, as Leonidas LaFayette admonished audience after approving audience, was what Thomas Jefferson had warned against: the government's propensity to diminish the role of farmers and to promote those people favored by Alexander Hamilton, the manufacturers and captains of industry. Hamilton's policies had become those of government after government and of both political and market forces beyond the control of farmers. The numbers, Leonidas LaFayette pointed out, told much of the story.

In 1850 the farmers owned seventy per cent of the wealth of the country, and paid eighty-five per cent of the taxes; in 1880 they owned one-half the wealth, and paid eighty-seven per cent of the taxes; today [in 1890] they own less than twenty-three per cent, and still pay over eighty per cent of the taxes.

Bad as the current situation was, the whole agricultural sector was in a downward path. And not just economically. Farm families were not only losing wealth but much more important were losing their ability to profit from education facilities. This was a disaster, Leonidas LaFayette said, not only for farmers but for the whole nation, since "That nation which neglects to educate its masses of people to higher ability and to a higher plane of thought and action is on a sure road to inevitable decay and death."

The growing disparity of the rich and the poor was thus not only unjust but also profoundly antidemocratic. "Today [1890]," he pointed out, "6,600 men control two-thirds of the wealth of the United States, and the other one-third belongs to over sixty millions of people." This economic cleavage would surely provoke a social and political split far more grievous than the Civil War.

Why was this so? he asked rhetorically. It was in large part, he suggested gently but firmly, due to the lethargy of the farmers themselves. They had proved unable or unwilling to organize to achieve common objectives and to rise above their differences. Farmers throughout the

United States must realize, he exhorted his audiences, that the problems, culture and hopes they shared rose above the divisions of the past. "I want to tell you people of Kansas here today," he said in one speech,

> that the farmer of North Carolina, Georgia, Texas, South Carolina is your brother, whether you want it so or not . . . we have a common interest, and must make common cause . . . The struggle is *not* between the North and the South . . . And so long as we live there will *never* be a North and South! . . . never give prominence to any man who stirs up this question which was settled by Lee and Grant at Appomattox.

Remarkable words. Particularly given Leonidas LaFayette's own background. Born late in his father's life and to a second wife, he lost both of his parents before he was fifteen. He had little formal education but briefly attended Davidson College in 1855, where, interspersed in a rigorous religious program, he was exposed to a modest classical education and, like his cousin James K. Polk at Chapel Hill, took an active part in a debating society. At the end of the first year, probably for financial reasons, he dropped out of college and went to work on a farm. Then at twenty he got married. The next year, when he was twenty-one, he came into his modest inheritance, some 353 acres of moderately good farmland, then worth about $2,400, and seven black slaves.

His early twenties were hard years and taught him much of the troubles of agricultural America. His farm was too small to support all his dependents and to pay the operating costs; so he worked part-time off the land. Increasingly, he found himself drawn into discussions and arguments with his neighbors on local and national issues. He was a natural debater and had honed his skills in his brief academic career; so he quickly became accepted as a spokesman and leader despite his youth. Perhaps he would have found a different path forward, but with the whole country being drawn into the vortex that became the Civil War, he had to grapple with the problem that had bedeviled James K. Polk and other men of the previous generation and so many of his own. Was there a viable position that encompassed both ''states' rights'' and ''unionism''?

In the last few years before the Civil War, the edge between these two concepts did not appear so sharp as it would shortly become. And there were local issues that complicated the grander question: Leonidas LaFayette found much about the South to be reprehensible. From his perspective, the most galling was the way the planter aristocracy manipulated taxation to favor its own interests to the detriment of the yeomen. Taxes were drawn primarily from assessments on land, whereas slaves, the most valuable asset of the larger owners, were assessed only a poll tax; even when slaves were hired out as artisans (as Andrew Jackson Polk, for example, hired out a slave blacksmith), they paid no license fee, whereas free artisans did. Anger over such discrimination, discrimination that is within the white ruling race rather than between white and black, was widespread among the less wealthy southern whites. This, together with growing anxiety about the deepening national division, drove Leonidas LaFayette into state politics, and at just twenty-three years of age, he was elected a member of the North Carolina House of Commons.

North Carolina was then, in 1860, deadlocked over the issue of union or secession; as late as March 1861, two-thirds of the delegates to a state convention charged with reaching a decision on this issue were in favor of staying in the Union. Leonidas LaFayette was among them. It was, to his mind, the deeper issues set forth by Jefferson and followed by James K. Polk, rather than the emotional reaction to Lincoln's election, that were crucial. His position was more conservative than that of his namesake, Bishop Leonidas, who already thought that the Union was doomed. As Leonidas LaFayette later wrote, ''I was then a Union man, exerting all my power to aid in averting civil war, and continued to labor untiringly until the last hope was extinguished.'' That hope was extinguished, to his horror, when President Lincoln called for troops to suppress the rebellion. However much he had opposed secession, he, like many southerners, particularly among the Polk family, were swept into the war. Almost in the same words as Bishop Leonidas, he sadly wrote, "We are not battling for any minor consideration but for our lives, our property, our honor, in short, *our all.*"

His battle began in the North Carolina House of Commons, where in August of 1861, he played a major role in organizing North Carolina's militia into a regular standing army and in instituting conscription. There he announced a theme that would run through his liberal political philosophy throughout his life: he insisted upon a clause being inserted in the conscription bill allowing for conscientious objection to bearing arms. Liberty could not be preserved at the cost of personal freedom. Then, feeling that his job in the House was finished and that there was work to be done in the field, he left to organize the militia regiment of his home county.

Like others in the Confederate army, his position or rank wildly gyrated. Lucius Eugene had gone from private to general in the heat of battle, and Leonidas LaFayette, having organized the Anson County militia regiment as the "colonel-commanding," entered the regular army as a private. After having served on the staff of soon-to-be-elected-governor Zebulon Baird Vance as a sergeant major, he was promoted lieutenant in another regiment. In that capacity, he fought through most of the battles of northern Virginia, including the carnage of Gettysburg and the attack on Washington, D.C.

From the start, he had no romantic fantasies about war. He hated it as a ghastly, miserable, stupid and exhausting experience, unrelieved by glamour or heroism. Like many soldiers, he also hated the military life not only for the terrible privations under which he and his colleagues served but also because of the petty tyranny of the military bureaucracy. Perhaps because of his political experience, he clashed with several of his commanding officers. He ascribed his problems with his general and many of the vexations under which the soldiers served to the same class division he had seen in unfair taxation: the plantation oligarchy sought to impose its code and to protect its own parochial interests. Of course, in wartime, no one wanted to hear such opinions, and he was twice court-martialed. Despite the fact that he was both times honorably acquitted and was commended for bravery under fire, he would later be charged by his political enemies with a variety of wartime crimes.

The reality was more prosaic but was also formative in his thinking. The ordeal of the war served to solidify his already "populist"—the word was not yet in fashion—politics. He came, particularly, to hate "heartless speculators" when, as he found in the terrible campaigns of 1863, "I am nearly naked & my money cannot clothe me decently & feed me . . . to buy a coat & pants costs over 2 months wages . . . Ordinary shoes are selling in V[irgini]a markets for $50 pr . . ."

That his sentiments were those of many of his fellows was demonstrated when in April of 1864 he was nominated by the North Carolina regiments for reelection to the House of Commons. Although he was elected in August, he was not released from the army for nearly half a year. During much of that time, in another personal clash with a senior officer, he was placed under arrest for allegedly deserting his post. In fact, he had helped a wounded comrade to a field hospital and then returned to lead a charge against the Federal forces, for which he was commended for gallantry. For him, it was one more instance of the stupidity and tyranny of the war, but, as he wrote to his wife, he took solace in the fact that being under arrest may have saved his life.

Returning to North Carolina in the last phase of the war, he took up his post as a member of the North Carolina House; there he voted in October 1865 to repeal the Ordinance of Secession and to abolish slavery.

When the session ended, he returned to try to restore his farm, which had been devastated in the last weeks of the war by a unit of Sherman's army. If the damage was less impressive than in George Washington Polk's Rattle & Snap, it was only because there was less to destroy. But without animals, workers and money for seed, rebuilding was just as daunting a task. Leonidas LaFayette and his wife devoted themselves to it. For them, there would be no "West" to which to retreat.

Being forced to make do with what they had, however, brought a certain benefit. No longer able to rely upon slave labor and unable to move to new lands when the old was exhausted, Leonidas LaFayette had to learn a new approach to farming. As he learned, he became more and more influential among the farmers who were his neighbors. And as they copied his relatively enlightened methods, the economy gradually picked up, so that in 1873 a railroad began to be constructed. Its projected path was right through his farm. Bowing to the inevitable, he realized that this would spoil the farming, but with a flash of insight he recognized the opportunity for different use of the land. The railroad would bring people, so he began to lay out a housing project that soon became known as Polkton. He had become a property developer.

To serve the needs of the budding community, he converted his house into a combination of store and post office; then, to advertise his property, he set up a small printing press and began to publish a weekly newspaper. Within two years, his farm had truly become a town, and as his principal biographer has written, "he was farmer, merchant, express agent, postmaster, editor, juror, Mason, Sunday School teacher, holiday and commencement speaker, town commissioner, mayor, and politician."

In state politics in 1876, in part no doubt as a sign of his increasing prosperity, he sided with the conservatives. "I am," he wrote, "by birth, education, habit, thought, feeling, and interest—a Conservative." But he still felt himself kin, as his Jeffersonianism demanded, to "Those who labour in the earth." It was a true farmer's position, and he backed it up by joining the Patrons of Husbandry, a coalition of farmers begun just after the Civil War by Oliver Hudson Kelley and familiarly known as the Grange.

Leonidas LaFayette's plan to get the state back on its feet went a great deal further. He set out the emerging elements of it in a series of articles in his own newspaper and in the Grange's *State Agricultural Journal*.

Like farmers all over the South, he believed that a major aspect of the agricultural problem was racial. There was little hope, he wrote, that the newly liberated blacks could do the job on their own. "Guided, directed and controlled by the intelligent white man," he wrote, "he has no equal in the world as a field laborer," but under the circumstances and with his educational and cultural endowment, he could not successfully work on his own.

He did not like the revolutionary changes then being imposed upon the South by the victors in the Civil War, but he also believed in protecting the civil rights of the liberated blacks. As he wrote, "We intend to make good our promises and declarations, and thus prove to the negro, that the white men of the South are his very best friends." Only through intelligent, self-interested black suffrage, he argued, could something like a normal life be re-created in the South.

Like most Americans of that era and like his guide Thomas Jefferson, he believed in the innate inferiority of blacks. He thought that rapid progress in agriculture could be made only by whites and that, therefore, it would be better for the South if the black sharecroppers were replaced by white workers. It was an opinion long shared not only by southern yeomen (that is, by those more or less in competition with blacks) but also by members of the aristocracy. But what Leonidas La-Fayette proposed then appeared radical: to encourage the migration to the South of northern farmers and of northern capital to invest in reconstruction and new developments. It was an idea whose time appeared to have come, and the North Carolina House actually set up the office of "commissioner of immigration."

Leonidas LaFayette saw racial relations essentially in this economic guise. He affirmed that equal treatment under the law was right and proper, but legal equality did not carry with it the likelihood of economic success. Moreover, the stigma of slavery had operated both to undermine the productivity of white farm labor and also to make whites fearful that they would lose their dignity and freedom if they became working farmers.

To get around this dilemma, he urged landowners to avoid the residue of slavery, sharecropping, and themselves go to work on that part of their lands that they personally could cultivate; then, having themselves set the example of self-respecting farm labor, they should divide and sell off lands the tilling of which was beyond their personal capacity. Like Bishop Leonidas, he had been influenced by seeing neat, highly productive fields tended by whites—Leonidas in England and Leonidas LaFayette in Pennsylvania. What he wanted was essentially a prosperous, dignified and white agricultural establishment. Unconsciously, he was echoing the position the antislavery congressman Wilmot had taken half a century before with James K. Polk: America would be better off without slaves.

As slavery and its aftermath were burdens on the economy, so, Leonidas LaFayette believed, was the production of cotton. King cotton indeed was a tyrant. As long as it completely dominated southern agriculture, that long was southern society going to be in thrall to market forces far beyond its control while being forced to purchase on the world market the foodstuffs and commodities it was thoroughly capable of producing for itself. In an article in his paper in 1877, Leonidas LaFayette taunted farmers who are

> preparing to plant a full crop of cotton, that will cost you 14 cents per pound and for which you will receive, perhaps, 10 cents, and will you rely on buying corn at $1.25 per bushel, that you ought to produce at 60 cents. And will you still complain of hard times?

The essence of his message was self-reliance or as latter-day economic development economists would call it, import substitution.

Neither the racial nor the self-reliance policies are those with which today we have much sympathy, but in their time, they were radical self-help proposals and appealed widely to middle- and lower-class white farmers. What we *can* empathize with was his emphasis on education. In line with the family tradition, he constantly urged the creation of schools and the spread of information on better techniques of farming through the creation and operation of a state department of agriculture. That department would also be charged, he proposed, with the task of policing such widely sold commodities as fertilizer (which was often so adulterated as to be of no significant value) and cooperating with educational institutions to experiment with improved seed. In 1877, the state legislature accepted his proposals and co-opted him to draft suitable legislation; he was then appointed North Carolina's first "commissioner of agriculture." As he conceived the task, it was then virtually without parallel in the United States. He threw himself into the task with such verve that one contemporary wrote that he

> comes nearer being a steam locomotive than any man we know in official station. With a keen analytical brain, a restless, nervous temperament, an eye that is always dancing like a racehorse, and a . . . spirit of *push* and *go* aheadativeness in him, he keeps every one around him moving at firery speed. The work which he has already accomplished . . . is marvelous.

But as in nearly all human endeavors, energy and success came at the price of stepping on the toes of those whose feet rarely moved. Moreover, some of the work of the department had hurt those who had the power to resist. Sales of bogus products were said to have saved farmers about $200,000, but that, of course, removed a similar amount from those who had profited from such sales. Envy and opposition grew—focusing not on serious issues but on the petty cost of printing circulars and carrying out tests on seed. While he was not directly attacked, his office was divided into three sections, of which only one was left to him, his clerical staff was eliminated and his educational publications were stopped. His expected response was forthcoming: he resigned.

That turned out to be a blessing in disguise, but it did not appear so for several years. During that period "in the wilderness," he cast about for means to earn a living—even selling patent medicine for diphtheria—and to reorganize his life. Then, in 1877, he got started on a path that would take him close to the nomination for president of the United States.

Building an approach to the issue of farmers' well-being, he created an organization and finally founded a journal, the *Progressive Farmer*. It was full of practical information, entertainment and political advice. It spoke to the then very large farm community in language it understood and appreciated. And it gained the credibility essential to political success. It took no advertisements for products of "questionable character in its columns; no swindles, no lotteries, no catches to cheat unwary people out of their money; nothing to harm or rob man, woman or child. And what is more, there never will be . . . We shall publish a *clean* paper."

The *Progressive Farmer* was more than a journal; it was the motor for the creation of a movement to implement the ideas he had begun to develop in the Department of Agriculture. And this time, he did not depend upon a legislature or state officials. He went straight to the farmers and helped them to organize themselves.

Today it is hard for us to realize how desperate a problem the lack of education was then in the South—and not only among the black community. As Leonidas LaFayette constantly pointed out to his audiences, the 1880 census showed that almost one white person in three was illiterate and only about one in four children of school age attended school regularly. As he had earlier warned, not only had no solutions been effective, but the problems were getting worse.

So despite the various leading men, ironically including the president of the University of North Carolina, who had opposed his organization of the state Department of Agriculture, Leonidas LaFayette pushed for the creation of a state agricultural and mechanical college. After a vigorous campaign, it was officially opened in the fall of 1889. He thus carried forward the family tradition of founding educational institutions that, begun by Thomas a century before, had been implemented by his cousins Will, James and Leonidas earlier in the century.

To bring all the problems he had identified together and subject them to a massive campaign of reform, Leonidas LaFayette turned to a new organization that would replace the old Grange, the Farmers' Alliance. Before this organization, he laid out his hopes and aspirations. Farmers, he argued, were even more important than Jefferson had thought: they were the backbone not only of American society but also of the whole economy. Every other American was a farmer and farmers as a group paid 80 percent of the taxes and furnished over 70 percent of the nation's exports. Yet they were the poor relations of the population. To improve their condition, they had to organize, and the Farmers' Alliance must be their answer.

In their first national meeting, delegates elected him to be their president. And the organization spread like wildfire through the farming areas of the nation. As one of the organizers wrote, "it was born of necessity, nurtured amid want and distress, and stands to-day as the champion of the down-trodden of [the] earth."

At first, he saw the movement as a pressure group rather than a political party, but as the two main political parties failed to take note of the demands of the Alliance, it quickly evolved into a full-scale party to challenge the existing division. By December 1899, it had over 2 million members. With this organization behind him, Leonidas LaFayette threw himself into the political campaigns through the farm belt in 1890 with what was almost a crusading zeal. Despite its mainly southern origins and antiblack beginnings, the Alliance meetings brought together both former Confederates and Unionists and whites and blacks in a movement unlike anything ever seen before in America.

Now alarmed by what they thought of as "hayseed socialists," Republicans and Democrats alike attacked both the new movement and

Leonidas LaFayette personally. Wild stories were published in the main party newspapers accusing him of everything from cowardice in the Civil War to torturing or massacring prisoners, of embezzling public funds and failing in business and of being at the same time a vicious capitalist swindler and a socialist. He must have been amused by at least one article which promoted him from his wartime rank of lieutenant to brigadier general and took him out of the line at Gettysburg to put him in charge of running a military prison. If we, in our day, are not always delicate in our political invective, we can only laugh at what was then common. A Republican Party newspaper found Leonidas LaFayette and his associates to be "worthless schemers," "tramps," "regular renegades," "designing demagogues and disreputable scoundrels," "disturbers of the peace," "pests to communities," "enemies of God and man," "co-conspirators," "political and visionary schemers," "wolves in sheep's clothing," "designing, wicked mo[u]ntebanks," and "would-be revolutionists," who gave "pernicious advice" and wielded "hellish influence."

And all this in a single article! But the campaign of slander could not stem the tide. "Populist" candidates by the hundreds were elected to local and national offices. At least thirty-eight members of the new Congress were Alliance candidates. The next year, a strong push was being made to create "the People's Party" to contest the presidency. What to do was the question posed for the huge national convention held in Cincinnati in May 1891. The convention delegates decided to become a regular political party in the following year at a proposed mammoth convention at St. Louis. There Leonidas LaFayette received a standing ovation when in the keynote address he said,

> The time has arrived for the great West, the great South and
> the great Northwest, to link their hands and hearts together
> and march to the ballot box and take possession of the govern-
> ment, restore it to the principles of our fathers, and run it in

the interest of the people . . . we intend to have it [justice] if we have to wipe the two old parties from the face of the earth!

From that speech onward, there was a strong tide running that seemed destined to carry a second member of the family into the White House. All over the country, groups favoring his election sprang into existence. Then, just as the campaign reached fever pitch, it was announced that Leonidas LaFayette had a cancerous tumor in his stomach and that his bladder had hemorrhaged. There was nothing that could be done to save him, and he died on June 11, 1892, just on the brink of what might have been his triumph.

WAR, BOOM AND BUST

"The worst of enemies"

JUST AS "MR. POLK'S WAR" IN 1846 HAD TRAINED THE soldiers who would fight the Civil War, so President Woodrow Wilson's intervention in Mexico in 1916 would prepare the U.S. Army for the First World War. Both Lee and Grant learned their craft in the first Mexican intervention, while General John "Black Jack" Pershing won his right to command the American army in France in the Mexican "punitive expedition." Here, too, the Polk family played its part. One of Pershing's junior officers was Lieutenant Harding Polk, a troop commander in the U.S. 11th Cavalry regiment. Harding's second cousin Frank L. Polk played a far grander role as counselor of the Department of State and, during much of the time, acting secretary of state. In their experiences, we can see the emergence of America as a world power, a people beginning to look outward.

MEXICO PRESENTED PRESIDENT WILSON WITH THE FIRST OF his stunning, and ultimately tragic, failures. It stemmed from his inability to perceive what is perhaps hardest for the mighty to understand: that the weak do not usually share their perceptions. This is a lesson that each generation must learn for itself, but it proved particularly corrosive to Wilson's philosophy. He had staked out for himself, and for the United States, a lofty moral position in which the values of freedom and national self-determination were claimed to be not only fundamental but self-evident. In American policy toward Mexico, they were neither.

In shocking contrast to the ringing proclamations that caused people all over the world to regard him as a living saint, Wilson demonstrated in Mexico that split political personality that would so mystify his admirers. While he spoke in thrilling terms about human freedom, his administration was the most racist since the Civil War, and while he identified with men who shared his liberal ideals, he turned over action responsibility to those who followed his adviser in *Realpolitik,* Colonel Edward M. House. Among the latter was Frank Polk.

Recommending Frank to Secretary of State Robert Lansing on August 14, 1915, House said, "He has a good deal of political instinct and can speak the language of the members of Congress. At the same time, he is such a cultured gentleman that he will be of great value to you in dealing with the Diplomatic Corps . . ."

Lansing took House exactly at his word and turned Frank into a sort of one-man version of what today we would call an operations center. For the Wilson administration, he dealt with every sort of problem that came before the government, from Mexico through the Palestine conflict, from race relations affecting Japanese Americans in the Idaho Mixed Marriage Bill to anti-Jewish pogroms in Poland, from the problems of American banks to mining concessions, from the perils to the neutral powers of submarine warfare to the parole of sailors on impounded ships, from the trivia of granting or withholding passports to the issues of war and peace. But Mexico was a problem that he could not solve, and it would not go away. The troubles began just before the outbreak of the First World War.

In response to a series of minor incidents and misunderstandings, President Wilson sent American forces into the Mexican port city of Veracruz on April 21, 1914. The action was dramatic, but of longer-term import were two attitudes that underlay and were accentuated by the action. They would later provide the trigger—the Zimmermann telegram—that got the United States into the First World War. The first of these attitudes was American: President Wilson's self-proclaimed crusade to bring democracy to the world. He began with Latin America. In one of his first proclamations, he said that a central aim of his administration was to "cultivate the friendship and deserve the confidence of our sister republics of Central and South America." As he interpreted this, it meant that he would rid the hemisphere of dictatorships. His first target was the president of Mexico, General Victoriano Huerta, who had come to power in a coup d'état.

The second attitude was Mexican, a fear and hatred of the United States that was common not only to the governments that followed one another in tumultuous sequence but also to the whole people. Mexicans of all classes believed that behind the facade of morality and high-sounding declarations, the United States was simply an imperialist state bent on taking still more territory from its weaker neighbor, and they bitterly resented the officious, condescending attitude of Americans toward them.

These attitudes were thrown into sharp relief in 1914 when Wilson went to Congress for authority to punish Mexico for "grave affronts" to "American honor." He received a standing ovation and authority to carry out condign punishment by the occupation of Tampico and Veracruz.

Veracruz had been repeatedly sacked by foreign invaders; it was, indeed, the Mexican symbol of resistance to the predatory foreigner.

More significant, it was the primary gatherer of the revenues on which the Mexican government then lived. On April 21, the American invasion began, and within a few days about six thousand American troops had taken control of the city and killed at least two hundred Mexicans. Throughout Mexico, every newspaper called for vengeance. And everywhere mobs sacked American property and attacked resident Americans. In Tampico, some two thousand Americans had to be evacuated, and property damage was estimated at not less than $200 million.

Shocked that the Mexicans resisted, President Wilson insisted, "We have gone down to Mexico to serve mankind." True to his beliefs, he called for elections, but, true to his estimate of the Mexicans, he also insisted that General Huerta not stand as a candidate. Whether or not they liked Huerta, Mexicans resented this lordly interference in their affairs. As the Mexican foreign minister wrote, Wilson's note to his government was of a "humiliating and unusual character, hardly admissible even in a treaty of peace after a victory . . ." Huerta was forced from power in July 1914, and Wilson's choice as Mexico's democrat, Venustiano Carranza, seized the presidency.

With the central government weakened, Mexico became a collection of virtually autonomous military baronies plotting, acquiring arms and feuding with one another and with the Carranza government. The one thing they shared was a smoldering hatred of the United States. Then, on March 9, 1916, one of the most successful of the military leaders, Doroteo Arango, who fought under the *nom de guerre* Pancho Villa, did what all of them secretly wanted to do: he struck out on a raid against the United States.

As guerrillas nearly always are, Villa's forces were wildly exaggerated. The raiders numbered exactly 484 men, but the United States government attributed to Villa an army in the thousands. The damage they did to the little frontier town of Columbus, New Mexico, was relatively small-scale—they killed ten American soldiers and eight civilians, looted the town and stole about a hundred horses. It was not a great military feat, and it cost Villa's guerrillas at least four times as many lives as they took. But the political affront was more than Americans were prepared to tolerate, and President Wilson, unchastened by the costly and unpopular Tampico-Veracruz affair, ordered a massive punitive expedition.

The punitive expedition was assigned to the seven regiments of the U.S. Army Cavalry stationed along the frontier, all of which had won their spurs in the wars against Geronimo's Apache Indians. The American expedition, the last major campaign of the U.S. Cavalry, was under the command of General Pershing, and among his young officers were two VMI roommates, Lieutenants Harding Polk and George Patton.

For nearly a year, American forces occupied or ranged over the entire north-central plains and mountains of Mexico, penetrating some five hundred miles from the border south toward Mexico City. During that time, they fought a number of small engagements with Pancho Villa's supporters, but they never defeated or caught him because he was supported by the people of his province. But much more important, the invasion of Mexico was bitterly protested even by President Carranza's government and brought the Americans into two major engagements with Mexico's regular army. In June 1916, Mexico and the United States were at the brink of war.

Still proclaiming (and apparently believing) that he had acted in accord with his principles and in the best interests of Mexico, Wilson withdrew the American forces from their southernmost lines northward to Chihuahau, and then in January 1917, as events were rapidly leading toward American involvement in the war in Europe, he ordered them back across the frontier.

In one of the more bizarre episodes of the campaign, long classified and withheld from public knowledge, Wilson's government, or at least his military command, attempted to poison Villa. The attempt, like most espionage, was bungled, and the only poison that took effect was in Mexican feelings toward the United States. With much of this, Frank Polk had to cope.

RANK POLK WAS BORN IN NEW YORK CITY IN 1871 AND WAS the son of Dr. William Mecklenburg ("Meck") and the grandson of Bishop/General Leonidas. Far from his southern relatives, he attended Groton and Yale and then trained as a lawyer at Columbia University. After just a year of legal practice, he enlisted in the New York National Guard and served as a captain in Puerto Rico in the Spanish-American War. Returning to civilian life, he began what would become a long and distinguished legal career and also became active in New York City politics. After helping to defeat the Tammany Hall machine, he became the corporation counsel of the city in 1914. It was from that position that President Wilson called him to take the number two position in the Department of State in 1915. His first major challenge in office was the Mexican crisis.

As acting secretary of state on March 14, 1916, Frank telegraphed all American consular agents in Mexico that "This Government's expedition will shortly enter Mexico with sole objective of pursuing and capturing Villa and his band for the outrage committed at Columbus, New Mexico, on March 9 . . ." The impact of the message was softened by the more or less hypothetical grant to "Mexican soldiers to cross international boundary in pursuit of lawless bands who may enter Mexico from the United States . . ." The Mexicans rightly saw this as a sop, and their damaged pride was not assuaged by it.

Meanwhile, the president informed Congress that he had "obtained the consent of the *de facto* Government of Mexico [which, ironically, the United States did not recognize] for this punitive expedition." But the Mexican government immediately denied, as it would continue to do for months to come, that this was true, saying, "the Mexican Government cannot authorize right off the crossing into our territory of expeditions of American forces," and pointing out that, to the extent an agreement had been reached on reciprocal bandit chasing, any expedition was to be confined to fewer than one thousand men and not to last more than five days. As protest followed protest, Frank met with the Mexican foreign minister in Washington and, on behalf of President Wilson, bluntly "told him that as the original agreement called for American troops being withdrawn, a discussion of that agreement was useless at the time, as our troops were already far in the country."

At a subsequent meeting, Frank officially informed the Mexican foreign minister that "we had 150,000 men there now and, if necessary, could send 100,000 more, and that no discussion was necessary on that subject." He warned that Mexico had better settle the problem with America then, "as it was unlikely there would be another President as friendly to his country as President Wilson."

Unconvinced, Mexican officials continued to complain about American action. One official ended his meeting with Frank "by asking how we would feel if a Mexican expedition of 10,000 men pursued some American marauders all the way to Washington. I told him that I would guarantee to stop both the marauders and the Mexicans before they got out of Texas, if not before."

What really terrified the Mexican government, as the Mexican foreign minister wrote to the U.S. Secretary of State, was the possibility that "some incident might occur which would give an aspect of legality to the indefinite stay of American troops on Mexican soil" despite the fact that "The American Government for some time past has been making assurances of friendship to the Latin-American people, and has taken advantage of every opportunity to convince them that it wishes to respect their sovereignty absolutely." The Mexican government was convinced, moreover, that most "rebels against this Government are cared for and armed, if they are not also organized, on the American side [of the border] under the tolerance of the authorities of the State of Texas, and, it may even be said, that of the Federal authorities of the United States."

Reacting to this démarche as acting secretary of state, Frank cabled the American "special representative" in Mexico, "Long note just delivered by Mexican Agent. Tone aggressive and recriminatory. Will not be given out here at present. Secure copy if possible for your own information and report whether in your opinion expresses attitude of Government. Tone and style bound to create irritation here.''

The American commanding general in Mexico reported from Fort Sam Houston on December 8, 1916, that ''From reliable information I am sure that Villa gets nine-tenths of his arms, ammunition and supplies of all kinds as well as the majority of his recruits from the Carranza forces'' (that is, from the official Mexican government). In a foretaste of America's later dilemma in Vietnam, Frank commented to the Mexican ambassador that ''as soon as we let them [the Mexican government] have ammunition, the revolutionists very shortly after were to get it.'' There was no doubt that the Mexican people supported the guerrillas.

CERTAINLY, LIEUTENANT HARDING POLK ON THE FIRING LINE had no doubt. The elder son of James H. and Molly, Harding was born in Fort Worth in 1887 and attended first VMI and then West Point. Commissioned a lieutenant in the cavalry, he began his service in the Philippines. Then he was assigned to the 11th United States Cavalry, one of the regiments stationed along the frontier which had been charged with trying to chase down Pancho Villa.

The campaign was hard on men and horses. In his letters, Harding repeatedly mentions that each trooper typically carried only what he could put in his saddlebags, usually three days of rations and 150 rounds of rifle ammunition. Harding rode over a thousand miles, nearly always short of food and nearly always far from water, often without maps and far from support or protection. Supply was a nightmare. The terrain was appalling: sweltering heat and suffocating dust alternated with violent rainstorms that left an almost impassable sea of mud. Trucks, horses and even mules foundered. This campaign was probably the last time that regular American troops had to hunt game for their food. The only saving grace was that occasionally mail arrived from home in the new army airplanes, soaring a few hundred feet above the plains at the breakneck speed of seventy miles an hour.

As Harding found, "every man, woman and child was an enemy of the Americans," and even while he suffered the privations of the campaign, he agonized over the moral and legal ambiguity of his position. As he wrote, the American force was formidable,

> four regiments of cavalry, one of infantry, and three batteries of artillery. Behind them, but within supporting distance, were three regiments of infantry and one of cavalry. It was a force well calculated to arouse suspicion in the minds of a far less suspicious people than the Mexicans . . . The flimsy excuse that our troops have been bandit chasing, will not hold water. Our troops have been kept in Mexico because the present administration lacked the cold nerve to withdraw them. It meant the defeat of the Democratic party if such action were taken.

Every armed man, as virtually all Mexican men then were, was considered a bandit. At least some had no relationship to Pancho Villa. Of one group, he wrote, "With such a force we had no right to interfere, yet we attacked and killed forty-two of them and put the remainder to flight." Over all, Harding concluded, the American troops "are a thorn in the side of the Mexican nation, an embarrassment to the Carranza government, a chip on our shoulder that may cause war with our neighboring republic, and an invading army that no strong and self-respecting people would tolerate for one moment." "Quagmire" was hardly an appropriate term for the Mexican deserts, but for America it was a moral and legal wasteland. Harding was disgusted. What he saw violated the code of military conduct by which he lived. As he lamented,

> At Colonia Dublan at the present time there are twenty-one Mexicans in a wire enclosure . . . All of them are called

bandits. We captured them in an alien land without the authority of any known law. Can any of our courts try them? If so, for what offense? If not, what are we to do with them? If we turn them over to the Carranza government, they will be placed against an adobe wall and shot. This would simply mean our approval of such high handed methods of murder. Our Punitive Expedition is avowedly not one for the policing of Mexico. Yet this is the only thing our troops have been doing for the past three months.

Time after time, the Mexican government asked for the withdrawal of the American force; it made every effort to avoid confrontation with the American troops, but the incident that almost caused war between the two countries, and did result in the call-up of the National Guard, was an American assault on Mexican government troops in the town of Carrizal. Face-to-face with the Mexicans, Harding wrote,

The Mexicans are a proud people and love their native land. Let no one mistake this fact. Our soldiers in Mexico with ''a place in the sun'' have had their eyes opened to this. The lowly and half starved peon is glad to get the money our Punitive Expedition brings him, and yet he intensely resents our presence in *his* country. They look upon us as the worst of enemies.

Their wounded pride and anger were to play a significant role in the events unfolding far away in Europe.

WHILE THE BULK OF THE AMERICAN ARMY AND MOST OF THE energies of the Wilson presidency were focused on Mexico, the effects of the war that had begun in Europe in August 1914 were spreading throughout the world. On the surface, the issues that most directly affected America, and consumed much of Frank's time, were the challenges to American neutrality.

Relations with Germany were coolly correct. When, for example, a German raider brought a captured ship into Norfolk harbor, Prince Hatzfeldt, the counselor of the German embassy in Washington, called Frank's attention to the 1799 American treaty with Prussia regulating the handling of naval prizes. Frank was obviously surprised at this ghost from the distant past and, lawyerlike, replied that "we did not have sufficient facts as yet to state our position, but if the Treaty he showed me was still in effect and not qualified, they would be entitled to have the ship remain in port." At the same time, however, he "personally and unofficially" advised the counselor not to go to Norfolk to visit the crews of German warships interned there.

The German torpedoing of the passenger liner *Lusitania* on May 7, 1915, outraged many Americans, but their anger dissipated as negotiations over reparations and apologies dragged on inconclusively for months. American public opinion remained deeply divided. German-speaking immigrants to America were numerous and influential; by and large, they were pro-German. The English-speaking population, by and large, empathized with at least the British part of the Anglo-French-Russian alliance, but at the same time, they bitterly resented the high-handed actions of the Allies. Among these was British and French tampering with international mails. Meeting with Frank, the French ambassador justified their tampering as mere extensions of "the principles established by us [the Americans] in the Civil War." This must have rung particularly ironic to the grandson of General Leonidas. Frank blandly pointed out that "this Government had never, in the Civil War, claimed the right to interfere with neutral mail and that the British and French Governments had gone far beyond anything that had ever been attempted."

In the conflicting actions, sometimes literally a minefield, of the Germans and the Allies, the Wilson administration was constrained both by American public opinion and by the beliefs of the president. Frank was the point of contact of the various forces. But, already in October 1915, he and Colonel House discussed a plan House had devised to either force a peace conference or to justify American entry into the war on the Allied side. As House wrote,

> I thought we had lost our opportunity to break with Germany [by not acting immediately after the sinking of the *Lusitania*], and it looked as if she had a better chance than ever of winning, and if she did win our turn would come next; and we were not only unprepared, but there would be no one to help us stand the first shock. Therefore, we should do something decisive now—something that would either end the war in a way to abolish militarism or that would bring us in with the Allies to help them do it. My suggestion is to ask the Allies, unofficially, to let me know whether or not it would be agreeable to them to have us demand that hostilities cease. We would then put it upon the high ground that the neutral world was suffering along with the belligerents and that we had rights as well as they, and that peace parleys should begin upon the broad basis of both military and naval disarmament . . . The Allies, after some hesitation, could accept our offer or demand and, if the Central Powers accepted, we would then have accomplished a master-stroke of diplomacy. If the Central Powers refused to acquiesce, we could then push our insistence to a point where diplomatic relations would first be broken off, and later the whole force of our Government—and perhaps the force of every neutral—might be brought against them.

Wilson did not act upon House's suggestion, which was not fully developed; so on October 11, House enlisted Frank to try to persuade the president, ending on the ominous note that

It will not do for the United States to let the Allies go down and leave Germany the dominant military factor in the world. We would certainly be the next object of attack . . . Polk thought the idea was good from every standpoint, and he hoped the President would finally put it through . . .

The major obstacle, as soon began to become evident and as was later to become destructive in the 1919 Paris Peace Conference, was that

> House's proposition would not meet the approval of those Allied statesmen who looked forward to utilizing their prospective victory as a means to extensive annexations and crushing indemnities . . . The Russians, British and French had signed treaties which carved up the regions of the Near East with little regard for the interests of their inhabitants, they had brought Italy to their side by promising territories which were certainly not Italian in character; French aspirations extended far beyond Alsace-Lorraine, and Tsarist Russia had plans for the Poles who might be liberated from Austria and Prussia, which did not include independence.

So the American government, with Frank as its diplomatic point man, tried to protect its rights as a neutral, to maintain a cosmetically acceptable position between the Allies and the Germans but to do what it could both to keep the Allies from defeat and to prepare the American public for the coming conflict. The way out of this impasse was created by Germany and effected by the British release of the so-called Zimmermann telegram of January 17, 1917.

German Foreign Minister Arthur Zimmermann had begun to negotiate with the Mexican government in November 1916 to acquire safe bases for submarines by hinting at some sort of alliance. Germany had hit upon the most sensitive nerve of the Wilson presidency. The American government did not then know of the German contact, but the British, who had broken the German diplomatic codes, did. Their opportunity to use their knowledge came in January when Zimmermann sent a telegram to his ambassador in Washington announcing Germany's decision to begin unrestricted submarine warfare and setting out a plan, in the event America reacted as expected by declaring war, to create a diversion by fomenting a war with Mexico.

Code breaking is a very old tool of diplomacy. It is highly valued because it enables the interceptor to learn the most intimate thoughts and actions of the sender in a way that rises above propaganda, since the sender presumes that his message is known only to his most intimate associates. But the dilemma of code breaking is precisely that: if the interceptor makes use of the information, the sender will realize that his method of transmission is not secure, and he will stop using it. Consequently, the interceptor makes every effort to protect his source even if that means he cannot use the information. Only in the most dire circumstances will he risk compromising it. Just such a circumstance caused the British to share their decoding of the Zimmermann telegram with the United States.

During 1916, the British government was beginning to believe that the Allies were facing likely defeat. The German government concluded that it was also facing defeat and that if the war continued, Germany would collapse by August 1917. Both sides were suffering horrendous losses. Both grasped for some means of effecting a decisive blow: the Germans thought they had found their answer in the submarine, and the British, theirs in America's entry into the war. Germany gambled that while unrestricted submarine warfare would bring America into the war—as Frank told the Austrian ambassador on February 26, 1917, it definitely would—so many ships would be sunk that Britain and France would be starved into a negotiated peace before America could get mobilized. Britain thought that the Germans were right, and so they sought to speed up America's entry before they starved. They found the perfect tool in the almost pathological concern of the Wilson administration with Mexico: they wanted to show that the diabolical "Huns" were inciting the Mexicans to avenge Mr. Polk's War and President Wilson's two attacks. Code breaking was their tool.

The text of the Zimmermann telegram was given to Frank, who was then acting secretary of state, through the American ambassador in London on February 24. He immediately took it to the president. The telegram could not have come at a more opportune time for Wilson, as he was facing a revolt of his Democratic supporters in the Congress against his proposal to arm American merchant ships. His bill was heading for certain defeat. So he "leaked" the telegram through the Associated Press to American newspapers. Typical of the press headlines reporting was the *New York World* of March 1.

MEXICO AND JAPAN ASKED BY GERMANY TO ATTACK
U.S. IF IT ENTERED THE WAR; [German Ambassador
Johann] BERNSTORFF A LEADING FIGURE IN PLOT.

The British gamble paid off: America declared war on Germany on April 6, 1917.

WHILE THESE GRAND EVENTS WERE UNFOLDING ON THE world stage, Sarah Polk Bradford of Nashville had started on a very different route that would lead her to Europe. The daughter of a Tennessee judge and the granddaughter of Lucius Polk and President Andrew Jackson's niece, Mary Eastin, Sarah attended schools in Switzerland and France. In Paris, she met the son of the president of the Canadian Pacific Railway, Alfred Shaughnessy, whom she married in 1912.

When the war broke out, Alfred joined the Canadian militia. War seemed very far away to him as to most Canadians. Rumors were rife but no one knew how to evaluate them. He was shocked when his close friend and business associate German Prince Alfred Hohenlohe was arrested as an enemy alien. Suddenly, the war began to seem more real. Soon thereafter, Alfred was inducted into the army and sent to England.

Alfred, also like most Europeans and Americans, saw the war as a short, "traditional" campaign full of parades and martial music to be followed soon by a negotiated peace. And delighted by London, he begged Sarah to join him. Sarah's mother, vicariously aware of "real" war from the tales of the American Civil War, was adamantly opposed. Among other things, she worried about the exotic and terrifying zeppelin raids, and she urged Alfred, whether or not Sarah went over, to "get a position on some General's staff. You would be in much less danger. I see in the papers there is much talk of peace. I sincerely hope it may be true and you will not have to go to the Front."

Even relatively safe London in those days presented an eerie sight. As Sarah confided in her diary on January 17, 1916,

> London at night is now in nearly total darkness, the tops of the street lamps are painted black throwing only a shadow below, and the windows of the buildings and houses have black shades and curtains to conceal the light, while the searchlights are at work in the sky looking for Zeppelins. It is all so weird and exciting. The people, however, are very calm and don't seem to worry at all about the "baby killers" as the Zeppelins are called.

Death in the trenches came quickly for Alfred: he was hit by a bullet in the heart and killed instantly on March 31, 1916. Sarah was then seven months pregnant and quickly left London to return to Nashville to pick up her children, whom she had left with her mother. Then she returned to London, where she became a sort of Merry Widow and found consolation in what her son later called a "relentless round of amusement." Soon she was the subject of "talk" as she was courted by Queen Victoria's son the Duke of Connaught, Lord Beaverbrook and a host of younger officers, married and unmarried.

London was then known as a man's city. Pretty young women were considered the prey of an endless and delightful hunt, but like several of the smarter women, Sarah was no mere fox to their hounds. And if chase was merry, it was usually she rather than they who set the course. As her diary makes clear, her winning formula consisted of beauty, wealth and connections; more alluring, she exhibited just the right amount of being nearly but not quite "available." In her diary of February 9, 1919, she remarked, perhaps somewhat self-consciously, as she was an irrepressible flirt, of one gentleman suitor, "The General is too awful with his stories of wine, women and song. Curious how many men's brains are so developed on those lines."

But her outstanding ability was stamina. As the diary also makes clear, she must have had the strength of a mule. Every day was filled with a sequence of luncheons, exhibitions, cocktail parties, dinners and the theater and was nearly always climaxed with a midnight dance. She was everywhere, all day and night, the belle of London society. All doors were opened for her.

So when her brother arrived in France with the American army, and asked her to visit, she was undeterred by the government ban on travel. She went right to Prime Minister David Lloyd George, and as she wrote in her diary in December 1917,

> I was invited to go with the Prime Minister, Mr. Lloyd George, and all the members of the great Allied Conference that was to be held in Paris. It was the most important gathering of the "Entente" powers since the beginning of the war . . . I was, of course, thrilled and shall always remember the interesting history-making conversation . . . Lloyd George is a most charming person to meet and impressed me with his keenness, extraordinary vitality and quick wit . . . On our arrival in Paris we were met by [the French premier] M. Clemenceau. It was a wonderful trip.

Meanwhile, the war dragged on. In her diary for February 18, 1918, Sarah wrote, "Bad air raid on London last night. 60 killed. We heard the guns and barrage from here [Surrey, her house in the country]. The crocuses and primroses are in bloom. They give a breath of spring."

She never lost the breath of spring. Cut off from the war, Sarah continued what the older women, particularly the Canadian women who were friends of her late husband's family, regarded as that of a "flighty widow who ought to be leading a quieter life." Undeterred, she kept up what her son later called, discreetly, "a busy social life in London." Finally, probably reacting to the "talk" and her in-laws' bitter comments on her conduct, she thought of getting properly married again. But as she commented of one suitor, "I am very fond of him but feel I can never care for any of these men enough to marry them. Wish I could but it is hopeless."

A S A NEWLY APPOINTED MAJOR, HARDING WAS SENT TO France in April 1918 where he commanded the headquarters troop of the 5th Division; then after a short course at the General Staff College, he became assistant chief of staff of the 92nd Division and went into combat at Vosges and at the Battle of the Argonne. But on November 11, 1918, hostilities ceased. For Harding, the war had ended almost before it had begun, and for his younger brother, George, who had joined him in France as a captain of artillery, it truly had: George never made it to the front.

Almost immediately, the whole attention of the world was shifted to Paris, where President Wilson began his great struggle for world peace. But just as Harding and George had hardly seen the war, so Frank appeared unlikely to take part in the peacemaking. During the year when Wilson and his entourage were in Paris attempting to convince the Allied leaders of his plan for peace, Frank was left in Washington to "mind the store" as the acting secretary of state. Then their roles were reversed. On July 21, 1919, Frank and his wife sailed for France, where he was to become "Commissioner Plenipotentiary of the United States of America to Negotiate Peace and to be Head of the Peace Mission." The tumultuous riptide of enthusiasm for everything American on which President Wilson had ridden had already ebbed when Frank arrived; the great issues had been pushed aside by a multitude of relatively small but more practical questions that were the subject of the sordid ambitions and deals among the Allies. Frank found that he had to fight even for the right of the American commissioner to attend key meetings. Soon he clashed with British Prime Minister Lloyd George, who was trying to dissolve the peace conference. But most of his time was spent, as it had been in Washington, dealing with a plethora of insistent issues that, in sum, would shape the postwar world. His daily calendar is a litany of the world's woes. Many of the issues were familiar to him from his years in Washington, but some were new to all Americans. None was more exotic than the problem of the Near East.

Before Frank arrived, Wilson, over the objections of the British and the French, had sent the King-Crane Commission to the Near East to try to ascertain the wishes of the inhabitants. The commissioners delivered their report on August 28, but Frank was so involved with the Russian Revolution, the virtual outbreak of war in the Adriatic, starvation in eastern Europe and the creation of Czechoslovakia that he made no comment on it in his papers.

He was aware that Britain and France had made a secret deal (the so-called Sykes-Picot Agreement) to divide the Near East between them and that they were united in adamant opposition to any American interference. He soon learned that the Arab delegation under the colorful leader of the Arab Revolt against the Ottoman Empire, Amir Faisal of Mecca, was equally adamant on being heard at the peace conference and appealed to Frank to implement the Wilsonian call for "self-determination of peoples." To bolster the Arab case, Faisal passed to Frank copies of what later came to be known as the Hussein-McMahon correspondence, in which the British had promised the Arabs their independence. The British reneged on the agreement and reverted to their imperialist deal with the French. Amir Faisal asked that Frank or another senior American be appointed as arbitrator between them. In reply, Frank said he was sure that America would not interpose itself in this issue unless all parties requested it, which of course the British and French would not do, but he also assured the Arab envoy that "The United States had notified France and Great Britain that it did not regard itself bound by any such arrangements made between them." Desperate, weak and isolated, the Arab delegate

> pressed me to tell him whether Americans regarded the claims of the Emir [Faisal] as extravagant. I replied that I could give no official opinion on this subject but that, as a purely personal opinion, I considered that the Emir would greatly increase the difficulties of his position if I [mistyped for "he"] totally disregarded certain claims, for instance those of the Zionists.

Faisal then called on Frank to press the claim that America had "incurred a moral responsibility toward the people of Syria" and in order to prevent war, should attempt to get France and Britain to agree to arbitration. Frank recommended that Faisal bring the issue before the Supreme Council and he agreed to do so. Shortly thereafter, Frank told the Arabs that "we were going to keep out of it [the Anglo-French-Arab conflict over the Near East] but intimated that I sympathised with his difficulties." To Frank's lawyer mind, America could have no role in the conflict, since the United States had not declared war on the Ottoman Empire of which the Arabs had been a part and "we had not been able to persuade the French to give [Faisal] a hearing." The Near East was an issue then overshadowed by others but one that would persist long after many of the greater issues of the peace conference had been forgotten.

America was near the end of Wilson' foray onto the world stage. The president's health had failed, the Congress had turned against him and the public was anxious to devote itself to what became the Roaring Twenties. Finally on December 4, 1919, Frank noted in his diary,

[French Premier Georges] Clemenceau said, when I told him we were all leaving, that it was a desperate situation for France and they felt as though they were being abandoned. He said the English were saying it just proved that you cannot depend on the Americans, and kept telling me he knew I had done all I could to help.

What Frank had so struggled to achieve seemed to him to go to dust in his hands, but, for his cousin Sarah, the signing of the peace at Versailles was all pomp and glory. She followed up her earlier excursion to Paris with the prime minister by getting herself invited to attend the signing of the Treaty of Versailles and so had a ringside seat on the opening of the new era.

A MONTH LATER BEGAN THE FIRST OF A SERIES OF ENCOUNTERS that might have changed the shape of the British monarchy. Sarah met Edward, the Prince of Wales, who was then in the midst of one of his many love affairs with married women, Freda, Mrs. Dudley Ward. As Sarah wrote of her encounter, "We dined at 8:30. The Prince brought his gramophone and we danced a bit afterwards. It was a most delightful evening and we all enjoyed ourselves. They stayed until 12.0. 'The Boy' [that is, the Prince of Wales] has great charm and personality. He seems very young but there isn't much he doesn't know." Or intended to find out. A close friend of Sarah's, Lady Joan Mulholland, wrote on October 30, 1919, "the Prince [of Wales] is very *épris* [smitten, in love with] Sarah and dances with her most of the time . . . and, if only 'it' would happen, it would be the most wonderful thing in the world and save the British Empire. We are going to try our best to bring it off . . ."

Sarah's son commented much later, "One can't help reflecting on the fuss that the prince caused seventeen years later when, as king, he decided to marry an American. Sarah might have proved marginally more suitable, for at least she was a widow and not a double divorcée. Furthermore she was the daughter-in-law of a British peer.'' Had they ''brought it off,'' England might today have had a very different royal family. But Mrs. Dudley Ward was soon replaced by Mrs. Wallis Simpson.

Meanwhile, Sarah drifted slowly into a marriage with Edward's equerry, Piers ''Joey'' Legh. The marriage, as appears in the diary, was a rather intermittent affair as Joey was constantly taken away by the prince on one months-long ''loyalty building'' tour of the empire after another. After Edward's abdication, Joey was summoned back to court by George VI; so descendants of a family that had fled the English king's wrath 257 years before were now living at court.

For Harding, the end of the First World War, what he had been trained for, was to be followed by a long ''dry'' period in which the U.S. Army was allowed to atrophy: without a role to play— the Indians were all dead or on reservations, the Mexicans were quiet and Wilson had made the world safe for democracy—it withered away to about the size of the New York City police force. With few troops to command, officers were stuck in rank with little to do; Harding remained a major for sixteen years. They were years in which many previously dashing but then bored young officers followed a pattern vividly outlined by the hero of the cavalry, Colonel Tommy Tompkins, with whom Harding had served in Mexico. ''Nobody minds a man having a morning eye-opener,'' he wrote,

> and its OK to have a bracer around 10 A.M., and a couple of drinks before lunch. And a few beers on a hot afternoon to keep a man healthy or at least happy. And, of course, everyone drinks at cocktail hour. And a man can't be criticized for having wine with his dinner, a liquor afterwards and a highball or

two during the evening. But this damn business of guzzle, guzzle, guzzle all day long has GOT TO STOP.

Harding's career, like those of many of the officers of the "old" army,
ground to a halt just on the eve of the Second World War when he was
retired.

Meanwhile, Harding's younger brother, George, who had also
gone to Virginia Military Institute, had turned aside from a military career to study law at Columbia (like his cousin Frank) and subsequently at
the University of Texas. Returning to his hometown, Fort Worth, he began to practice law and then became the public prosecutor.

In 1912, he had married one of the wealthiest young women in
Texas, Adelaide Roe, whose father had followed the railway to Texas in
the 1880s after riding shotgun on stagecoaches, wandering through the
West and dealing in land grants. By the time George and Adelaide met,
Addison Roe had acquired a vast amount of land in Texas and had lum-
beryards all over the state. He had also built a great house, a sort of
Texas version of Rattle & Snap, from which his formidable wife strug-
gled to bring culture to the natives of the little cow town.

In the spring of 1917, George followed Harding into the army and,
as a captain in the field artillery, was shipped to France, where he arrived in July, but his unit was held in reserve, so he was too late to take
part in the final battles. Perhaps because of that, the military life, of
which he had only this fleeting taste but of which he knew through family legends, always captured his imagination.

As did the memory of the Old South. For George, who had grown
up in what his mother described as a "shack" but who was haunted by
the memory of Rattle & Snap, his wife's family, the Roes, were the
grandees of Texas. They were. Addison left his three daughters over a
million dollars' worth of ranches and other property. But George was
an intensely proud young man, and soon, with his growing law practice
and his wife's inheritance, he also built a Texas version of Rattle & Snap.

In the heady days of the boom in the 1920s, it looked like he was on the way to recapturing the halcyon days of the Old South. His law practice was profitable, he was regarded as a "comer" and he stood at the center of the new-style fellowship of the country club, which had, to some extent, replaced the plantation society. On the crest of the 1920s wave, he put Adelaide's money into what appeared to be a solid and lucrative business venture, a "sure thing," a large building that was leased to a major national furniture chain.

Then came the stock market crash of 1929 and the Great Depression of the 1930s. The furniture company went bankrupt and defaulted on the lease for the building. In quick succession, the bank foreclosed because George and Adelaide could not keep up the large mortgage payments. George's law practice also began to dry up. And soon, like his grandfather George at Rattle & Snap, George found himself living in the grandest house in the area with no money. By 1936, the inevitable happened: he was forced to declare bankruptcy.

Bankruptcy, which today has become almost a business strategy, was then regarded as shameful. For George, it was crushing. In the time of his father and in his own time, the Old South—both the mythic Old South and the one he was trying to rebuild—had crumbled to dust. Like his grandfather, he was reduced to "genteel poverty." His law practice died and he went to work as a counsel for a bus company. Just before his death, he began to negotiate for a commission in the Texas National Guard. For him, there was no "West" to go off to. No new beginning. America had come of age.

Frank meanwhile had resigned from the Wilson administration in 1920, and together with John Davis, who had been solicitor general of the United States from 1913 to 1918 and Wilson's ambassador in London from 1918 to 1921, he founded the New York law firm of Davis Polk, which quickly became one of the most prestigious in New York. When Davis ran for the presidency in 1924 (against Calvin Coolidge), Frank acted as his principal adviser.

A very different career indeed was that of a Harding cousin of Molly Polk's. The great-great-grandson of John Harding (1777–1865), the founder of Belle Meade, "Smiling Jack" Harding became a pioneer in the new field of aviation. Just when Frank was finishing up his work in Paris and Harding and George were on their way back to America, Jack took part in the first demonstration of the army's budding airpower.

Airplanes in the First World War had limited range and even more limited capacity to carry anything aloft. So the army was anxious to show that there was a future very different from the recent past. The means to do this was a radically new airplane designed by Donald Douglas known as the MB-1. Intended to be a bomber, it was relatively huge, with a wingspan of 148 feet, and was powered by two 400-horsepower engines. To demonstrate what then seemed its awesome capacity, it was to fly around the entire frontier of America. Jack was signed on as the copilot in the summer of 1919.

The flight was a great success and was instrumental in getting the Congress to appropriate money to build up the air wing of the army. So, aiming at congressional relations and public acclaim, the army decided to send off a mission to try to circumnavigate the globe. The planes for this mission were also designed by Donald Douglas, and thus began what became a huge American air industry. So it was that in 1924, Jack became copilot of the Douglas *New Orleans,* the first airplane to fly around the world.

The *New Orleans* was a custom-built, open-cockpit biplane designated a "World Cruiser." It had a wingspan of fifty feet and could fly at a maximum speed of 103 miles per hour. By today's standards, the World Cruiser was not only slow and cumbersome but astonishingly fragile. Virtually everything on the plane was to be changed at least once—and the motors almost after each "hop"—along the route. Indeed, perhaps the most impressive aspect of the flight was the remarkable logistical support it received. New engines, spare parts, even pontoons were pre-positioned at key points, and navy ships dotted the wider expanses of the seas over which the planes flew.

Of the four planes that started out on the mission, two quickly crashed and had to be virtually rebuilt. At Seattle, the remaining planes caught up with the *Chicago* and the *New Orleans,* and all had their wheels replaced with pontoons. Then they jumped off "into the wild blue yonder." When they reached Alaska, one plane crashed beyond repair and the crew had to walk, nearly frozen, across the Alaska Peninsula to a Bering Sea fishing village. The weather that April had been particularly foul, and while the crews of the remaining planes sat on the ground way out at the end of the Aleutians, forlornly awaiting a bit of clear sky, Jack asked an old-timer when the seasons could be expected to change. The old man snapped back, "Don't be funny, young fellow. We have only two seasons up here. This winter and next winter." In despair, they took off on what would be the first flight across the Pacific.

Forced northwest by bad weather, they landed in the Pacific, just offshore from the Komandorskiye Ostrova. The Russian officials were friendly to Jack and his colleagues, but since the United States had not recognized the Soviet Union, the planes were encouraged to take off after a night's rest.

In Japan, to the contrary, they received a heroes' greeting by a Tokyo crowd estimated at 100,000 who waved Japanese and American flags. While they were receiving the adulation of the crowds, and, it was said, the charming attentions of geishas, they repaired the planes, changed the already worn engines and replaced the pontoons.

After stops in Shanghai and Hong Kong, they landed in French Indochina in what is now Vietnam, where one more of the American planes came to grief. Having been forced down with engine trouble, the *Chicago* was towed, in what must have been a colorful sight, by three oar-powered sampans to the nearby city of Hue for a new engine.

Crossing India in the searing heat of the first week of July, they headed up the southern coast of Iran, along some of the most desolate land of the planet, an area that almost destroyed the army of Alexander the Great, to the steam bath known as Bandar Abbas. Then up the Persian Gulf to Baghdad and across the Great Syrian Desert to Aleppo and northward toward Paris, which they had promised to reach on the French national holiday of July 14.

Flying westward across the stormy Atlantic, the *Boston*'s engine lost oil. As the pressure fell, the plane slowed to less than fifty miles an hour and could not maintain its altitude. Soon it was forced down into the Atlantic. When the two remaining planes radioed for help, an American cruiser and a destroyer were sent to the rescue.

Meanwhile, the two planes slowly made their way westward. When they reached Greenland, they were on the ground for three weeks of virtual rebuilding. And by this time, thoroughly alarmed at the pattern of engine failures and accidents, the navy formed a virtual bridge of ships ahead of them. Every hundred miles or so was a destroyer or even a cruiser. The ships must have been almost as useful for flight navigation as for lifesaving: so close to the water were the planes often forced by poor visibility that they performed virtually as boats themselves, barely able to avoid the fate of the *Titanic* as they threaded their way through fields of icebergs. Between Quebec and Newfoundland, they had to fly so low that Jack nearly collided with a freighter.

The flight across America was a series of triumphs as city after city turned out to welcome them with banquets, boxes of gold coins, medals, and even landing strips strewn with roses. Finally, back in Seattle where they had begun, Jack and his colleagues had posted 26,345 miles in 363 hours of flight spread over nearly six months. It was truly an epic event in the history of flight.

In 1926, Jack and Captain Eddie Rickenbacker formed one of the first of the new airways to carry mail throughout the South. Truly a character out of Antoine Saint-Exupéry's novel *Vol de Nuit,* Jack Harding instead inspired the comic strip character Smiling Jack.

ADOPTED BY HER STEPFATHER, SARAH'S DAUGHTER BETTY grew up in the court and knew everyone in the royal family as childhood companions. It was a very social existence, and Betty's youth was nearly a fairy-tale existence with a constant whirl of parties as she moved into London society.

But filled with energy and wit, she wanted more out of life than parties, so as a young woman, in 1929, she decided to break out of the social whirl and go abroad to learn a language. Partly by plan and partly by accident, she picked Germany and set off to learn German in Munich. There she met one of the young women she had known in London, a member of the talented and eccentric Mitford family. Unity Mitford was already well connected in Germany and had become what today we would call a groupie of a then relatively unknown political leader and street fighter by the name of Adolf Hitler.

One evening, Unity decided to introduce Betty to her hero. She set up a rendezvous in a Munich beer hall much frequented by Hitler and his coterie of followers. It was a good chance for Betty to practice her German, and having heard rumors of Hitler, she wanted to meet him. So together with Unity, she entered the hall. Sitting with Hitler was one other man, but Hitler so dominated the conversation that the other man did not make much of an impression on her. It was only much later that she figured out that he must have been Joseph Goebbels.

That was, of course, before Hitler became chancellor and before the Nazis had taken power, and Hitler spoke little of his own plans and ambitions, but knowing that Betty lived in the English court, an institution that apparently would continue to fascinate him until the end of his life, he asked detailed and exact questions about Buckingham Palace and Windsor Castle. How big were they, when did the court move from one to another, who lived there, what was life there like? By the end of the evening, Betty had begun to get the impression that Hitler's interest was not just casual. As they walked out, she remarked to Unity Mitford, "I think that man means to go to war with us." Unity was shocked and emphatically denied that Hitler, whom she idolized, could even contemplate such a thing. "Why," she said, "if he did, I would kill myself." That is exactly what she later did: she shot herself when England and Germany went to war.

AMERICA IN A
NEW WORLD

"They die often in abject fear in the dirt"

A T THE END OF 1911 WAS BORN THE FIRST OF THREE DESCEN-
dants of Will Polk who would play significant roles in the new
world into which America was launched by the Second World War.
Jimmy was born on December 13, 1911, Lucius Burch on January 15,
1912, and George on October 17, 1913. Their births demonstrated the
wide dispersion of the Polk family over the previous half century. Jimmy
was born on an American army base in the Philippines, where his father
was stationed as a young cavalry officer; Lucius, who was born in Nashville, represented the part of the family that had remained in Tennessee
after the Civil War; and George was the grandson of the James who left
Tennessee for Texas after the Tennessee plantation on which he was born
was taken from the family. Much about their lives fit into a tradition that
was at least a century in the making, but like the country itself, they

were inevitably shaped by forces beyond even the imagination of their parents.

JIMMY WAS OFTEN OUT OF CONTACT WITH HIS ARMY OFFICER FA-ther during his youth. As a baby, he was sent home from the Philippines because his parents were worried about his health; then, when his father was mustered to fight against Pancho Villa and to serve in France during the First World War, he was left behind. But he spent his teenage years at VMI, where many of the family members had been trained and where his father had become the commandant. When he was ready for college, as he later said, "I nearly went to VMI . . . but I got an appointment to West Point so dad said, 'I'm just a Major and it's free, so you go to West Point.' " It was not a happy choice. He was constantly in trouble for breaking the academy's strict rules, but he scraped through to be commissioned a second lieutenant in 1933.

The America into which he graduated was deep in the slump of the Depression, but compared to many Americans, Jimmy was well off—he had a secure job with a salary of $125 a month (plus a $12 allowance for owning his own horse). Life in the tiny American army was easy and comfortable but unexciting. Officers were frozen in rank for years—many second lieutenants like Jimmy remained that for a decade or more, while few senior officers ever progressed beyond the parade ground. Practically no officer was even aware of the dramatic changes then taking place in the reconstituted German army, and none studied the new tactics. The only man in the American cavalry who knew anything about tank warfare was Colonel—still the same rank he had held twenty years earlier in the First World War—George Patton. The army professional school for cavalry at Fort Riley, Kansas, Jimmy said, was almost entirely focused on "horsemanship, horse doctoring and shoeing horses and studying [pre–First World War horse] cavalry campaigns." Training still called for charges with sabers. Even against machine-gun nests. Jimmy would make his first mark in the army by winning the

U.S. military horse jumping championship at Madison Square Garden in 1939.

With little public interest in the military and money in short supply, the lessons and equipment of the First World War, and even of the Indian wars, were the staples of professional life. For his passion for tanks, Patton was regarded as an oddball; it did not pay to follow his lead. Far better to be regarded as a team player, "a hale fellow well met" and a good companion at bridge or polo. Not surprisingly, many officers gave themselves up to daily cocktail parties. The 1930s were a period in which the American army nearly died of boredom. And drink.

Lucius and George faced quite different challenges. Their lives were to be anything but routine or protected. Lucius's father, who was dean of the Vanderbilt University medical school, wanted him to become a doctor, but by his own account, Lucius was a poor student and was particularly bad at just those subjects required for medical school. As he later said of this period of his life, it took him four years to pass a course in freshman mathematics. George's father similarly wanted him to follow his footsteps. That meant becoming a lawyer. But George hated that prospect and dropped out of college before graduating. Neither Lucius nor George could foresee a clear path ahead, and, without knowing one another, ventured far afield.

The Alaska to which both escaped was the very antithesis of Jimmy's cavalry post. Raw, anarchic, violent, it was America's last frontier. Lucius, who was an expert marksman, got a job hunting predators, wolves, grizzly bears, eagles and hair seals for the U.S. Biological Survey. As he later remarked, what he did would become not only "environmentally incorrect" but even a felony; at that time, however, exterminating "pests" was government policy. "Taming the Wilds" was as current a thought in the 1930s as it had been in the 1730s when Charles Polk, "the Indian Trader," moved into his frontier. What was to be new was that years later Lucius would become an ardent champion of conservation.

When George arrived in Alaska a few years after Lucius, he got a summer job in a salmon canning factory, then, having become aware that for almost any work beyond canning salmon he would need a college degree, he entered the University of Alaska. That institution, to judge from his letters, was more boisterous but not more academic than VMI, from which he had fled. Ironically, he supported himself there by teaching the military "science" he had so hated at VMI. And no matter how exotic the places he visited, it was hard to top being a graduate of the University of Alaska. Having got his degree, George took off for the real wilderness as Lucius had done: he joined a survey mission on the Yukon River.

For Lucius, Alaska was a stage in maturing. As he later said, "For the most part I was alone and the only social intercourse that I had was with loggers, Filipino cannery workers, and native women. This gave me a self-confidence and a maturity that I might not have gained otherwise and certainly not nearly so quickly." For George, the payoff of Alaska was quite different. It was there that he took his first tentative steps toward journalism by writing a series of letters on his experiences which were published in a hometown newspaper, the *Fort Worth Press*. For both men, Alaska was a wild and colorful life and each was transformed by it.

Having learned to fly in Fort Worth and later in California, George hung around the bush pilots who were then the only means of communication for much of the frozen wasteland. He was mesmerized by their tales and experimented with their daring feats. Flying with skis instead of wheels was a major challenge, but even getting an engine going in the bitter cold was no small chore. "The warm-up process is a long drawn out one," he marveled, "for the oil must be heated with a blow torch . . . and a gasoline stove is placed under a funnel of canvas, so that the heat will be directed against the motor parts. Often this takes an hour or more [since temperatures often hit] 55 to 60 degrees below zero—not far from the stove!"

But it was the land and the people that really caught his imagination. The high point of his experience was the survey mission down the Yukon River in June 1938. That part of Alaska was then "the back of beyond," and had he seen it, the young George Washington might have altered his comment on the Indian territory in Pennsylvania where Charles Polk had lived—"I believe y. worst Road that was ever trod by Man or Beast." There were perhaps worse in Alaska, and wild Alaska was populated by trappers, gold prospectors, fugitives from justice and plain outlaws who would have been quite at home in the cabin of Charles.

George was fascinated by them, tried to catch their peculiar turns of phrase and to learn their stories. He wrote down their tales and dreamed of following the literary path of Jack London. But he was also pulled, as Lucius had been, in the opposite direction. His youthful diary is full of nostalgia for his former life, yearnings for the string of girlfriends he had left behind and worries about what direction he could hope to take for his life. "I'm all mixed up again over my life desires. I don't know what I want to do." Full of self-doubt and confusion, he wrote on August 1, 1938,

> I'd like to teach in college maybe, or do newspaper work, or travel and work in between trips. The American Foreign Service calls, too. I question the advisability of going back to Texas and going to work for [relatives, since there] . . . I'd be an embarrassing fixture—the down-at-the-heel relation. Far better to try writing—maybe the [Fort Worth] Press would give me a job and then maybe Scripps-Howard contacts would result in something. I'll be damned if I know what I'll do . . .

In this confused frame of mind, George set off in March 1939 for Japan and China on what he planned to be a trip around the world, his "vagabondia," as he called his period of wanderlust, before settling down to a "stable" life in Texas. He would never make it. Instead, he would get caught up in some of the greatest events of this century and would spend most of the rest of his short life in exotic places.

ALREADY ON THE SHIP GOING TO THE FAR EAST, GEORGE WIT-nessed one of the great controversies on the eve of the Second World War, the sale of American scrap iron to fuel the steel mills of Japan. The *Tai Shan* carried eight thousand tons of the iron that would soon be made into the bombs and shells that would be dropped on Pearl Harbor. Well might George have pondered a remark attributed to Lenin that "the capitalists will sell the very rope used to hang them." This was the first of the ironies that would shock him into a political sophistication he could never have achieved in college.

After a brief tour of Japan, where he was exposed to its remarkable military discipline and industrial organization and began to sense, as so few then did, the likelihood of the coming conflict, he went on to Shanghai. There, in place of Japanese order, he found chaos. And chaotic it would have been, as it was a huge, bustling, almost formless city, and it was also divided among the Japanese, the British and the French, with large areas given over to what amounted to guerrilla warfare. Running low on the small amount of money he had managed to save on the Yukon survey mission, George got a job as a cub reporter on the English-language *Shanghai Evening Post & Mercury*. It wasn't much of a job, but it was another small step toward what was to become his life's mission, journalism, and it exposed him to another ugly and brutal aspect of what would become the Second World War in the Pacific.

Shanghai was then filled with refugees. White Russians (fleeing the Communists) led the way, but they were being joined by German Jews (fleeing the Nazis). The human tragedy appalled him. And as he always was to do in his later writing, he chose not to allow the ugly reality to be covered over by euphemisms. He felt that one of the reasons people do such hateful things to one another is that they avoided talking about them in plain language. If the truth was repulsive, so must the words be. As George put it,

> There is a new crop of whores in the Far East. I allude to the young, beautiful Jewesses. Their plump, shapely young bodies will soon be for rent . . . I saw one walking down the Bund today with tears streaming down her face, and sobbing quite audibly. It is wicked, desperately cruel, and yet nothing but history repeating itself. The 20's saw beautiful young Russians, and today . . . [I learned] that 5,000 Jews in Vienna expect to depart for Shanghai in the near future . . ."

George ached over the stories of those victims he got to know, but in Shanghai the effects of tyranny soon came to seem almost hackneyed. George could relate to individual Russians and Jews but was numbed by Shanghai's hundreds of thousands of Chinese who were fleeing one another, the Japanese and famine: starving children hovering by the doors of restaurants made meals almost impossible, but there were too many for him to feed. Surfeited with suffering, he retreated to a table away from the door. But he was never insensible to men's violence to their fellows. In Shanghai, it was latent on every street, but official violence was the worst and most inexcusable. George watched with horror the casual brutality with which the Japanese treated the Chinese. One day, he wrote, he watched powerless as Japanese soldiers, having learned their trade in the rape of Nanking, "beyoneted a poor devil, probably because he didn't bow low enough [and] quite casually the sentinels flattened the Chinese's face and knocked out his teeth with a rifle butt." To his diary, he confided, "I still believe the Japanese nation will pay through the nose for all this . . ." In 1939, that was more a hope than an expectation.

Sickened by Shanghai, George left for Europe, pausing in virtually every city along the route. Many of these Asian cities and towns would soon come under the Japanese heel or be hoisted on the Japanese bayonet, but in them in the spring of 1939, life flowed languidly in graceful habit. War was unimaginable. It had begun to seem more likely, however, when George arrived in Paris, and his first newspaper stories dealt with the dread of war. After his arrival, he had flaunted his journalistic experience, but it was his hobby as a ham radio operator that he parlayed into a job on the *Herald Tribune.* On August 29, 1939, he wrote that "The shadow of war hangs like a dark and heavy cloud over Paris today. No one knows when the storm may break. Parisians await the dreaded drone of high flying German bombers. The attack is expected to come without warning." France had already begun to prepare for defeat.

Meanwhile, he found that wealthy Frenchmen, mobile foreigners and tourists were desperately trying to get out. Some had even booked passage on German ships and were stunned when the ships failed to arrive. "After waiting in Havre for 12 hours for the arrival of the Hamburg-America liner Hansa, 200 vacationists have returned here. No explanation has been offered concerning the ship's failure to arrive on schedule from Hamburg. None is needed." But ticket scalpers were doing a brisk business, selling reservations on other ships to the desperate would-be refugees for as much as $1,000.

When war came, it was in the guise of the "phony war." Nothing military seemed to be happening. The Germans, as we now know, were hard at work preparing their panzer *Blitzkrieg,* but the French remained bewildered. In despair, officials led their citizens in prayer. Theirs was an old answer to danger. Just as medieval churchmen had tried to stave off the Huns by parading relics of saints and praying, so the modern French consecrated a special church. The Sacré-Coeur in Paris had been dedicated to continuous prayer from the first German invasion in 1870 through the German invasion of 1914, and as George wrote on January

23, 1940, "As in the [First] World War, so today, the procession of the devout to the Sacre-Coeur is uninterrupted."

A few days later, George sent a dispatch on the major French preparation, the removal of the art treasures of the Louvre.

> Among the works of art stored in special safety deposit vaults are the Mona Lisa of da Vinci, the Winged Victory of Samothrace, the lush and grandiose portraits of Rubens and the armless Venus de Milo . . . 3,000-odd paintings have been taken from the walls and carried away . . . The Galerie d'Apollon, once considered the finest and most ornate room in the Louvre, is just a long empty corridor, decorated with pictureless frames . . . The Louvre is today a hollow shell.

Next on his agenda was a visit to the troops on the Maginot Line, from which he was able to look across no-man's-land into the Siegfried Line. At the front, he was astonished by military apathy and triviality. He found the commanding British general very concerned about the high price his troops had to pay for English beer and about the length of the soldiers' jackets. Local customs also bothered him. Englishmen, he said, will simply "have to learn the Continental custom of dipping [their bread] into soup and coffee." Coping with these urgent tasks apparently kept the defending troops from doing anything else. "You journalists," the general lectured, "should not give the impression that the men are having a soft war, for they aren't. It is quite true that we are not yet in the thick of fighting but waiting is the hardest part of warfare." The general would soon learn that there are harder parts. Such was the phony war in Europe as 1940 began.

With eyes hardened by the sights of what Japan was doing in China and with ears filled with the radio rantings of Hitler, George, who was still a reserve officer in the American army, decided that it was time for him to return to America. There, in February 1940, he got a job on the

New York Herald Tribune and also began first to study at Columbia University and then to teach a class in journalism at New York University. In each of these activities, he followed events closely as they rushed toward general war in the Far East and Europe, and on the day after Pearl Harbor, anxious to get into combat, he volunteered for what seemed the fastest route, the U.S. Naval Air Force.

M EANWHILE, THE AMERICAN ARMY'S VIEW OF THE WORLD was not much different from that of the English general in France. As Jimmy later wrote, "I don't think we [the junior officers of the American army] were aware of it [the onset of the European conflict] at all. We were in a little, enclosed enclave you might say, living our own lives. It didn't cross our mind that we'd be going to war" even after the German invasion of Poland in 1939. After Pearl Harbor, to his surprise given his spotty cadet record, Jimmy found himself stationed back at West Point as an instructor in tactics. He hated being there. As the army began to expand, he saw opportunities for advancement slipping past him and tried repeatedly to escape by volunteering for a combat assignment. But West Point's commandant fought tenaciously to hang on to his staff, so Jimmy was stuck, as he thought, in limbo. It wasn't until 1943 that he would manage to get assigned to a division that was being shipped to England and prepared to invade Europe. By that time, George's war was nearly over.

During this time, Lucius was the most insulated of the three cousins from the events beyond the Americas. Like George and Jimmy, he had attended military school, and like George he turned away from it early in life. Having found his vocation as a lawyer, he plunged into practice, joining the firm of his uncle in Memphis. There his penchant for causes soon got him in the whirlpool that swirled around the virtual dictator of Memphis, Boss Crump.

But long before he crossed swords with the Boss, he had become a maverick. His concern with social and political injustice began, as he remembered, in college. As the scion of an old southern family, growing up under the care of a black mammy on a plantation outside of Nashville, he had taken a benign but patronizing view of blacks. As he later wrote,

> . . . though all my early playmates were black, the suggestion that they were not genetically and in every other important way different from me would have seemed ridiculous. Indeed, I remember one evening at dinner when the Episcopal Bishop of Tennessee was visiting and President Theodore Roosevelt was being criticized by all present for having had Booker T. Washington at the White House. The Bishop in buttressing the argument reminded the company that the difference was Biblically ordained blacks being descended from the lost Tribe of Ham and sentenced for all time to be "hewers of wood and drawers of water."

Those were the ideas he took with him to Vanderbilt University; there he happened into a course given by a sociologist who challenged him with the idea that difference in ability between whites and blacks was a result of social conditioning rather than race. His text was an intelligence test administered to soldiers during the First World War which showed that, on average, northern blacks outperformed southern whites.

Disturbed by this radical notion, Lucius went to his father for guidance; his father's answer was that "a selective migration had occurred and the more intelligent and vigorous blacks had moved to the North and that they were in effect the best of the breed." Armed with this insight, Lucius returned to counter the ideas of his professor,

> . . . but he was ready for me. Extensive studies had been made of identical twins in situations where one twin had migrated and the other had stayed in the South, yet the conclu-

sion was the same—the intelligence of the more advantaged twin was greatly in excess of the Southern twin. I read everything I could get my hands on to get around this but it was impossible and I concluded at the age of eighteen that a monumental injustice had been done and it was something that ought to be changed. We all know how violently young people react to perceived injustice and I made myself very unpopular with a great many people by arguing my new found conviction.

That was to be Lucius's habit throughout his long and active life. He was always a combative person, three times the heavyweight boxing champion of Vanderbilt, and was never afraid to march to his own drumbeat. He believed his independence was, in part, a result of the time he spent far from society or guidance in the wilds of Alaska, but his independence quickly led him into trouble with the Crump machine that then ruled Memphis specifically and Tennessee generally.

Like a number of American cities, Memphis suffered from the problems of integrating foreign immigrants, many of whom felt exposed by not knowing the law and the customs of the city and by not having strong local contacts, and the blacks, who, although about 40 percent of the population, were a repressed minority. E. H. Crump in Memphis, like bosses in other cities, provided what these exposed people desperately wanted: protection. In return he got their votes and extorted from them and others various kinds of graft. In Memphis, Crump came into power in 1909 and except for one interlude of ten years, stayed in power until his death in 1954.

Crump could boast civic achievements; if he didn't make the trains run on time like Mussolini, he at least cleaned up the streets. And like Mussolini, he was popular. That was almost the most frightening aspect of his rule. As the *Washington Post* editorialized on May 13, 1946, "Memphis, Tennessee, should be a warning to the whole country. The city is a perfect example of the ease with which Americans with a philosophy of efficiency and materialism can succumb to fascism and like it."

But at a price. And not only freedom in the abstract. Those who challenged the machine routinely had their tax rates raised, were often warned indirectly by their banks or employers or were sometimes beaten up. Those who particularly paid the price were the blacks.

Annoyed by a mild show of restlessness in the black community, Crump had his police commissioner publish a warning, identifying the leaders and saying, "this is a white man's country, and always will be and any Negro who doesn't agree to this better move on." Crump himself then told the editor of the black newspaper, "You have a bunch of niggers teaching social equality, stirring up social hatred. I am not going to stand for it . . . We are not going to tolerate a bunch of niggers spreading racial hatred and running things their way. Tell them Mr. Crump said so. You understand me?" The editor left town hurriedly.

Lucius first fell afoul of the Crump machine by trying to defend some of its victims. He was told in no uncertain terms that "no young man can succeed in Memphis unless he is friendly to the Crump organization," and when he did not come into line, Crump sent one of his henchmen to Lucius's largest client, the Illinois Central Railroad, "to point out the danger of retaining an attorney who could not get along with the city administration.

Undeterred, Lucius kept on practicing law as the city grew and as the political opinions of its citizens slowly came closer to his own way of thinking during the Second World War.

HAVING LEARNED TO FLY YEARS BEFORE IN TEXAS, GEORGE claimed some rusty skills as a pilot, but the navy was not impressed by them; he admitted years later that he had tried to help the navy by padding his flight records to show more hours than he had actually flown and by memorizing the eyesight chart so that he was able to pass that test. Those efforts got him into flight training; but at his age, nearly thirty, he was not a prime candidate for the combat role he sought. So after finishing flight training, he was sent to the South Pacific, destined to be a radio officer on a reconnaissance flying boat. But fate and the Japanese aborted that destiny. He arrived during the very depths of American defeat with the Japanese right on Australia's doorstep. If Australia was lost, the fate of the Pacific region seemed sealed; so every available man and machine was being readied for the first American counterattack of the war, and George found himself in the vanguard of the action.

The invasion of Guadalcanal began in disaster when the Japanese fleet ambushed the American naval force. Among the casualties were four cruisers, three American and one Australian, along with many lesser craft, while the Japanese suffered virtually no damage. The catastrophe rivaled Pearl Harbor. The Battle of Savo Island, a stunning Japanese victory, lasted just long enough for the American transports and supply ships to dump a part of their cargoes of men and matériel on Guadalcanal. But without naval or air protection, they, too, beat a hasty retreat, leaving the marines stranded with only one-month's supply of food, only four days' supply of ammunition and no heavy long-range artillery. There was little prospect of their getting any more, since the Japanese controlled the sea and air. Worse, the Japanese could reinforce their garrison at will.

The American navy was, understandably, battle-shy and refused to risk any more of its few remaining transports or cargo ships, and it had no way to land anything from the air. In a frantic attempt to avoid losing the whole 1st Marine Division, it dispatched three old destroyers to dash in on August 15 with ammunition. George was on one of the destroyers as the commander of a 120-man force (prudently divided among the three ships in case one or two were sunk) charged with opening and running the yet-to-be-built airfield. Theirs was a desperate mission: without an airfield, Guadalcanal, the 1st Marine Division and perhaps Australia, too, were doomed.

Having almost no equipment to build the airstrip, the marines fell to filling in potholes and craters by hand and clearing the brush and high grass with their sharpened bayonets. They soon needed their bayonets for other purposes. The Japanese quickly reacted and penned them into their beachhead. For months to come, the marines were to hold little more than the perimeter of the airfield, so that Japanese machine guns fired on planes as they took off and landed and pilots got no warning of Japanese air raids until the bombers were overhead. As their planes began to arrive, the pilots learned with dismay that they were outclassed by the faster, better-armed, more maneuverable Japanese aircraft. To avoid massacre, American planes often took off at dusk and landed at night by the dim light of flashlights. Even then, they usually came under sniper fire. Worst of all, there were few available pilots.

So George, then an old man by air combat standards and not trained as a fighter or dive-bomber pilot, had to become both. Everyone who could fly, flew. And flew anything that was available. When an air raid happened, every man who knew how to fly anything rushed out to the nearest available aircraft, of any kind, in any state of repair, fueled or not, to take it into the relative safety of the air. In one of these raids, George did not make it. A bomb fell just in front of the plane he was trying to take off, exploded and trapped him in the wreckage. He was very lucky not to be burned to death right there. As it was, he had to be cut out of the wreckage. As he told the story, a marine medic wanted to get him out quickly by leaving one of his legs behind—George swore he ended that medical consultation by brandishing his .45 automatic.

Not for saving his leg but for trying to save the aircraft as the bombs were falling, Major General A. A. Vendegrift, the commander at Guadalcanal, wrote, "You are to be highly commended for your brave actions," and awarded him the Order of the Purple Heart. The award was a continuation of a family tradition: George Washington originated the decoration and is thought to have awarded it to Will Polk during the Revolution.

George was wounded and soon came down with malaria, but as a pilot, he was too valuable to be sent out of the island. That is the way the

Japanese also felt about the American pilots. They concluded that the best way to shut down the airfield was to kill the pilots; so they set up special forces whose task it was to infiltrate the American lines to kill pilots as they lay asleep in their foxholes. One moonless night, an infiltrator fell upon George, slashing at him with a trench knife. Momentarily delayed by the mosquito netting, the man missed as George, awakening with his pistol in hand, fired. The shot probably only panicked the infiltrator, who ran and was cut down by fire from the machine gun of a nearby marine guard. That terrifying episode would haunt George's dreams to the end of his life. It was but one of the more personal nightmares he was collecting.

Since the American navy had virtually no major combat ships nearby in the early days of the campaign, the pilots on Henderson field worked out a routine with the patrol torpedo boats: George and his colleagues would fly their slow, cumbersome, twin-winged, pontoon-equipped "SOCs" as decoys over the battleships of the "Tokyo Express" at night.

> We couldn't carry bombs, so all we could do was skim low over their decks and strafe 'em. We had one other weapon—Japanese beer bottles, empty, left behind by the enemy when we took the islands. These we tossed down on the Express. Our object was to get the enemy to open up on us, of course, so that they would reveal themselves by gun flashes.

When their tracers pinpointed the Japanese ships, the torpedo boats would race in to attack them. Each flight of the planes was nearly a suicide mission, and the casualties in George's squadron were appalling. *Life* magazine commented that the pilots "were performing feats of aerial valor that would rank with the greatest deeds of the R.A.F. pilots in the Battle of Britain."

In straight aerial combat, the pilots, who were often flying as much as eleven or twelve hours a day, lost count of their "victories," and most occurred, of course, far from any acceptable witnesses, but George was credited officially with having downed three enemy aircraft and several "smokers." Additionally, in a dive-bomber (an SBD), he managed to disable and so set up a Japanese cruiser to be sunk the following day.

The most dramatic of his missions was not intended to be combat but rescue: he was often sent out to pick up other pilots who had gone down at sea or sailors whose ships had been sunk. The plane used for this mission was the same slow, two-man pontoon scouting plane used to provoke fire for PT-boat attacks. Usually, after spotting a man in the sea, the pilot would put his plane down in the water close to him. Then, with the man, who was likely to be wounded, clinging on the pontoon or resting on the wing—sometimes he would pick up half a dozen in this way—he would taxi to a nearby American ship. But on one occasion, George was ordered out on a mission to pick up a downed pilot who was far from any friendly base or ship. He would have to fly the man out; so George had to leave the rear-gunner cockpit empty for the downed man. Even with a rear-gunner, the old, slow SOC was already vulnerable, but without a rear-gunner, as the pilots said, it was a sitting duck.

Night was falling when George reached the spot where he was to find the pilot. He had been briefed that an American fighter plane was circling overhead and that he should flash his landing lights as a signal that he was "friendly." When he spotted a circling plane, he did as told only to be met by a hail of machine-gun fire: the American fighter had run low on fuel and gone home, and two Japanese planes, realizing what was happening, waited in ambush.

As George dodged and twisted, at less than half the speed of the Japanese, they shot his plane full of holes. Miraculously, he was only slightly wounded, but his plane's instrument panel and radio were shot away. Thus began one of the remarkable adventures of the Pacific war. As he recounted,

. . . forty minutes after the shooting got under way, I climbed into some rain clouds and started home—only I didn't know where home was. I had got lost during the fight . . . The weather got dirtier and dirtier; it was very dark, of course. I could not land in the sea and float, for I knew my float was badly shot up; had it not been, I could have landed and waited for dawn, taking a chance that I could get the engine turned up by myself. I flew until I had enough gas left for forty minutes of flying—and suddenly sighted land ahead.

I started to follow the coast line. In a few minutes I sighted a lagoon which should not have been there, and then I knew that it was not Guadalcanal; I had to land in strange territory, lost, and perhaps I would land in the midst of Japs.

I landed by instruments (it was raining) some five miles offshore in order to insure that the plane would sink and not be available to the Japs. Then I inflated my rubber boat (the strong hiss of that CO2 plunging into that boat was a great cheerer, for it meant that I had a lifeboat, anyway). The surf was roaring and tumbling when I reached it . . . Finally I did get ashore, having lost my boat, been almost drowned, and after having been battered about quite a bit on the coral . . .

Then I ducked into the bush and carefully cleaned my .45 . . . It was as dark as the inside of a cow. I spent two hours getting some 300 yards into the interior; the volcanic character of the land made faster and farther progress impossible. I crept under some dense foliage and tried to get some sleep . . . About an hour before dawn I heard voices . . .

[Several lines were censored out here and are lost.]

My position was in between the roots of a banyan tree; the roots were about four feet high and over my position were twined heavy runners and vines . . . I sat there until almost noon, not daring to stir except to lift myself from time to time in order to twist my head for a peep in the direction of the village. You will know how my heart sank when a lithe brown body suddenly stepped over my position; it was a native . . . In his hand he carried a three-foot-long knife. He crept away noiselessly and then started doubling back.

He came closer and closer to me, cutting grass which he piled in his arms . . . (By this time I had smeared my face and hands with thick coatings of mud so that my skin would not show up so well in my hideout). When his face was some three feet from mine I hissed softly and tapped the vine across my face with my pistol. He looked up and looked right down the barrel of my gun.

He looked at me with stark terror in his eyes, and for a moment [I] thought he would run. I would have killed him. Then he said something with his lips that did not get out. He was as scared as I was. Then he said: "Friendly."

I asked if there were Japs around. He said not near. I asked if he would take me to British or American. He said yes. (All of this was in my best Shanghai pidgin English.) I explained to him that I would kill him instantly if he shouted or made any noise, or if we saw any Japs. I made him turn his back while I climbed out of my hideaway. I took the knife away from him and made him walk right in front of me.

When he reached the village, the villagers were indeed "friendly." "I was given food and my numerous cuts were bandaged. A magnificent bushy-headed fellow—six feet and some 180 pounds of him—came and announced that he was a 'British soldier' scouting the Japanese positions to the north," that he had the entry trails watched and that he would organize the return to Guadalcanal.

"We started out and walked some three miles. Then, two racing canoes, manned by the most superb boatmen I had ever met, took us aboard and we went speeding down the coast." Arriving at the next village, George was told that the same group had rescued a pilot "some three weeks earlier. When they told me his name proudly, I didn't have the heart to tell them he had been killed just a week after they had rescued him.

> I was by then known as "Mr. America," "Mr. Pilot," etc. Excited groups brought odds and ends from my pockets to me—piece by piece, and not even a scrap of paper was missing. My clothes were brought. They had been washed and the ragged bottoms cut and mended. I had a quick breakfast and as the racing canoes were held ready the chief took me by the hand and placing his left on his heart he told me gravely that he hoped I would "crash down" near his village again.

Rescued by a plane just like the one in which he had been shot down, George returned to Gaudalcanal and his war resumed; he did not "crash down" again there, but he sustained further injuries including a broken back. Repeated attacks of malaria so disabled him that, after nearly a year on Guadalcanal, during which time he buried nearly half of his squadron, he was airlifted to the first of many hospitals in which he would spend the following year.

MEANWHILE, A DEEPLY FRUSTRATED JIMMY WAS COOLING HIS heels at West Point. At last, about the time George was being invalided out of Guadalcanal, Jimmy was allowed to leave West Point, joined a division and was dispatched to England to prepare for D-Day.

Like many young Americans going abroad for the first time, Jimmy found his thoughts often turning to simple and familiar staples of American life—warm socks, comfortable underwear and, above all, soft toilet paper. He mentioned these in one of the first of a long stream of affectionate letters he would write to his wife, Joey, and her response on May 22, 1944, came as something of a shock. As he wrote,

Our mail was delivered in the field and I got a wonderful looking package. All the officers clustered around my offer of ci-
gars and candy which I thought was what was going to be in it.
It was going to be a great feast in that cold and sodden
meadow. So I opened it up and what was it but toilet paper.
What a roar went up. You funny lovable woman. We all
laughed until we were sick. When I ask for something, you
really send it. However, all the headquarters officers are most
greatful and we are all revelling in the softness of our imported
American luxury.

The division to which Jimmy was attached in England was assigned the
mission of landing on "Utah Beach" shortly after D-Day, then driving
southwest toward the Atlantic, to cut the German forces on the Brittany
peninsula off from those in Normandy. At the last minute, as the *Wehrmacht* panzers tore into the Americans on the beach, that plan was
aborted. A good thing too. As Jimmy wrote later, "I've often wondered
what would have happened had we done that. Probably we'd be dead."
Landing on the beach on "D-Day + 14," he wrote his wife that

the carnage of battle was around us; burned out tanks, broken
gliders, broken LSTs, ammunition boxes. There weren't any
American dead, but there were some German dead that hadn't
been all cleaned up. Busted airplanes. Well, you know, really
scary. Burned up trucks. Foxholes all around the place . . .
The night we got ashore, two troops lined up at angles and
fired at each other. That's how spooked we were.

And with good reason. A direct hit destroyed the radio van Jimmy
had been using, killing the whole crew. "After that," Jimmy wrote,
"we all slept in slit trenches below ground level."
On a day of continuous downpour, Jimmy's command post was visited by a group of reporters. He was not happy to see them, since

the dumb reporters all walked to my observation post in a big herd. And I knew damn well it would draw fire. I had no more than finished giving them hell about it and here it came. I really had plenty of company in my hole. They nearly trampled me to death jumping on top of me . . . They also took my picture and I look just like a complete pirate.

It wasn't only the German army or American reporters that distracted the American soldiers. "The refugees here are a terrific problem. Nearly all of them are destitute and it is very hard to eat when they watch with hungry eyes, particularly the children. All of our soldiers give away some of their food . . ."

Getting ready to break out of the beachhead, Jimmy was given command of the 6th Mechanized Cavalry, whose missions included protecting the headquarters of General Patton's newly created 3rd Army and of providing communications for the by-then-widely-scattered American divisions. That role enabled Jimmy to watch almost hour by hour the unfolding of the Normandy campaign. But for him as for most soldiers, the majestic events of the huge armies colliding was nearly eclipsed by the little pleasures of daily life. Indeed, of just staying alive. "I have access to a shower-bath," he delightedly wrote Joey,

and am now completely cleaned up and bathed—my first shower in three weeks. It's amazing the importance that cleanliness takes on when it is impossible to obtain it . . . I have become an old man overnight with all sorts of service and all sorts of comfort, like a canvass cot and a chair . . . and actually today got some white bread.

He was not to enjoy this luxury for long.

As the 3rd Army began its lightning attack across France, Jimmy wrote that

It is really an awesome sight to see what our air [force] has done to them in the last few days. The roads are littered with German tanks, trucks, guns and with all the trash that men throw away when they are retreating . . . They simply cannot move in daylight in any strength or our air will get them. So we go like hell in daylight and have trapped them by the thousands. All their stragglers seem glad to quit.

But the German army had a great deal of fight left in it, as Jimmy would find in the dreary, dangerous and exhausting months to come. As he assessed his own performance in a letter to his wife,

I have not found it hard to be personally brave. It is really easy as everyone expects it of me, so I am. What I do find hard and terribly hard, is to order men in to do a thing in which I know some will be killed. To see the looks on their faces, to see the sometimes terrific heroism that they nonchalantly display, makes you proud and humble all at once. It is tough to be nonchalant and impersonal at such times. Pray for me my dear, that I will be smart and courageous and ready to command, for it is a hard job. It is so difficult to write even of love and home and soft things for my life now is so unlike that.

General Patton, who had known Jimmy since he was a young boy and had been a friend of Jimmy's father's since they were roommates at VMI and classmates at West Point, decided to put him in what was probably the most difficult job in the 3rd Army, the command of the spearhead of his forces, the 3rd Mechanized Cavalry. As Jimmy later recounted, Patton brought him to his mobile headquarters, and after Jimmy had saluted and they had shaken hands, he asked Jimmy how old he was and

I said 32. He said that seems awfully young for a Command and I was being kind of brash and I said, "Sir, as I remember, you were 31 when you were Col." And he said, "That's correct" and laughed. Then he said to me, "Are you lucky?" and I said, "Yes sir, I think I am lucky." And he said, "Well, you're going to need it." Then he said, "Now I want to be serious for a minute. I want you to know I will not put up with a beaten Commander. So if you're ever overrun or your outfit is ever overrun and badly beaten up, you're going to be relieved. If it's the fault of some bad orders and you were doing things you weren't trained to be doing, on account of a higher command decision, I'll get you a job someplace, but you'll still be relieved. And if it's your fault, I never want to see you again—you understand?" I said, "Yes sir," saluted and left.

Shortly thereafter, Mrs. Patton wrote to Jimmy's mother saying, "This is what Georgie wrote about Jimmy's assignment. 'Jimmy Polk has just gotten a Regiment. He earned it having done a wonderful job. He is 32, I was a Col. at 31 but when I looked at Jimmy I wondered if I ever looked as young.' "

As Jimmy sized up his new regiment, he liked what he found. It was composed of draftees, farmers and factory workers from northern New York and Pennsylvania, mostly first-generation Poles,

a tough, resourceful, rough and ready [group of] men, not strong on discipline, but knowlegable of the Germans and knowing them as their natural enemies. Each troop had soldiers who between them could speak almost every central European language including Yiddish, but excluding French, so translation or prisoner interrogation was no problem. They could move, shoot and in some degree communicate, made natural soldiers and quickly learned combat skills . . . They treated me with respect; we admired each other and I came to love them.

Task Force Polk, as Jimmy's command came to be designated, soon grew from just the 3rd Mechanized Cavalry to include a combat engineer battalion, two companies of tanks from another regiment, two assault gun troops, a tank destroyer battalion and the French 1st and 2nd "Regiments of Paris." Communications intercepts reveal that the Germans thought Task Force Polk was an entire armored division.

With this group, Jimmy began a hard-fought, American version of *Blitzkrieg,* a drive that would take him across eastern France, into brutal combat with such German divisions as the 2nd S.S. and the 11th Panzer, through the Siegfried Line and into Germany. Leading Task Force Polk, Jimmy was the first American commander to get into Germany. As the fighting ebbed and flowed, he probed deep into enemy formations and territory, occasionally as much as sixty miles ahead of the main units of the 3rd Army.

So far out in front and often necessarily scattered over relatively vast distances, Jimmy was an aggressive commander; he had to be, he explained, because his forces were too small ever to be caught on the defensive. This attitude delighted Patton, who was, himself, so aggressive that his tanks ran out of fuel. ". . . tank by tank behind us when we were going up to the Moselle," Jimmy wrote, "every time we got running, we would have halt lines issued, the reason being that we didn't have enough gasoline to keep going." Patton was furious and engaged Generals Dwight Eisenhower and Omar Bradley almost as bitterly as he did the Germans. It was politics not strategy that determined the fuel allocation: Patton was starved to satisfy Field Marshal Bernard Montgomery. Starved, the 3rd Army was stopped. Jimmy's unit was often ordered to retreat from hard-won victories, but, given its head, the 3rd Army advanced so rapidly that the Germans did not have time to re-form and establish defensive positions. Allied *amour propre* came at the terrible price of prolonging the war by weeks or even months.

Generals were not frequent visitors to the fluid and often ragged front, but Jimmy had cause to remember one visit vividly. General George Marshall, the chief of staff of the American army, joined General Patton in a morale-building visit to the unit commanders of the 3rd Army in October 1944. Marshall, who was not known for his personal warmth, walked down the line of generals and colonels, shaking hands and mumbling greetings "in a very cursory and cold sort of way. He finally came to me and said, 'Well, Jimmy, goodness sakes, what are you doing here? How are you? How's your mother? I'm sorry to hear about your father's death. How is this Division treating you?' And I said, 'They treat me just fine, Sir. I like to be with this Division.' " Meanwhile, "Gen. Patton put his arm around me and said, 'This boy is doing damn good work. He will be the youngest Colonel in my Army soon, about my age in the last war when I was a Colonel, but God damn, doesn't he look young!' " Marshall looked at Jimmy "and said, 'Well, let me know if they give you any trouble, will you?' And believe me, from then on, I was a very special person."

The little luxuries were rare and the moments of morale building were even rarer; the reality was grim and furious combat with an increasingly desperate but far-from-defeated *Wehrmacht*. It was in a mood of exhausted anguish that Jimmy poured out his heart to his wife late one night. "You should understand," he wrote,

> that men don't die in the glory of battle in some gallant charge amidst the music of bugles and the roll of drums. They die often in abject fear in dirt, in mud, in filth and exhaustion and in the taking of some miserable little hill or some dirty little town. There are some glorious moments that transcend all the badness of it, but they are few and far between.

One great advantage the American and British armies had was their knowledge of German plans and capabilities from listening to and breaking German coded communications, the so-called Ultra intercepts. That they existed was the most closely guarded secret of the Second World War, and Jimmy, as a relatively junior officer, was not told about them, but he would be informed that "intelligence" showed that a certain German unit would be at a given location. Often the information was lifesaving, but occasionally it was terrifying. On the eve of the Battle of the Bulge, Jimmy got a message from the corps to which his unit was attached warning him that the seasoned and still-powerful 11th Panzer Division, fitted out with the latest and best of the German tanks, was going to attack his lightly armed reconnaissance regiment the next morning. Jimmy called for reinforcements and was told that there were none available. He waited through a sleepless night for what promised to be the end of his military career and probably of his life.

Fortunately, as dawn broke, no attack materialized; as Jimmy later learned, Ultra had correctly reported that Field Marshal Gerd von Rundstedt *had* ordered an attack on Jimmy's sector, but he had been overruled by Hitler. "Hitler reportedly said, 'No, I don't want to broaden the attack that much. I want you to go deep, not broad.' And so I was quite grateful to Hitler."

The German offensive on the Ardennes Forest was a desperate gamble, and Patton was quick to seize the opportunity it offered for a counterattack. As the historian of the campaign wrote, Patton began "the boldest and most insolent armoured blitz of the western war," thrusting "from Trier to Koblenz and the Rhine in a single bound on 6 and 7 March . . ." Task Force Polk was again in the lead. But the front was so fluid that Jimmy came close to being killed by fellow American soldiers. As he recounted,

> I was inspecting our front line positions and they are frequently a mile or two miles apart, generally in little villages or

clumps of woods, and there was a main road that ran along our positions. I decided when I reached the far flank of the 3rd Squadron [a unit of the 3rd Mechanized Cavalry], foolishly as it later seems, to go and visit the adjoining strongpoint held by the 90th Division. I wasn't worried because we had run up and down this road when the 3rd Squadron had held that strong-point for some weeks. As we neared the 90th Division posi-tion, they called a general alert, swung all their guns on us, brought us to a screeching halt and made us stick our hands up. A Sgt. who was half out of his mind, almost frothing at the mouth, dirty, unkempt and obviously frightened, thought that we were some of the Skorzeny German troops in American uniforms. He just couldn't believe that a full Col. would be running around the front lines like this and he was certain that I was a German spy. While the other people held their guns on Sabu and Icekant [Jimmy's driver and gunner], this guy put his rifle about 6' from my breastbone, took off the safety and was absolutely ready to shoot me right on the spot. I really thought he was going to shoot me dead, right then. I begged him not to shoot me. I begged him—almost got down on my knees and I had my hands over my head and I said, "For God's sake, take me to one of your officers." He finally consented. He got the three of us out of the jeep, marched us with our hands up about a quarter of [a] mile down into the village where the Command Post of the Company was located. The Captain checked me out and realized I was Col. Polk of the 3rd Cav-alry; but it took some talking even with him. In the meantime, the Sgt. was standing around there, still just dying to shoot me. He really thought he had captured a German spy . . . It was as near to death as I ever came.

At about this time, Jimmy got word that his brother Jack was com-manding a battalion in the 1st Cavalry Division and his brother-in-law,

Harry Wilson, was commanding a battalion in the 11th Airborne Division, both in the Philippines, under General Douglas MacArthur, while his younger brother Tommy was an officer on the battleship *Colorado* in the Philippine Sea. Like other soldiers, Jimmy occasionally complained about those who stayed at home. "It really makes me sort of mad," he wrote Joey on February 7, 1945, just before the big push into Germany,

> that so many of your friends and my friends are still in El Paso going about their daily lives as same as usual. Why haven't they been drafted? How will this work or fight law affect them? Will they be drafted now because we are getting replacements that are older and not nearly as physically fit as they used to be. Oh, it's just that I envy them and the existence they lead.
>
> It is now 2:00 am and I have been out on the river as we had a little exciting activity. I am waiting for the final reports to come in so my ear is sort of cocked to the telephone to know how bad it was. Those damn mines. It makes me so bitter to see good, fine, brave men mangled. It makes me bitter as hell and mad as hell at this fiendish enemy we fight. I want to smash them all, wipe them off the face of the earth and show them no mercy.

These somber thoughts were underlined as Jimmy's command began to pick up groups of slave laborers. As he wrote Joey,

> If you could see the released slave labor we have freed, Russians, Poles, Czechs, Italians, French, all completely starved and tattered. All taking to the highways to get home after five bitter years. They are pitiful and terrible creatures, men, women and children . . . the Germans fear them and well they might for they will steal and kill to eat, rape to satisfy their lust. We are collecting them to feed them and get them to the Red Cross, but as yet they are like wild things, like ani-

mals released from pens who will not be penned again. They beg any kind of food and wolf it down . . . The crime of this slave labor stinks up the whole world, this crime that the Germans can never pay enough for. You cannot conceive of how they have made beasts of people . . . I am bitter, bitter, bitter, tonight.

Having crossed the Rhine, the 3rd Army raced south across Bavaria and into Austria. There they came into contact with a concentration camp at Ebensee with "17,000 poor starving humans. They are dying at the rate of 300 a day from starvation. I have seen suffering before, I thought, but I really didn't know the depth of despair and deprevity that people can sink to . . . I really would like to turn the whole German Army over to the Russians."

In the nearby little town of Vocklabruck, Austria, after 252 days in the front line, Jimmy's troops fought their last battle against a unit of Hungarian S.S. troops and Jimmy won a Silver Star, his third decoration for personal bravery.

Jimmy's last European campaign was over the Alpine passes to Trieste. For that operation, Task Force Polk again grew almost to division size, to include three new battalions, infantry, artillery and tank destroyer, in addition to the 3rd Cavalry regiment. "We didn't know," he wrote, "who the heck we were going to run into, Tito's Yugoslav partisans, Mihailovic's Serbian Chetniks or units of the German army." Once over the Alps, they were recalled before making contact with any but German Army stragglers. Then, returning from that short and fruitless campaign, Jimmy was sent off to make contact with the Russians who had reached the Enns River. For him, the European war had ended.

For his services, General Walton H. Walker, his immediate commander, recommended Jimmy to be promoted to brigadier general. Patton approved the recommendation, but General Bradley vetoed it as premature, since Jimmy would have been the youngest general in the

American army. Instead, as the war ended, Jimmy reverted to the last "regular" rank he had held, a captain; he was not to achieve his wartime rank of colonel in the regular army for another ten years.

AFTER A LONG STINT IN VARIOUS NAVAL HOSPITALS AND months of convalescence in Texas, George returned to his old life as a reporter on the *New York Herald Tribune*. For him, the transition was difficult. His bodily wounds remained painful, but those encoded in his memory were nearly incapacitating. Night after night he dreamed of burning to death in an airplane or being knifed in a foxhole. In contrast, his daytime experiences were virtually a catalog of reporters' dream assignments. He covered the formation of the United Nations at San Francisco and the Dumbarton Oaks conference that did so much to shape the postwar world. Then he decided to return to the Far East, this time by way of Europe. Setting up his own syndicate, he also became a "stringer," or part-time correspondent, for *Newsweek* and CBS.

Passing through Germany in January 1946, he had the probably unique experience of having moved from a Guadalcanal foxhole to the press gallery of the Nuremberg war crimes tribunal, sitting within a few paces of the rogues' gallery of Nazidom. He wrote that the men appeared so prosaic, indeed so trivial, that it was difficult to imagine that they had been the rulers of much of the world.

By the time he had crossed Europe and reached the Middle East, he was asked to join the elite team of radio journalists assembled by Edward R. Murrow and Howard K. Smith for CBS.

The Middle East was then still under the domination of the British, and George, having seen the British overseas in Shanghai, Singapore, Burma, India and Egypt before the war, understood the sharp separation between the *English* commitment to democracy at home and the *British* commitment to imperialism abroad. Much of what he saw in Egypt and Palestine disgusted him. The old habits were again in full operation. Much as he admired the English, he had not, he wrote to his brother (the author of this book), fought in World War II to see the old British system of imperialism perpetuated.

Then, when he moved over to Greece in 1947, he was even more disturbed: he felt that much of what he and others had fought and suffered for in the war was being thrown away in the peace. In the Balkans, particularly, he saw a return to what he regarded as something like fascism. Worse, it was a form of tyranny in which, because of America's growing fear and hatred of Russian imperialism and communism, it was blindly following the British lead.

The Greece to which George came in 1947 was to baffle many observers. George worked hard to understand it, but the closer he got to understanding, the more dangerous he became to those who profited from the confusion. Finally, on May 8, 1948, he was murdered to ensure his silence.

Even today, over half a century later, much about his death remains shrouded in mystery. The relevant British, Greek and American official documents are still highly censored; those few of the CIA documents that have been released are mostly blanked out (see illustration for a typical instance), and those who have tried to find out the truth have been sternly discouraged. I myself have received numerous threats, including death threats, to dissuade me from following the trail. This is not the place to tell the whole story, or as much of it as I know, but while it is complex and demanding, it assumes an importance that requires at least a sketch here. I say this both because George's report of the events resulted in his death and because the attempts by America both to understand the complexities of the "old world" and to work out a reasonable and just policy toward its tragic dilemmas were themes that ran through George's life since his first experience in Shanghai. They were then a challenge, with which George struggled as hard as he had in the battles of Guadalcanal, and they have left a legacy that, today, is far from resolved. So I must ask the reader's indulgence as I set the stage on which he was murdered.

RITISH GOVERNMENTS HAD TRADITIONALLY TRIED TO PROTECT the part of Asia they dominated by blocking the access of other European powers. One after another, the British regarded Napoleon's France, Habsburg Austria and tsarist Russia as jinn that had to be kept bottled up to prevent them from moving south to threaten British-controlled India, the Middle East and Egypt. As "stoppers" to prevent these jinn from escaping, the British used the Afghans and the Turks. With the rise of Hitler, the jinn in the bottle was seen to be German, and the only available stopper was Greece. But there was a problem: on the eve of World War II, Greece was ruled by a dictatorship no less antidemocratic than the German Nazis or the Italian Fascists; however, when the Greeks tried to resist the German invasion, the British idealized Greece as a bastion of freedom.

When Greece was overrun, the British brought out with their retreating army the king and as much of the former dictatorship as they could carry and set them up as a government-in-exile in Egypt. Meanwhile, in Greece itself, a quite different government was formed in the struggle against the German and Italian occupying forces. A new generation of leaders and new ideas of freedom energized the Greeks as never before in this century. Although a tiny country, Greece had one of the largest anti-Nazi undergrounds of any country in Europe. When much larger France could hardly count twenty thousand "freedom fighters," Greece had hundreds of thousands. The British realized that the Greek underground tied down several *Wehrmacht* divisions that just might have turned the fortunes of war at El Alamain, but in British eyes, these people had one fatal flaw: they were unwilling even to consider a return, as Britain sought, to the days of the dictatorship under the monarchy.

This upsurge of self-determination was an entirely new development to which the British were as profoundly hostile in Greece as they were in Egypt, Palestine, Iraq and India. It was not just, although this was a factor, that the British did not much care what the "natives" wanted, but that in Greece, as in much of occupied Europe, it was the Left that most effectively fought the Nazis and proved most successful in rallying people into the underground.

That *was* indeed a fatal flaw in the estimation of Winston Churchill. For him, Greece had one importance in the planned-for postwar world: to stop the slide toward Russian domination. And he had good reason to fear this slide, since, despite his reputation as the architect of Western strategy in the Cold War, it was his 1944 "pact with the Devil" that had made Russian domination of the Balkans inevitable: he had offered the Soviets a free hand in the Balkans in return for their giving Britain one in Greece, and they had accepted the British offer.

Having made that deal, Churchill absolutely could not "lose" Greece. It was the only stopper he could find to contain the now much larger jinn in the Eastern European and Balkan bottle he had helped to provide. So the policy he set out was designed to control Greece no matter what the cost. The cost would be high. One of his attempts almost broke up the fragile Anglo-American military structure designed to create the second front in Europe: he tried to divert the Anglo-American invasion forces destined for France to the eastern Mediterranean, and when America refused, Churchill threw all the available British forces into the Greek campaign. This diversion of men and equipment degraded the invasion of France and probably cost many lives. But it was the second aspect of his policy that is of more concern here: he believed he had to impose on Greece a "friendly" government—that is, as he defined it, the old monarchy.

The Resistance, known as the EAM, and those in exile who supported them tried to work out a compromise with the British, but the British tried to sabotage their movement, even arming and financing a quasi-fascist rival organization in Greece. This provoked a revolt in the Greek army in Egypt which the British ruthlessly put down and, at Churchill's personal order, hanged its leaders. Indeed, so enraged was Churchill—describing the Greek anti-Nazi Resistance as "treacherous, filthy beasts'' and ''miserable Greek banditti''—that he determined to destroy them root and branch.

At this point, it appears—the documents (if there were any) are not available—that the Soviets informed the EAM that they had made a deal with the British and told them to reach an understanding with the British. Isolated, feeling betrayed by the Russians and exhausted by the underground war, the EAM caved in and agreed to place its military force under the British-supported royalist government-in-exile. With the way thus prepared, some six thousand British troops and the remainder of the Greek army-in-exile arrived in October 1944 under the command of an English general.

Greece at that time potentially had three governments: in addition to the monarchy they brought with them, the British found in-country the EAM, which controlled those areas not occupied by the German army, and the collaborationist administration that remained from the former dictatorship.

The EAM was then a loose coalition which included every faction and shade of opinion from the conservative hierarchy of the Orthodox Church to pro-Soviet communists. Given legitimacy by its struggle against the Nazis, it was then *the* national institution. Its natural enemy was the remaining cadres of the old dictatorship who had supported, fought for and acted as the henchmen of the Nazis. They remained in control of the areas that had been occupied by the Germans. They were less political, and so less popular, but more administrative, and so more effective than the EAM. Thus, they provided a suitable platform onto which to mount the monarchy. Typical of their leaders was the chief of police of Athens who, as George pointed out, ''has held his post without a break since the early 1930's—serving in turn the Greek dictators, the king, the Germans during the occupation, and the king again.''

As they retreated, the Germans had left chaos behind them—Greece was starving, there was no work and the currency was worthless. Opinions were already bitterly divided, loyalties were conflicting and suspicion was deep. In this explosive mixture, the British struck a spark by attempting to disarm the underground (who were then legally a part of the national army) while leaving the former collaborators free and armed.

Push came to shove in the central square of Athens on December 3, 1944. The police fired into crowds of demonstrators, and in reprisal EAM units attacked their posts. The push of the British and the shove of the EAM threatened civil war. A last-minute cease-fire was worked out in the first days of 1945, and a month later a more comprehensive deal was reached in which EAM agreed to turn in its weapons in return for a British-guaranteed amnesty and the promise to prosecute collaborators, guarantee fundamental freedoms and hold a plebiscite on the monarchy before general elections.

Almost before the ink was dry, this compromise broke down. Vigilante bands and "security battalions" left over from the Nazi occupation, particularly of an organization known as X (pronounced in Greek *khi),* and the so-called National Guard began hunting down and killing the now unarmed EAM members. Mass executions of the veterans of the underground dispirited the survivors and terrified the moderates who tried to stand aside.

In this climate of violence, elections were finally held; not surprisingly, the British-supported Right won an overwhelming victory. As George wrote, "The inside story is that . . . long before the plebiscite took place, the army and police had rounded up or scared away all persons known to harbor any anti-monarchist sentiments. Thus the Greek government . . . were able to proclaim stoutly that the plebiscite was free. It was, but well rigged." Massive arrests and summary executions became the order of the day.

By October 1946, Greece was plunged into full-scale civil war. And a bitter and divisive war it was. Since Thucydides, Greeks have not been known for their kindness to one another, and if cities were not razed and populations enslaved, it was not for want of trying. Even by the standards to which, lamentably, we have become accustomed, the Greek war became especially savage.

Both sides had major disadvantages. When I first visited Greece in the spring of 1947, it was jokingly said that the rebels had been "confined" to the mountains—that is, to about 70 percent of the country—but the joke contained a serious point. In the mountains, the Left became isolated from the people as it had not been during the war against the Nazis, when it dominated most towns: gradually, it was being worn down, and virtually all Greeks, even those who hated or feared the royal government, desperately wanted peace at virtually any cost. The loose coalition that had made up the Resistance rapidly unraveled, so that, by the end, the remainder was little more than the communist minority. That was fatal, since most Greeks, no matter how much they feared the heirs of the old dictatorship, did not want the communists as their rulers. Absent the nationalist cause against the Nazis, the EAM had insufficient support among the general population. To adapt Mao's metaphor on guerrilla warfare, the water had dried around the fish.

The British-imposed government got little popular support, but being supported by the British was less in need of popular support. Like the Left, so the Right was dominated by extremists. The royal family, originally German and still regarded as alien, had never been popular; the sequence of prime ministers was thought to be little more than a parade of British puppets; and the operative parts of the administration were at least disliked by those who had suffered under the Italians and Germans. Corruption was endemic everywhere and was blatant at the higher reaches. Having little belief in their future in Greece, the leaders were preparing their getaways and padding their foreign bank accounts as George reported. But the government had one overwhelming asset: British steel.

The moderates, who might have given Greece both peace and freedom, had no allies, few leaders and little coherent support. They were quickly crushed between the extremes. As George wrote on January 4, 1948, "Certainly nothing positive is being done by anybody to rescue the vast majority of democratic-minded Greeks from the clutches of the

Right and/or the Left." Money was poured into Greece "without changing anything much except the size of a select few bank accounts."

It was this tragic mess, for which certainly it had to take a large measure of blame, that in the early days of 1947 Britain decided to turn over to America. And it was this impasse that George sought to analyze for his listeners on CBS.

THE TRUMAN DOCTRINE WAS ANNOUNCED IN MARCH 1947 "TO help free peoples resist subversion by armed minorities," and the Congress authorized $400 million in aid for Greece, but well into 1948, the only *effective* foreign presence was British, and as George wrote in 1947, "There is no doubt that in Greece—as throughout much of this part of the world—the USA policy is a blurred rubber stamp of British policy."

The resident British officials regarded themselves as realists about Greece. They knew the government was shaky, corrupt and tyrannical, but they could not let it collapse; the Americans also saw the corruption, weakness and ineptitude, and many were dismayed. The key officials, however, were so focused on the danger of communism that they thought the government, any government, simply had to be supported at whatever cost.

A few observers, including George, took a different stand: without any sympathy for the by-then-communist-dominated EAM, they saw the Greek government as so antidemocratic as not to be of the sort America *should* support and so corrupt that, in any event, without massive American financial and military support, it was unlikely to win the civil war. George detailed his observations in the article in *Harpers Magazine* in December 1947 that so infuriated the Greek government it demanded that CBS recall him. George was undeterred, and Edward R. Murrow of CBS backed him up. In subsequent reports, George detailed corruption on such a monumental scale, and at the very center of the government, that he believed it could not win the civil war, and even if it won the war with massive American help, he was convinced that its victory would be a defeat for what he had fought for and what he wanted America to stand for.

In the months after the publication of the *Harpers* article, George received numerous death threats. Having received a few myself, I know that it is an unnerving experience. Years later, on getting one when I was president of the Adlai Stevenson Institute and professor of history at the University of Chicago, I called in the FBI and Chicago and university police to advise me on the danger. It never occurred to me that they might be involved. I had at least that comfort. But George, of course, did not. In the conditions prevailing in Greece in 1947 and 1948, no one, not even the prime minister, could trust *all* of the several virtually autonomous secret police organizations and their informal or *parakratic* hit-men "friends." A foreign journalist was almost defenseless.

In a broadcast on January 30, 1948, George commented that not only the journalists but even the officials of the American aid mission were under constant attack. "Yes, you guessed it," he said. "The Greek royalists are charging that the American aid mission is staffed by Communists! . . . So it goes in this unhappy and confused land . . . The problem [highlighted by a U.S. congressional committee report on Greece] is how to save the Greek people from their own government. It is a tough assignment."

George was due to leave Greece in May. CBS offered to make him its chief correspondent in Washington. That offer was widely known in Greece; indeed, he informed the rightist leader and sometime prime minister Constantine Tsaldaris in an unpleasant interview that he intended to take the Washington post. Tsaldaris, whom George had caught padding his own bank account with illegally acquired American aid dollars, was rightly scared.

Before leaving for America, George decided to take a last look at northern Greece. As he wrote the family just three days before he was killed,

We plan to leave Greece between May 20 and June 1st . . . Between now and then, Rea [his second and Greek wife] and I are going to visit some places in Greece I have never seen. On Friday, we are off by air to Kavalla . . . We'll be in Kavalla for three days. Next, we are going to Crete . . . Finally I plan a quick junket to Konista, that ever turbulent Greek Albanian date line. I've just got to see the place that's being called the "fuse of world war III" . . . Then we'll be ready to shuffle off to New York . . . My greatest wish is that we will all be together next Christmas—lets plan now on a gala [family] festival somewhere—OK?

He never made it. He was murdered in Salonika on May 8, 1948, becoming, as the American journalist I. F. Stone put it, "the first casualty of the Cold War."

THE YEAR THAT GEORGE WAS KILLED, JIMMY WAS ASSIGNED TO Japan. During the Korean War, he served as assistant chief of staff for the 8th Army. Hard and brutal as that war was, it was for Jimmy a sort of poor sequel to the grand crusade in which he had played so brilliant a role: in Korea, he commanded no troops and earned no glory. Korea has often been termed America's forgotten war.

It was with relief that Jimmy returned to Europe in 1956; his first assignment was to become the assistant chief of staff for NATO Land Forces Central Europe. By then the Cold War was in full swing, and many, particularly in the army, had come to share the belief first set forth by General Patton in 1945 that Russia was America's principal enemy. It was Jimmy's job to supervise the development of a European defense.

In 1961, having been promoted to major general, he returned to Germany to take command of the 4th Armored Division. For him, it was nearly a return to the tasks and challenges of the Second World War and on nearly the terrain over which he had then fought, but his field command was short. With one career success after another, he was a natural choice, in December 1962, to become the U.S. commander in Berlin.

Berlin was one of the anomalies created by the Second World War. Deep inside territory controlled by Russia, it was an international enclave as sharply divided as Shanghai was when George visited it nearly twenty years before. The Western Allies, who had recognized the Federal Republic, allowed their zones to be partly amalgamated into it in 1949, while the Soviet Union fostered a similar move of its zone into its puppet state, the German Democratic Republic. From 1958, Soviet Premier Nikita Khrushchev had pressed for a peace treaty to make the division of East and West Germany permanent, but the Western powers had rebuffed him. Then in 1961, in his meeting with President Kennedy in Vienna, he escalated the action: unless the West agreed to a treaty whose terms would effectively have ended the free status of West Berlin, he would enable East Germany to choke off the access routes. Then it was not so widely recognized that this was a move of defense on the part of the Soviets, since Berlin was the "hemorrhage" point of East Germany. Germans from the East were migrating to the West in the millions. What was particularly bad for the communists was that many of the 3.5 million who had left by the fall of 1961 were both educated and young; their flight virtually crippled the East German economy. The Russians and the East Germans were desperate.

With only a "trip wire" force, a single brigade, under his command in Berlin, Jimmy was in the most exposed position of the Cold War and one that called for a high degree of diplomatic skill in dealing not only with his Russian and East German counterparts but also with the sensitive French and British commanders and finally with the charismatic mayor of Berlin, Willy Brandt.

Still smarting from the psychological defeat he had suffered, or thought he had suffered, in his Vienna encounter with Khrushchev, and aware he could not get his Allies to do more to protect Berlin, President

Kennedy decided to make a major propaganda demonstration: he would visit Berlin. Jimmy was called to West Germany to escort him back. As Jimmy later wrote,

> About halfway to Berlin, President Kennedy came in and sat down on the arm of my seat. I started to get up and he said, "No, don't get up." He said, "Are we going to have any problems on arrival in Berlin?" I answered, "Well, yes we have one problem, Sir, everyone thinks he should shake hands with you first—the British [general] because he's the Commandant of the Month, the French because it's his airfield, Adenauer because he's the Chancellor of Germany and Willie Brandt because you're his guest." And he said, "Well I'm glad you told me; don't worry about it." I didn't know what he was going to do but I watched him. When he got off the plane he just rushed down the stairs and threw his arms around the four and really didn't shake hands with anyone so no one was offended.

It was an adroit beginning and Kennedy went on, due to an accident in translation, to score the greatest imaginable propaganda coup. In his speech in English, he said, "The greatest boast of the ancient world was 'I am a Roman citizen' "—but, as Jimmy observed, those words were missed in the translation into German; the translator skipped to the next phrase when

> the President said, "And the greatest boast today is '*Ich bin ein Berliner.*' " Because the early part wasn't translated, the whole crowd of 500,000 thought that he said '*he* was a Berliner,' which he didn't intend. At the end of his speech (he was a very smart politician) he said, "You've taken me to your heart in such a great way that I can, I think, in all honesty say, '*Ich bin ein Berliner.*' " And, of course, the crowd of 500,000

roared and chanted "KEN-E-DEE, KEN-E-DEE, KEN-E-DEE . . ."

In September 1964, as a lieutenant general, Jimmy took command of the 5th U.S. Army Corps in Germany and then briefly returned to Washington as assistant chief of the army staff in 1968. Finally, he returned to Germany, where in 1969 he became, as full general, commander in chief, commander of the 7th Army and commander of NATO's Central Army group. Without exaggeration, Jimmy could be said to have been the "point man" in the Western forces in the Cold War with the Soviet Union.

Shortly before his death in 1992, I went to see him at his house in El Paso, not far from where he had begun his military career nearly sixty years before, and as we swapped family jokes and stories, he suddenly produced the four Silver Stars he had worn as a general, saying, "I'll bet you've never seen anything quite like these."

I laughed and, recalling my own government service, retorted, "Jimmy, I've seen lots of generals."

"Not like these," he continued, handing them to me. "These were General Patton's stars. Mrs. Patton gave them to me when I got promoted. Look at them closely. Patton was really quite a snob, you know. He didn't like silver. He liked gold. But the army regulation called for generals to wear *silver* stars; so he had these made of gold and then silver-plated!"

FAR FROM THE SCENE OF MOST OF JIMMY'S CAREER, LUCIUS seemed to have been blessed with a relatively tranquil life. True, he often made it very interesting by scuba diving for sunken treasure in the Caribbean, by horse- and mule-back expeditions into the Wyoming mountains and by what seemed to his friends daredevil flying in his own airplane, but his law practice could only be described as lucratively conventional. That it was tranquil, however, would be a misleading impression. From his move to Memphis in 1936, he had periodically clashed with the city's dictator, Boss Crump. That was often a dangerous thing to do; worse, it was not popular, as Crump was a master at winning support for his machine by keeping taxes low, providing security on the streets and hiding the seamier side of his administration.

The Second World War, however, brought about changes in Memphis. Large numbers of new people arrived, major industries from the North set up plants, unions began to operate and returning veterans bridled at the coerciveness of the Crump machine. In 1948, the anti-Crump forces, by then led by Lucius, were ready to challenge it. They did so first by organizing a campaign that elected Estes Kefauver, from Chattanooga, to the U.S. Senate. Instead of seeking to co-opt the reformers, Crump became even more reactionary, following his opposition to the reelection of Harry Truman by joining the Dixiecrat movement.

By the middle of the 1950s, the resistance to Crump had begun to focus on treatment of blacks; Memphis had, by that time, acquired a chapter of the NAACP, and it asked the city administration to respect the recent U.S. Supreme Court decisions on civil liberties by opening the parks and a few other public facilities to blacks. Little was done, and Lucius took the lead in forming a "Good Local Government League," but he found himself way out in front of the white community. No one really wanted to face the racial issue. The most powerful citizens group advocated maintaining racial segregation "by all lawful means." But the black community was beginning to find its own voice, and Martin Luther King, Jr., made his first visit to Memphis in 1959.

Lucius kept hammering away, and modest steps toward desegregation were achieved on buses, in various public places including the zoo (which had not been open for blacks) and in the city libraries. But white reformers were branded by such slogans as "Race-Mixing is Communism." Undeterred, Lucius made another significant push in the early 1960s, calling on the white community to end segregation forthwith.

"It is now clear beyond argument," he wrote in a paper that stands as his credo,

> that no public institution has the right to deny equal facility of use to any citizen because of color . . . In the lives of most of us there are not many opportunities to play a perceptible part in the greatest of human roles—the peaceable extension of human liberty and the creation of a climate having a greater reverence for human dignity . . . but what we do here can stand as a beacon throughout the South and indeed the world as an example of how these problems can be solved by men with courage to take a stand . . .

Lucius could not bridge the widening gap between the increasingly frightened whites and the increasingly militant blacks. The garbage strike of 1968 brought the long-simmering issues to a head: crowds organized by the local black churches and spurred by black civil rights activists began a peaceful protest march, led by Dr. Martin Luther King, but militants turned it into a riot. Police moved in with tear gas and force: one black was killed, sixty were injured and three hundred were arrested.

King was deeply distressed at the violence and set about organizing a second and nonviolent march. The city authorities banned it, and King needed a lawyer to secure the permit to march. To represent him, he chose Lucius. And to the horror of Memphis white society, Lucius agreed to do so. He had just successfully accomplished the task when King was assassinated.

THREE LIVES, VERY DIFFERENT, BUT EACH IN ITS OWN WAY pursued with vigor, determination and zest by men who cared. Each rose not only to the top of his profession, which after all is not so unusual, but in doing so kept that sense of purpose, decency and commitment that is far more rare. And finally, each was recognized by his peers for these qualities. Jimmy has gone down in military annals as one of America's truly great generals and played a significant role in preserving the delicate balance of power on which peace rested in Europe for half a century. Lucius Burch carried the story full cycle from slavery to freedom, working carefully, constructively and modestly to achieve a peaceful transition in his community from segregation to integration, and ultimately defending the constitutional rights of the great black leader Martin Luther King. His life has been commemorated by having a mountain peak in his beloved Wyoming wilderness named for him, Burch Peak, and his fellow Memphians are erecting a statue to him in what will be the world's largest urban park, so the "aristocratic rebel/maverick/liberal," as he has been called, is taking a permanent place in the establishment. George, fearlessly probing into the murky subject of America's growing power in the world, opening what has been perhaps the most difficult and delicate problem America has faced in the second half of this century, is honored by what is perhaps the most prestigious accolade in journalism, the George Polk Award.

WITH THEIR STORIES, I END MY TALE. I HAVE THOUGHT OF this account as a saga because it chronicles generations of the family in what the dictionary calls "a long and leisurely narrative." In the medieval Norse sagas, it was customary to end on a note of fantasy: the fallen heroes go to Valhöll, or Valhalla, which was described as a splendid palace roofed with the symbols of their struggles in life—for the Vikings it was their shields—to reap the rewards of their valor by daily feasting on the flesh of a wild boar. I would like to think it is more than a coincidence that the crest of the Polk family, a wild boar pierced with an arrow, was established about the time the sagas were first composed. And I would particularly like to think that there is some sort of Valhalla in which Jimmy, George and Lucius were greeted by a gathering of relatives and friends, led perhaps by old Maccus, the distant patriarch, and including generations of wild Scots reivers. With them would stand Robert and Magdalen, several Williams and Charleses, the privateer Robert, Delilah, Thomas, Will and Sarah, James K., Leonidas, Lucius Eugene, Leonidas LaFayette, James H. and Molly, Meck, Frank, Harding, George and Adelaide, and that they would greet the newcomers with a chorus of "well done, you!"

Then, in a body, they would all turn toward us, the living, and shout, "Next!"

NOTES

CHAPTER 1

2 *infamous cutthroats.* These "Barbary" pirates were not only North Africans but renegade Europeans and were then using not galleys but sailing ships as fast as or faster than those in the best navies in Europe.

9 *Undwin the Saxon.* We know this about Undwin because he and his son Maccus are identified in a document that can be dated at roughly 1080, by which time they appear to have acquired both lands and status in the Scottish royal establishment.

13 *became Presbyterian.* The most powerful and famous of the lot, Lord Robert Maxwell, Earl of Nithsdale, remained a Catholic and even took up arms to hold his powerful fortress Carlaverock Castle against the forces of the Presbyterians.

13 *few records.* Many were destroyed by fire in 1921. What is left is mainly housed in the Irish Public Record Office.

13 *Robert de Pollok.* This and variant spellings first appear in the hearth money rolls in the 1660s.

18 *being as yet raw. An History of Ireland, from the Year 1599 to 1603,* quoted in Jonathan Bardon, *A History of Ulster* (Belfast: Blackstaff Press, 1992), 113.

19 *bitter Irish resistance.* The first attempt was made in 1572 by Sir Thomas Smith, who was provost of Eton and vice-chancellor of Cambridge University. No liberal academic, he published a pamphlet setting out his intent to drive away from his lands all the Irish except for useful peasants and to forbid them from wearing English clothes or carrying weapons on pain of death.

20 *the issue was religion.* Among the Anglo-Scottish royals, Henry VIII became an Anglican; Edward VI, a Calvinist; Elizabeth, probably worried by the threat she perceived from the Catholic Mary, Queen of Scots, became a sort of political Protestant; James I (as he was known in England) was personally Catholic but publicly favored the Church of England; Charles I publicly espoused a near-Catholic version of High Anglicanism known as Arminianism, which antagonized Catholics, Calvinists, Puritans and most Episcopalians. That was to cost him his head. Cromwell was a Puritan. Charles II was, covertly, a Catholic, and James II was an active Catholic.

21 *a covert Catholic.* While Charles II had proclaimed himself to be a Presbyterian, he made a secret treaty with Louis XIV of France for assistance that specified that he would proclaim himself a Catholic and bring England back into the Catholic fold.

22 *Meanwhile, in Ireland.* See Graeme Kirkam, "Ulster Emigration to North America, 1680–1720," in H. Tyler Blethen and Curtis W. Wood, Jr., *Ulster and North America: Transatlantic Perspectives on the Scotch-Irish* (Tuscaloosa: University of Alabama Press, 1997), 77.

22 *an angry and vengeful James II.* In the Act of Uniformity, Parliament began a program of persecution of Puritans (and later in 1673 was

to pass the Test Act, which barred all but Anglicans from public office). The core of the policy of revenge against Protestants was codified in the so-called Clarendon Code, four acts of Parliament passed between 1661 and 1665.

23 *fifty tons burthen.* Thus, it was almost exactly the size of *Dove,* which sailed to Maryland from Cowes in 1633.

25 *were much like his.* Half a century later, we hear of the *William & Mary* (thirty tons from Coleraine), *William and Elizabeth* (forty tons, sailing from Londonderry), *Dolphin* (seventy tons from Dublin), *Mc-Collom* (seventy tons from Londonderry) and *Beginning* (thirty tons from Waterford) sailing to America.

26 *Villany of Ship Masters.* Quoted in R. J. Dickson, *Ulster Emigration to Colonial America, 1718–1775* (London: Routledge & Kegan Paul, 1966), 221.

26 *the later slave ships.* David Hackett Fischer, *Albion's Seed* (New York: Oxford University Press, 1989).

29 *Irish servants.* Noted in Dickson, *Ulster Emigration,* 20.

29 *they had run out of beer.* See Bert L. Vallee, "Alcohol in the Western World," *Scientific American,* June 1998, 61ff.

30 *about half that.* A few years later, the ship *Nassau* carried forty-five pigs, a calf, three sheep, twenty turkeys, fourteen geese and more than a hundred chickens. See Arthur Pierce Middleton, *Tobacco Coast: A Maritime History of the Chesapeake Bay in the Colonial Era* (Baltimore: Johns Hopkins University Press and Maryland State Archives, 1994), 20.

30 *earmark of a cow.* William Harrison Polk, *Polk Family and Kinsmen* (Louisville, Ky.: Bradley & Gilbert, [1912]), 15, 31 (noting separate sources).

30 *official pamphlet.* It is reprinted in Clayton Colman Hall (ed.), *Narratives of Early Maryland* (New York: Charles Scribner's Sons, 1910), 93ff. A similar list is given by Captain John Smith in his widely read *The General History,* which was first published in London in 1624 and was reprinted in 1626, 1627 and 1632.

31 *Forks were not yet in use.* Even a century later, when Robert's grandson, Captain Robert Polk, died, the inventory of his property lists among other tableware, "6 table silver spoons, 6 tea d[itt]o, pair of salt shovels, tea tongs, mustard spoon . . . 6 pewter dishes, 12 pewter plates" but no forks. Baltimore County Will Book 3, page 347.

31 *to grace their house in Maryland.* According to William Harrison Polk, *Polk Family,* 52–53.

34 *Puerto Rico.* There is evidence, however, that a James "Poke" who may have been the brother of Robert Bruce Pollok had established himself and his family at St. Michaels, Barbados, sometime before 1680. On this point, see William Harrison Polk, *Polk Family,* 19–20.

34 *so foul weather.* "A relation of Richard Clarke of Wemouth master of the ship called 'The Delight,' " in Richard Hakluyt (ed.), *Voyages* (London: Dent, 1907), vol. 6, 40.

35 *extreme dangers.* Sir George Peckham, in Hakluyt, vol. 6, 20–21, 71.

35 *reached their destinations.* Middleton, *Tobacco Coast,* 11.

37 *the woman died.* Quoted in Middleton, *Tobacco Coast,* 20.

37 *one French writer.* Quoted in John Duffy, "The Passage to the Colonies," *Mississippi Valley Historical Review* 38 (June 1951–March 1952): 22.

37 *a later German traveler.* Carl T. Eben (trans.), *Gottlieb Mittelberger's Journey to Pennsylvania in the Year 1750* (Philadelphia, 1898), 20. Quoted in Duffy, "The Passage," 23.

38 *the old lady's antics.* "An Old Lady's Jottings," unpublished manuscript in the possession of the Polk family.

40 *The hammock.* Borrowed by the Spanish and English from Latin American Indians, it was observed by Sir Walter Raleigh at the end of the sixteenth century. Also known as Brasill beds, hammocks were regarded as a virtual necessity for ships in the tropics but spread slowly in the north.

CHAPTER 2

42 *quiet like a lake. Utopia,* book 2, translated from the Latin by H. V. S. Ogden (Northbrook, Ill.: AHM Publishing Co., 1949).

42 *account written in 1584.* Reprinted in Hakluyt, vol. 6, 131–32.

43 *twenty Thousand Ships.* Sir William Berkeley quoted in Middleton, *Tobacco Coast,* 40.

43 *Father Andrew White wrote.* In a manuscript in Latin entitled *Relatio Itineris in Marilandiam,* he described the trip. See Hall, *Narratives,* 40.

43 *down to her middle.* Lyon G. Tyler (ed.), *Narratives of Early Virginia* (New York, Charles Scribner's Sons, 1907), 88.

43 *he described Indians. The History and Present State of Virginia,* originally published in London by Richard Parker in 1705; new edition edited by Louis B. Wright (Chapel Hill: University of North Carolina Press, 1947), 159, 166.

44 *Amadas and Barlowe again.* Hakluyt, vol. 6, 121ff.

45 *bloudie Flixe.* Caused by *Endamoeba histolytica,* on which see Carville V. Earle, "Environment, Disease and Mortality in Early Virginia," in Thaddeus W. Tate and David L. Ammerman, *The Chesapeake in the Seventeenth Century* (Chapel Hill: University of North Carolina Press, 1979), 100.

45 *As he wrote.* Hakluyt, vol. 6, 191.

46 *Villages in England.* So stated a more or less official document, probably prepared by Lord Baltimore's brother-in-law and published in London in 1635. Reprinted in Hall, *Narratives,* 86.

46 *tribes.* As Richard White remarks *(The Middle Ground: Indians, Empires and Republics in the Great Lakes Region, 1650–1815* [Cambridge: Cambridge University Press, 1991], xiv), there actually were no tribes.

46 *even weeks of travel.* Helen Rountree and E. Randol Turner III, "On the Fringe of the Southeast: The Powhatan Paramount Chiefdom in Virginia," in Charles Hudson and Carmen Chaves Tesser, *The Forgotten Centuries: Indians and Europeans in the American South, 1521–*

1704 (Athens, Ga.: University of Georgia Press, 1994), 356–57, 363.

47 *their lethal effects.* See William Fenton, "Contacts Between Iroquois Herbalism and Colonial Medicine," Board of Regents of the Smithsonian Institution *Annual Report,* 1941.

47 *Violent theater.* In *Neighbors and Strangers* (Chicago: University of Chicago Press, 1997), 77ff. Captain John Smith describes such a battle. See Tyler, *Narratives,* 106–7.

47 *soldiers in formation.* Before the advent of firearms, Indians fought their battles in formations, not unlike European soldiers; it was only after firearms were used on them by Europeans that they adopted guerrilla-like tactics.

47 *gave them status.* See Daniel K. Richter, "War and Culture: The Iroquois Experience," *William and Mary Quarterly,* 3rd ser., 40, no. 4 (October 1983): 530.

47 *the pain of loss.* White, *Middle Ground,* 79ff.

47 *bodies might be eaten.* Cannibalism is well attested by Western observers from the time of Captain John Smith in the first years of the seventeenth century.

47 *this phase of violence.* Typical and probably accurate is the report by George Alsop, who had gone to America as an indentured servant *(A Character of the Province of Maryland* [London, 1666], reprinted in Hall, *Narratives,* 368–69. The psychological and quasi-religious role of torture is analyzed by Richard White *(Middle Ground,* 1, passim).

48 *to her Majestie.* Reprinted in Hakluyt, vol. 6, 232.

49 *Irish mantles.* See Tyler, *Narratives,* 99–100.

50 *One of our Gentlemen.* Quoted in Harold L. Peterson, *Arms and Armor in Colonial America* (New York: Bramhall House, 1956), 147.

51 *possess my Country.* Quoted by J. Frederick Fausz, "Merging and Emerging Worlds: Anglo-Indian Interest Groups and the Development of the Seventeenth-Century Chesapeake," in Lois Green Carr et al., *Colonial Chesapeake Society* (Chapel Hill: University of North Carolina Press, 1988), 52.

52 *our first worke.* Quoted by Fausz, "Merging and Emerging Worlds," 47.

52 *apartheid.* Philip Alexander Bruce, *Institutional History of Virginia* (New York: G. P. Putnam's Sons, 1910), 72.

52 *defray the expenses.* Bruce, *Institutional History,* 80, and J. Frederick Fausz, "Fighting 'Fire' with Firearms: The Anglo-Powhatan Arms Race in Early Virginia," *American Indian Culture and Research Journal* 3, no. 4 (1979): 41.

52 *Pequot's War.* The origins of the conflict are discussed in Alfred A. Cave, *The Pequot War* (Amherst: University of Massachusetts Press, 1996), 69ff.

53 *danger to their way of life.* See Fausz, "Merging and Emerging Worlds," 47ff.

53 *either killed or sold.* Colin G. Calloway, *New Worlds for All* (Baltimore: Johns Hopkins University Press, 1997), 35–36.

53 *ancestral lands.* See Douglas Edward Leach, *Flintlock and Tomahawk: New England in King Philip's War* (New York: Macmillan, 1958).

53 *Indians were rarely seen.* White, *Middle Ground,* 11.

53 *the essay argues.* Paragraphs 43–45.

53 *two thousand folde.* Thomas Heriot, in Hakluyt, vol. 6, 173.

54 *in the Chesapeake.* Middleton, *Tobacco Coast,* 105ff.

55 *the property remained.* Calloway, *New Worlds for All,* 23.

55 *European kings.* As among the bedouin, a paramount "chief" was addressed by his given name rather than his title; he also did ordinary labor alongside his fellows (Rountree and Turner, "On the Fringe of the Southeast," 365). As White wrote *(Middle Ground, 38),* "Chiefs were men with large responsibilities and few resources . . . The French desired to transform this noncoercive leadership into coercive leadership." "During the best of times, as the French noted, 'there is only voluntary subordination' [to the chiefs] among the western Indians. 'Each person is free to do as he pleases. The village chiefs and war chiefs can have influence, but they do not have authority . . .' " (206).

55 a "plantation" in the New World. Charles M. Andrews, *The Colonial Period of American History,* vol. 2 (New Haven: Yale University Press, 1936), 282, and Hall, *Narratives,* 16.

57 crude and uncomfortable houses. Alice Morse Earle, *Home Life in Colonial Days* (New York: Grosset & Dunlap, 1898), 23.

58 you cannot keep warm. In their *Journal of a Voyage to New York and a Tour in Several of the American Colonies in 1679–80,* quoted by Gloria L. Main in *Tobacco Colony: Life in Early Maryland, 1650–1720* (Princeton: Princeton University Press, 1982), 167.

58 A chair was a prized rarity. Raphael Semmes, *Crime and Punishment in Early Maryland* (Baltimore: Johns Hopkins University Press, 1996), 43–44, and David Freeman Hawke, *Everyday Life in Early America* (New York: Harper & Row, 1989), 56. But excavations carried out by Ivor Noël Hume (published as *Martin's Hundred* [New York: Knopf, 1982]) reveal a scattering of surprisingly rich ornaments and tableware in a Virginia settlement burned by the Indians in 1622.

58 samp. From the Algonquin *nasamp.* Roger Williams described it in 1643 as "a kind of meale pottage, unpartch'd. From this the English call their Samp, which is the Indian corne, beaten and boild, and eaten hot or cold with milke or butter." See Alice M. Earle, *Home Life in Colonial Days* (Stockbridge, Mass.: Berkshire, 1993), 134.

59 continued to struggle. In 1688, following the Glorious Revolution, the colonists petitioned William and Mary to make Maryland into a royal colony. They did but left the Baltimore family their rents and revenues. The monarchy reversed itself in 1715 and reappointed the Anglican 5th Lord Baltimore the proprietorship. This arrangement endured until the Revolutionary War.

59 people flooded into Maryland. Russell R. Menard, "British Migration to the Chesapeake Colonies in the Seventeenth Century," in Carr et al., *Colonial Chesapeake Society,* 101, and William A. Reavis, "The Maryland Gentry . . ." *William and Mary Quarterly,* 3rd series,

14, no. 3 (1957): 428. Somewhat lower figures are given by David W. Jordan, "Political Stability and the Emergence of a Native Elite in Maryland," in Tate and Ammerman, *The Chesapeake,* 246.

59 *at the whim of the master.* Hawke, *Everyday Life,* 123.

60 *jails were not introduced.* Semmes, *Crime and Punishment,* 32.

60 *as crowds ogled.* A high proportion of women were pregnant when they got married; even if they were not, if the baby was born before the normal term, they were considered guilty of fornication. Not surprisingly, large numbers of indentured women bore illegitimate children, and with parents struggling to survive, young people were given little supervision, so that promiscuity was common.

60 *the most bizarre case.* Bradford Smith, *Bradford of Plymouth* (Philadelphia: J. B. Lippincott, 1951), 222–23.

61 *lived even shorter lives.* Lois G. Carr and Lorena S. Walsh, "The Planter's Wife: The Experience of White Women in Seventeenth-Century Maryland," *William and Mary Quarterly,* 3rd ser., 34 (1977): 542; and Carol Berkin, *First Generations: Women in Colonial America* (New York: Hill & Wang, 1996), 8; and Hawke, *Everyday Life,* 59–60.

61 *a deadly, invisible ally.* Fausz, "Fighting 'Fire' with Firearms," 46.

62 *joined by a pilot.* The earliest identified pilot was a man by the name of John Rablie, who met incoming ships as early as 1644. See Middleton, *Tobacco Coast,* 89.

63 *his family would settle.* If this is true, it suggests that Robert must have known, before he left county Donegal, more or less the area on which he was expected to settle upon arrival. That, in turn, would indicate that he must have been in touch with the London office or a traveling agent. Such agents and other promotional devices are mentioned in Graeme Kirkam, "Ulster Emigration to North America, 1680–1720," in Blethen and Wood, *Ulster and North America,* 76.

64 *is recorded.* A document (now lost) mentioned in William Harrison Polk, *Polk Family,* 15.

64 *a separate livestock mark.* Lorena S. Walsh, " 'Till Death Us Do Part': Marriage and Family in Seventeenth-Century Maryland,'' in Tate and Ammerman, *The Chesapeake,* 143.

64 *"fevers" rose apace.* Darrett B. Rutman and Anita H. Rutman, "Of Agues and Fevers,'' *William and Mary Quarterly,* 3rd ser., 33, no. 1 (1976): passim.

65 *Feeling deprived.* See Michael G. Kammen, "The Causes of the Maryland Revolution of 1689,'' *Maryland Historical Magazine* 55 no. 4 (December 1960), 293ff.

CHAPTER 3

67 *destroy the nearby Indian societies.* As Helen Rountree and E. Randol Turner III comment in "On the Fringe of the Southeast'' (366), "When the English in Virginia turned to raising tobacco as a cash crop, around 1617, the doom of the Powhatans was sealed.''

68 *got the best land.* Charles A. Barker, "Property Rights in the Provincial System of Maryland: Proprietary Policy,'' *Journal of Southern History* 2 (February–November 1936): 60.

69 *many were Indians.* A 1708 census in Carolina indicates that about 15 percent of the population was composed of Indian slaves. On Indian slave hunters, see Joel W. Martin, "Southeastern Indians and the English Trade in Skins and Slaves,'' in Hudson and Tesser, *Forgotten Centuries,* 355ff. In Africa, the Kongo similarly preyed upon the Tio and Mbundu and unprotected groups known as *montamba* in Bobangi.

70 *Robert Beverley protested.* Colonists were always at pains to compare their actions with those of the home country, as Carole Shammas points out in "English-Born and Creole Elites in Turn-of-the-Century Virginia,'' in Tate and Ammerman, *The Chesapeake,* 279.

70 *shared their living quarters and meals.* Jack Larkin, *The Reshaping of Everyday Life* (New York: Harper & Row, 1989), 178.

70 *had black fathers and white mothers.* See Gloria L. Main's interesting and

well-researched book *Tobacco Colony: Life in Early Maryland, 1650–1720* (Princeton: Princeton University Press, 1982), 124, 139. One such union, "Irish Nell and Negro Charles," is told by Martha Hodes, *White Women, Black Men* (New Haven: Yale University Press, 1997), 19ff.

70 *having owned slaves.* Will dated January 23, 1739, and probated in Somerset County on February 24, 1739.

70 *to hunt them down.* As did the governor of Virginia in 1646 in setting a boundary for colonists at the York River. Neither this nor subsequent lines (the Appalachians in 1763 by the British and the Ohio in 1768 by the treaty of Fort Stanwix) held for long because of the land hunger of both the speculators and the colonists. In fact, both the colonists and the British government sought the same end, conquest of the American landmass, but they differed in timing and in method.

71 *less than five hundred acres.* David W. Jordan, "Political Stability and the Emergence of a Native Elite in Maryland," in Tate and Ammerman, *The Chesapeake,* 264.

71 *few houses were painted.* As Alice Morse Earle notes (*Home Life,* 27), "Painters do not appear in any of the early lists of workmen."

71 *more numerous than immigrants.* Jordan, "Political Stability," 246. Also see Shammas, "English-Born and Creole Elites."

72 *already pregnant.* Walsh, " 'Till Death Us Do Part,' " 128, 132.

72 *not up to growing tobacco.* His petition is noted in William Harrison Polk, *Polk Family,* 57. The various plots with the references to Maryland archives are given on page 61.

73 *things worth recording.* The inventory is recorded in 1703 in Liber EB no. 14, folios 294 and 295, in the Delmarva Research Center.

74 *Marginal land at best.* William Harrison Polk, *Polk Family,* 50–51.

74 *by a fire in 1847.* William Harrison Polk, *Polk Family,* 52.

74 *some form of title.* As Charles A. Barker points out ("Property Rights in the Provincial System of Maryland"), title was in process of tran-

sition from the feudal system of socage to private, but in 1715 it was ambiguous, as control of the colony was returned from the Crown to the lord proprietor.

75 *marriages seldom lasted more than a decade.* Carol Berkin, *First Generations: Women in Colonial America* (New York: Hill & Wang, 1996), 81.

77 *a woman could not legally own property.* Walsh, " 'Till Death Us Do Part,' " 137.

77 *left all adult children.* Walsh, " 'Till Death Us Do Part,' " 143.

78 *they probably heard tales.* On Indian-white relations at this time, see Charles A. Hanna, *The Wilderness Trail* (Lewisburg, Pa.: Wennawoods, 1995; reprinted from 1911 ed.), vol. 1, 36; Fausz, "Merging and Emerging Worlds," 48; Rountree and Turner, "On the Fringe of the Southeast" and Calloway, *New Worlds for All,* 169.

78 *have spoken "the Indian tongue well."* So said Captain Christopher Gist in a visit to a Delaware village in 1751, quoted in John G. Kester, "Charles Polke: Indian Trader of the Potomac, 1703–1753," *Maryland Historical Magazine,* 90, no. 2 (1995): 453–54.

79 *Nathaniel Bacon.* Charles M. Andrews (ed.), *Narratives of the Insurrections* (New York: G. P. Putnam's Sons, 1915).

80 *Sexual relations.* The Comte de Frontenac, mentioned in Hanna, *Wilderness Trail,* vol. 1, 201, and White, *Middle Ground,* 28, 58. The existence of this half-French, half-Indian society is one of the bases on which Richard White builds his insightful analysis of what he calls the Middle Ground.

80 *Indian hunting grounds.* The process not only began early but was repeated time after time. For the result of the settlement of Pennsylvania, see Francis P. Jennings, "The Delaware Interregnum," *Pennsylvania Magazine of History and Biography* 89, no. 2 (1965): 174ff.

80 *the Rum we get.* Quoted in Colin G. Calloway, *The American Revolution in Indian Country: Crisis and Diversity in Native American Communities* (Cambridge: Cambridge University Press, 1995), 13.

80 *Rum-debauched, Trader-corrupted.* "Narrative of the Late Massacres," in *Writings* (New York: Literary Classics of the United States, 1984), 553.

80 *James Adair wrote. History of the Indians in the South,* as quoted in Hanna, *Wilderness Trail,* vol. 2, 302.

81 *whom we call the Delawares.* Like the names of many Indian peoples, including the Illinois and the Iroquois, their name meant simply "the people." We often know the Indian tribes by geography, as the Susquehannocks (people living by the Susquehanna River) or sometimes by such unlikely names as Flatheads or by words used to describe them by their enemies, such as *Minquas* (a name given them by the Delaware, meaning "treacherous") or *Apache* (a name given the *Dine* by the *Ute* Indians, meaning "enemy"). Obviously, no people ever called itself Treacherous or Enemy.

81 *Charles A. Hanna wrote. Wilderness Trail,* vol. 1, 1.

82 *A few traders did talk.* Among them were James Adair, *History of the Indians in the South* (London, 1775); Alexander Henry (a cousin of mine), *Travels and Adventures in Canada and the Indian Territories Between the Years 1760 and 1776* (New York, 1809), and John Long, *Voyages and Travels of an Indian Interpreter and Trader, 1768–1782.* These all, unfortunately, deal only with a later period.

83 *so utterly destroyed.* James Logan, secretary of Pennsylvania from 1699, actively sought Indian traders who would seek out Indian hunters and buy their furs and identify choice locations for land speculation. "The effect on the Indians of Logan's land hunger can hardly be exaggerated," writes Francis Jennings in "The Indian Trade of the Susquehanna Valley," *Proceedings of the American Philosophical Society* 110, no. 6 (December 16, 1966). The Pennsylvania fur trade was a means of accelerating settlement. The Indians performed pioneer labor for him, clearing wilderness sites which he later acquired. By getting other settlers nearby, he raised the value of his holdings and drove out Indians. At least as early as 1685, we read complaint after complaint to the colonial authorities. In that year, Indians com-

plained to the Pennsylvania Council of traders employed by the Quakers who "supplied them with liquor, made them drunk, and then grossly abused them and debauched their wives" (quoted in Hanna, *Wilderness Trail,* vol. 1, 163). Also see Peter C. Mancall, *Deadly Medicine: Indians and Alcohol in Early America* (Ithaca, N.Y.: Cornell University Press, 1995). In addition to the reasons put forth by Mancall, alcohol created an imbalance in sugar, for which the Indians had little genetic tolerance. George Croghan, "the king of the traders," remarks on a series of encounters with the Indians in 1754, by which time liquor had become virtually a disease among the Indians: "we found the Indians all drunk," ". . . The Indians were all drunk . . ." and "From the sixteenth to the twenty-sixth we could do nothing, the Indians being constantly drunk" (all quoted in Hanna, *Wilderness Trail,* vol. 1, 274, 275).

83 *every hungry dog that approaches.* John Stuart in a dispatch to General Thomas Gage, May 23, 1772 quoted in Calloway, *American Revolution,* 11.

83 *called stroud.* Stroud in Gloucestershire was where a rough woolen cloth was made; it became a major item of commerce with the Indians.

83 *eight bucks worth of goods.* Hanna, *Wilderness Trail,* vol. 1, 370.

84 *interlaced trails.* "Pathfinding in Pennsylvania," *Papers of the Kittochtinny Historical Society,* vol. 13 (1957), 269–70. And see *Indian Paths of Pennsylvania* (Harrisburg: Pennsylvania Historical and Museum Commission, 1993), which includes a sketch map of known trails. Another account of Indian trails in Pennsylvania is given in Charles Morse Stotz, *Outposts of the War for Empire* (Pittsburgh: University of Pittsburgh Press, 1985), 25.

84 *Conestoga wagon.* W. P. Conrad, *From Terror to Freedom in the Cumberland Valley* (Greencastle, Pa.: Lilian S. Besore Memorial Library, 1976), 2.

85 *traders like Charles.* His name appears on the assessment rolls in 1724 and 1726.

85 *left an estate.* An inventory was filed on November 25, 1742, in the Prince George's County Register of Wills and is noted in Kester, "Charles Polke," 462. Charles was accused of stealing this amount, but the case was dismissed.

86 *Charles Polk's house.* William J. Hinke and Charles E. Kemper (eds.), "Moravian Diaries of Travels Through Virginia," *Virginia Magazine of History and Biography* 12 (1904): 55.

86 *young George Washington.* John C. Fitzpatrick (ed.), *The Diaries of George Washington, 1748–1799* (Boston: Houghton Mifflin, 1925), vol. 1, 6.

86 *Charles ate.* George P. Donehoo (ed.), *History of the Cumberland Valley* (Harrisburg: Susquehanna History Association, 1930), vol. 1, 39, and Thomas J. C. Williams, *A History of Washington County Maryland from the Earliest Settlements to the Present Time* (Chamberstown, Pa.: J. M. Runk, 1906; reprint, Baltimore: Regional Publishing Co., 1968), 12–13.

87 *Benjamin Franklin.* Letter to Peter Collinson, Philadelphia, May 9, 1753, in *Writings,* 470–71.

87 *forced to return.* See "The White Indians of Colonial America," in James Axtell, *The European and the Indian* (New York: Oxford University Press, 1981).

87 *whites were abducted.* Calloway, *New Worlds for All,* 155. Also see White, *Middle Ground,* 261, and Paul A. W. Wallace, *Indians in Pennsylvania* (Harrisburg: Pennsylvania Historical and Museum Commission, 1993), 50. Colonel Bouquet is quoted in the *Western Pennsylvania Historical Magazine* 42 (1959): 287–88. There is now a substantial literature on Indianization of whites.

89 *to extirpate this execrable race.* White, *Middle Ground,* 288. The quote is drawn from "Journal of William Trent," in John W. Harpster (ed.), *Pen Pictures of Early Western Pennsylvania* (Pittsburgh: University of Pittsburgh Press, 1938), 103–4.

89 *the Paxton Boys.* Wallace, *Indians in Pennsylvania,* and James H. Merrell, *Into the American Woods: Negotiators on the Pennsylvania Frontier* (New

York: Norton, 1999), 281ff. For an unflattering mention of Charles "Poke," see 205.

90 *bounty for Indian scalps.* See Ronald W. Clark, *A Biography of Benjamin Franklin* (New York: Random House, 1983), 173–75.

90 *Franklin spoke.* Reprinted in *Writings,* 540ff.

90 *in his own black heart.* See Carl van Doren, *Benjamin Franklin* (New York, 1938), 308–13.

90 *attempts to protect Indians.* One such act was carried out by Captain William Patterson in arresting the murderer of a Seneca Indian, but the murderer was immediately freed by a mob of his fellows. See Hanna, *Wilderness Trail,* vol. 2, 56–57.

90 *I appeal to any white man.* Jacob H. Stoner, *Historical Papers: Franklin County and the Cumberland Valley* (Chambersburg, Pa.: Craft Press, 1997), 21.

91 *could now become rich.* Already in the seventeenth century and increasingly in the eighteenth, the coastal establishment also speculated in titles to lands beyond the frontier. Louis B. Wright, *The Atlantic Frontier: Colonial American Civilization* (New York: Knopf, 1951), 74, comments that the Byrds "sold rum, guns, and iron pots to the Indians and bought furs from them, making a fat profit from these transactions."

91 *Who "invented" scalping.* The probably definitive answer is given by James Axtell and William C. Sturtevant in "The Unkindest Cut, or Who Invented Scalping?" *William and Mary Quarterly,* 3rd ser., 37, no. 3 (July 1980): 451ff.

91 *bounty for Indian scalps.* A century later, in the West, a similar offer resulted in the deaths of countless Mexican peasants whose scalps were claimed as Apache. The custom spread far afield: even Australians took it up and paid bounties for the scalps of Aboriginals.

92 *Clark's orders from . . . Jefferson.* Colin G. Calloway, " 'We have Always Been the Frontier': The American Revolution in Shawnee Country," *American Indian Quarterly* 16 (1992): 43.

CHAPTER 4

98 *weeks of hard slogging.* George Washington gives an account of the hospitality he received in his diary for November and December 1753 (Fitzpatrick, *Diaries of George Washington,* 43ff).

100 *would have disagreed.* William Henry Hoyt, *The Mecklenburg Declaration of Independence* (New York: G. P. Putnam's Sons, 1907), 67–68.

100 *the chief engineer.* In a letter quoted in Ernest Kipping, *The Hessian View of America, 1763–1783* (Monmouth Beach, N.J.: Philip Freneau Press, 1971), 34–35, quoted in Charles Patrick Neimeyer, *America Goes to War: A Social History of the Continental Army* (New York: New York University Press, 1996), 8.

101 *on the eve of the Revolution.* Richard Hofstadter, *America at 1750: A Social Portrait* (New York: Vintage, 1973), 67.

101 *develop into communities.* Marvin L. Michael Kay and Lorin Lee Cary, *Slavery in North Carolina, 1748–1775* (Chapel Hill: University of North Carolina Press, 1995), passim.

102 *land "Grows dearer."* Quoted in Parke Rouse, Jr., *The Great Wagon Road* (New York: McGraw-Hill, 1973), 35.

103 *a century before.* Ralph Lane's 1585 colony was abandoned and John White's 1587 group simply disappeared, but the English were not the first Europeans to visit the Carolinas. Hakluyt vol. 6, 233, mentions that in 1524 "John Verrazzano a Florentine was sent by King Francis the first, and by Madam the Regent his mother into these newe Regions, where he went on land . . ." When Hernando de Soto arrived in 1540, he saw evidence that other Europeans had been in contact before, because the diseases they imported had already devastated the Indians (E. Lawrence Lee, *Indian Wars in North Carolina, 1663–1763* [Raleigh: Carolina Charter Tercentenary Commission, 1963], 15).

103 *Fifty-four shiploads.* Alan D. Watson, *Society in Colonial North Carolina,* rev. ed. (Raleigh: Division of Archives and History, 1996), 5. Also see Duane Meyer, *The Highland Scots of North Carolina, 1732–*

1776 (Chapel Hill: University of North Carolina Press, 1957); Charles Knowles Bolton, *Scotch Irish Pioneers* (Boston: Bacon & Brown, 1910), and James G. Leyburn, *The Scotch-Irish: A Social History* (Chapel Hill: University of North Carolina Press, 1962).

104 *Locke's constitution.* His theme was "Life, Liberty and Property," which Jefferson and others later reconstituted as "Life, Liberty and the Pursuit of Happiness."

104 *Only those who acquired land.* Charles M. Andrews, *The Colonial Period of American History,* vol. 3, *The Settlements* (New Haven: Yale University Press, 1937), 214.

104 *of what opinion or religion soever.* Jeffrey J. Crow, *The Black Experience in Revolutionary North Carolina* (Raleigh: Division of Archives and History, North Carolina Department of Cultural Resources, 1996), 2.

104 *meals of meat.* Watson, *Society in Colonial North Carolina,* 38. As Jeffrey J. Crow wrote, (*Black Experience,* 12–13, 19), "By all accounts, North Carolina blacks in the colonial period were ill-fed, ill-housed, and ill-clothed . . . The better masters gave slaves 'a suit of coarse woolen cloth, two rough shirts, and a pair of shoes' once a year."

104 *enjoyment of a negro.* Josiah Quincy, quoted in Crow, *Black Experience,* 30.

104 *Thomas Jefferson complained.* William Peden (ed.), *Notes on the State of Virginia* (Chapel Hill: University of North Carolina Press, 1982), query 14, 139. Jack Larkin writes (*Reshaping of Everyday Life,* 163), "Most men and women also washed without soap, reserving it for laundering clothes; instead they used a brisk rubbing with a coarse towel to scrub the dirt off their skins."

105–6 *a bounty for Tuscarora scalps.* A contemporary Indian trader, John Lawson, is quite candid about this practice. See Hugh Talmage Lefler (ed.), *John Lawson's "A New Voyage to Carolina"* (Chapel Hill: University of North Carolina Press, 1967).

106 *sold into slavery.* Lee, *Indian Wars,* 26.

106 *hundreds of grants were made.* D. A. Tompkins, *History of Mecklenburg County and the City of Charlotte from 1740 to 1903* (Charlotte: Observer, 1903), 15–16.

106 *shortly after their arrival.* Polk Births and Deaths, manuscript in the Polk Papers, North Carolina Department of Archives and History, Raleigh.

106 *indomitable enterprise.* Draper Collection, State Historical Society of Wisconsin, Mecklenburg Declaration unpublished manuscript, 2ff, 161–75, subsequently reprinted in edited form by J. B. Alexander, M.D., *The History of Mecklenburg County from 1740 to 1900* (Charlotte: Observer, 1902), 387–88.

107 *registered in November 1764.* Patent Book 15 of the Colony of North Carolina, 1735–64.

107 *2 shillings an acre.* Deed registered in Mecklenburg County, "in the seventh year of the reign of our Sovereign Lord George 3d," January 5, 1767.

107 *a gristmill.* The size of his mill is shown by the fact that during the Revolution the British seized 28,000 pounds of flour and "a quantity of wheat" (Alexander, *History of Mecklenburg County,* 133).

107 *the then huge sum of £920.* C. L. Hunter, *Sketches of Western North Carolina, Historical and Biographical* (Baltimore: Regional Publishing Co., 1970), 155. To give a scale, a captain in the Revolutionary army, when he was paid, received $26³/₄ and a lieutenant $18 a month. Whiskey was 5s/gallon; calico 8s/yard; broadcloth 18s/yard.

107 *starving American troops.* They were described as "ill-trained, ill-fed, ill-housed, ill-clothed, without sufficient arms, ammunition, blankets, and tents" (Hugh F. Rankin, *The North Carolina Continentals* [Chapel Hill: University of North Carolina Press, 1971], 83).

107 *failed to come through.* Richard K. Showman (gen. ed.), *The Papers of General Nathanael Greene,* vol. 7, 26 December 1780–29 March 1781 (Chapel Hill: University of North Carolina Press, 1994), 122. Thomas resigned when he could not force the people of North Car-

olina to provide enough to sustain General Greene's forces. See his
letter of December 10, 1780, quoted in Showman, vol. 6, 560–61.

107 *vary a little*. Zack Spratt, "History of the Old Indian Fort, Retold,"
Fort Mill Times, September 20, 1962.

108 *against the Crown*. William Henry Hoyt (ed.), *The Papers of Archibald
D. Murphey* (Raleigh: E. W. Uzzell & Co., 1914), 400. The college
was burned during the Revolution by retreating British troops.

108 *half grown over with moss*. Quoted in Timothy Silver, *A New Face on the
Countryside: Indians, Colonists, and Slaves in South Atlantic Forests,
1500–1800* (Cambridge: Cambridge University Press, 1990), 103.

108 *Charles Woodmason*. Richard J. Hooker (ed.), *Charles Woodmason: The
Carolina Backcountry on the Eve of the Revolution* (Chapel Hill: University of North Carolina Press, 1953), passim.

109 *What Woodmason failed to notice*. Watson, *Society in Colonial North Carolina,* 22.

109 *pocketed most of what they collected*. "Governor William Tryon in 1767
expressed the opinion that 'the sheriffs have embezzled more than
one-half of the public money ordered to be raised and collected by
them' " (William S. Powell, *The War of the Regulation and the Battle
of Alamance, May 16, 1771* [Raleigh: Department of Cultural Resources, 1976], 7).

110 *were subdued*. War with the Cherokee ended in 1761; in 1767, Governor Tryon sent one hundred men of the militia with a surveying
party to mark the boundary with the Cherokee. The Indians, as
D. A. Tompkins wrote (*History of Mecklenburg County,* 37), "cheer-
fully accepted the line as run and gave no further trouble until the
white people began once more to encroach upon their territory."

111 *speculating in western lands*. Among whose principals were such lumi-
naries as George Washington, various members of the Lee family
and Benjamin Franklin. Other, less well known but comparable
ventures included the Transylvania Company, which drew support
from North Carolina. An older but still useful study is Kenneth P.

Bailey, *The Ohio Company of Virginia and the Westward Movement, 1748–1792* (Glendale, Calif.: Arthur H. Clark Co., 1939).

111 *The Regulation.* See William S. Powell, *The War of the Regulation and the Battle of Alamance, May 16, 1771* (Raleigh: Department of Cultural Resources, 1976), and his *The Regulators in North Carolina: A Documentary History, 1759–1776* (Raleigh: State Department of Archives and History, 1971).

112 *defeated the Regulators.* Magnanimously and wisely, he offered them a pardon, and some six thousand men accepted, but hundreds swelled the growing tide of settlers moving westward (Robert L. Ganyard, *The Emergence of North Carolina's Revolutionary State Government* [Raleigh: Department of Cultural Resources, 1978], 16).

112 *pamphlet itself superfluous.* William S. Price, Jr., *Not a Conquered People: Two Carolinians View Parliamentary Taxation* (Raleigh: Department of Cultural Resources, 1975).

113 *Liberty, Property and No Stamp-Duty.* The November 20 *North Carolina Gazette,* reproduced in Lindley S. Butler, *North Carolina and the Coming of the Revolution, 1763–1776* (Raleigh: North Carolina Department of Cultural Affairs, 1976), 19.

113 *at any Risque whatever.* Saunders, *Colonial Records,* quoted in Butler, *North Carolina,* 21.

114 *Thomas Polk.* Alexander, *History of Mecklenburg County,* 389.

115 *in October 1774.* Hoyt, *Mecklenburg Declaration,* 34.

115 *Pine Creek Declaration.* Leyburn, *Scotch-Irish,* 306, and Neimeyer, *America Goes to War,* 32–33. Pauline Maier, *American Scripture: Making the Declaration of Independence* (New York: Knopf, 1997), finds ninety of these.

115 *Mecklenburg Resolves.* It may be, as has been asserted, that an even clearer call for independence was issued ten days before. In 1800, the house in which various of the Revolutionary documents of western North Carolina were stored was destroyed by fire; some were reconstituted from memory and efforts were made to put

them in context. A committee of the North Carolina legislature in 1830–31 examined the most controversial, an alleged "declaration of independence" of May 21, 1775, which either echoed or presaged the one Jefferson wrote the following year. The issue was exhaustively examined by Hoyt (*Mecklenburg Declaration,* 34), who concluded that the only actual document was the one issued on May 31, 1775. The May 31 resolutions were printed in the June 13, 1775, *South-Carolina Gazette and Country Journal* and in the June 29, 1775, *New York Journal; or, The General Advertiser* and in the July 12, 1775, *Massachusetts Spy or American Oracle of Liberty.* Similar resolves were adopted by other counties and by the Provincial Congress of South Carolina in June.

116 *the Continental Congress.* Some of the delegates, including John Adams, shortly thereafter advised another group, also from the frontier, to be patient, since "We have petitioned and addressed the King, and have entreated him to point out some mode of accommodation."

117 *put it bluntly.* On July 31, 1775, a North Carolina delegate to the Continental Congress in a private letter, quoted in Hoyt, *Mecklenburg Declaration,* 97.

117 *production of war matériel.* Ganyard, *Emergence,* 51.

118 *was severely wounded.* Colonel Will Polk's pension application April 4, 1833, "Pension Declaration of William Polk," Revolutionary War Pension and Bounty Land Warrant Applications Files, 1800–1900, M804, roll 1945, National Archives, Washington, D.C. At the National Archives, there are some eighty thousand applications on file, in response to an act of Congress in 1832. This pension application process constituted "one of the largest oral history projects ever undertaken, with thousands of veterans being interviewed." See John C. Dann, *The Revolution Remembered: Eyewitness Accounts of the War for Independence* (Chicago: University of Chicago Press, 1980). I will draw much of the record of Colonel Will's war from this record.

118 *a contemporary described it.* Hoyt, *Papers of Archibald D. Murphey,* 403–4.

119 *naked and dead.* According to Jonas Clark (Revolutionary War Pension and Bounty Land Warrant Applications Files, 1800–1900, M804, roll 560, National Archives, Washington, D.C.), who two days later "Buried our dead which we found stripped of their clothes by the enemy."

119 *the words of Charles Stedman.* Quoted in Thomas E. Baker, *Another Such Victory: The Story of the American Defeat at Guilford Courthouse That Helped Win the War for Independence* (n.p.: Eastern National, 1981), 76.

120 *long "Kentucky" rifles.* As Jac Weller asserts in "Irregular but Effective: Partizan Weapons Tactics in the American Revolution, Southern Theatre," in Don Higginbotham (ed.), *Military Analysis of the Revolutionary War* (Millwood, N.Y.: KTO Press, 1977), 135, "The rifle in the North had some early propaganda value and was effective in a few isolated instances, but fell finally to such low estem that it was largely replaced by [smoothbore] muskets."

121 *Letters of Marque.* Papers of the Continental Congress, M247, rolls 202–3, Ships Bonds, 1776–83, National Archives, Washington, D.C.

122 *mere pirates.* See, for example, P.R.O. Admiralty, 1, vol. 4134, Dublin, June 30, 1777.

122 *impossible to trace.* Bernard C. Steiner, "Maryland Privateers in the American Revolution," *Maryland Historical Magazine* 3 (1908): 99ff.

123 *The sale of one of these.* William James Morgan (ed.), *Naval Documents of the American Revolution,* vol. 7 (Washington, D.C.: Naval History Division, Department of the Navy, 1976), 13. Vol. 8, 139, gives a list of the Maryland grants of Letters of Marque and Reprisal.

124 *a few months later.* John McLure to Colonel Mordecai Gist, Baltimore, November 2, 1777, in Michael J. Crawford (ed.), *Naval Documents of the American Revolution,* vol. 10 (Washington, D.C.: Naval Historical Center, Department of the Navy, 1996), 379.

124 *Declaration of Independence.* Ganyard, *Emergence,* 68ff.

125 *offering manumission.* Benjamin Quarles, "Lord Dunmore as Libera-
tor," *William and Mary Quarterly,* 3rd ser., 15, no. 4 (October
1958): 494ff. Various other English generals offered similar inducements later in the Revolution, but the British often did not honor
their offer, occasionally selling the blacks back into slavery or simply making them servants when they arrived to be freed. Eventually, some twelve hundred were shipped back to Africa and settled
in what became Sierra Leone. (Crow, *Black Experience,* 75, 82, and
Carole Watterson Troxler, *The Loyalist Experience in North Carolina*
[Raleigh: Division of Archives and History, Department of Cultural
Resources, 1996], 49ff.)

125 *James Madison.* William T. Hutchinson and William M. E. Rachal
(eds.), *The Papers of James Madison* (Chicago: University of Chicago
Press, 1932), vol. 1, 153.

125 *public order.* Ganyard, *Emergence,* 31. Also see Neimeyer, *America Goes
to War,* 69, 77, 80.

126 *were discharged.* Pete Maslowski, "National Policy Toward the Use of
Black Troops in the Revolution," *South Carolina Historical Magazine*
73, no. 1 (January 1972): 3.

126 *but no others.* Washington Papers, ser. 3A, Dec. 31, 1775, quoted in
Maslowski, "National Policy," 6.

126 *give them their freedom.* Stanley Elkins and Eric McKitrick, *The Age of
Federalism: The Early Republic, 1788–1800* (New York: Oxford University Press, 1993), 99.

126 *serving as soldiers.* Lorenzo J. Greene, "Some Observations on the
Black Regiment of Rhode Island in the American Revolution,"
Journal of Negro History 37, no. 2 (1952): 143ff.

126 *the freedom he had been promised.* Kitchen offered the slave, Ned Grif-
fen, his freedom if he went to war. He did, but when he was discharged at the end of the war, Kitchen reneged and sold him to
another slave owner. In 1784, the General Assembly reviewed the
case and passed a law freeing him. (Crow, *Black Experience,* 65.)

127 *black former slaves.* By Baron von Closen, an aide-de-camp to French General Rochambeau; cited in Benjamin Quarles, *The Negro in the American Revolution* (Chapel Hill: University of North Carolina Press, 1961), viii–ix.

127 *a contest for liberty.* Crow, *Black Experience,* 69.

128 *rung especially hollow.* Papers of the Continental Congress, reel 91, item 78, 2:41, cited by Neimeyer, *America Goes to War,* 91–92.

128 *joining the American side was appalling.* Andrew McFarland Davis, ''The Employment of Indian Auxiliaries in the American War,'' *English Historical Review* 2 (1887): 709.

129 *Ezekiel Polk.* The essential details are given in Charles Grier Sellers, Jr., ''Colonel Ezekiel Polk: Pioneer and Patriarch,'' *William and Mary Quarterly,* 3rd ser., 10, no. 1 (January 1953): 80ff.

130 *dirty, mutinous and disaffected.* Quoted by Neimeyer, *America Goes to War,* 24.

130 *a discharge of their duty.* Blackwell P. Robinson, *The Revolutionary War Sketches of William R. Davie* (Raleigh: Department of Cultural Resources, 1976), 59–60.

130 *felons paroled.* John Shy, *A People Numerous and Armed: Reflections on the Military Struggle for American Independence* (Ann Arbor: University of Michigan Press, 1990).

131 *three thousand soldiers deserted.* Neimeyer, *America Goes to War,* 24.

131 *Colonel Will Polk.* Hoyt, *Papers of Archibald D. Murphey,* vol. 2. He is quoted in Chalmers Gaston Davidson, *Piedmont Partisan: The Life and Times of Brigadier-General William Lee Davidson* (Davidson, N.C.: Davidson College, 1960[?]), 52.

131 *their bounty money.* Rankin, *North Carolina Continentals,* 343.

132 *composed principally of those men.* Leyburn, *Scotch-Irish,* 305–6, and Neimeyer, *America Goes to War,* chap. 2.

132 *George III was told.* Sir John Fortescue, *The Correspondence of King George the Third, from 1760 to December 1783* (London: Macmillan, 1928), no. 2492, vol. 4 (1778–79), 245ff.

133 *exact a damn.* Abner Nash to Greene, April 7, 1781, Autographs of

Americans Collection, Pierpont Morgan Library, New York; quoted in Rankin, *North Carolina Continentals,* 341.

133 *supposed to be fighting for.* Rankin, *North Carolina Continentals,* 135ff., from which the material in this paragraph is drawn.

133 *finally collapsed.* See E. Wayne Carp, *To Starve the Army at Pleasure: Continental Administration and American Political Culture, 1775–1783* (Chapel Hill: University of North Carolina Press, 1984), and E. James Ferguson, *The Power of the Purse: A History of American Public Finance, 1776–1790* (Chapel Hill: University of North Carolina Press, 1961).

133 *purchasing goods.* Reproduced in Showman, *Papers of General Nathanael Greene,* vol. 7, 348.

134 *avoided if possible.* Leonidas Polk Papers, Southern Historical Collection, University of the South, Sewanee, Tennessee.

134 *what the army needed.* See Mark A. Clodfelter, "Between Virtue and Necessity: Nathanael Greene and the Conduct of Civil-Military Relations in the South, 1780–1782," *Military Affairs* 52, no. 4 (October 1988): 169ff. As Greene wrote, "The Great Laws of Necessity must Justify the Expedient Till we can be otherwise furnished."

134 *resume a fighting command.* Horatio Gates Papers, New York Historical Society, Thomas Polk to Major Pinckney, Charlotte, August 6, 1780.

134 *on the Yadkin River.* Horatio Gates Papers, New York Historical Society.

134 *uncertain and unpleasant means.* Robinson, *Revolutionary War Sketches,* 41–42.

135 *are daily discharged.* Robinson, *Revolutionary War Sketches,* 59–60, n. 137.

135 *to tip the balance.* As General Greene wrote to George Washington on March 18, 1781; see Showman, *Papers of General Nathanael Greene,* vol. 7, 451–52.

135 *tired of the Rebellion.* Fortescue, *King George,* no. 2492, "Proposal for

Covering and Reducing the Country as the British Army Shall Pass Through It.''

135 *a campaign strategy*. Martin thought he could raise at least three thousand Highland Scots and former Regulators if he had adequate arms to give them. See Rankin, *North Carolina Continentals,* 28, and Ganyard, *Emergence,* 22–23.

136 *newly arrived Highlanders*. Meyer, *Highland Scots,* 157ff.

136 *young Will Polk fought*. Recounted in his pension declaration, M804, roll 1945, National Archives, Washington, D.C.

136 *letter to General Nathanael Greene*. February 20, 1781; reproduced by Odell McGuire: ''Many were sore chased and some cut down: Fighting Cornwallis with the Rockbridge Militia,'' Internet, http// wwe.wlu.edu/~omcguire/mass.html. October 1995.

137 *the salvation of our Countrey*. Reproduced in Showman, *Papers of General Nathanael Greene,* vol. 7, 380.

137 *We fight, get beat, rise, and fight again*. Rankin, *North Carolina Continentals,* 327.

139 *Manufacturers would leave*. Fortescue, *King George,* vol. 4, 500–1, dated Kew, June 11, 1779. Also see no. 2161, where the king speaks of the narrow scope of his ability to bargain, given parliamentary opinion.

CHAPTER 5

141 *founded by Will Polk*. Wallace Evan Davies, ''The Society of the Cincinnati in New England, 1783–1800,'' *William and Mary Quarterly* 5, no. 1 (January 1948): 3, 23. Also see William S. Thomas, *The Society of the Cincinnati 1783–1935* (New York, 1935); *The Writings of George Washington* (New York, 1889–93), vol. 11, 157, and Edgar Erskine Hume, *Washington's Correspondence Concerning the Cincinnati* (Baltimore, 1941).

141 *their association*. Gordon S. Wood, *The Creation of the American Republic, 1776–1787* (New York: Norton, 1972; original edition Chapel

Hill: University of North Carolina Press, 1969), 399–400. The society was attacked by Noah Webster (later to become known for his dictionary) and Sam Adams, who called it "as rapid a Stride towards an hereditary Military Nobility as was ever made in so short a time." (*Writings,* vol. 4, 301. [New York: Octagon, 1968: reprint of 1904–8 edition edited by Harry A. Cushing].)

142 *society had to be formed anew.* The Massachusetts constitution of 1780, for example, specified that "the whole people covenants with each citizen, and each citizen with the whole people." Describing the agreement, Thomas Dawes told a Boston audience that "We often read of the original contract, and of mankind, in the early ages, passing from a state of nature to immediate civilization . . . the people of Massachusetts have reduced to practice the wonderful theory" and signed "a glorious covenant." (Quoted in Wood, *Creation,* 289.)

142 *As Gordon Wood wrote. Creation,* 285.

142 *From Montesquieu.* Whose very title, *Considérations sur les causes de la grandeur des Romains et de leur décadence,* ensured its success in an age with a penchant for classical Rome.

142 *Emmerich de Vattel.* In *Le Droit des gens,* 1758.

142 *merely "our embassy."* Quoted by Wood, *Creation,* 357.

143 *Pancakes on Sundays.* In a letter to John Steele of November 28, 1800, in the A.L.S. John Steele Papers, Collections of the North Carolina Historical Society, *The Papers of John Steele,* edited by H. M. Wagstaff (Raleigh: Publications of the North Carolina Historical Commission, 1924), vol. 1, 192.

144 *one common mass.* Quoted in Wood, *Creation,* 357.

144 *theatre of public action.* Quoted in Wood, *Creation,* 498.

145 *Articles of Confederation.* Stanley Elkins and Eric McKitrick, *The Age of Federalism: The Early Republic, 1788–1800* (New York: Oxford University Press, 1993), 32ff.

146 *Thomas Jefferson would probably not have voted either.* Joseph J. Ellis,

American Sphinx: The Character of Thomas Jefferson (New York: Knopf, 1996), 103. On seeing the draft Constitution, he commented that "there is a great mass of good in it . . . , but there is also to me a bitter pill or two," so he expressed himself as neutral.

146 *we would probably not have a constitution.* Elkins and McKitrick (*Age of Federalism,* 22) play this down: "its impact, if very much in any case, was largely limited to New York."

147 *the bedrock of America.* Query 19, "Manufactures," in *Notes on the State of Virginia,* edited with notes by William Peden (Chapel Hill: University of North Carolina Press, 1982), 165.

148 *supervisor of internal revenue.* John C. Fitzpatrick (ed.), *The Writings of George Washington from the Original Manuscript Sources* (Washington D.C.: United States Government Printing Office, 1931–4), vol. 31. In a proclamation dated City of Philadelphia, March 15, 1791. The revenue in question, the only one then collectable, was on liquor, and for his work, Will was to be paid $700 a year plus a commission of 1 percent.

149 *in North Carolina.* Chartered in 1810; before then there was no state banking institution, but there were two private banks (at New Bern and Cape Fear); the capital stock was not to exceed $1.6 million, of which $250,000 was to be reserved for the state.

149 *Will's reply.* A broadsheet issued on November 26, 1818, in Raleigh, North Carolina, and contained in "Polk Family of North Carolina," ms. 16,734, the Library of Congress.

149 *lack of currency.* Tompkins, *History of Mecklenburg County,* vol. 2, 93ff.

150 *only at a premium.* It was to avoid this problem that modern dollar bills have printed on them "This note is legal tender for all debts, public and private."

151 *the notorious Sedition Act of 1798.* See Elkins and McKitrick, *Age of Federalism,* 20, 700.

151 *Shays's Rebellion.* It was in reference to Shays's Rebellion that he coined his famous statement that "The tree of liberty must be re-

freshed from time to time with the blood of patriots and tyrants. It is its natural manure." And what he enjoyed in America from his vantage in Paris, he either did not observe, or did not wish to see in France, the Revolution's Terror. On the eve of the Terror, he reported to Secretary of State John Jay that "The great crisis now being over, I shall not have a matter interesting enough to trouble you with as often as I have lately." Then, on July 11, 1789, he told Tom Paine that "the French Revolution was effectively over." Moreover, when he became aware of it, he condoned the Terror. "Rather than see the Revolution fail," he wrote, "I would have seen half the earth desolated." He was obviously embarrassed by this and other statements of support for the bloody events, because when later, in 1821, he was preparing his autobiography, he went back and changed the wording of some of his dispatches, as Joseph Ellis points out in *American Sphinx,* 108.

152 *What is to be done? The Correspondence of James K. Polk* has been printed (to date) in nine volumes, of which the first four were edited by Herbert Weaver and the last five by Wayne Cutler. Volumes 1–7 were published in Nashville by Vanderbilt University Press from 1969 to 1989. Volumes 8 and 9 were published in Knoxville by the University of Tennessee Press in 1993 and 1996. Citations will be given only by volume and page numbers. This citation is *Correspondence,* vol. 1, 554–55.

152 *that of the United States.* Madison famously wavered in his position. Having written in *Federalist 44* that "No axiom is more clearly established in law, or in reason, that wherever the end is required, the means are authorized", i.e., agreeing with Hamilton, he reversed his position to support Jefferson and urged President Washington to veto Hamilton's program. Soon he would become an even more determined foe of Hamilton than Jefferson.

153 *arteries of communication.* Charles Sellers, *The Market Revolution, Jacksonian America, 1815–1846* (New York: Oxford University Press, 1991), esp. chap. 1. Also see Larkin, *Reshaping of Everyday Life,* and

George Tucker, *Progress of the United States* (New York: Press of Hunt's Merchants' Magazine, 1843).

154 *repeal a treaty*. Negotiated between the Cherokee nation on the one hand and North Carolina and Virginia on the other in July 1777 (Francis Paul Prucha, *American Indian Treaties* [Berkeley: University of California Press, 1997], 35–36).

154 *land was literally dirt-cheap*. Charles Grief Sellers, Jr., "Colonel Ezekiel Polk: Pioneer and Patriarch," *William and Mary Quarterly*, 3rd ser., 10 (1953): 87.

154 *ultimately, vast riches*. Thomas Perkins Abernethy, *From Frontier to Plantation in Tennessee* (Chapel Hill: University of North Carolina Press, 1932), 36–37.

154 *Blount himself*. Robert V. Remini, *Andrew Jackson and the Course of American Empire, 1767–1821* (New York: Harper & Row, 1977), 51.

155 *the locus was shifted to Middle Tennessee*. Lloyd DeWitt Bockstruck, *Revolutionary War Bounty Land Grants Awarded by State Governments* (Baltimore: Genealogical Publishing Co., 1996), v, xviii.

155 *lands for his children*. So wrote J. B. Alexander *(History of Mecklenburg Country, 395)*.

155 *worth reading in part*. Leters [sic] Patent issued to Thomas Polk, State of North Carolina, no. 2383.

156 *by the score*. Advance surveying gave such an advantage to the speculator and caused so much resentment among the Indians that it was banned in the March 30, 1802, Trade and Intercourse Act.

156 *relatively great wealth*. A letter from his father-in-law, Phil. Hawkins, on March 12, 1821, says that he sold about $50,000 worth of warrants and "entrys" in the area around Nashville in that year. Letter in the possession of the heirs of Mrs. J. A. Moore of Fayetteville, North Carolina. The buildup of the Polk estate is described in *Impartial Review and Cumberland Repository*, Nashville, November 22, 1806.

156 *price of nine Cents*. Abstract: Charlotte, N.C., Contract of Sale,

1796–97, William Polk Papers, North Carolina State Archives, Raleigh.

157 *rich Tennessee land.* When he died in 1824, according to Charles Grier Sellers, Jr. ("Colonel Ezekiel," 97), he left an estate composed of thousands of acres of land, twenty-four slaves, nine horses, 123 hogs, thirty-six cattle, twenty-two sheep, and a library of seventy books.

158 *sadly not recorded.* William Harrison Polk, *Polk Family,* 516ff.

159 *after the Revolution.* Bradford Perkins, *The Cambridge History of American Foreign Relations,* vol. 1, *The Creation of a Republican Empire, 1776–1865* (Cambridge: Cambridge University Press, 1993), 81ff.

160 *with a tiny navy.* Perkins, *Cambridge History of American Foreign Relations,* vol. 1, 137.

160 *Billy Philips.* Marquis James, *The Life of Andrew Jackson* (Indianapolis: Bobbs-Merrill Co., 1938), 143.

160 *Will became a leader of the "Peace Party."* Sarah McCulloh Lemmon, "Dissent in North Carolina during the War of 1812," *North Carolina Historical Review* 49 (1972): 103ff.

160 *he turned it down.* Sarah McCulloh Lemmon, *Frustrated Patriots: North Carolina and the War of 1812* (Chapel Hill: University of North Carolina Press, 1973), 28.

161 *in any capacity.* George Washington Polk Papers, Southern Historical Collection, University of North Carolina, Chapel Hill.

161 *into the political wilderness.* Letter to General John Steele on November 28, 1800, in *Papers of John Steele,* vol. 1, 192.

162 *to eat elsewhere.* News and Observer, April 4, 1929.

162 *As James wrote to Will.* November 2, 1832; reprinted in Paul H. Bergeron, "My Brother's Keeper: William H[awkins] Polk Goes to School," *North Carolina Historical Review* 44 (1967): 190–92.

162 *he would study hard.* William to James, letter of December 26, 1832; reprinted in Bergeron, "My Brother's Keeper," 197.

162 *an ultimatum.* Bergeron, "My Brother's Keeper," 202–4.

163 *inevitably destroy you.* Apparently, that warning, like many young students receive from worried parents or guardians, worked, since young William subsequently graduated from the University of Tennessee, studied law, was admitted to the bar, served as a major during the Mexican War and represented the United States in negotiating a treaty with one of the European powers. On the eve of the Civil War, he ran for governor of Tennessee on a pro-Union ticket and then joined the Union army.

163 *school commissioners.* Polk Family of North Carolina, Manuscript Division, Library of Congress.

163 *cant trust him an inch.* Letters to Davison McMillen; from James R. White; to Pryon Lea, et al., in *Correspondence,* vol. 1, 229ff.

163 *At the "liberal" extreme.* Reprinted in Francis Paul Prucha (ed.), *Documents of United States Indian Policy* (Lincoln: University of Nebraska Press, 1975), 22. Also see Bernard Sheehan, *Seeds of Extinction: Jeffersonian Philanthropy and the American Indian* (New York: Norton, 1973), part 2.

164 *Sac and Fox Indians.* In return for the cession of most of the tribal lands, the chiefs received presents valued at $2,234.50. See William T. Hagan, *The Sac and Fox Indians* (Norman: University of Oklahoma Press, 1958), 24.

164 *President Monroe.* Reprinted in Prucha, *Documents,* 39–40.

165 *the borders of states.* The Cherokee in North Carolina, Tennessee, Georgia and Alabama; the Creek in Georgia and Alabama; the Chickasaw and the Choctaw in Alabama and Mississippi.

165 *Cherokee Nation v. Georgia.* United States Supreme Court, 1931, 5 Peters 1; text reprinted in Prucha, *Documents,* 58–60.

166 *Worcester v. Georgia.* United States Supreme Court, 6 Peters 534–36, 558–63; text reprinted in Prucha, op. cit., 60–62.

166 *Jackson was said.* Horace Greeley, *The American Conflict: A History of the Great Rebellion in the United States of America, 1860–'64* (Hartford: O. D. Case & Co., 1866), vol. 1, 106.

166 *coercive and often barbaric.* Robert V. Remini, *The Legacy of Andrew Jackson: Essays on Democracy, Indian Removal and Slavery* (Baton Rouge: Louisiana State University Press, 1988), 45, 80.

166 *Indian Removal Act. U.S. Statutes at Large,* 4:411–12; cited in Prucha, *Documents,* 52–53.

166 *Genl.* Because Will Polk had been offered appointment as a general, he was usually given the title.

166 *destroyed the serpent. Correspondence,* vol. 1, 325–26, 330–31. The treaty was not ratified, so another had to be negotiated in October 1832.

166 *the Trail of Tears.* On which tragic story, see the eyewitness account of Alexis de Tocqueville, *Democracy in America* (New York: Knopf, 1966), vol. 1, 336ff.; Ronald N. Satz, *American Indian Policy in the Jacksonian Era* (Lincoln: University of Nebraska Press, 1975), particularly 64ff.; John Ehle, *Trail of Tears: The Rise and Fall of the Cherokee Nation* (New York: Doubleday, 1988); Arrell M. Gibson, *The Chickasaws* (Norman: University of Oklahoma Press, 1971), 179ff.; Michael Paul Rogin, *Fathers & Children: Andrew Jackson and the Subjugation of the American Indian* (New York: Vintage, 1976), and Grant Forman, *Indian Removal* (Norman: University of Oklahoma Press, 1972).

166 *cheated on their contracts.* As Daniel Graham, who was Tennessee secretary of state and controller and at one time touted as a candidate for governor, wrote to James from Alabama on March 1, 1831 (*Correspondence,* vol. 3, 521–22).

167 *the learned of Europe.* Tocqueville, *Democracy in America,* vol. 1, 339.

167 *extremely desireable. Correspondence,* vol. 4, 526.

168 *nearly killed together.* President-elect Andrew Jackson greeting Will in Washington said, "My dear old friend, how glad I am to see you! I fancy I can see your red face during [the British cavalry officer] Tarleton's raid upon the Waxhaw settlement, when you and I were running down the lane, closely pursued by the British cavalry!"

This was told by Major Donelson, private secretary to the president-elect, to Jackson's godson and ward, Colonel E. G. W. Butler, who is quoted in William M. Polk, *Leonidas Polk* (Longman, Green, 1894), vol. 1, 89.

168 *White House wedding.* Letter from Andrew Jackson to Will Polk of April 11, 1832, in which he describes the wedding and sends Andrew Jackson Polk a silver medal "bearing my likeness" (George Washington Polk Papers, Southern Historical Collection, University of North Carolina).

168 *fairly and honestly.* Will Polk to Willie P. Mangum, Raleigh, January 26, 1824; reprinted in Henry Thomas Shanks (ed.), *The Papers of Willie Person Mangum* (Raleigh: State Department of Archives and History, 1950), vol. 1, 111.

169 *prepare his report.* August 23, 1834, in *Correspondence,* vol. 2, 455–58.

169 *examine their books.* Congressman John Y. Mason to James, May 10, 1834, in *Correspondence,* vol. 2, 409.

169 *instrument of the federal government. MuCulloch v. Maryland.* MuCulloch was the cashier of the Baltimore branch of the Bank and had been jailed for refusing to pay Maryland taxes; although he took his stand on a matter of principle or at least bank policy, he was known to have engaged in various corrupt transactions, including improperly lending money to himself and his business associates. See Daniel Feller, *The Jacksonian Promise: America, 1815–1840* (Baltimore: Johns Hopkins University Press, 1995), 49.

169 *Alexander Hamilton.* "Report on the National Bank," in Henry Cabot Lodge (ed.), *The Works of Alexander Hamilton* (New York: G. P. Putnam's Sons, 1885–86), vol. 3, 424.

170 *James was told.* Letter from Terry H. Cahal, May 4, 1832, in *Correspondence,* vol. 1, 471.

170 *interested in investing.* Will Polk to Willie P. Mangum, Raleigh, February 1, 1832, in Shanks, *Papers of Willie Person Mangum,* vol. 1, 467.

170 *below par.* At that time, Will had not been a member of the board of

his bank for many years and would die two years later. As his son Leonidas wrote of his death, after so adventuresome and long a life, "He seems to have expired like a candle."

170 *no chance.* December 23, 1833, *Correspondence,* vol. 2, 196–97.

170 *Democratic Party.* Letter from Stephen Adams of Mississippi, March 24, 1834, in *Correspondence,* vol. 2, 374.

170 *attacking newspapers.* The *Washington National Intelligencer* and the *National Banner* in Nashville. James to Francis P. Blair, August 8, 1833. The practice was apparently widespread. See the letter from Edward Kavanagh of Maine dated September 10, 1834, who mentions that "two presses which had heretofore supported me were bought up by Partisans of the Bank (one of them 3 weeks before the election)" *(Correspondence,* vol. 2, 97–98).

170 *mamoth of corruption. Correspondence,* vol. 2, 106.

170 *no compromise.* Arthur Schlesinger, Jr., *The Age of Jackson* (Boston: Little, Brown, 1945), 74ff.

170 *letter to the president.* August 23, 1834, *Correspondence,* vol. 2, 455ff.

171 *speech in June 1840.* Letter from Levin H. Coe to James K. Polk, in *Correspondence,* vol. 5, 486–87.

172 *James Walker. Correspondence,* vol. 4, 213.

173 *close to treason.* Remini, *Andrew Jackson,* 47ff; 443, n. 63, reviews the evidence for what appears to have been near treason. See also James, *Life of Andrew Jackson,* 121–23.

173 *colorfully did.* When his superior officer, General Winfield Scott, was informed of Jackson's disobeying orders, he said Jackson was mutinous and deserved "a reprimand . . . of the President." At that, Jackson blew up and wrote Scott a letter in which he referred, with his always colorful and usually confused hyperbole, to *"the intermeddling pimps and spies of the War Department . . ."* Quoted in James, *Life of Andrew Jackson,* 279.

174 *nullies.* Letter to James of May 12, 1835, in *Correspondence,* vol. 3, 191.

174 *As he wrote to James. Correspondence,* vol. 3, 184.

174 *The spoils system.* Letter to Will Polk in June 1829; quoted in William M. Polk, op. cit., vol. 1, 96.

175 *As James wrote. Correspondence,* vol. 1, 331.

175 *Andrew Derryberry.* It turned out that the only problem was that his name had been misspelled and James was able to help *(Correspondence,* vol. 1, 420–21).

176 *like a military command.* See, for example, his letters of August 3, 1835, and September 15, 1835: "You must be in Nashville some days before the assembly meets, every arrangement ought to be made, and as soon as the House is formed the resolutions ought to be offered, or the opposition will forestall you by a set prepared for their own pallate. Be prompt and do not permit yourself to be out generalled" *(Correspondence,* vol. 3, 251–54, 299–300).

176 *rather than in a preemptive style.* For example, in a letter to Felix Robertson et al., September 26, 1835 *(Correspondence,* vol. 3, 309–14).

176 *Archibald Yell. Correspondence,* vol. 1, 161.

176 *a quality he showed. Correspondence,* vol. 5, 309–14.

176 *his electoral district. Correspondence,* vol. 8, 545.

177 *one of Will's neighbors.* Letter from John Haywood to John Steele, in *Papers of John Steele,* vol. 2, 533.

177 *most European peasants.* Larkin, *Reshaping of Everyday Life,* 178.

178 *a pass.* A typical example of such passes was one written in 1794 by Colonel William for "Joe a Negro Man the property of Mr. John G. Blount." Reprinted in Alice Barnwell Keith (ed.), *The John Gray Blount Papers* (Raleigh: State Department of Archives and History, 1959), vol. 2, 349.

178 *"other moveables."* Property to be distributed on the death of the owner—as his were distributed *(Notes on the State of Virginia,* 137).

179 *State v. Mann.* The facts were these: Mann had hired for one year the young female slave belonging to another owner, and when she tried to evade his "chastisement" for what the court called "some small offense" by running from him, he shot her. The court decided that the issue was not the rights (if any) of the slave or the crime (if any)

of the defendant but the right of compensation (if any) of the owner.

179 *dependent upon slavery.* It was estimated that each acre of cropland required at least one slave (Robert Lacour-Gayet, *Everyday Life in the United States Before the Civil War, 1830–1860* [New York: Frederick Ungar, 1969], 173). On sugar lands, it was higher still (J. Carlyle Sitterson, *Sugar Country: The Cane Sugar Industry in the South, 1753–1950* [n.p.: University of Kentucky Press, 1953], 60).

180 *inherently inferior and always alien. Notes on the State of Virginia,* 138–49. "Never yet," Jefferson wrote, "could I find that a black had uttered a thought above the level of plain narration; never seen even an elementary trait of painting or sculpture" (140).

180 *American Colonization Society.* William M. Polk, *Leonidas Polk,* vol. 1, 93–95.

181 *and New York.* Sellers, *Market Revolution,* 126–27.

181 *he was nearly right.* Quoted in Feller, *Jacksonian Promise,* 62–63.

181 *have to assume that James read them. Correspondence,* vol. 2, 144, 187, 190, 204, 235, 574, 580.

183 *some owners refused to hire them.* A contemporary, Thomas Harding, the grandfather of Molly Harding Polk, "would never have an overseer because they were so cruel. He had one of his sons to spend two years on the plantation taking turns. He never allowed anyone to whip his negroes." So wrote Molly in "Jottings," 10.

183 *Silas M. Caldwell. Correspondence,* vol. 3, 474.

183 *what to do with him. Correspondence,* vol. 5, 715.

184 *to gow back to tennessee. Correspondence,* vol. 5, 746–47.

184 *than being whipped.* A graphic account of this experience is given by Solomon Northup in Sue Eakin and Joseph Logsdon (eds.), *Twelve Years a Slave* (Baton Rouge: Louisiana State University Press, 1968).

184 *385,000 owners of slaves.* Kenneth M. Stampp, *The Peculiar Institution, Slavery in the Ante-Bellum South* (New York: Vintage Books, 1989), 30–31. Stampp points out that 88 percent of slave owners held

fewer than twenty slaves and that fewer than three thousand families owned as many as one hundred slaves, while 1.5 million whites owned no slaves.

CHAPTER 6

186 *one of America's greatest presidents.* Arthur M. Schlesinger, Jr., "Rating the Presidents: Washington to Clinton," *Political Science Quarterly: The Journal of Public and International Affairs,* Summer 1997, 179ff.

188 *larger than 2,500.* A convenient summary of this information is in Larkin, *Reshaping of Everyday Life,* 1–6.

189 *In a letter. Correspondence,* vol. 6, 143.

189 *assemblies of the people. Correspondence,* vol. 6, 332.

190 *"Lean Jimmy."* As West H. Humphreys warned James in a letter of May 17, 1840, *Correspondence,* vol. 5, 456.

191 *more on their campaigns.* As John Kane reports from Philadelphia in *Correspondence,* vol. 8, 219–21.

191 *Cave Johnson. Correspondence,* vol. 6, 170. He wrote again in the same vein on February 17, 1843 *(Correspondence,* vol. 6, 213–14).

191 *he failed financially everywhere. Correspondence,* vol. 6, 340–41.

191 *Needing that amount. Correspondence,* vol. 6, 353.

192 *a perfect confidence. Correspondence,* vol. 5, 593.

192 *and we are theirs. Correspondence,* vol. 5, 723.

193 *Paul Bergeron. The Presidency of James K. Polk* (Lawrence: University of Kansas Press, 1987), 15.

193 *lawyers.* Charles Sellers writes *(Market Revolution,* 43) that "Less than a third of the first Congress, lawyers moved into a majority after about 1813."

193 *As he wrote.* To his cousin John Bills on September 14, 1843, in *Correspondence,* vol. 6, 333.

193 *Martin Van Buren. Correspondence,* vol. 6, 332.

194 *believed in "Jacksonianism."* Milo Milton Quaife (ed.), *The Diary of*

James K. Polk During His Presidency, 1845 to 1849 [Chicago: A. C. McClurg & Co., 1910], vol. 1, 426). Further citations to President Polk's diary will be given as *Diary* with the volume and page numbers.

194 *not come and endorse him.* Letter to Andrew Jackson, February 7, 1839, in *Correspondence,* vol. 5, 52–54.

195 *fewer than five hundred people.* Sellers, *Market Revolution,* 37.

195 *private secretary.* James's sister's son J. Knox Walker, who subsequently represented Tennessee in the House of Representatives.

195 *vice presidential nomination.* See his letter to his principal adviser, Cave Johnson, on May 4, 1844, in *Correspondence,* vol. 7, 118–20.

195 *that post in 1840.* Cave Johnson to James K. Polk, February 24, 1840, and Andrew Jackson Donelson to James K. Polk on March 4, 1840, in *Correspondence,* vol. 5, 394–96 and 400–1.

196 *he had bowed out.* Letter to Felix Grundy of May 27, 1840, in *Correspondence,* vol. 5, 470–71.

196 *in no event be voluntarily withdrawn.* As he clearly set out in a letter to Cave Johnson on May 4, 1844 (*Correspondence,* vol. 7, 118–20).

196 *John J. Goodman. Correspondence,* vol. 6, 267.

196 *his visit to Andrew Jackson. Correspondence,* vol. 7, 134–35.

197 *Michigan's Lewis Cass.* Cass had been governor of the Michigan Territory from 1813 to 1831, then secretary of war and minister to France. He was to be elected senator from the new state of Michigan in 1845 on the Democratic ticket.

197 *like a campaign manager. Correspondence,* vol. 7, 145–47.

197 *Mr. Morse's Electric magnetic telegraph.* As B. B. French wrote James on May 29, "¹/₂ past 6 o'clock p.m. We have now in operation between the R. Road depot in Baltimore & the Capitol, Mr. Morse's Electric magnetic telegraph which gives any item of news between this & Baltimore in less than a second. About 10 minutes since it announced Mr. [Silas] Wright as the nominee for V.P. Mr. Wright immediately returned an answer by telegraph that he would not ac-

cept." A year before, Congress had appropriated $30,000 to establish this experimental line.

197 *may take that turn yet. Correspondence,* vol. 7, 154–57.

197 *almost breathlessly. Correspondence,* vol. 7, 158–59.

198 *not to seek a second term. Correspondence,* vol. 7, 241.

199 *do so with propriety. Correspondence,* vol. 7, 265.

199 *entire course of the campaign.* His one, but very important, letter was to John W. Goode et al., written on September 25, 1844 *(Correspondence,* vol. 8, 122–24).

199 *J. George Harris.* A Democrat, Harris had worked for a number of New England newspapers before becoming editor of the *Nashville Union.*

199 *wrote to him. Correspondence,* vol. 8, 118–19.

200 *"nativism." Correspondence,* vol. 7, 215.

200 *a conciliatory posture.* Letter of June 21, 1844, in *Correspondence,* vol. 7, 270–71.

200 *Jackson wrote to James. Correspondence,* vol. 7, 299–300.

201 *after the party convention. Correspondence,* vol. 7, 168–69.

201 *James adopted the gist. Correspondence,* vol. 7, 267.

201 *Polk doctrine. Correspondence,* vol. 6, 156–57.

202 *hurt James deeply. Correspondence,* vol. 8, 12, 14, 53.

202 *tyrannical to his slaves. Correspondence,* vol. 8, 334–35.

202 *a grave offense. Correspondence,* vol. 8, 97.

202 *Adam Huntsman. Correspondence,* vol. 8, 164.

203 *Cave Johnson. Correspondence,* vol. 8, 455, 482.

203 *in which other citizens do. Correspondence,* vol. 9, 66.

203 *a skilled artisan. Correspondence,* vol. 6, 59.

204 *lost heavily betting on him. Correspondence,* vol. 8, 370.

204 *Smithsonian Institution.* Toward which the Englishman James Smithson had recently given $600,000 in gold coins.

204 *discovering relatives. Correspondence,* vol. 8, 371–72.

205 *The inaugural address.* James engaged Amon Kendall, a former mem-

ber of Andrew Jackson's Kitchen Cabinet and postmaster general from 1835 to 1840, to help draft it. James mentions in his diary entry of December 13, 1845, that he usually wrote all of his messages to Congress and had them copied by his private secretary after having had them reviewed by the cabinet.

206 *Texas.* James and others argued that the territory that became Texas had, in fact, been acquired by the Louisiana Purchase but wrongly given up.

206 *John N. Mars.* From Salem, Massachusetts, in *Correspondence,* vol. 9, 274–75.

207 *cabinet.* On April 10, 1845, in *Correspondence,* vol. 8, 455–56.

207 *led the pack. Correspondence,* vol. 9, 56.

208 *presidential or vice presidential ambitions.* Letter to James Buchanan on February 17, 1845, in *Correspondence,* vol. 9, 110–11.

208 *As he wrote.* In a letter to Martin Van Buren on March 1, in *Correspondence,* vol. 9, 157.

209 *he wrote at one point. Diary,* vol. 2, 382.

209 *to warn James. Correspondence,* vol. 9, 201.

212 *a ride on horseback. Diary,* vol. 1, 442.

212 *the tomb of Washington. Diary,* vol. 2, 84.

212 *who at my request accompanied me. Diary,* vol. 2, 87–88.

212 *previous thirteen months. Diary,* vol. 4, 78.

212 *must be faulted.* He recorded in his diary on July 21, 1846, the biting criticism of a senator that he was "poorly employed in the pitiful and little business of appointing clerks & messengers."

213 *makes my duties very great. Diary,* vol. 4, 261.

214 *before he voted. Diary,* vol. 2, 44–45.

214 *James confided in his diary. Diary,* vol. 2, 55.

215 *express my astonishment. Diary,* vol. 2, 49. The tariff bill passed the Senate on July 28, 1846.

216 *John Quincy Adams. Diary,* vol. 1, 129.

216 *the last two hundred years. Diary,* vol. 1, 155.

216 *Texas was believed. Correspondence,* vol. 9, 347.

217 *James Hamilton, Jr. Correspondence,* vol. 9, 129–30.

217 *Jacob L. Martin. Correspondence,* vol. 9, 385–86.

217 *To counter the British moves.* As he wrote to the American agent there, Andrew Jackson Donelson, on May 26, 1845 *(Correspondence,* vol. 9, 408–9).

218 *as he wrote Donelson. Correspondence,* vol. 9, 449–51.

218 *James then moved. Diary,* vol. 1, 386.

219 *through negotiation.* He believed that if he were allotted $2 million by the Congress, he could work out a settlement with Mexico *(Diary,* vol. 1, 307).

220 *As he wrote. Diary,* vol. 1, 401.

220 *from the Mexicans. Diary,* vol. 1, 419–20.

220 *for a higher command.* For his opinions on Taylor, see *Diary,* vol. 2, 119, 140, 181, 249.

221 *strong hint of corruption. Diary,* vol. 3, 79–81.

222 *in my power to do. Diary,* vol. 2, 430–31.

222 *information on these points. Diary,* vol. 2, 139.

223 *by later writers.* See, for example, Glenn W. Price, *Origins of the War with Mexico: The Polk-Stockton Intrique* (Austin: University of Texas Press, 1967), 88–89.

223 *January 5, 1847. Diary,* vol. 2, 308.

224 *Secretary of State Buchanan. Diary,* vol. 1, 495–97.

224 *He deplored. Diary,* vol. 2, 458–59.

225 *Northwest Ordinance.* ". . . neither slavery nor involuntary servitude shall ever exist in any part of said territories, except for crime, whereof the party shall first be duly convicted."

225 *James met with Wilmot. Diary,* vol. 2, 288–90.

225 *For Wilmot's part.* Quoted in Sellers, *Market Revolution,* 426–27.

226 *and great was the fall of it.* Matthew 7:27.

226 *the question of religion. Diary,* vol. 1, 86.

226 *Churches. Diary,* vol. 3, 42, 71, 72.

226 *Mormons. Diary,* vol. 1, 445.

226 *to censure the administration. Diary,* vol. 1, 408–9.

226 *James was furious.* Diary, vol. 2, 189–90.

227 *United States Postal Service.* Diary, vol. 4, 371–72.

227 *In one telling entry.* Diary, vol. 4, 200.

228 *retirement in private life.* Diary, vol. 3, 210.

228 *a somber philosophical note.* Diary, vol. 4, 177.

228 *four years of incessant labour.* Diary, vol. 4, 331–32.

229 *he virtually collapsed.* Diary, vol. 4, 400, 408, 411, 413.

CHAPTER 7

230 *and other Polks did.* "An Old Lady's Jottings," by Mary Harding Polk, manuscript in the possession of the author's family; and George W. Polk, "Some Reflections and Reminiscences," Manuscript #2976 in the Southern Historical Collection, University of North Carolina Library. Where they are quoted, the source will be these manuscripts.

234 *these ugly brutes.* Charles Dickens, *American Notes* (London: Chapman & Hall, 1898), 102. "They are never attended upon, or fed, or driven, or caught," he wrote, "but are thrown upon their own resources in early life, and become preternaturally knowing in consequence."

235 *retired from the table.* Her trunks also revealed the latest Paris scandal: instead of dainty ruffled pantaloons then the height of fashion in Tennessee, she showed off knee-length drawers (from Frances Ann Polk Dillon as told to her daughters, Frances and Eliza Dillon).

236 *"Reminiscences of a Pioneer in Louisiana."* Reprinted in Herbert Bemerton Battle (ed.), *The Battle Book* (Montgomery, Ala.: Paradon Press, 1930), 51ff.

236 *As one social historian has remarked.* Larkin, *Reshaping of Everyday Life,* 92.

237 *James K. Polk . . . was informed.* By G. W. Campbell, *Correspondence,* vol. 2, 153–55.

238 *the European Colleges.* So wrote John D. Hawkins in an untitled pamphlet dated September 28, 1829 (Raleigh: Lawrence & Lemay), 8.

239 *Governor Charles Polk of Delaware.* Quoted in William Harrison Polk, *Polk Family,* 461ff.

239 *as Charles Dickens noted. American Notes,* 162.

240 *in her care to read.* See, for example, Sir Charles Lyell, *A Second Visit to the United States of North America* (London: John Murray, 1849), vol. 1, 275.

240 *or from the North.* Lyell, *Second Visit,* vol. 1, 297.

241 *The mails were slow.* Stamps came into use after 1847 when domestic postage was about what an artisan earned in an hour or so, and international postage was what he earned in a day. See Lacour-Gayet, *Everyday Life,* 59–60.

242 *in her diary.* Reprinted in Battle, *Battle Book,* 52.

243 *not worth saving.* Quoted in William M. Polk, *Leonidas Polk,* vol. 1, 140–41.

243 *Stephen and Austin.* Austin was listed as "the colured man"—that is, a mulatto—whereas the others were specified as "negro."

244 *great estates.* "The Polk family alone enriched the neighborhood of Columbia with no less than four great houses" (Gifford A. Cochran, *Grandeur in Tennessee: Classical Revival Architecture in a Pioneer State* [New York: J. J. Augustin Publishers, 1946], 13).

244 *John Ruskin, who wrote.* In *The Seven Lamps of Architecture* (New York: Wiley, 1865).

245 *throwing of the dice.* The legend is more or less confirmed by Mary Polk Branch, *A Genealogical Record and Annals of My Past* (Wasukesha, Wisc., 1905), 13.

245 *on the plantation.* Rattle & Snap has often been the subject of architectural histories. See, for example, J. Frazer Smith, *White Pillars* (New York: Bramhall House, 1961). It is illustrated in Reid Smith, *Majestic Middle Tennessee* (Prattville, Ala.: Paddle Wheel Publications, 1975), and Henry Wienck, *Great American Homes* (Birmingham, Ala.: Oxmoor, 1988).

246 *the great house of Belle Meade.* The original house burned and was rebuilt in 1853.

247 *guided by a vision.* But, Leonidas lamented, ''There are some things that we cannot make, such as Bibles, Prayer Books, Baptismal fonts, organs and such trimmings.'' For these things, he turned to his family and they generously contributed.

247 *Aunt Patsy.* Aunt Patsy, who as recounted above had lost her leg in a savage operation without anesthetics, was Molly's favorite companion as a young girl. Molly later recalled her cork leg ''played a regular tune while her cane and myself helped her along . . . She was a splendid woman and won the hearts of young and all who came in contact with her.''

248 *but I have it.* It is now owned by James H. Polk III.

249 *George Washington Polk's.* This George was the son of Lucius and the namesake and nephew of the George who was the son of Will.

251 *Andrew Jackson gave away the bride.* Marie Smith and Louise Durbin, *White House Brides* (Washington, D.C.: Acropolis, 1996).

252 *Charles Dickens. American Notes,* 133–34.

254 *her line earned 300 percent on the original investment.* William M. Polk, *Leonidas Polk,* vol. 1, 131.

255 *local railway spurs.* William M. Polk, *Leonidas Polk,* vol. 1, 132.

257 *produced by nonslaveholders.* It is true that the British and others produced cotton in Egypt and India without using people legally classified as slaves, but the peasants could hardly be differentiated from slaves socially, economically or culturally. While it is certainly no justification for the abominable treatment of black slaves by American whites, it is worth noting that it was by no means unique. In India, for thousands of years and for generations after the Americans had emancipated their slaves, the millions of ''untouchables'' were subjected to treatment that was at least as degrading, dangerous and mutilating. Untouchables were not allowed to leave the village in which they lived, and there they were paid a bare life-sustaining wage, were unable to own any property and were forced to perform a variety of menial tasks linked to waste, excrement and

death. "Contact with them thus polluted the high castes, who had to avoid touching them, but also avoid going near them, or even sometimes seeing them: some castes were thus 'unseeables' so to speak. In some areas of India, their very shadow was polluting . . . they could not cover their head, or chest, nor the legs below the knees. Gold and silver were also prohibited to them, as well as shoes and parasols. They constantly had to maintain a respectful attitude in the presence of the high castes, an attitude which verged on humiliation. They had to speak to a superior with eyes lowered and holding their hand to the mouth. They had to cross their arms over their chest—also a sign of humility—and could not raise their voice . . . An untouchable could not sit down in the presence of a member of a high caste, or could sit only in an inferior position. When an untouchable encountered a high-caste man in the street, he had to go down into the ditch, in order to leave the street clear. He had to carry out all the tasks which he was ordered to do and allow himself to be beaten if a high-caste man had decided so." Robert Deliège, *The World of the 'Untouchables'* (Delhi: Oxford University Press, 1997), 147–8.

257 *"best case" plantation*. J. D. B. De Bow, *Resources of the Southern and Western States,* vol. 1 (New Orleans: De Bow's Review, 1853), 151ff.; quoted in Emory Q. Hawk, *Economic History of the South* (New York: Prentice-Hall, 1934), 256–58.

258 *were actually returned*. With often tragic results. Many of the immigrants died of tropical diseases, and those who lived, and set up the Republic of Liberia in 1847, themselves enslaved the interior tribesmen. Their slavery was not stopped, of course, by the Civil War but lasted until 1930.

259 *of the plantation houses*. Cochran, *Grandeur in Tennessee,* 10.

260 *wrote Sir Charles Lyell. Second Visit,* vol. 1, 293–94.

261 *knell of the Union*. Quoted in Feller, *Jacksonian Promise,* 62–63.

261 *letter to Lucius J. Polk*. He wanted Lucius to give him three hunting

dogs. So in his letter, dated Columbia, June 13, 1839, he wrote, "Disappoint me not. I am ever thine[.] Truly, Sam Houston." The letter was signed with a flamboyant flourish.

262 *participated in many.* As relentless in dueling as in warfare, on May 30, 1806, Andrew Jackson challenged Charles Dickinson; Dickinson hit Jackson in the shoulder. "Then the relentless Jackson slowly aimed at his opponent, who was standing with folded arms, and pulled the trigger. The hammer stopped at half-cock, but he coolly recocked the pistol and killed his enemy."

262 *letter to James K. Polk. Correspondence,* vol. 4, 627–31.

263 *James Hilliard Polk.* Letter to Dr. William Mecklenburg Polk, dated Fort Worth, Texas, August 23, 1913.

CHAPTER 8

264 *wrote James Monroe Polk.* "Memories of the Lost Cause, Stories and Adventures of a Confederate Soldier in General R. E. Lee's Army 1861–1865," manuscript in the possession of the Polk family.

264–65 *going over our heads.* The .69-caliber explosive minié ball was fired from muzzle-loading muskets which were standard among Federal troops.

266 *obsessed with the Civil War.* James M. McPherson, "The War That Never Goes Away," in James M. McPherson (ed.), *Drawn with the Sword: Reflections on the American Civil War* (New York: Oxford University Press, 1996), 55ff.

266 *debated the causes.* See, for example, Gabor S. Boritt (ed.), *Why the Civil War Came* (New York: Oxford University Press, 1996).

266 *the manufacturing capacity.* James M. McPherson, *Battle Cry,* 91.

267 *mainly just depots.* Jack Coggins, *Arms and Equipment of the Civil War* (Wilmington, N.C.: Broadfoot, 1990), 65. In a letter to General Leonidas Polk on September 2, 1861, President Jefferson Davis remarked that "The great difficulty is to supply arms, we can get more men for the war than we can arm and equip."

267 *were unusable.* Stanley F. Horn, *Tennessee's War, 1861–1865* (Nashville: Tennessee Civil War Centennial Commission, 1965), 19.

267 *to manufacture cartridges.* Clement A. Evans (ed.), *Confederate Military History,* extended ed. (Wilmington, N.C., Broadfoot, 1987), vol. 2, 374–76. After VMI was burned in 1864, the workshop was transferred to Richmond, where it functioned until 1865 when the Confederacy surrendered.

267 *one cannon foundry.* Horn, *Tennessee's War,* 26.

267 *to manufacture it.* Coggins, *Arms,* 35.

267 *multinational arms producer.* Samuel Colt wrote to Major William Hawkins Polk, the brother of President James K. Polk, who was serving in Mexico with the United States Army Dragoons, on October 19, 1847, saying, "I at last have finished yor pistols which were ordered by you a long time since . . . I should like to here from you my dear fellow after you have practiced a little with them & I hope you will be enduced to use your valuable influence to get a reception of them to arm your whole regiment." After mentioning that each pistol cost about $35, he asked William for a publishable endorsement. For the Crimean War, Colt set up a factory in London to produce pistols for the British army.

268 *to the flames.* McPherson, *Battle Cry,* 57.

268 *Kentucky and Missouri.* There Trusten Polk, who had been elected governor in 1856, and subsequently became a senator, resigned as a member of the U.S. Senate in 1861 to join the Confederate army, in which he served, until captured in 1864, as judge advocate general.

268 *positions of command.* In the Battle of Perryville, General Leonidas Polk was in command of the southern forces and faced Captain (later Colonel) Burr Harrison Polk of the 6th Kentucky Infantry and other Polks (RG94 National Archives, Washington, D.C.).

268 *her Confederate relatives.* Jimmie Lou Sparkman Claxton, *Eighty-Eight Years with Sarah Polk* (New York: Vantage, 1972), 153.

269 *warfare in America.* James M. McPherson, *Battle Cry,* 9.

269 *to avert the war.* This and other documents are preserved in collections in the Library of Congress, the Southern Historical Collection in the University of North Carolina and the Leonidas Polk Collection of the University of the South at Sewanee and have been reproduced in various publications, including William M. Polk, *Leonidas Polk, Bishop and General* (New York: Longsmans, Green, 1894), and Joseph H. Parks, *General Leonidas Polk, C.S.A., the Fighting Bishop* (Baton Rouge: Louisiana State University Press, 1990).

270 *the month before.* Lincoln received only 40 percent of the popular vote, but his 180 electoral votes won the presidency by 28.

270 *Andrew Jackson Polk.* As remembered by Captain W. T. Hardison in the *Confederate Veteran* 27, no. 11 (November 1919): 430.

272 *William Harrison Polk.* Then eighteen-year-old William Harrison Polk wrote that "like all excited, patriotic youths, [he had] enlisted in the [United States] army, making three attempts before he succeeded" (*Polk Family,* 617). He remembered Grant for having "drilled the Regiment diligently, punishing all infractions."

272 *Joseph E. Johnston.* It is an amusing sidelight on Scots-Irish history that the Johnston clansmen were the most bitter enemies of ancestors of the Polks in Scotland.

273 *the battle is not always to the strong.* Horn, *Tennessee's War,* 22–23. Leonidas viewed the military appointment as a temporary interlude before returning to the church and wrote to Jefferson Davis to resign on November 6, 1861; for privacy, he sent the letter by his son and aide, Alexander Hamilton Polk. Davis refused to accept his resignation. He again tried to resign on January 30, 1862.

275 *forces in Missouri.* See Bruce Catton, *Grant Moves South* (Boston: Little, Brown, 1960), 70ff.

276 *Grant later wrote. Personal Memoirs* (reprint, New York: Library of America, 1990), 185.

277 *many years later.* Letter to Dr. William M. Polk of May 7, 1913.

278 *wrote to his wife.* Parks, *General Leonidas Polk,* 195.

279 *Tennessee Cavalry.* Federal regiments tended to be designated by numbers, while Confederates were known by the names of their commanders; so this unit is also, confusingly, listed as the 7th, the 6th and the 1st.

279 *to paralyze them.* Horn, *Tennessee's War,* 111.

280 *had temporarily stopped.* Mauriel Phillips Joslyn, *Immortal Captives: The Story of Six Hundred Confederate Officers and the United States Prisoner of War Policy* (Shippensburg, Pa.: White Mane Publishing Co., 1996), 15.

282 *the so-called Lieber Code.* It set the legal context of the treatment of Governor Trusten Polk, Captain James H. and other Confederate prisoners. Born in Berlin in 1800, Franz (or as he Americanized it, Francis) Lieber enlisted in the Prussian army and fought at Waterloo. Twice seriously wounded, he learned firsthand the perils of warfare. Much later, in 1861, while a professor at Columbia University, he met Abraham Lincoln and became his adviser on legal aspects of the war. His code called for humanitarian treatment of prisoners, their exchange (a personal matter for Lieber who had sons in both armies) and protection of the lives and property of civilians.

282 *General William T. Sherman.* Quoted in Horn, *Tennessee's War,* 109.

282 *A war correspondent.* Reprinted in Horn, *Tennessee's War,* 123.

282 *later wrote.* In what she called "An Old Lady's Jottings," a manuscript of which was found in a trunk long after her death and of which I have a copy.

284 *and at Christmas.* I have cuff links made from two of the coins.

284 *the bottom of a well.* George W. Polk, "Some Reflections and Reminiscences," Manuscript #2976 in the Southern Historical Collection, University of North Carolina Library, 25.

284 *men of color.* Noah Andre Trudeau, *Like Men of War: Black Troops in the Civil War, 1862–1865* (Boston: Little, Brown, 1998), 9–10.

284 *hide their slaves.* In his remarkable account of his three-month trip through the South during the war, Lieutenant Colonel James Ar-

thur Lyon Fremantle of the Coldstream Guards, in Walter Lord (ed.), *The Fremantle Diary* (London: Andre Deutsch, 1956), 63, 65, 68, 81, etc.

285 *deem most beneficial. The War of the Rebellion: A Compilation of Official Records of the Union and Confederates Armies;* quoted in Trudeau, *Like Men of War,* 12.

285 *Emancipation Proclamation.* "The president promised to consider insurrection ended in any area which had Congressional representation by January 1, 1863, thereby exempting those areas from emancipation." James D. Richardson (ed.), *A Compilation of the Messages and Papers of the Presidents, 1789–1897* (Washington, D.C., 1896–97), vol. 5, 3298, cited by John Cimprich, "Military Governor Johnson and Tennessee Blacks," *Tennessee Historical Quarterly* 39 (1980): 462.

285 *in favor of Union victory.* James M. McPherson, "Who Freed the Slaves?" in James M. McPherson (ed.), *Drawn with the Sword,* 193.

287 *disorderly gatherings.* Trudeau, *Like Men of War,* 8.

287 *white backlash.* Trudeau, *Like Men of War,* 14.

289 *we must make free men of them.* His position was not unique: Robert E. Lee reached a similar conclusion, and even a Georgia brigade ("Thomas' Brigade," the 14th Georgia) urged enlistment of blacks. Although generally not allowed to enlist until near the end of the war, several thousand blacks served in Confederate armies (Charles Kelly Barrow et al. [eds.], *Forgotten Confederates: An Anthology About Black Southerners* [Atlanta: Southern Heritage Press, 1995]).

289 *ef I was a soldier.* Quoted by Ervin L. Jordan, Jr., *Black Confederates and Afro-Yankees in Civil War Virginia* (Charlottesville: University Press of Virginia, 1995), 218.

289 *Will Polk.* Service Record of William Polk, 48th Tennessee Infantry, Record Group 109, National Archives, Washington D.C.

290 *like the Englishman.* Lord, *Fremantle,* 81 and passim.

291 *achieved their independence.* In the presidential elections of that year,

General George B. McClellan ran on a peace program that would have given the Confederacy its independence. As James M. Mc-Pherson has written ("Why Did the Confederacy Lose?" in Mc-Pherson, *Drawn with the Sword,* 133), "If the election had been held in August 1864 instead of November, Lincoln would have lost."

291 *Where Lee attacked.* Alan T. Nolan, *Lee Considered: General Robert E. Lee and Civil War History* (Chapel Hill: University of North Carolina Press, 1991), 106.

291 *McPherson has written.* "Why Did the Confederacy Lose?," 133.

292 *for his own mistakes.* As one of his staff officers, M. R. Tunnard, wrote many years later, on January 23, 1902, to Dr. William Mecklenburg Polk. While acknowledging Bragg's physical courage Tunnard commented that Bragg "would never acknowledge a grave mistake, or even error, but place them on innocent shoulders if he could. For instance—note his conduct when the army was moving from Corinth to Shiloh. General Polk carried out the orders he received as far as it was possible to do, but on account of General Bragg's tardiness in arriving at the point designated, General Polk could not form upon Bragg's line, for Bragg had no line formed . . . Bragg's tardiness caused the miscarriage of plan, and General Beauregard, who was probably told by General Bragg that General Polk was to blame, sent for General Polk and expressed his disappointment. General Polk's reply must have opened his eyes, but there sat Bragg, silent, when he knew that he, himself, was to blame; yet quite willing that the innocent should suffer."

293 *President Davis, saying.* Quoted in Horn, *Tennessee's War,* 218.

293 *arrest and courts-martial.* Horn, *Tennessee's War,* 73–74, 217.

293 *usually rejoined.* For example, the 3rd (Brown's) Tennessee Volunteer Infantry regiment lost roughly 10 percent casualties in the battle at Fort Donelson. They surrendered a few weeks later and were imprisoned; when released on parole, they immediately reorganized with the entire former complement. (Civil War Centennial Commission, *Tennesseans in the Civil War* [Nashville, 1964], 181.)

294 *to the rebel leaders.* Horn, *Tennessee's War,* 124.

295 *Antoinette's famous ride. Memoirs of a Southern Woman "Within the Lines"* (Chicago: Joseph G. Branch Publishing Co., 1912), 23–24.

296 *Sam Watkins . . . saw. Co. Aytch: A Confederate Memoir of the Civil War* (New York: Touchstone, 1997), 63.

296 *Watkins wrote.* Watkins, *Co. Aytch,* 158–59.

298 *reconnoitered those fellows pretty closely.* The story is recounted by Colonel Fremantle in Lord, *Fremantle,* 132–33.

298 *to manufacture many cannons.* Colonel Fremantle describes a newly constructed cannon foundry at Augusta that was then turning out one "Napoleon 12-pounder" every two days and seven thousand [pounds] of powder daily (Lord, *Fremantle,* 140).

298 *Lieutenant E. W. Rucker, recounted.* In a letter dated April 21, 1913, to Dr. William Mecklenburg Polk.

302 *Leonidas was described.* Lord, *Fremantle,* 111.

304 *He later wrote.* Letter to William Mecklenburg Polk of October 21, 1908, in Leonidas Polk Papers, University of the South, Sewanee, Tennessee, Microfilm Reel #3.

305 *happened to be on the spot.* Watkins, *Co. Aytch,* 154.

305 *the fighting goes well.* After the war, Sherman gave his version of the death of Leonidas in *Memoirs of General W. T. Sherman* (reprint, New York: Library of America, 1990), 524–25. "It has been asserted that I fired the gun which killed General Polk, and that I knew it was directed against that general. The fact is, at that distance we could not even tell that the group were officers at all; I was on horseback, a couple of hundred yards off, before my orders to fire were executed, had no idea that our shot had taken effect, and continued my ride down along the line to [General] Schofield's extreme flank, returning late in the evening to my headquarters at Big Shanty, where I occupied an abandoned house. In a cottonfield back of that house was our signal-station, on the roof of an old gin-house. The signal-officer reported that by studying the enemy's signals he had learned the 'key,' and that he could read their signals.

He explained to me that he had translated a signal about noon, from Pine Mountain to Marietta, 'Send an ambulance for General Polk's body;' and later in the day another, 'Why don't you send an ambulance for General Polk?' From this we inferred that General Polk had been killed, but how or where we knew not, and this inference was confirmed later in the same day by the report of some prisoners who had been captured.''

308 *Only 7 of the original group were still there.* Watkins, *Co. Aytch,* 243–44.

CHAPTER 9

309 *marks of bullets.* James's letters are in the possession of the author and other members of the family. Shortly before he got there, a Federal officer had written, ''This is a dreary, desolate, barren and deserted looking country,'' and another Federal soldier commented that ''There are no fences left at all. There is no corn and hay for the cattle and horses, but there are no horses left anyhow and the planters have no food for themselves'' (quoted in Stephen V. Ash, *Middle Tennessee Society Transformed, 1860–1870* [Baton Rouge: Louisiana State University Press, 1988], 85–86).

311 *former slaves.* Ash, *Middle Tennessee,* 107–8.

311 *wartime tragedies.* Mary Harding Polk, ''An Old Lady's Jottings,'' manuscript in the possession of the author's family.

312 *let him go.* ''Recollections,'' by Prudence Polk, in William Waller (ed.), *Nashville in the 1890s* (Nashville: Vanderbilt University Press, 1970), 191.

312 *charged with piracy.* Daniel E. Sutherland, *The Confederate Carpetbaggers* (Baton Rouge: Louisiana State University Press, 1988), 12.

312 *be executed.* Hans L. Trefousse, *Andrew Johnson* (New York: W. W. Norton, 1989), 192.

314 *a new branch of the family.* Antoinette married Baron Athanase de Charette de la Contrie.

314 *Esther Polk recounts.* ''Memories,'' by Esther Winder Polk Lowe,

Manuscript MS 1949 in the Maryland Historical Society Library, transcribed by Dr. John F. Polk in 1998, 23.

316 *as Meck did.* Sutherland, *Confederate Carpetbaggers,* 2.

316 *a sort of archtype.* Sutherland, *Confederate Carpetbaggers,* 4–5.

316 *after Robert E. Lee's surrender.* Sutherland, *Confederate Carpetbaggers,* 11.

317 *and log huts.* Arthur Benjamin Chitty, Jr., *Reconstruction at Sewanee* (Sewanee, Tenn.: University Press, 1954), 41.

318 *Stephen Ash has written. Middle Tennessee,* 61.

319 *have been collected.* For example, John W. Blassingame (ed.), *Slave Testimony: Two Centuries of Letters, Speeches, Interviews, and Autobiographies* (Baton Rouge: Louisiana State University Press, 1977; reprinted 1997).

319 *being called "mister."* Eric Foner, *Reconstruction, America's Unfinished Revolution, 1863–1877* (New York: Harper & Row, 1988), 78ff.

320 *murdered on the streets.* Foner, *Reconstruction,* 32–33.

320 *Andrew Johnson.* The story persisted that he was an illegitimate descendant of Will Polk—Will's daughter accepted it as a fact—and, because looked down upon by "polite society," hated the southern aristocracy.

320 *die so believing.* Trefousee, *Andrew Johnson,* 165.

320 *blotted out of space.* Quoted in Trefousee, *Andrew Johnson,* 166.

321 *future of the freedmen.* Trefousee, *Andrew Johnson,* 188.

321 *dead in its tracks.* Trefousee, *Andrew Johnson,* 226–27.

321 *insulting language.* Foner, *Reconstruction,* 199–200.

322 *confiscated lands.* Foner, *Reconstruction,* 68ff.

323 *Radical Reconstruction.* Foner, *Reconstruction,* 251, 262ff.

323 *a sort of social club.* Allen W. Trelease, *White Terror: The Ku Klux Klan Conspiracy and Southern Reconstruction* (Baton Rouge: Louisiana State University Press, 1971; reprinted 1995), 3ff.

324 *condemned and dissolved.* An anonymous letter to the *Richmond Enquirer & Examiner,* April 30, 1868; reprinted in Trelease, *White Terror,* 6.

324 *Nathan Bedford Forrest.* Trelease, *White Terror,* 10.

325 *described the episode.* Mary Jones Polk Branch, *Memoirs of a Southern Woman "Within the Lines"* (Chicago: Joseph G. Branch Publishing Co., 1912), 49.

325 *had "degenerated."* Ash, *Middle Tennessee,* 247.

326 *a typical plantation.* U.S. Senate Committee on Agriculture and Forestry, *Report on Conditions of Cotton Growers in the United States, the Present Price of Cotton, and the Remedy,* 53rd Cong., 3rd sess., Rept. 986, vols. 1 and 2; noted in Emory Q. Hawk, *Economic History of the South* (New York: Prentice-Hall, 1934), 451.

326 *made money.* J. D. B. De Bow, *Resources of the Southern and Western States,* vol. 1 (New Orleans: De Bow's Review, 1853), 151ff; quoted in Hawk, *Economic History,* 256ff.

326 *entire reconstruction period.* Hawk, *Economic History,* 429.

327 *another namesake.* Mary Roe Scruby, the sister of George W. Polk's wife; unpublished manuscript in the possession of the family.

328 *a Mr. Stevens.* John J. Stevens, secretary and treasurer for the railway in 1882; quoted in C. L. Sonnichsen, *Roy Bean, Law West of the Pecos* (New York: Macmillan, 1943), 81–82.

330 *As Molly wrote,* "An Old Lady's Jottings."

335 *climbed onto the cot.* While I cannot vouch for every detail of the story, whose source was James's wife, Molly, and was not written down, I still have his pistol in my possession and as a boy learned to shoot with it (see illustration).

336 *in the world.* J'nell L. Pate, *Livestock Legacy: The Fort Worth Stockyards, 1887–1987* (College Station, Tex.: Texas A&M University Press, 1988), 99.

336 *at least once.* Walter Gann ("War Horses for the British," *Old West* 9, no. 3 [Spring 1973]: 20ff.) said that the British required his relatives to furnish rather more trained and broken horses.

340 *Some thought it was suicide.* Marsh's nephew Van Leer Polk was not charged with any crime and was subsequently elected to the Tennessee Senate; he also served as U.S. consul general at Calcutta, In-

dia, took part as one of the U.S. commissioners at the Pan American Conference and became editor of the *Memphis News and Scimitar.*

340 *Jefferson had pinned his hopes.* William Peden (ed.), *Notes on the State of Virginia* (Chapel Hill: University of North Carolina Press, 1982), "Query XIX. Manufacturers," 164–65.

342 *audience after approving audience.* A typical speech (on July 4, 1890, at Winfield, Kansas) was recorded in the *Winfield Courier* of July 10, 1890, and is partly reproduced in Stuart Noblin, *Leonidas LaFayette Polk, Agrarian Crusader* (Chapel Hill: University of North Carolina Press, 1949). These quotations appear in Chapter 1. His papers are collected in the North Carolina State University Libraries in Raleigh, collection no. MC 13.

345 *carnage of Gettysburg.* He recounts his experiences in letters to his wife, Sallie, and in a series of articles called "The 43rd N.C. Regiment During the War: Whiffs from My Old Camp Pipe," published in the *Ansonian* in April 1877. He also kept a diary.

345 *no romantic fantasies about war.* He was several times wounded, and as he wrote to his wife at one time in the campaign, "We had no bread and the raw bacon was greatly relished without it . . . heat and dust almost beyond endurance . . . men actually dropped dead in ranks." His unit marched six hundred miles and fought nine engagements in one month.

347 *his principal biographer has written.* Noblin, *Leonidas LaFayette Polk,* 79.

348 *work on his own.* Leonidas LaFayette shared the low opinion of blacks' capacities then common in the South. See Noblin, *Leonidas LaFayette Polk,* 92.

349 *in England.* As a young man, the future bishop and general (the other Leonidas) had written to his father, Will Polk, "The more I see of those who are without slaves, the more I am prepared to say that we are seriously wronging ourselves by retaining them" (reprinted in William Mecklenburg Polk, *Leonidas Polk, Bishop and General* [New York: Longmans, Green, 1894], vol. 1, 122.

350 *one contemporary wrote.* John S. Long in the January 24, 1878, *Farmer and Mechanic;* quoted in Noblin, *Leonidas LaFayette Polk,* 121.

352 *champion of the down-trodden.* Noblin, *Leonidas LaFayette Polk,* 207.

353 *A Republican Party newspaper.* The *Topeka Weekly Capital,* July 24, September 18, and October 16, 1890; reprinted in Noblin, *Leonidas LaFayette,* 225.

CHAPTER 10

355 *Harding Polk.* Harding was the son of James H. and Frank was the son of Meck, so both were great-grandsons of Will.

356 *since the Civil War.* His administration sponsored twenty bills creating or extending segregation and by executive order required black federal employees to use separate eating and washing facilities.

356 *House said.* Charles Seymour (ed.), *The Intimate Papers of Colonel House* (Boston: Houghton Mifflin, 1926), vol. 2, 11.

356 *every sort of problem.* His official papers and diaries are collected in the Frank L. Polk Papers, Manuscripts and Archives, Yale University Library.

357 *Veracruz.* Robert E. Quirk, *An Affair of Honor: Woodrow Wilson and the Occupation of Veracruz* (Lexington: University of Kentucky Press, 1962).

358 *Mexican foreign minister wrote.* Quoted in Colonel Frank Tompkins, *Chasing Villa: The Last Campaign of the U.S. Cavalry* (Harrisburg: Military Service Publishing Co., 1934; reprint, High-Lonesome Books, 1996), 14.

358 *Pancho Villa.* See Friedrich Ketz, *The Life and Times of Pancho Villa* (Stanford: Stanford University Press, 1998).

359 *to poison Villa.* Charles H. Harris and Louis R. Sadler, ''Termination with Extreme Prejudice: The United States Versus Pancho Villa,'' in *The Border and the Revolution* (Silver City, N.M.: High-Lonesome Books, 1990).

360 *Frank telegraphed.* This and subsequent quotations from State Department documents are drawn from *Papers Relating to the Foreign Rela-*

tions of the United States (Washington, D.C.: Government Printing Office, 1925) unless otherwise noted.

361 *already far in the country.* The memorandum of this conversation was not published. Dated May 10, 1916, it is contained in the Frank Lyon Polk Papers, Manuscripts and Archives, Yale University Library; hereafter cited as *Papers.*

361 *as President Wilson.* July 19, 1916; *Papers.*

361 *if not before.* December 26, 1916; *Papers.*

361 *Secretary of State.* On May 22, 1916; *Papers.*

361 *special representative.* May 31, 1916; *Papers.*

362 *Mexican ambassador.* February 17, 1919; *Papers.*

362 *hunt game for their food.* Clarence C. Clendenen, *Blood on the Border: The United States Army and the Mexican Irregulars* (London: Macmillan, 1969), 250.

363 *enemy of the Americans.* Clendenen, *Blood,* 266.

363 *As he wrote.* Letter to Esther Polk on March 28, 1916, from "Same Place."

363 *American force was formidable.* Lieutenant Harding Polk, "Notes from the Mexican Punitive Expedition," typescript, 1916.

365 *remain in port.* February 1, 1916; *Papers.*

365 *outraged many Americans.* Colonel Edward House happened to be visiting British Foreign Minister Sir Edward Grey on that day and "We spoke of the probability of an ocean liner being sunk, and I told him if this were done a flame of indignation would sweep across America, which would in itself probably carry us into the war." Seymour, *House,* vol. 1, 432.

365 *justified their tampering.* May 22, 1916; *Papers.*

366 *As House wrote.* Seymour, *House,* vol. 2, 82–86.

367 *House's proposition.* Seymour, *House,* vol. 2, 86–87.

367 *the so-called Zimmermann telegram.* Frank refers to it as "a telegram sent by [German Ambassador Count Johann von] Bernstorff to the German Minister in Mexico City, dated January 19, 1917 [which] . . . offered an offensive and defensive alliance with Mexico and

held out the hope that Mexico take certain lands from the United States'' (in a meeting with the Japanese ambassador on February 28, 1917, contained in *Papers*).

367 *some sort of alliance.* Barbara W. Tuchman, *The Zimmermann Telegram* (New York: Ballantine, 1979). The text of the telegram is given on pages 141 and 142.

368 *unrestricted submarine warfare.* Frank met with the Austrian ambassador on February 26, 1917. ''We got on the subject of war and I told him I did not think there was any possibility [in that event] of war with Germany being avoided . . . if we sent the armed ships over it was almost certain that they would either sink a submarine or they would be sunk by a submarine. It seemed to me that all that was wanted was an act of war, which was inevitable.'' *Papers*.

368 *very old tool of diplomacy.* I have discussed it at length in *Neighbors and Strangers: The Fundamentals of Foreign Affairs* (Chicago: University of Chicago Press, 1997), 187ff.

370 *Sarah confided.* Her diary, supplemented by letters to and from her family, husbands and admirers, has been edited by her son, Alfred Shaughnessy, as *Sarah: The Letters and Diaries of a Courtier's Wife, 1906–1936* (London: Peter Owen, 1989). Unless otherwise noted, all quotations relating to Sarah are drawn from Shaughnessy's book.

373 *attend key meetings.* Note on August 29, 1919, in *Papers*.

373 *dissolve the peace conference.* Note on September 16, 1919, in *Papers*.

373 *promised the Arabs their independence.* October 17 meeting with Abdul Hadi, in *Papers*. On the context, see William R. Polk, *The United States and the Arab World* (Cambridge, Mass.: Harvard University Press, 1964 and subsequent editions).

376 *hero of the cavalry.* John M. Carroll, *The 7th U.S. Cavalry's Own Colonel Tommy Tompkins* (Mattituck, N.Y.: J. M. Carroll & Co., 1984), 90.

380 *This winter and next winter.* Lowell Thomas and Lowell Thomas, Jr., *Famous First Flights That Changed History* (New York: Doubleday, 1968), 68.

382 *eccentric Mitford family.* Among the Mitfords, Nancy is perhaps the

best known as the author of *Love in a Cold Climate* and *The Pursuit of Love.* Her sister Diana married the British Fascist Party leader, Sir Oswald Mosley, and another sister became the Duchess of Devonshire.

CHAPTER 11

384 *he later said.* Unless otherwise indicated, quotations from James H. "Jimmy" Polk, are drawn from Jesse Stiller and Rebecca Craver, *An Oral History of James H. Polk, General, U.S. Army, Retd.,* typescript, 1988), or from the mimeographed typescript of his wartime letters to his wife, "Letters and Notes of James H. Polk, Colonel U.S.A. Commanding, 1944–1945," a copy of which is in the possession of the author.

384 *George Patton.* A longtime friend of Jimmy's father, Harding, and whom Jimmy had known since he was a little boy.

385 *died of boredom.* As Jimmy later commented during the war in Europe, "Some of the Captains in the 8th Cavalry had been in World War I and they were still Captains 15 years later . . . they didn't have any ambition. They weren't going anyplace and they knew it. Just putting in their time."

385 *Lucius.* In "Valedictory of a Maverick," a lecture in Memphis on May 21, 1992. Unless otherwise indicated, quotations from him will be from this source.

385 *becoming a lawyer.* Unless otherwise indicated, all quotations will be from George's letters and diaries in the possession of the author.

394 *the* Washington Post *editorialized.* Reprinted in David M. Tucker, *Memphis Since Crump: Bossism, Blacks, and Civic Reformers, 1948–1968* (Knoxville: University of Tennessee Press, 1980), 39.

395 *sometimes beaten up.* One who was, was Turner Catledge, then a reporter on the *Commercial Appeal* and later the managing editor of the *New York Times.*

396 *reinforce their garrison at will.* So wrote Samuel Eliot Morison, *The Struggle for Guadalcanal, August 1942–February 1943,* vol. 5 of *History*

of United States Naval Operations in World War II (Boston: Atlantic-Little, Brown, 1954), 65.

397 *came under sniper fire.* Command, Advanced Naval Base, Ringbolt, dispatch to Commander South Pacific Forces, December 22, 1942. The dispatch commended George for "outstanding heroism" when he assumed charge of all the ground activities at Henderson Field.

397 *to have awarded it.* George Washington's order book is missing, so this cannot be definitely proved.

397 *to be sent out of the island.* Major General A. A. Vandegrift, the commander at Guadalcanal, wrote, "You are to be highly commended for your brave actions," and awarded him the Order of the Purple Heart, on September 23, 1942.

398 *by gun flashes.* John G. Norris in the *Washington Post*, December 1, 1943.

399 *The most dramatic.* The account was published in the *New York Herald Tribune*, February 14, 1943.

405 *to be personally brave.* This was written to his wife while Jimmy was flying in General Patton's airplane.

409 *grateful to Hitler.* Ralph Bennett, *Ultra in the West: The Normandy Campaign of 1944–1945* (London: Hutchinson, 1979); see map of the German attack on page 193. The 3rd Cavalry was just below the axis of attack, south of the city of Trier, between the Moselle and Saar Rivers.

409 *in a single bound.* Bennett, *Ultra,* 219.

410 *Skorzeny.* S.S.-Obersturmbannführer Otto Skorzeny, a flamboyant German officer, was famous for having rescued Mussolini in a daring airborne commando raid, and then commanded a detachment of English-speaking German soldiers in American uniforms operating behind American lines.

412 *Vocklabruck, Austria.* It was at this time that Jimmy met Baron Hermann von Oppenheimer, the father of the later wife of the author.

413 *He wrote.* In the *Los Angeles Daily News,* January 21, 1946.

415 *Greece was ruled by a dictatorship.* The Greek dictator Metaxas and the

policies he advocated differed from those of Hitler mainly in that Metaxas (who had studied at the Prussian war college and had un- bounded admiration for all things German) was Greek. In the pre- war years, he had tried to remake the Greeks by imposing upon them a Greek version of Nazism. For Hitler's Third Reich, read Metaxas's "Third Hellenic Civilization." What Hitler had hoped to do with the Hitler Youth, Metaxas tried to do with his National Youth Organization (*EON*). Greeks were to be purged of all cor- rupt ideas, in which Metaxas sweepingly included parliamentary democracy, the free press, women's rights and even the Boy Scouts. Those unfortunate enough to be caught opposing him, by the Greek equivalent of the Gestapo, were exiled, sent to concen- tration camps or shot.

416 *in the Cold War.* In his March 5, 1946, speech at Fulton, Missouri, Churchill proclaimed that "an iron curtain has descended across the Continent." This, he continued, "is certainly not the liberated Europe we have fought to build up." For those who then knew of his deals with the Russians and his actions in Egypt, India and Greece, his words rang false, but few then knew.

416 *accepted the British offer.* In May 1944, Churchill ordered Anthony Eden to propose to Stalin a swap—a Soviet free hand in Romania in return for a British free hand in Greece. Churchill went even fur- ther when he met with Stalin in October of that year: in exchange for Greece, Churchill legitimated Soviet control over virtually all of eastern Europe. It is from this—Churchill's—deal that the Russian hegemony may be dated; long before the much despised Yalta Con- ference in which Roosevelt is alleged to have given away much of Europe, the great cold warrior, Churchill himself, had planted the corner post of the iron curtain.

417 *from the former dictatorship.* During the Axis occupation, quasi-mili- tary formations, known as the Rallis Security Battalions, armed and directed by the Germans, Italians or Bulgarians, were notorious for rounding up and shooting Greek hostages.

417 *as George pointed out.* In a letter to Howard K. Smith of CBS on November 7, 1946.

419 *between the extremes.* George wrote that "As always, the British servicemen individually were pleasant guys. A good many of them told me frankly they were appalled by the atrocities being perpetrated by Greek soldiers and policemen on Greek captives. One lt. col. complained that he and other British officers often made full reports of these atrocities to London but that diplomatic word never came back to Athens to curb these excesses."

420 *foreign presence was British.* A large British police mission continued to dominate the Athens and Salonika security forces at least through the first half of 1949. The CIA, which would later play such a role in Greek affairs, was then just being created out of the debris of the wartime OSS.

421 *almost defenseless.* By the end of 1947, the American reporters, George reported to Howard K. Smith, were being denounced in the rightist press as communists. "Our names were used in the daily articles and our private affairs (or believed to be private affairs) were bluntly examined. We had quite an exciting time apparently, because the Royalist-Rightwing press said we did terrible things from 'dawn to dusk but almost unbelievable things from dusk to dawn.' This rabid press attack included charges that we wrote under instructions from our Communist controlled organizations (CBS, New York Daily News, NY Her[ald] trib[une] etc.!!!)."

426 *of the Crump machine.* Among other things, the machine censored books and films so that, for example, the Unitarian Church was not allowed to show a Charley Chaplin movie because the censor regarded Chaplin as "a dirty, filthy character." See Tucker, *Memphis Since Crump,* 75.

427 *courage to take a stand.* Burch to Members of the Executive Committee, June 5, 1963; quoted in Tucker, *Memphis Since Crump,* 134–35.

INDEX

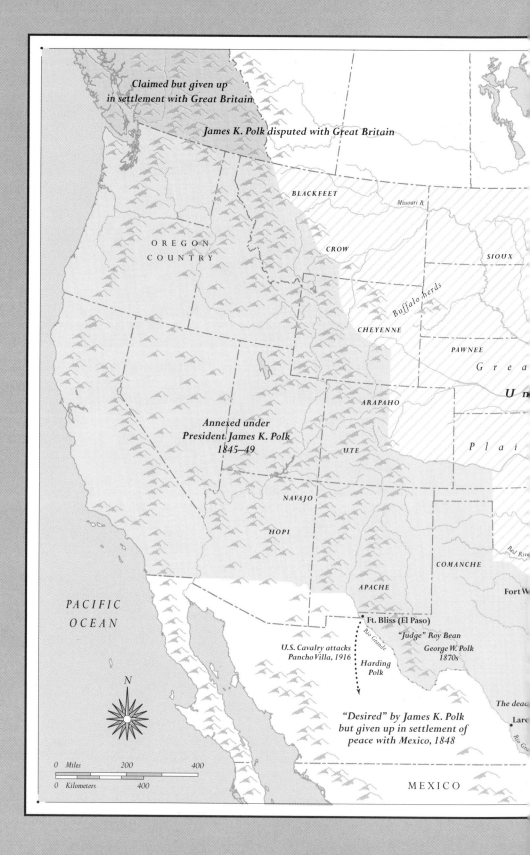

Claimed but given up
in settlement with Great Britain

James K. Polk disputed with Great Britain

BLACKFEET

Missouri R.

OREGON
COUNTRY

CROW

SIOUX

Buffalo herds

CHEYENNE

PAWNEE

Grea

ARAPAHO

Un

Annexed under
President James K. Polk
1845–49

UTE

Plai

NAVAJO

HOPI

Red Rive

COMANCHE

APACHE

Fort W

PACIFIC
OCEAN

Ft. Bliss (El Paso)

Rio Grande

"Judge" Roy Bean

U.S. Cavalry attacks
Pancho Villa, 1916

George W. Polk
1870s

Harding
Polk

N

The dea

Lare

"Desired" by James K. Polk
but given up in settlement of
peace with Mexico, 1848

Rio Gra

0   Miles   200   400

0   Kilometers   400

MEXICO